Computers
from logic to architecture

R.D. Dowsing
F.W.D. Woodhams
I. Marshall

School of Information Systems
University of East Anglia
Norwich

Computers
from logic to architecture

second edition

The McGraw-Hill Companies

London • Burr Ridge, IL • New York • St Louis • San Francisco • Auckland • Bogotá
Caracas • Lisbon • Madrid • Mexico • Milan • Montreal • New Delhi • Panama • Paris
San Juan • São Paulo • Singapore • Tokyo • Toronto

Published by
McGraw-Hill Publishing Company
Shoppenhangers Road, Maidenhead, Berkshire, sl6 2ql, England
Telephone: +44(0) 1628 502500
Fax: +44(0) 1628 770224
Web site: http://www.mcgraw-hill.co.uk

British Library Cataloguing in Publication Data
A catalogue record for this book is available from the British Library

First edition published in 1990 by Van Nostrand Reinhold
First published in 1985 as *Computer Architecture: A first course*

ISBN 007 709584 7

Library of Congress cataloguing in publication data
The loc data for this book has been applied for and may be obtained from the
Library of Congress, Washington, d.c.

Web site address: http://www.mcgraw-hill.co.uk/textbooks/dowsing

Publisher:	David Hatter
Page design:	Mike Cotterell
Typesetting:	Mouse Nous
Illustration origination:	Mike Cotterell
Peripherals illustrations:	Martyn Ford
Production:	Steven Gardiner Ltd
Cover:	Hybert Design

The McGraw·Hill Companies

To Anita, Christine and Gill

Contents

	Preface	xiii
1	**Introduction**	1
1.1	Introduction	1
1.2	What is computer system?	1
1.3	Understanding computer architecture	1
1.4	Translation and interpretation	4
1.5	Languages and abstract machines	6
1.6	Sequentiality, concurrency and distribution	6
1.7	The speed of technology change	7
1.8	Summary	8
2	**Introduction to digital logic**	11
2.1	Introduction	11
2.2	Combinational and sequential logic	11
2.3	Basic logic gates	12
2.4	Example: a 1-bit half adder	17
2.5	Boolean algebra	17
2.6	NAND/NOR logic	20
2.7	Positive and negative logic	23
2.8	Logic implementation	24
2.9	Logic families	28
2.10	Summary	36
2.11	Exercises	36
3	**Combinational logic design**	39
3.1	Introduction	39
3.2	Problem specification	40
3.3	Design example: a parity generator	40
3.4	Design example: a 7-segment decimal decoder	43
3.5	Minimization of Boolean functions	45
3.6	Medium scale integrated functions	50

3.7	Programmable logic arrays	56
3.8	Read-only memories	59
3.9	Summary	60
3.10	Exercises	60

4	**Sequential logic design**	**63**
4.1	Introduction	63
4.2	Synchronous and asynchronous sequential circuits	64
4.3	State diagrams and state variables	65
4.4	Memory elements	68
4.5	Sequential logic systems using D-type flip-flops	73
4.6	Sequential logic circuits using read-only memories	77
4.7	Sequential logic circuits using EPLDs	80
4.8	Counter design	84
4.9	Design of a register bank	88
4.10	Summary	91
4.11	Exercises	91

5	**The structure of a computer**	**93**
5.1	Introduction	93
5.2	The operation of a computer	94
5.3	System packaging	95
5.4	The bus	96
5.5	The central processing unit	97
5.6	The arithmetic and logic unit	98
5.7	Examples of processors	104
5.8	Input and output	110
5.9	Summary	110
5.10	Exercises	111

6	**Memory systems**	**113**
6.1	Introduction	113
6.2	Memory	113
6.3	Architectural considerations and memory	122
6.4	The 80x86 memory organization	131
6.5	Summary	132
6.6	Exercises	133

7	**Input–output**	**135**
7.1	Input–output interfaces	135
7.2	Controlling input–output devices	144
7.3	Peripheral devices	150
7.4	Summary	165
7.5	Exercises	166

8	**Control & microprogramming**	**169**
8.1	The fetch cycle	169

8.2	The execute cycle	172
8.3	The control unit	173
8.4	Horizontal and vertical microcoding	177
8.5	Emulation	178
8.6	Microcoded versus hardwired implementation	178
8.7	Summary	179
8.8	Exercises	179
9	**Design of a small computer system**	**181**
9.1	Connecting the components together	181
9.2	A minimal Intel 8088 system	185
9.3	A Motorola 68000-based microcomputer	186
9.4	Summary	189
9.5	Exercises	190
10	**Data representation & manipulation**	**191**
10.1	Introduction	191
10.2	Number systems	191
10.3	Binary arithmetic	195
10.4	Representation and manipulation of data in a computer	196
10.5	Arithmetic using integer representations	201
10.6	Real numbers	207
10.7	Summary	212
10.8	Exercises	213
11	**Instruction sets & addressing modes**	**215**
11.1	Instruction sets	215
11.2	The programmer's models	217
11.3	Assembly code	221
11.4	Instruction types	223
11.5	Operands	231
11.6	Addressing modes	234
11.7	Instruction encoding	239
11.8	Use of addressing modes	240
11.9	Examples to illustrate assembly code and addressing modes	244
11.10	Summary	252
11.11	Exercises	252
12	**Introduction to system software**	**255**
12.1	Introduction	255
12.2	Assembly language and assemblers	255
12.3	Translating from assembly code to machine code	257
12.4	Relocation	261
12.5	Linking	262
12.6	Loading	264
12.7	High-level languages	265
12.8	The translation environment	269

12.9	Summary	272
12.10	Exercises	272
12.11	Longer programming exercises	274

13	**Concurrency**	**277**
13.1	Introduction	277
13.2	Multiple processor systems	278
13.3	Hardware controlled interrupts and input–output	279
13.4	Software interrupts	279
13.5	Types of concurrency	279
13.6	A warning	283
13.7	Systems with multiple processors	283
13.8	Summary	287
13.9	Exercises	287

14	**Protocols & data transmission**	**291**
14.1	Introduction	291
14.2	Protocols and protocol hierarchies	291
14.3	Data transmission and the physical layer	297
14.4	Multiplexing of signals	298
14.5	Types of transmission media	299
14.6	Framing and synchronization	300
14.7	Signal attenuation and noise corruption	303
14.8	Telephone system	304
14.9	Modulation	305
14.10	Modems	306
14.11	Example protocol	307
14.12	Summary	310
14.13	Exercises	311

15	**Computer networks**	**313**
15.1	Introduction	313
15.2	Topology	315
15.3	Local area networks (LANs)	318
15.4	Wide area networks	328
15.5	Example – the Internet	338
15.6	Summary	341
15.7	Exercises	342

16	**Error correction**	**345**
16.1	Introduction	345
16.2	Error control	346
16.3	Backward error correction	349
16.4	Time-out control	356
16.5	Forward error correction	356
16.6	Flow control	359
16.7	Error and flow control in HDLC	360

16.8	Transaction control protocol (TCP)	362
16.9	Summary	363
16.10	Exercises	363
17	**Architectural trends**	365
17.1	Introduction	365
17.2	Reduced instruction set computers (RISC)	366
17.3	Webcentric computing	376
17.4	The future of architectures	378
17.5	Summary	380
17.6	Exercises	381
	Appendix	383
	Further reading	389
	Glossary	393
	Answers to selected exercises	403
	Index	421

Preface

With the ever increasing use of computers there is an increasing need for specialists who are familiar with computer technology. The insatiable demand for such people has led to increasing number of students seeking education and training in the techniques and applications of computing. One specific area that has been targeted by many colleges and universities is computer systems engineering, the interface area between computing and electronics, hardware and software. The specific requirements of this area are a knowledge of the interaction of software and hardware, often with particular relevance to microprocessors and their applications.

This book is aimed at providing a first course in computer architecture and exploring hardware-software interaction. The reader does not need any specific prior knowledge but the student who has at least a little experience of programming in a high level language will find the latter half of the book easier reading. The book covers the spectrum of computer architecture from basic technology through systems software to communications. This material is essential for computer systems engineering and is also central to other computing courses.

The approach we have taken in this book is to concentrate on the principles of computer architecture. One reason for this is that we believe that fundamentals are more important than particular details of current technology. Another reason is that the details of current technology change very rapidly, whereas the principles are applicable over a much longer time scale. We have taken deliberately simple examples in many cases; for example, we have used only very simple logic circuits and small integrated circuits for much of the discussion rather than the larger circuits that current technology allows. Once the basic fundamentals have been understood, these same principles can be applied to larger, more modern circuits where they still apply, although implementation details differ.

As in previous editions of this book, we had the problem of deciding what hardware to use for examples throughout the book. We decided that, since the two most commonly used processors in use in higher education today for teaching this type of material are the Motorola 68000 series and the Intel 80x86 series, we should use these processors and their support components as examples. The use of these two architectures helps to highlight some of the different decisions made by the two design teams at approximately the same dates.

The book takes a bottom-up approach, starting with the lowest level, electronics, and building up a typical architecture layer by layer from this starting point. This edition of the book has been updated and expanded to include more material on communications, thus giving a wider view of computer architecture, although the central focus of the book is still computer architecture.

Chapter 1 introduces some of the key concepts in understanding computer architecture. The succeeding chapter describes the basis of electronic logic as the foundation for combinatorial and sequential logic circuits. It includes descriptions of primitive electronic components and the theory — Boolean algebra — underlying the composition of these components into larger units. Chapter 3 concentrates on combinatorial logic design, that is, the design of circuits whose outputs depend solely on the present circuit inputs. It illustrates how the combinatorial elements of a computer such as decoders and multiplexors can be formed from networks of the primitive components. Chapter 4 describes sequential logic design, that is, the design of circuits whose outputs depends on the history of circuit inputs. Typical sequential elements of a computer such as registers and memories are discussed. This is followed, in the next chapter, by the description of the organization of a simple computer system built by interconnecting the components discussed in the previous two chapters.

Chapter 6 describes the different types of memory that can be built and examines their behaviour. It also introduces the idea of a hierarchy of memories to overcome the disparity in the price, speed and capacity of different memories and shows how the notion of a single level virtual memory simplifies the use of memory for the programmer. Input–output processing techniques such as polling, interrupts and direct memory access are introduced in the succeeding chapter. This is followed in the next chapter by consideration of different methods of implementing the control within a processor. This naturally leads to the consideration of microprogramming and its role in computers. Chapter 9 presents the design of two simple computer systems built around the two processors we have chosen to illustrate computer architecture; the Motorola 68000 and the Intel 80x86.

Chapter 10 concentrates on a description of the different types of data that can be manipulated in a computer and the operations that can be performed on them. Detailed discussion of number systems is given in this chapter. Instruction sets and addressing modes are considered with particular reference to the two example processors in the succeeding chapter. Many examples are given for illustrative purposes and several complete programs are given at the end of the chapter. Chapter 12 discusses some of the system software to be found in any computer system, such as assemblers, linkers and loaders. The discussion is necessarily brief but includes details of the algorithms on which this software is based. The next chapter in concerned with concurrency in computer systems and describes a few of the more common places in the architecture where concurrency is to be found in modern computers. Pipelining is considered in this chapter.

Chapter 14 is the first of three chapters that discuss computer communications. This chapter is concerned with the basic principles of data communication. Chapter 15 considers the development of wide area and local area networks and discusses their organization. The final chapter of this group, Chapter 16, is devoted to the detection and correction of errors in communication systems.

The final chapter, Chapter 17, considers the future of computer architecture in the light of current trends. The conclusion is that there are unlikely to be major changes in the underlying architecture of computers in the near future but that architectures at the applications level will continually evolve to meet new user requirements.

R. D. Dowsing
I. Marshall
F. W. D. Woodhams

2000

1
Introduction

1.1 Introduction

Before considering computer architecture in detail, it is useful to look at some of the basic principles underlying the study of the subject, and that is the theme of this chapter. Important topics will be introduced briefly so that the reader will have an overview of some of the topics that permeate the study of computer architecture. Having a basic understanding of these topics will make it easier to comprehend the rest of the book and will also give some insight into the development of computer architecture. Most of the topics in this chapter are discussed in more detail later in the book.

1.2 What is computer system?

A computer consists of hardware and software components. Hardware comprises a set of interconnected electronic components such as memory, processor and input–output devices and software is a collection of programs, each of which consists of a number of instructions that the hardware 'understands', that is, the hardware performs a set of predefined actions for each instruction.

Both hardware and software consist of interconnected components that have structure. Many different organizations of these structures are possible and this gives rise to many different computer architectures.

1.3 Understanding computer architecture

Humans understand complex topics using a 'divide and conquer' strategy. Any complex topic is decomposed in a set of less complex subparts hierarchically until the subparts are simple enough to be understood. Once these simple subparts are understood they are composed into more complex units whose behaviour can be explained by the action of the subparts and their interaction. The process is continued hierarchically until the behaviour of the complex object can be explained. This process is illustrated in Figure 1.1 where the circles represent the actions.

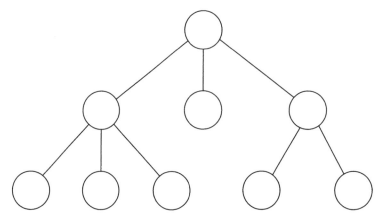

Figure 1.1   A hierarchy of abstractions – a tree in computer terminology.

Computer architecture is a complex topic and the way to understand it is to subdivide it into smaller topics. There are many different ways to subdivide it and hence the many different approaches found in different textbooks. Here, two approaches to computer architecture are considered to show why a mixture of these approaches is used in this book.

1.3.1 A layered approach

One approach to computer architecture is to consider a computer system as consisting of a set of layers of abstraction, each layer of which relies on the layers below for its components. For example, one or more of the lower layers in this model are concerned with the logic elements used to implement the hardware of the system. One level could be solely concerned with the types of element used, for example, AND and OR gates, and the design methods for using these logic elements. If the computer system is implemented in very large scale integration (VLSI) circuits then a lower level might be appropriate where the concerns are for physical parameters such as the width of tracks and type of technology. At a somewhat higher level is the machine level, which is the interface between the lower level hardware abstractions and higher level software abstractions and is normally the lowest level accessible to the computer user. At this level the software consists of strings of bits, which are interpreted as instructions and data by the hardware. Abstraction levels above this are concerned with the operating system, high level programming languages and applications. One possible hierarchy of levels of abstraction is given in Figure 1.2. Higher levels have more complex abstractions than lower levels and each level relies on the level below to implement its primitive operations. Each level has its own set of primitive components and its own set of design methods to interconnect these primitive components. In addition each level ideally has its own basic theory that underpins the construction method, although the theories at the higher levels tend to be less formal than those used at the lower levels. For example, at the logic level, the propositional calculus and Boolean algebra are the basis of the synthesis and analysis of logic circuits. This layered approach is appealing since it relegates details of the synthesis and analysis of components to the appropriate level, thus giving rise to a hierarchically structured approach.

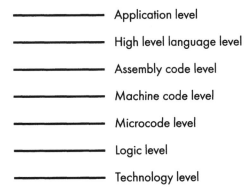

Figure 1.2 Levels of abstraction.

1.3.2 Functional decomposition

Another approach to understanding computers is to adopt a functional decomposition. In this scenario a computer consists of a set of functional components, for example, processor, memory and input–output devices, as shown in Figure 1.3, where each component is considered to be a functional block. Taking memory as an example, it can be further subdivided into different types, such as random access memory (RAM) and read-only memory (ROM) and each of these types can be divided further into different types of RAM and ROM. In effect, this decomposition gives a hierarchical structure, a tree, where each subtree consists of functionally related items. This decomposition is attractive since concerns about physically related components are grouped together and hence, easy to compare.

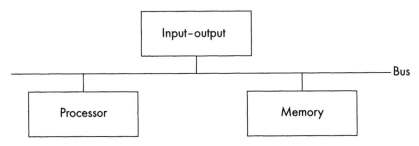

Figure 1.3 Functional block diagram of a computer.

To illustrate the advantage of functional decomposition, consider memory. In functional decomposition this would occupy a large subtree and, in terms of the structure of a book, would appear as a single chapter or group of chapters that describe memory at different levels of detail. In the layered approach different aspects of memory would be found in different layers and hence in different chapters. It would thus seem that the functional approach is the best way to understand computer architecture but there are many cases, especially at the lower levels of abstraction, where abstractions are more important than function. For example, logic design would appear as a single entity in the layered approach but would be scattered throughout all the components in the functional approach. Logic design is a subject in its own right and it makes sense to consider it as a whole in a separate chapter. Since it depends on the viewpoint as to which is the best approach, a mixture of approaches is taken in this book, depending on the particular view the authors wish to take of a particular topic.

1.4 Translation and interpretation

Consider the structure of a computer as a series of abstraction layers. Some method of implementing the highest level of abstraction by means of components of the lower levels is required. For the following discussion, only two levels are considered but the principles discussed can be applied to a hierarchy of levels.

1.4.1 Translation

There are two basic methods of implementing the higher level in terms of the lower. One technique is called translation and involves decomposing the higher level abstraction into a set of lower level abstractions. Consider, for example, how to evaluate the arithmetic expression $7 \times 3 + 8 \times 4$. The high level abstraction is 'calculate value of arithmetic expression' whilst the low level abstractions are 'multiplication' and 'addition'. The action of calculating the value of the arithmetic expression can be translated into a set of simpler multiplication and addition operations. The multiplication and addition operations can be carried out by a specialized device that knows only how to perform multiplication or addition and nothing about how to calculate the value of arithmetic expressions. Thus to calculate the value of this arithmetic expression the sequence of actions below could be performed:

> Compute 7×3 and remember the result
> Compute 8×4 and remember the result
> Add the result of the two previous operations

1.4.2 Interpretation

An alternative way of implementing the higher level requirement is to build a high level machine – in the above example this would be a calculator – out of lower level components. This higher level machine understands the abstraction 'calculate the value of an arithmetic expression'. This technique is called *interpretation*.

It appears that these two approaches produce the same result, as indeed they must if they are to implement the high level abstraction, but they do so in different ways. Consider the case of translation in the above example. The result of the translation is a set of lower level instructions detailing how to evaluate an arithmetic expression. This set of instructions can be implemented by a simple device that has to understand only the lower level instructions – multiplication and addition, not how to evaluate an expression. In the case of interpretation, the objective is to build a machine that understands just the operation 'calculate the value of an arithmetic expression'. The machine may be built up of the same primitive operations as before – multiplication and division – but these are hidden and are not provided as operations of the machine. In terms of this example, the machine understands only one command, calculate the value of the given expression.

How are these ideas used in the implementation of a computer architecture? Figure 1.4 shows the relationship between two abstraction levels in an architectural hierarchy and translation and interpretation. Both

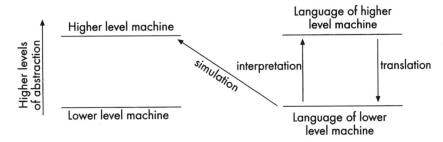

Figure 1.4 Interpretation and translation in computer architecture.

translation and interpretation can be used to implement layers of abstraction. Assuming for the moment that the hardware understands only machine code, that is, bit patterns, then a higher level language, a higher level of abstraction, may be implemented by means of translation or interpretation. Using translation the high level language program can be transformed into the equivalent machine code, which the hardware can then execute. Using interpretation, a high level language machine would be built out of the hardware and some software, that is, a program would be written to run on the hardware to imitate the actions required of the high level language machine. This new machine would then understand the high level language and so would be able directly to execute programs written in that language.

The distinction between translation and interpretation is central to the problem of realising an architecture. In most computer systems the lower levels of abstraction are realized by interpretation, that is, by building a machine using lower level primitives, whilst the higher level abstractions are realized by translation, that is, creating a set of lower level constructs equivalent to the higher level abstraction. The basic difference between the two approaches in terms of the user's perception is that translation produces a faster implementation although debugging has to be performed at a lower level, whereas interpretation, although slower, can produce diagnostics more easily. A more detailed example is given in Chapter 12.

1.5 Languages and abstract machines

It may appear at first sight that a computer language and a computer architecture do not have very much in common. However, the discussion above has shown that a language and architecture go together. Given a computer language, a machine can be built, in hardware and/or software, to 'understand' it; this is essentially what an interpreter is. Thus a machine is equivalent to a language in the restricted context of computers. The various levels of computer abstractions may be thought of in terms of either languages or machines, whichever is the more convenient. For example, a washing machine controller can be considered either in terms of the set of instructions it will obey such as wash, rinse and spin, or in terms of a machine that understands the instructions wash, rinse and spin. This does not imply that the design should be implemented in a particular way; only that it is convenient to think about the object in that way. This ability to consider designs as either languages or machines gives the designer the flexibility to explore the design space in a number of different ways.

1.6 Sequentiality, concurrency and distribution

One of the major issues of computer design at present is the subject of concurrency and distribution, especially at the higher levels of abstraction. If two actions occur concurrently then these actions occur 'at the same time', whereas if they occur sequentially at most only one of them can be active at any one time. Concurrent operation implies potential overlap in the execution of a set of tasks. At the lower levels of abstraction, that is, hardware, concurrency exists naturally. Some electronic components react immediately to a change on their inputs. Thus if inputs to several components change 'at the same time' then those components will be active concurrently. At this level considerable concurrency is possible. However, most high level programming languages do not provide constructs for the user to express concurrency in a program; most high level languages are purely sequential. Due to the search for higher performance, there has been increased interest in allowing the user to be able to specify concurrency, for example, by adding concurrent programming, constructs to programming languages or for implementing software to extract concurrency from sequential programs. Both of these techniques would allow concurrent implementation. Up until now most of the improvements in the performance of computers has arisen from technological improvements at the lower levels of abstraction but physical limits are expected to be reached sometime early in the 21st century. There is thus a need to identify other techniques for performance enhancement of which concurrency is the prime candidate.

For a computer system to execute multiple instructions concurrently, multiple processors are required. There are many different architectures possible with many processors and there are many ways of classifying them. One important feature of these systems is the degree of distribution, that is, physically how far apart the components are. The Internet can be considered as a very large distributed computer with the processors spread all over the world! The feature of a distributed computer is that a single computation is spread over many different interconnected processors. This implies that the separate units have to communicate with each other and this is the focus of Chapters 14, 15 and 16. The units of distribution may be large or small and the processor may be interconnected in many different configurations. Much of the current interest in the Internet and World-Wide Web is centred on the use of distributed computing. This is discussed further in the final chapter of the book.

1.7 The speed of technology change

One noticeable feature of computing over the last 30 years has been the rapid changes that have been seen, perhaps most notably in the emergence of the personal computer in the last twenty years. The changes have been largely driven by improvements in technology, which mean that is has been increasingly possible to produce cheaper, faster and smaller circuits. This is encapsulated in Moore's Law which states that the circuit density on a piece of silicon doubles approximately every 18 months. Since cost and speed depend largely on the size of circuits, technology improvements have been constantly driving down costs, reducing size and improving performance.

This speed of change inevitably means that the parameters that affect hardware and software designers have also been changing fast and thus the industry is constantly upgrading and improving hardware and software. One effect of this is that if a computer is designed at a point in time it will rapidly become obsolete. Manufacturers cannot allow that to happen so products are constantly updated. However, both manufacturers and users have considerable resources devoted to a particular architecture and cannot afford to change the architecture as rapidly as technology changes. Hence most manufacturers introduce a new architecture only very infrequently and mostly just update their current architectures at frequent intervals. This means that instead of having a single product for a particular architecture a manufacturer will have a range of implementations of the architecture over a period of time. This gives rise to families of processors, later members of which have additional features over the earlier members although they have the same basic architecture. This allows for backwards compatible, that is, programs written for earlier members of the family still work correctly on later members. This can be seen in the example processors used in this book; both the Motorola 68000 and the Intel 80x86 are families of processors with families of support components. Both these processor families are based on 8-bit processors which first appeared in the 1970s; the 6800 from Motorola and the 8080 from Intel. The 16-bit Motorola 68000 and Intel 80x86 first appeared in the mid to late 1980s as the Motorola 68000 and the Intel 8086, together with their 8-bit versions, the Motorola 68008 and the Intel 8088. The basic architecture of these processors was gradually improved and extended to include, for example, 32-bit addressing and virtual memory as described in Chapter 6. The Motorola 68000 became the 68010, 68020, 68030, 68040 and 68050 over a period of approximately 10 years. Similarly, the Intel 8086 became the 80186, 80286, 80386, 80486 and the Pentium and its derivatives over about 15 years. In many cases in this book one of the simpler processors is used as an example, rather than the later, more complex ones because it uses the same basic architecture and is simpler to comprehend.

The speed of technology change is still evident today and shows little signs of slowing. Rapid changes in the technology of computers are likely to occur for the foreseeable future and some possible developments are discussed in Chapter 17.

1.8 Summary

The process of design is one of hierarchical decomposition. There are many different criteria for the decomposition, which give rise to many different approaches to computer architecture. One of the most common decompositions gives rise to a layered approach to architecture where successive layers are built from primitives provided by the lower levels. Using this approach, computers are built from logic devices that are used to implement a processor that executes programs to implement higher level machines. A contrasting decomposition is the functional approach where a computer is considered as a set of functional components and the total design is in terms of the interconnection of functional units. Which approach is taken depends on the particular importance placed on facets of the design.

Using the layered approach there are two methods of implementing a higher level using the lower level primitives; translation and interpretation. In a computer architecture the lower levels of abstraction are implemented by hardware and by interpretation and the higher levels are implemented by software and by translation.

Central to current computer architecture discussions are the notions of concurrency and distribution. Concurrency implies that two or more actions occur at the same time and for this to be possible in a computer system the system must contain more than one processor. A class of concurrent architectures is known as distributed architectures where processors are physically distributed and interaction among them takes place by message passing over communication systems.

The technology of computation has been changing rapidly over the last 30 years and is expected to continue into the future. Whilst this affects the implementation of an architecture, which changes rapidly, it does not have such an immediate impact on the architecture itself since users have considerable investment in a particular architecture and are unwilling to throw this investment away. Thus manufacturers normally use developments in technology to produce new implementations of architectures rather than new architectures. This gives rise to families of processors and support circuits.

2
Introduction to digital logic

2.1 Introduction

Digital logic systems are used to process information, to control plant and machinery, and in communications systems in the 'real world'. The use of digital systems, particularly computers, has become increasingly widespread over the past few decades, and the rate of expansion shows no signs of slowing. This has occurred for two simple reasons. Firstly, information can be easily represented, stored, and manipulated in binary form, using very simple electronic circuits. Secondly, the ability to fabricate integrated circuits onto silicon chips, containing many thousands of these simple circuits, has meant that the cost of a digital logic system has continued to fall in real terms. In this chapter the fundamentals of Boolean algebra, or switching theory, are considered, together with the families of gates that are available for implementing logic systems. This chapter provides all the background knowledge necessary for understanding Chapters 3 and 4, which consider the design and implementation of combinational and sequential logic. The only assumptions made are that the reader has a basic knowledge of binary codes and binary arithmetic, and some elementary understanding of simple circuit theory, current, voltage, Ohm's law, etc.

2.2 Combinational and sequential logic

At an abstract level a digital logic system may be regarded as a black box, as shown in Figure 2.1. This box has a number of inputs, shown on the left, and a number of outputs, shown on the right. Each input and each output may take only one of two values, which are referred to as TRUE or '1', and FALSE or '0'. When a logic system is implemented with an electronic circuit, voltages are used to represent these values. Usually a low voltage, close to

0 V, is used to represent FALSE, and a high voltage, usually in the region 3 V to 5 V, is used to represent TRUE.

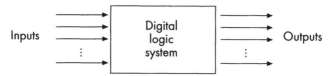

Figure 2.1   Basic digital logic system.

The words HIGH or ON are frequently used as analogous to TRUE, and LOW or OFF as analogous to FALSE. It will be shown later that a transistor may be used as a switch, having two stable states, which correspond to the transistor being switched either ON or OFF. These two states, are used to represent TRUE and FALSE. Thus:

$$TRUE = HIGH = ON = 1$$

$$FALSE = LOW = OFF = 0$$

Digital logic circuits are divided into two distinct types, namely combinational logic circuits and sequential logic circuits. Most real logic systems, such as computers, are a mixture of both combinational and sequential logic circuits. A combinational circuit is one where the values of the outputs depend only on the present values of the inputs. Such circuits have no memory, so the outputs cannot depend on the order in which the values of the inputs are changed, or on any previous values of those inputs. The design of combinational circuits is discussed in Chapter 3.

A sequential circuit, on the other hand, is one in which the outputs depend not only on the present values of the inputs, but also on the past values of those inputs, that is, on the history of the circuit. Sequential circuits require memory to store the necessary history of the circuit. In practice, sequential logic circuits contain both combinational logic and memory elements, as shown in Figure 2.2. Such sequential logic systems are often referred to as finite state machines (FSM), and are discussed in Chapter 4.

2.3 Basic logic gates

Figure 2.3 shows the simplest possible combinational logic circuit with a single input labelled A and a single output labelled Z. The circuit of Figure 2.3a is known as a buffer. The output Z always has the same logic level as the input, so the Boolean equation defining its behaviour is:

$$Z = A$$

and is read as Z is A. Although the use of such a circuit is not immediately apparent, it is in fact widely used.

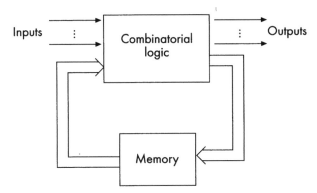

Figure 2.2 Block diagram of a sequential logic circuit.

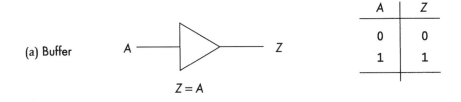

A	Z
0	0
1	1

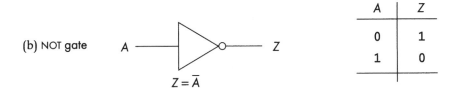

A	Z
0	1
1	0

Figure 2.3 The basic 1-input logic gates.

Figure 2.3b is an inverter or NOT gate. The value of the output is always the inverse, or complement, of the input, that is, the output is FALSE when the input is TRUE, and vice-versa. The logic equation is:

$$Z = \overline{A}$$

and is read as Z is NOT A. The line, or bar, over the A implies NOT, in this case NOT A. The logic symbol of the NOT gate is really composed of two parts, a triangle and a circle, or bubble as it is usually called. The triangle means that the element is a buffer, and the bubble that this buffer is an inverting buffer so that the element performs the NOT function. Note for the present that the bubble may be drawn either on the input to, or the output from, the buffer. The use of the bubble notation will be discussed more fully in

Section 2.6. The simplicity of the NOT gate hides its importance: without the NOT gate, the design of many useful digital logic systems would not be possible!

Slightly more complicated are the combinational circuits shown in Figure 2.4, each of which has two inputs, labelled A and B, and one output, labelled Z. Although there are actually 16 logic functions that have two inputs, or variables, only five are fundamental elements: AND, OR, NAND, NOR and EOR. Figure 2.4 shows the logic symbols of four of these five basic elements, or gates as they are frequently known. Each circuit is defined by a Boolean logic equation and by a truth table; both definitions are shown in Figure 2.4. These gates will now be considered in more detail.

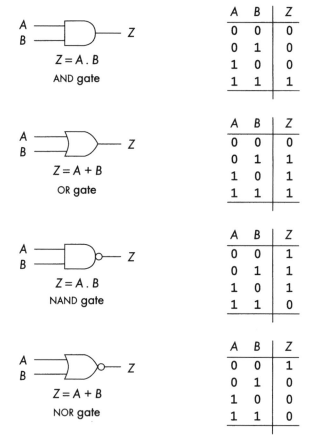

A	B	Z
0	0	0
0	1	0
1	0	0
1	1	1

$Z = A . B$

AND gate

A	B	Z
0	0	0
0	1	1
1	0	1
1	1	1

$Z = A + B$

OR gate

A	B	Z
0	0	1
0	1	1
1	0	1
1	1	0

$Z = \overline{A . B}$

NAND gate

A	B	Z
0	0	1
0	1	0
1	0	0
1	1	0

$Z = \overline{A + B}$

NOR gate

Figure 2.4 The basic 2-input logic gates.

2.3.1 The AND gate

The output Z is TRUE (that is, 1) only when both the inputs are TRUE. The logic equation is:

$$Z = A.B$$

where the operator dot symbol (.) means and. The equation is read as Z is A AND B. The truth table gives the output of the gate for each of the possible inputs. In this case it has three columns, one for each input, A and B, and one for the output Z, and four rows since there are $2^2 = 4$ possible input combinations of A and B. The truth table is usually written using 0s and 1s, although TRUE and FALSE could equally well be used. The number of inputs can be increased to n, say, to give an n-input AND gate. The generalized logic equation then becomes:

$$Z = A.B.C....$$

and the truth table will have 2^n rows. The output Z will be 1 only when all the inputs are 1.

2.3.2 The OR gate

The output of the OR gate is TRUE when either input A or input B is TRUE or when both are true. The logic equation is:

$$Z = A+B$$

where the operator + (the plus symbol) means 'or'. The equation is read as Z is A or B. The OR gate can be generalized to an n-input OR gate with the logic equation:

$$Z = A+B+C+...$$

In this case the output Z will be 1 if any of the inputs is 1.

2.3.3 The NAND gate

The NAND gate performs the function NOT–AND and is best thought of as an AND gate followed by a NOT gate. The truth table is obtained by complementing the output column Z of the AND gate, that is, changing all 0s to 1s, and 1s to 0s. The logic equation is:

$$Z = \overline{A.B}$$

and is read as NOT(A AND B). Note the use of the bar over the whole expression to symbolize inverting the whole function. Do not confuse it with (NOT A) AND B, which is $Z = \overline{A}.B$, and which has a different action and truth table.

2.3.4 The NOR gate

Similarly the NOR gate may be thought of as an OR gate followed by a NOT gate. The logic equation is:

$$Z = \overline{A + B}$$

and is read as NOT (A OR B).

Both the NAND and the NOR gates may be expanded to n-inputs, and both gates are of great importance. Although it is useful to think of a NAND (NOR) gate as a NOT-AND (NOT-OR) gate, it is designed and implemented directly as a NAND (NOR) gate. Later it will be shown that all logic functions and systems may be implemented using only NAND gates or only NOR gates. At present, for example, it should be clear that the NOT function can be implemented directly with either a NAND gate or a NOR gate by joining both inputs together. This is shown in Figure 2.5a for a NAND gate. The truth table for the NAND and NOR functions shows that if both inputs are 0 then the output is 1, while if both inputs are 1 then the output is 0. An alternative way to implement NOT using a NAND gate is shown in Figure 2.5b. Here one of the inputs is tied permanently to the logic value 1. Again, inspection of the truth table shows that this performs the NOT function.

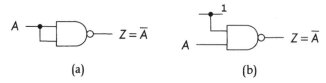

(a)   (b)

Figure 2.5 Implementing the NOT function with a NAND gate.

2.3.5 The EOR gate

Earlier it was pointed out that there are 16 possible logic functions of two variables that can be generated. So far four of these have been discussed, namely AND, OR, NAND and NOR. Of the remaining 12 only one other is commonly implemented, the exclusive-OR, EOR function. The logic symbol and the truth table for the EOR gate are given in Figure 2.6. The first three rows of the EOR truth table are identical to those of the OR function. The fourth row is different: if both inputs are logic 1 then the output is logic 0. Thus the output is 1 only if either A or B, but not both, are 1. Strictly speaking, the ordinary OR function should be called the inclusive-OR function (symbol +) to distinguish it from the exclusive-OR function (symbol ⊕).

A	B	Z
0	0	0
0	1	1
1	0	1
1	1	0

$$Z = A \oplus B$$

Figure 2.6 The exclusive-OR logic gate.

2.4 Example: a 1-bit half adder

Before proceeding with a formal discussion of Boolean algebra, a very simple but widely used combinational circuit, the 1-bit half adder shown in black box form in Figure 2.7, will be considered. The circuit has two 1-bit inputs,

Figure 2.7 The 1-bit adder.

A and *B*, and performs binary addition. The circuit generates two outputs, the sum *S* and the carry *C*. Table 2.1 shows the relation between the outputs *S* and *C*, and the inputs *A* and *B*, for all possible combinations of input values. The truth table has four columns, two for the inputs *A* and *B*, and two for the outputs *S* and *C*. There are four rows, one for each of the possible $2^2 = 4$ input combinations.

Table 2.1   Truth table for a 1-bit half adder

A	B	S	C
0	0	0	0
0	1	1	0
1	0	1	0
1	1	0	1

Logic equations for each of the two outputs *S* and *C* can now be derived from the truth table in terms of the inputs *A* and *B*. The procedure for determining these logic equations from the truth table will be discussed in detail in Chapter 3. In this example it leads to:

$$S = \bar{A}.B + A.\bar{B}$$

$$C = A.B$$

A combinational circuit may be constructed using basic gates to generate *S* and *C*. In fact, *S* is just the exclusive-OR ($\oplus$) of *A* and *B*, while *C* is the AND of *A* and *B*, as may be seen by reference to Figures 2.4 and 2.6. An implementation of this simple circuit is shown in Figure 2.8.

2.5 Boolean algebra

The specification and design of digital logic systems requires a set of basic propositions and rules. The mathematics that is used for digital design is called Boolean algebra, or switching theory, and is based on Boole's work on

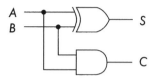

Figure 2.8 The 1-bit adder circuit.

the algebra of propositions published in 1854. Boolean algebra is also known as propositional calculus, and the form in which it is now used was developed by Shannon in 1938.

2.5.1 Propositions and rules of Boolean algebra

The Boolean algebra operators NOT, AND and OR have already been described. NOT operates on only a single variable to give its complement, while AND (.) and OR (+) operate on pairs of variables. There are four basic propositions in Boolean algebra:

1. Commutative proposition:

$$A.B = B.A$$
$$A + B = B + A$$

where A and B represent Boolean values (that is, 0 and 1).

2. Distributive proposition:

$$A.(B + C) = A.B + A.C$$
$$A + B.C = (A + B).(A + C)$$

3. Identity proposition:

$$A + 0 = A$$
$$A + 1 = 1$$
$$A.1 = A$$
$$A.0 = 0$$

4. Inverse proposition:

$$A + \bar{A} = 1$$
$$A.\bar{A} = 0$$

With these propositions a large number of Boolean algebra theorems may be developed. The most important, which will be used where necessary in the text, are:

1. De Morgan's theorem:

$$\overline{A + B} = \bar{A}.\bar{B}$$

$$\overline{A.B} = \bar{A} + \bar{B}$$

2. Simplification theorem:

$$A + A.B = A$$

$$A + \overline{A}.B = A + B$$

Any of the theorems of Boolean algebra can be verified by evaluating the truth tables for both sides of the equation, and showing that they are identical. This method is demonstrated in the Table 2.2 for the first of De Morgan's theorems, $\overline{A + B} = \overline{A}.\overline{B}$.

Table 2.2   Truth table for De Morgan's first theorem.

A	B	$A + B$	$\overline{A + B}$	$\overline{A}$	$\overline{B}$	$\overline{A}.\overline{B}$
0	0	0	1	1	1	1
0	1	1	0	1	0	0
1	0	1	0	0	1	0
1	1	1	0	0	0	0

As column 4 is identical to column 7, the theorem is verified. An alternative method is to manipulate the theorem using the propositions and any previously proven theorems, until the new theorem is proved. For example, to prove the first of the simplification theorems:

$$A + A.B = A$$

the third identity proposition can be used and $A.1$ substituted for A. The left hand side then becomes:

$$A.1 + A.B$$

A is a common factor so this can be rewritten as:

$$A.(1 + B)$$

Finally, using the identity proposition $B + 1 = 1$, the left-hand side of the original equation is then just $A.1 = A$, and as this is equal to the right-hand side the proof is complete.

2.5.2 Sum-of-products

When designing combinational logic systems, one logic equation is derived for each output. These equations will have a single logical variable on the left hand side, the output variable, while the right-hand side will be a Boolean expression of the input variables. The complexity of the right-hand side of each equation will depend on the complexity of the logic function to be implemented. Boolean equations may be written down in many ways. For example, in the 1-bit adder discussed above, the equation for the result S for the binary addition of A and B is:

$$S = \bar{A}.B + A.\bar{B}$$

This equation is written down in what is called the sum-of-products form, that is, in this case a sum (+) of two products (.).

A general Boolean function of two variables, $f(A,B)$, may be written in a sum-of-products form in the following way:

$$f(A,B) = A.B.f(0,0) + A.B.f(0,1) + A.B.f(1,0) + A.B.f(1,1)$$

where each of the terms $f(0,0)$, $f(0,1)$, $f(1,0)$ and $f(1,1)$ can take only the value 0 or 1. Again, for example, in the 1-bit half adder $S = f(A,B)$ and so:

$$S = f(A,B) = \bar{A}.\bar{B}.0 + \bar{A}.B.1 + A.\bar{B}.1 + A.B.0 = \bar{A}.B + A.\bar{B}$$

that is, $f(0,0) = 0$, $f(1,1) = 0$ and $f(0,1) = 1$, $f(1,0) = 1$

The equation for $f(A,B)$ is said to be in canonical form since it contains all possible combinations of the input variables. Each term is called a minterm, which is a (.) product containing each of the input variables, or its complement, just once.

2.6 NAND/NOR logic

The design of combinational logic circuits proceeds from the truth table to the logic equations, and then to the implementation. The form of the logic equations used in this text is the sum-of-products form, which could be implemented directly if all the different types of basic logic gate are available. For example, returning to the 1-bit half adder, the logic equation $S = \bar{A}.B + A.\bar{B}$ could be implemented directly, as in Figure 2.9, using a mixture of NOT, AND and OR gates (assuming, of course, that an exclusive-OR gate is not available). However, such an implementation would be very

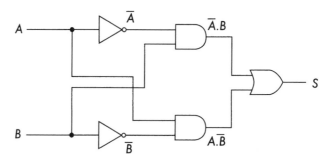

Figure 2.9 1-bit adder circuit using a mixture of NOT, AND and OR gates.

inefficient since it requires two AND gates, one OR gate, and two NOT gates. This is because gates are implemented in integrated circuits, often called chips, which in general contain only groups of a single type of gate. (A 2-input AND gate is generally available only in a package containing four such gates.) A much more efficient implementation would result if it were possible to implement the logic equation with just NAND gates, or just NOR gates. It has already been demonstrated how a NAND gate can implement the NOT function by joining its inputs together (Figure 2.5). De Morgan's theorem states that it is always possible to convert a NAND function to a NOR function, and vice versa. The theorem will now be applied to the equation for S to eliminate the OR operation, as follows. First, both sides of the equation are complemented, giving:

$$\bar{S} = \overline{\bar{A}.B + A.\bar{B}}$$

Note that, just like normal algebra, performing the same operation to each side of an equation does not affect its validity. De Morgan's theorem is now applied to the right-hand side of the equation to change the OR function to the AND function:

$$\bar{S} = \overline{\overline{\bar{A}.B}.\overline{A.\bar{B}}}$$

Finally, both sides of this equation are complemented to leave S on the left-hand side:

$$S = \overline{\overline{\overline{\bar{A}.B}.\overline{A.\bar{B}}}}$$

Remembering that a 2-input NAND gate acts as a NOT gate if both its inputs are joined together, then S has now been expressed in such a way that it can be entirely implemented with NAND gates, as shown in Figure 2.10a.

It is quite easy to make mistakes in this type of algebraic manipulation; an alternative approach is to use a diagrammatic technique. This technique begins with the original logic gate diagram of Figure 2.9. Again it is assumed that the circuit will be implemented with only NAND gates. The first stage is to identify the two AND gates and change them to NAND gates by adding bubbles to their outputs. Clearly, this completely changes the logic function of the circuit. To maintain the correct logic function a second bubble (an inverter) must be added into each of the lines leading to the OR gate. If the bubbles are added at the inputs of the OR gates then the logic diagram is as shown in Figure 2.10b. Although it may not be apparent at first sight, this simplifies the circuit, since the combination of the OR gate symbol with the bubbles on the two input lines is actually a NAND gate. If the two inputs to the two bubbles at the OR gate are labelled X and Y (refer to Figure 2.10b) then this gate performs the logic function:

$$\bar{X} + \bar{Y}$$

which by De Morgan's theorem is just $\overline{X.Y}$, that is, the NAND function of X and Y. This completes the conversion, since again the original circuit has been converted to one containing only NANDs. Figure 2.11a shows two equivalent ways of drawing a NAND gate, following directly from De Morgan's first theorem:

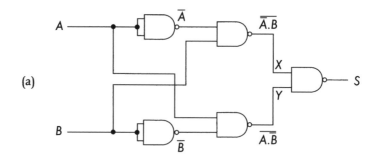

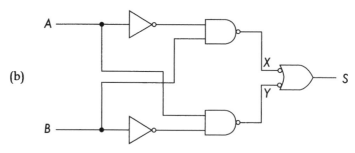

Figure 2.10 (a) Implementation of 1-bit adder using only NAND gates;
(b) Illustration of the 'bubble' technique.

Figure 2.11 Equivalent ways of drawing (a) NAND and (b) NOR gates.

In a similar way, the second of De Morgan's theorems:

$$\overline{A + B} = \overline{A}.\overline{B}$$

gives two different ways of drawing the NOR gate symbol, shown in
Figure 2.11b. The gate symbol that should be used for NAND and NOR
depends on the circumstances. The first NAND symbol implies that the
output is active low when both the inputs are active high, while the second
NAND symbol implies that the output is active high when the inputs are
active low. Similar arguments apply to the NOR gate symbols. The meaning
of active high and active low will be discussed in the next section. The
example described above has shown how implementation using a single type
of logic gate, namely NAND gates, is possible. The design could equally well

have been implemented with only NOR gates, and the reader is recommended to try this as an exercize. The idea of being able to move bubbles around in a design, and of adding pairs of bubbles when necessary, is extremely useful, and one which will be used in Chapter 3.

2.7 Positive and negative logic

So far it has been assumed that positive logic is being used, that is, TRUE is represented by logic 1 and FALSE by logic 0. This leads to Table 2.3, the truth table for the NAND function

Table 2.3   Truth table for NAND function

A	B	NAND		A	B	NAND
F	F	T		0	0	1
F	T	T		0	1	1
T	F	T		1	0	1
T	T	F		1	1	0
	(a)				(b)	

where (b) is obtained directly from (a) by making the substitutions $F = 0$ and $T = 1$. This is known as positive logic. Logic schemes can also be implemented using negative logic by making the substitutions $F = 1$ and $T = 0$. Making these substitutions, that is, $0 = T$ and $1 = F$, in Table 2.3(b) above gives Table 2.4.

Table 2.4   Truth table for NAND, using negative logic

A	B	Z
T	T	F
T	F	F
F	T	F
F	F	T

Examination shows that Z is the NOR function, and so leads to the conclusion that a positive logic NAND gate can also be regarded as a negative logic NOR gate. In the same way, if the same substitutions are carried out to a NOR gate it becomes clear that a positive logic NOR gate can also be regarded as a negative logic NAND gate. Although logically straightforward, negative logic does seem intuitively to be more difficult to handle than positive logic, and so will not generally be used in this text.

2.8 Logic implementation

We will now consider the practical implementation of the basic logic gates. Although there are several ways of implementing digital logic systems, including fluidic logic, relay logic and electronic logic gates, only the last will be considered here. The aim of this section is, firstly, to introduce the concept of using a transistor as a digital switch and, secondly, briefly to introduce families of electronic logic gates. This will only be taken to the extent that the reader will feel confident to implement simple logic designs by interconnecting logic chips, and have an appreciation of the differences among available logic families.

2.8.1 The field effect transistor as a switch

Transistors are the basic 'building blocks' of all integrated electronic logic circuits. There are two main types of transistor family available, field-effect transistor (FET) and bipolar, each with several variants. All transistors have the ability to act as digital switches, and it is this capability that is exploited in all digital logic circuits. Figure 2.12 shows the circuit symbol used for the FET. The device has three terminals, called the source, gate and drain. The

Figure 2.12 FET symbol.

basic transistor switch circuit using a FET is shown in Figure 2.13a. Although there are several different types of FET available, only one, the 'n-channel enhancement mode FET', will be considered. In addition to the FET, the circuit contains a resistor R_L, known as a load resistor, and a battery, whose voltage is labelled V_{cc}. The battery, the resistor R_L, the drain–source resistance of the FET, and the connecting wires form a simple series circuit. In this circuit no current flows because there is no voltage on the gate (since no connection has been made to the gate) and the transistor is turned off. The drain-source path thus acts like an open switch, and so the drain-source current, i_{ds}, is zero. Moreover, because no current flows in this circuit there is no voltage drop across R_L (by Ohm's law) and so the voltage across the drain-source of the FET, V_{ds}, is V_{cc} volts. Since no connection was made to the gate, the gate-source voltage $V_{gs} = 0$ V. Note that voltage differences are defined relative to the source of the FET.

Consider now what happens when a non-zero voltage is applied to the gate relative to the source, that is, $V_{gs} > 0$. It turns out that if V_{gs} is greater than a threshold voltage, V_t, then the transistor is turned on. There is now a

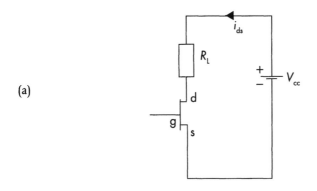

(a)

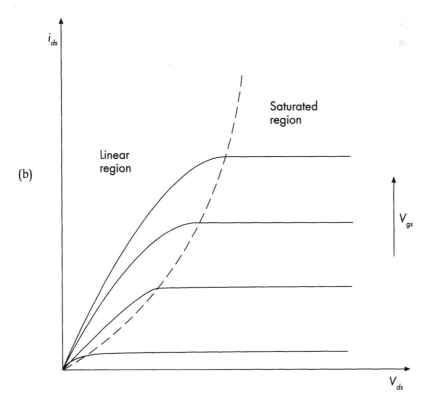

(b)

Figure 2.13 (a) Basic FET transistor circuit;
(b) Characteristic curves for a typical n-channel enhancement
mode FET. Each curve is a plot of the drain–source current, i_{ds},
as a function of the drain–source voltage, V_{ds}, for given values
of the gate–source voltage, V_{gs}.

conducting path between the drain and the source which completes the
circuit so that a current can now flow around the battery, R_L, and FET circuit,
that is, $i_{ds} > 0$. The threshold voltage, V_t, varies from a few tenths of a volt to
a few volts, depending on the design of the FET. Figure 2.13b shows how the

drain-source current i_{ds} varies with the drain-source voltage V_{ds} for a number of values of the gate-source voltage V_{gs}. Each curve, corresponding to a constant value of V_{gs}, falls into two distinct regions, namely the linear region and the saturation region. As V_{ds} is increased from zero, the drain current, i_{ds}, initially increases approximately linearly with V_{ds}. However, above a certain value of V_{ds} the curve 'flattens out', or saturates, so that i_{ds} remains constant for any further increase in V_{ds}. FETs used as digital switches are operated in the saturation region. This is achieved if V_{gs} is much greater than the threshold voltage V_t, by making $V_{gs} = V_{cc}$, say. The drain–source path then behaves like a closed switch, with a small resistance which can be neglected. If this is the case then $V_{ds} = 0$ and the voltage drop across the resistor equals V_{cc}. This is the basic FET digital switch, and is re-drawn in Figure 2.14. The input voltage V_{in} is applied to the gate, so $V_{gs} = V_{in}$. The output is taken from the drain terminal, so $V_{out} = V_{ds}$. There are only two possible values for V_{in}; either 0 volts or V_{cc}. Thus the two following cases are possible:

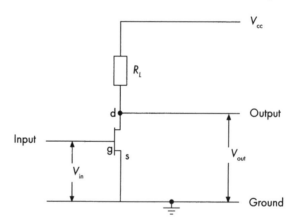

Figure 2.14 Basic FET switch circuit.

1. $V_{in} = 0$. The FET is switched off, so $i_{ds} = 0$ and $V_{out} = V_{cc}$.

2. $V_{in} = V_{cc}$. The FET is switched hard on, so $i_{ds} > 0$, and $V_{out} \sim 0$. From Ohm's law, $i_{ds} = V_{cc}/R_L$

These two conditions can be expressed as a truth table in Table 2.5 where, as usual, 0 represents logic level **0**, and V_{cc} logic level **1**. This is clearly the truth table for a NOT gate, and so a single FET can be used to implement the NOT function.

2.8.2 Field-effect transistor NAND and NOR logic gates

NAND and NOR logic gates may be constructed very simply from the basic FET switching circuit just described. The circuit of Figure 2.15 is a 2-input NAND gate. The inputs are A and B, while the output Z is taken from the

Table 2.5 Truth table for FET circuit

V_{in}	V_{out}	or	V_{in}	V_{out}
0	V_{cc}		0	1
V_{cc}	0		1	0

junction between the drain of the top FET and the load resistor R_L. The V_{cc} power supply and the connecting wires have been omitted for simplicity. There are four possible input conditions. Consider first $A = B = 0$. Both transistors are switched off so no current flows down the chain comprising the load resistor R_L and the two transistors. Thus the output Z is at the supply voltage V_{cc}, so $Z = 1$. A similar argument applies for $A = 0$, $B = 1$ and for $A = 1$, $B = 0$. Only for the case $A = B = 1$, when both FETs are turned on, can a current flow so that $Z = 0$. The circuit is clearly that of a NAND gate. Figure 2.16 shows a 2-input NOR function constructed from two FETs in parallel. The reader should be able to verify that this circuit does indeed perform the NOR function. These two circuits are easily extended to have any number of inputs.

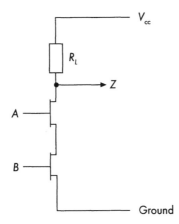

Figure 2.15 2-input FET NAND gate.

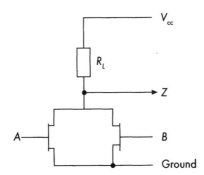

Figure 2.16 2-input FET NOR gate.

Bipolar transistor logic circuits are constructed in a similar way to implement the basic logic functions, but they will not be considered in this text (see, for example, *The Art of Electronics*, by Horowitz and Hill).

2.9 Logic families

2.9.1 Introduction

Before discussing particular logic families, consider the characteristics of an ideal gate, as follows:

1. In all positive logic systems, logic level 0 is nominally represented by 0 V, and logic level 1 by a positive voltage, often +5 V. However, it is essential that the two logic levels be represented not by fixed voltages but by voltage ranges. These ranges should be as wide as possible, but must not overlap, otherwise the 0 and 1 logic levels will be indistinguishable. In addition, there must be a voltage gap between the two ranges. The reasons for these requirements will become clear later in this section.

2. Each gate should dissipate the least amount of power possible (ideally zero). This is because power is dissipated as heat, causing systems containing many integrated circuits to require cooling fans or in extreme cases, water cooling. Moreover, 'hot' integrated circuits are less reliable than 'cold' ones, and in addition systems requiring large currents necessitate large power supplies which are costly and cumbersome.

3. The propagation delay through a gate should be kept to a minimum (ideally zero). Figure 2.17a shows the ideal input and output signals of a simple NOT gate, and Figure 2.17b the actual signals observed for a real NOT gate. In Figure 2.17a there is no delay between the change of state of the input from 1 to 0, and the corresponding change in the output from 0 to 1. Moreover, the changes are instantaneous. In a real gate these changes are not instantaneous and values called the rise time and fall time are given for each logic family. These times are defined as the time taken for a logic level to change from 10% to 90% of its final value, and are typically a few nanoseconds. Figure 2.17b also shows that the output does not change until some time after the input changes. This is known as the propagation delay, and is typically several nanoseconds. Considerable effort is made to make the propagation delay as short as possible since such delays limit the speed at which logic can operate. In practice it is found that, for a particular fabrication technology, the product of the power consumption of a gate and its propagation delay is approximately constant. Consequently a trade-off can always be made between a lower power consumption and a larger gate delay, or vice versa.

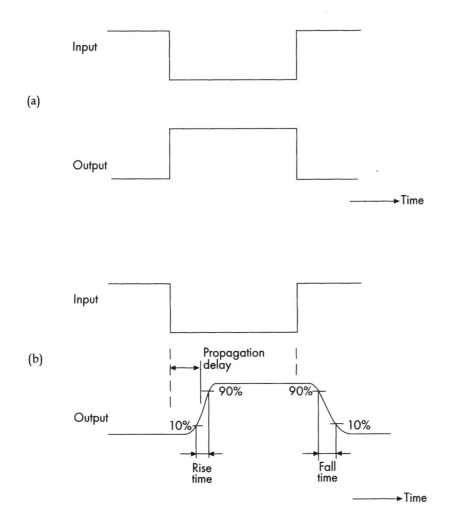

Figure 2.17 Input and output signals of an (a) ideal and (b) actual NOT gate.

4. The output from a single gate should be able to drive a large number (ideally an infinite number) of similar gates in parallel. This is known as the fan-out capability of a logic family.

5. Each gate should have a high 'noise immunity'. In a real digital system the logic levels do not remain steady with time but are perturbed by noise. Logic families have to be designed to deal with noise, so that noise within a stated margin cannot cause a gate to operate incorrectly; for example, by giving a logic 1 when it should be 0.

The two most widely available logic families, known as TTL (transistor-transistor logic) and CMOS (complementary metal oxide semiconductor) logic, will now be discussed.

2.9.2 Transistor-transistor logic

Although TTL has been available since the 1960s, continuing development has produced a number of different families of TTL over the years, some now obsolete, so that it remains a popular choice for building small scale logic systems. The most popular family of TTL at present is low-power Schottky, or LS, based on bipolar transistor technology. Within this family there is a wide range of chips available, with individual chips being referred to as 74LSxx, where xx is a symbol referring to a particular chip. For example, the 74LS00 is a 2-input NAND gate, and the 74LS04 is a NOT gate. In practice the 74LS00 chip is a 14-pin device that contains four 2-input NAND gates, while the 74LS04 contains six NOT gates. Full details of these chips are given in TTL data books and device sheets.

The TTL parameters most relevant to users are logic levels, fan-out, fan-in, gate propagation delay and power requirements.

(a) Logic levels

TTL LS logic levels have the following voltage ranges:

Output:	Logic 1	V_{OH}	2.7 to 5.0 V
	Logic 0	V_{OL}	0 to 0.5 V
Input:	Logic 1	V_{IH}	2.0 to 5.0 V
	Logic 0	V_{IL}	0 to 0.8 V

These values mean that the output of a TTL gate for logic level 1 (the symbol is V_{OH}, where O represents output and H a logic 1) is guaranteed to be greater than 2.7 V even when it is supplying its maximum possible current. In practice, it is more likely to be closer to 3.5 V, referred to in data sheets as the typical V_{OH} value. However the input to a gate for logic level 1, symbol V_{IH}, need only be 2.0 V, that is, 0.7 V less than the minimum logic level 1 output voltage, V_{OH}. This difference is called the noise immunity margin. Consider Figure 2.18, which shows the output of a NOT gate being fed into the input of a second NOT gate. Suppose the output of gate A is a

Figure 2.18 Noise immunity example.

logic 1, and is actually the minimum value of 2.7 V. If this output is viewed on an oscilloscope, it may well be seen that the output is not a steady voltage of 2.7 V, but comprises two components: the steady level of 2.7 V and a randomly fluctuating noise voltage of perhaps several hundred millivolts. Gate B will still recognize the input to be a logic 1 provided that the amplitude of the noise voltage does not exceed 0.7 V. Now suppose the output of gate A is logic 0, and is actually 0.5 V, that is, at the top of the logic 0 range. What digital noise can be tolerated on this output? The answer is an amplitude that does not exceed $0.8 - 0.5 = 0.3$ V. These figures are referred to as noise margins. Finally, note that voltages in the range 0.8 to 2.0 V are not defined and must not occur. The output of a gate whose input does lay in this range will be undefined, and may be interpreted as either logic 0 or logic 1.

(b) Fan-out

The current-driving capabilities of TTL logic will now be discussed. Consider the TTL NOT gate shown in Figure 2.19a. The output is shown driving a load,

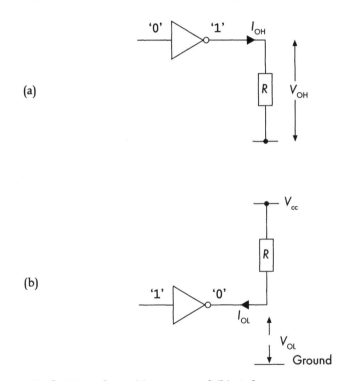

Figure 2.19 Definition of TTL (a) source and (b) sink currents.

represented by the resistor R, to ground. Let the input to the gate be logic 0 so the output is logic 1. The output current flowing through the resistor R to ground, I_{OH}, is related to V_{OH} and to R by Ohm's law:

$$I_{OH} = \frac{V_{OH}}{R}$$

Suppose R is initially 'large', that is, several thousands of ohms or more, and is then progressively decreased. The above equation shows that I_{OH} will increase as this happens. However, as I_{OH} increases it is found that V_{OH} starts to decrease. This is allowable of course, provided that it does not fall below 2.7 V. I_{OH} is known as the source current, and the maximum value allowed is −400 μA. The negative sign is used by convention to mean that the current is flowing out of the gate. When the maximum source current is drawn, V_{OH} will still be above (although perhaps only just) the minimum value of 2.7 V.

Now consider the situation shown in Figure 2.19b where the load R is connected between the output of the gate and the TTL power supply, nominally +5 V, with the gate input logic 1 so the output is logic 0. Current will flow from the power supply through the load resistor R and into the gate. This current is known as the output low current I_{OL} and is usually referred to as the sink current. If the output low voltage is V_{OL} then the voltage drop across the load resistor is $V_{cc}-V_{OL}$. Applying Ohm's law to R gives:

$$I_{OL} = \frac{V_{cc} - V_{OL}}{R}$$

Again, if R is initially 'large' and then progressively decreased, I_{OL} will increase. However, this time as I_{OL} increases, V_{OL} begins to rise above 0 V. Eventually it reaches the maximum TTL value allowed of 0.5 V. The maximum sink current I_{OL} is (+)8 mA. Note that the maximum sink current is much greater than the maximum source current.

Fan-out is defined as the maximum number of gates whose inputs may all be connected to the output of a single gate, that is, it is the maximum number of gates that the output from a single TTL gate will drive.

(c) Fan-in

In the same way as discussed above for output currents, the input current requirements of TTL gates must be considered. It is important to realise that for a TTL gate to work some current must flow into the input circuit of the gate. Consider again the two interconnected NOT gates shown in Figure 2.18. If the input to gate A is logic level 1 then its output will be logic 0. The input to gate B is thus logic 0, and its output, logic 1. The input circuit of gate B provides a load to the output of gate A, with the result that a current flows out of gate B into gate A. This current is called the input low current I_{IL} and for a LS TTL gate has a value less than −0.4 mA. Now suppose the input to gate A is changed to logic 0. Its output is logic 1 so that now a source current will flow out of A and into the input circuit of B. This current is the input high current I_{IH} and is less than 20 μA for LS TTL. Comparing these input currents with the output drive current capabilities of LS TTL shows that the LS TTL fan-out is 20, that is, a standard LS TTL gate can drive 20 standard LS TTL gates.

Figure 2.5 showed the two ways in which a NAND gate can be used as an inverter. The circuits differ in that Figure 2.5a has a fan-in of 2, since the preceding gate must drive both the inputs, while Figure 2.5b has a fan-in of 1. For this reason the second circuit is usually preferred.

(d) Speed versus power

In the introduction to logic families it was argued that the ideal gate should consume no power, and have zero propagation delay. In practice, neither of these requirements can be met, and trade-offs have to be made. The LS TTL family of TTL integrated circuits has a typical gate propagation delay of 10 ns, and a power consumption of 2 mW.

Other popular TTL families include FAST TTL, 74Fxx, with gate propagation times of 5 to 6 ns, and advanced low-power Schottky, 74ALSxx.

2.9.3 Complementary metal oxide semiconductor logic

(a) Introduction

The second logic family widely used for implementing digital logic is complementary metal oxide semiconductor logic, CMOS. Figure 2.20 shows the basic CMOS inverter circuit, or NOT gate. Although the circuit may look

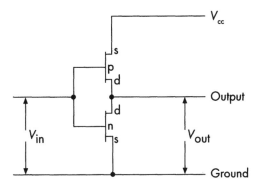

Figure 2.20 Basic CMOS NOT gate.

strange at first sight, it is conceptually very simple. It consists of only two FET transistors, connected in series between the logic power supply. The bottom transistor is an n-channel FET similar to the one discussed above in Section 2.8.1, while the top transistor is a p-channel FET. The main difference between an n-channel and a p-channel FET is that the p-channel FET is turned on when the gate voltage is more negative than the source voltage (that is, $V_{gs} < 0$) and is turned off when $V_{gs} = 0$. The input is applied to the gates of both transistors, which are joined together. The power supply lines are labelled V_{cc} and ground, although frequently V_{dd} is used in place of V_{cc}, and V_{ss} in place of ground. Unlike TTL the supply voltage V_{cc} can be varied between +3 and +15 V, or even higher in the case of some CMOS family circuits. To see how this circuit works consider the two possible logic values that V_{in} can take.

1. $V_{in} = 0$ V, corresponding to logic 0. The bottom transistor is switched off, while the top transistor is switched on. The ratio of the off/on source-drain resistance of a FET is very large, and so there is effectively a short-circuit path between V_{cc} and V_{out}, and an open-circuit path between ground and V_{out}. Thus $V_{out} = V_{cc}$.

2. $V_{in} = V_{cc}$, corresponding to logic 1. The bottom transistor is switched on, the top transistor is off, so V_{out} is effectively connected to ground, that is, $V_{out} = 0$.

The circuit thus acts as a NOT gate, and is the fundamental building block used in CMOS circuits. Note that only one transistor is on in both logic states, so in the quiescent state no current flows and hence the power dissipation is zero. Although there are a number of CMOS families available, the main series is the 74HCTxx family, which is compatible with LS TTL, so the two families can be used together.

(b) Logic levels

In CMOS logic the output changes state when V_{in} is approximately $\frac{1}{2}V_{cc}$. As the family is compatible with LS TTL, the V_{IH} and V_{IL} are 2 V and 0.8 V respectively. However, the maximum current output is 4 mA, which does differ from LS TTL.

(c) Fan-out

Because the transistors used in a CMOS gate are FETs, CMOS circuits have negligible current requirements (in practice less than 1μA), and can usually be neglected. Thus the output from a CMOS gate can drive any number of CMOS gates in parallel, that is, the fan-out is theoretically infinite. In practice this is not true. The input gate of a FET behaves like a capacitor: when the logic level of a gate is changed from 0 to 1, current flows into the gate capacitance, charging the gate until its voltage equals V_{cc}, and conversely when the level is changed from 1 to 0 current has to flow out of the gate capacitance.

Consider the circuit shown in Figure 2.21, where the output of the first CMOS NOT gate is used to drive a second NOT gate. Assume the input to the first gate is logic 1, so that its output is 0. Transistors $n1$ and $p2$ are switched on, while $n2$ and $p1$ are off, so that the gate of the second NOT gate is at 0 V. Changing the logic level at gate 1 from 1 to 0 switches $n1$ off and $p1$ on. The gate of the second FET is now connected to the supply voltages V_{cc} through $p1$, which has a low effective resistance, R_{eff} say. For the 74HCT series R_{eff} is about 100Ω. Current now flows through R_{eff} and charges the effective capacitance, C_{eff}, of the second FET's gate. The voltage on the gate V_g then increases with time according to the equation:

$$V_g = V_{cc}(1 - e^{t/(R_{eff}C_{eff})})$$

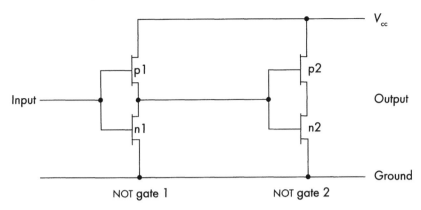

Figure 2.21 CMOS circuit illustrating fan-out.

Thus V_g increases in an exponential fashion towards V_{cc} with a time constant RC. The value of C is of the order 10 pF, so:

$$R_{eff}C_{eff} = 10^2 \times 10 \times 10^{-12} = 1 \text{ ns.}$$

If, however, n more gates are added in parallel with the second gate, the effect is to multiply C_{eff} by n, thus increasing the charge/discharge time. It is this effect which limits the fan-out in a real CMOS system. The input current requirements of LS TTL gates, discussed above, is such that 74HCT series can drive up to 10 LS TTL gates directly.

(d) Fan in

This term is not really applicable to CMOS circuits, since effectively no gate current is required. Although outside the scope of this book, the interfacing between different logic families that are not compatible, such as TTL and CMOS (other than the 74HCT series), is an important subject. See, for example, Horowitz and Hill in the bibliography.

(e) Speed versus power

The maximum speed at which a CMOS circuit can be switched is complicated by the fact that it depends not only on the capacitance of the load being driven, but also on the supply voltage V_{cc}. Basically, as V_{cc} increases, the gate delay for a given load decreases. The quiescent power consumption of a CMOS gate is very small, since one of the two gates is always off, and is typically much less than 1 μW at $V_{cc} = 5$ V. However, when the gate is being switched, current is required to charge the load that the gate is driving (usually the gate of another FET of course), and power is dissipated while this occurs. The power consumption is proportional to the switching frequency f and is given by the equation:

$$P_{ac} = C_{eff} \cdot V^2_{cc} \cdot f$$

where C_{eff} is the load capacitance being driven. The subscript ac is used to differentiate the switching from the quiescent power consumption. Taking $C_{eff} = 10$ pF and $f = 100$ kHz gives $P_{ac} = 10 \times 10^{-12} \times 25 \times 10^5 = 0.025$ mW for $V_{cc} = 5$ V. This will be increased by the factor 225/25, or nearly 10 times, if $V_{cc} = 15$ V.

Both TTL and CMOS circuits, such as the LS and HCT series discussed above, are widely available from many semiconductor manufacturers, and have been extensively used in the past in the design of small digital logic systems. Although this is still the case, programmable devices and gate arrays, which are discussed in a later chapter, are now widely used.

2.10 Summary

The basics of digital logic have been discussed in the first half of this chapter. After an introduction to the basic logic gates, NOT, AND, OR, NAND, NOR and EOR, which form the 'basic building block' of digital logic systems, the necessary mathematics of logic systems, Boolean algebra, was given. An understanding of this algebra, and in particular the use of the basic propositions and De Morgan's theorem, are the basic tools of the digital logic designer.

The implementation of digital logic systems, with emphasis on the two most popular logic families available, namely TTL and CMOS, were discussed from the user's point of view in the second half of the chapter.

2.11 Exercises

Exercise 2.1 Simplify the following expressions algebraically.

$$\bar{A}.\bar{B} + A.B + \bar{A}.B$$

$$\bar{A}.B.C + A.\bar{B}.C + A.B.\bar{C} + A.B.C$$

Exercise 2.2 Obtain the truth table of the following function.

$$X = A.B + A.\bar{B} + B.\bar{C}$$

Exercise 2.3 In Section 2.6 it was shown how to implement a 1-bit adder using only NAND gates by (a) applying de Morgan's theorem, and (b) using the 'bubble' technique. Using both techniques implement the 1-bit adder using only NOR gates.

Exercise 2.4 Implement an OR gate using only

(a) NAND gates

(b) NOR gates.

Exercise 2.5 How many different switching functions exist with two input variables and a single output? (AND and OR are two examples.)

Exercise 2.6 Simplify the following logic expressions to the minimum number of variables.

$$X.Y.Z + \bar{X}.Y + X.Y.\bar{Z}$$

$$(\overline{A+B}).(\overline{\bar{A}+\bar{B}})$$

Exercise 2.7 Determine whether the two logic expressions given are equivalent in each of the following two cases.

$$A.B + C.(A+B) \text{ and } A.B.\bar{C} + A.\bar{B}.C + B.C$$

$$\bar{A}.\bar{C} + B + A.C \text{ and } \bar{A}.\bar{B} + \bar{A}.\bar{C} + A.B + A.C$$

Exercise 2.8 Convert the circuit in Figure 2.22 to one using only NAND gates.

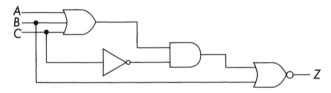

Figure 2.22 Example combinational circuit 1.

Exercise 2.9 Using Boolean algebra find a simpler circuit with the same function as that given in Figure 2.23.

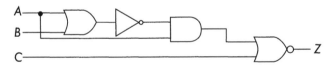

Figure 2.23 Example combinational circuit 2.

3

Combinational logic design

3.1 Introduction

A combinational logic circuit with m outputs, as shown in Figure 3.1, is one whose outputs depend entirely on the current values of the inputs. The

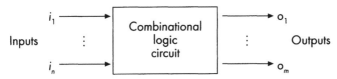

Figure 3.1 Typical combinational logic circuit.

behaviour of each output is given by a Boolean equation of the form:

$$\text{Output}_j = f(i_1, i_2, \ldots, i_n)$$

where the n inputs are labelled either $i_1, i_2 \ldots, i_n$, or $i_0, i_1 \ldots, i_{n-1}$. Thus, the function of the combinational circuit is totally specified by these m equations, one for each output. At this point it will be assumed that the outputs respond immediately to any change in an input signal. In practice this is not quite true. Combinational circuits are implemented with logic gates and since each gate has a small propagation time, there will inevitably be a small delay between an output signal changing as a result of a change of one or more of the inputs. In a complex combinational circuit containing many gates, this delay must be taken into account when designing a system, as it limits the maximum frequency at which an input may be changed.

3.2 Problem specification

All circuit design begins with a specification of the problem. It is necessary to appreciate that, at this stage, with 'real' designs the specification will almost certainly be incomplete and may even be somewhat vague. Before the circuit can be designed and implemented, requirements must be completely understood and the specification must be complete without any ambiguities. Experienced designers know that specification is often the most difficult stage of a project, because it involves persuading the customer to state exactly what the requirements are, and then translating them into an unambiguous and complete specification. In the case of combinational circuits the specification of a circuit should be written in the form of either a truth table or a set of Boolean logic equations.

The following design procedure should be adopted:

1. list the outputs required;

2. list the inputs available, or required;

3. state the functions required to obtain the outputs from the available inputs;

4. for each output draw a truth table.

All possible input combinations must be shown on this truth table, including those labelled 'don't care' or 'can't normally occur'. They are usually marked with a cross, '×'. The table must have one column for each input, one column for each output, and 2^n rows, where n is the number of inputs, since 2^n is the number of possible input combinations. Truth tables must be completely filled in, since 'can't normally occur' input conditions may actually occur under unusual or fault conditions. Such input conditions must be properly considered so that the combinational circuit always produces a known output for every possible combination of the input.

The next stage in the design process is implementation. If the design is a simple one, then this may be done directly, using either suitable gates or a programmable device. For more complex designs the implementation is preceded by a further stage, called minimization, in which techniques are applied to eliminate any redundant terms in the Boolean equations, so that an implementation can be achieved with the minimum number of gates. Before outlining minimization techniques, two design examples, a parity generator and a 7-segment decoder, will be presented.

3.3 Design example: a parity generator

3.3.1 Description

Data transmitted over long distances is prone to corruption, that is, individual bits might be lost or changed, and it is essential to know when such corruption has occurred. Many techniques, of varying degrees of sophistication, exist, the simplest being to add an additional bit at the sending end, to make the number of 1 bits in the pattern even or odd, and to check this bit at the receiving end. This extra bit is known as a parity bit. A single parity bit transmitted with a group of data bits allows the detection of a single-bit error, that is, a 0 corrupted to a 1 or vice versa.

In this example, a circuit is required to accept a 3-bit binary number and to generate an odd parity bit P. Figure 3.2 shows a block diagram of the system required. If the number of 1s in the data is odd, $P = 0$, while if the number of 1s is even, $P = 1$.

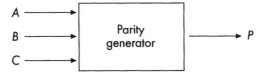

Figure 3.2 Block diagram of parity generator circuit.

3.3.2 Outputs

The circuit has a single output P.

3.3.3 Inputs

The three inputs are labelled A, B and C.

3.3.4 Truth table

The truth table can be written down immediately, as follows:

Input	A	B	C	P
0	0	0	0	1
1	0	0	1	0
2	0	1	0	0
3	0	1	1	1
4	1	0	0	0
5	1	0	1	1
6	1	1	0	1
7	1	1	1	0

3.3.5 Boolean equation for P

A Boolean equation is now written down in sum-of-products form for the output P in terms of the inputs A, B and C. This is done by identifying the rows in the truth table for which P is 1. These are rows 1, 4, 6 and 7. The input logic combinations of A, B and C corresponding to these rows are 000 $(\bar{A}.\bar{B}.\bar{C})$, 011 $(\bar{A}.B.C)$, 101 $(A.\bar{B}.C)$ and 110 $(A.B.\bar{C})$. The equation for P is then the sum of these combinations or products:

$$P = \bar{A}.\bar{B}.\bar{C} + \bar{A}.B.C + A.\bar{B}.C + A.B.\bar{C}$$

This equation may be rewritten in the shorthand notation:

$$P = 0 + 3 + 5 + 6$$

where the numbers correspond to the appropriate input values that give $P = 1$. Note that there are four product terms, since there are four input combinations that give $P = 1$.

3.3.6 Implementation

P can be implemented directly, using a combination of NOT, AND and OR gates, as shown in Figure 3.3a. Although this implementation is

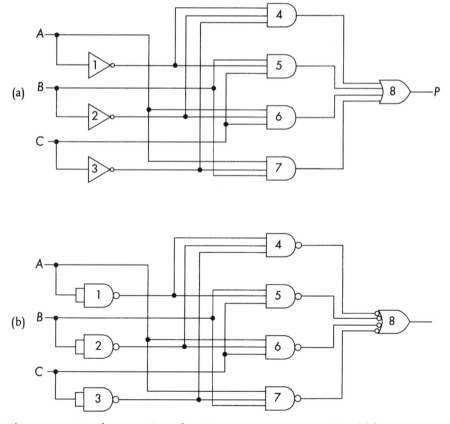

Figure 3.3 Implementation of parity generator circuit using (a) basic gates; (b) only NAND gates.

straightforward, it is not ideal, since it uses three different types of gate. Now, usually only three 3-input AND gates are normally available in a single integrated circuit, so two such packages must be used to give the necessary four AND gates. A number of simplifications can be made to this circuit. In Chapter 2 it was shown that all combinational circuits can be implemented with either NAND or NOR gates. Consider the implementation of the above circuit using only NAND gates. This may be done either by applying De Morgan's theorem directly to the equation for P to change the OR terms into AND terms, or equivalently by applying the graphical technique, discussed in Chapter 2, to Figure 3.3a. The inverting gates 1, 2 and 3 can be implemented with n-input NAND gates, with the n-inputs tied together. Using the graphical technique, the AND gates are converted to NAND gates by adding bubbles to each of the gate outputs. However, to keep the function of the circuit the same, bubbles must then be added at the other ends of the output lines from gates 4, 5, 6 and 7. Gate 8 then becomes a 4-input OR gate with negative true input logic, which is just a 4-input NAND gate with normal positive true logic. The final circuit can thus be implemented using only NAND gates, and is shown in Figure 3.3b.

3.4 Design example: a 7-segment decimal decoder

3.4.1 Description

A frequently used circuit is the 7-segment decoder used to drive 7-segment LED or LCD displays (Figure 3.4). Although this function is available as a

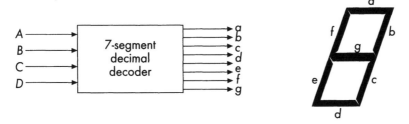

Figure 3.4 Block diagram of 7-segment decimal decoder and labelling of segments.

medium size integrated (MSI) chip, its design and implementation using standard gates provides a valuable example. The function of the decoder is to accept four bits of data representing the binary code of the number to be displayed (that is, 0 to 9), and to generate the appropriate outputs to drive the seven segments of the display. Figure 3.4 shows the black box representation of the circuit required together with the conventional labelling of the segments of the display. For example, to display the digit 4, the segments *b*, *c*, *f* and *g* are turned on, that is, **1**, while the remaining segments *a*, *d* and *e* are turned off, that is, **0**.

3.4.2 Truth table

The truth table of the combinational circuit required can be written down directly from an inspection of Figure 3.4b, as shown in Table 3.1.

Table 3.1 Truth table for Figure 3.4b.

Decimal number	*Binary representation*				*Segments*						
	A	*B*	*C*	*D*	*a*	*b*	*c*	*d*	*e*	*f*	*g*
0	0	0	0	0	1	1	1	1	1	1	0
1	0	0	0	1	0	1	1	0	0	0	0
2	0	0	1	0	1	1	0	1	1	0	1
3	0	0	1	1	1	1	1	1	0	0	1
4	0	1	0	0	0	1	1	0	0	1	1
5	0	1	0	1	1	0	1	1	0	1	1
6	0	1	1	0	0	0	1	1	1	1	1
7	0	1	1	1	1	1	1	0	0	0	0
8	1	0	0	0	1	1	1	1	1	1	1
9	1	0	0	1	1	1	1	0	0	1	1

The main difference between this example and the previous one is that there are several outputs, instead of just one. However, as these outputs are independent, a Boolean equation may be written down for each output, *a* to *g*, in sum-of-products form directly from an inspection of the truth table. For example, the Boolean equation for *a* is:

$$a = \bar{A}.\bar{B}.\bar{C}.\bar{D} + \bar{A}.\bar{B}.C.\bar{D} + \bar{A}.\bar{B}.C.D + \bar{A}.B.\bar{C}.D +$$
$$\bar{A}.B.C.D + A.\bar{B}.\bar{C}.\bar{D} + A.\bar{B}.\bar{C}.D$$

or in shorthand notation:

$$a = 0 + 2 + 3 + 5 + 7 + 8 + 9$$

Similarly for the other segments:

$$b = 0 + 1 + 2 + 3 + 4 + 7 + 8 + 9$$

$$c = 0 + 1 + 3 + 4 + 5 + 6 + 7 + 8 + 9$$

$$d = 0 + 2 + 3 + 5 + 6 + 8$$

$$e = 0 + 2 + 6 + 8$$

$$f = 0 + 4 + 5 + 6 + 8 + 9$$

$$g = 2 + 3 + 4 + 5 + 6 + 8 + 9$$

3.4.3 Implementation

Clearly it would be perfectly possible at this stage to implement the seven circuits required to drive the segments using NAND or NOR gates, in a similar fashion to that of the previous example. However, the circuit will be cumbersome, containing a large number of gates, many of which turn out to be redundant. In the next section, methods to minimize the number of gates required to implement a given logic function are discussed and these methods are applied to the implementation of the current example.

3.5 Minimization of Boolean functions

The aim of minimization is to simplify Boolean expressions and to eliminate any redundant terms, using the rules of Boolean algebra. The resulting expression will usually have fewer terms. In addition, each of the remaining terms will often have fewer variables, which leads in turn to a simpler implementation with either fewer or simpler gates. It is rarely worthwhile to take this process to the extreme, that is, to minimize the amount of logic required. This is particularly the case in designs that are to be implemented with larger scale integration, where the cost of using extra gates is minimal, and where the cost in design time of minimization will often outweigh the savings in hardware. Consider the Boolean equation for driving segment a of a 7-segment display:

$$a = \bar{A}.\bar{B}.\bar{C}.\bar{D} + \bar{A}.\bar{B}.C.\bar{D} + \bar{A}.\bar{B}.C.D + \bar{A}.B.\bar{C}.D +$$
$$\bar{A}.B.C.D + A.\bar{B}.\bar{C}.\bar{D} + A.\bar{B}.\bar{C}.D$$

In reducing a Boolean expression, one aim is to combine terms with common factors to give expressions of the form $X + \bar{X}$, which reduce to 1. For example, $\bar{A}.\bar{B}.C$ is a common factor in both terms 2 and 3, and so can be combined to give:

$$\bar{A}.\bar{B}.C.(\bar{D} + D) = \bar{A}.\bar{B}.C$$

Similarly, the last two terms can be combined to give $A.\bar{B}.\bar{C}$ leading to:

$$a = \bar{A}.\bar{B}.\bar{C}.\bar{D} + \bar{A}.\bar{B}.C + \bar{A}.B.\bar{C}.D + \bar{A}.B.C.D + A.\bar{B}.\bar{C}$$

Can this expression be simplified further? Has it been reduced in such a way that the simplest implementation is given? These questions are difficult to answer even when there are only four variables, as in the present example, and become even more so when the number is increased. Moreover, if there are any 'don't care' terms they can always be added to the Boolean equation if it leads to a further simplification, but it is often quite difficult to see which ones, if any, to add to do this. The graphical technique discussed in the next section allows this to be done in a straightforward manner.

3.5.1 Use of Karnaugh maps

A Karnaugh map or K-map is a diagram on which the sums-of-products of a Boolean expression are plotted, and which allows the elimination and reduction of terms to be made visually. A K-map for n variables contains 2^n squares, one for every combination of the input variables. K-maps for two, three and four variables are shown in Figure 3.5. The squares are labelled in such a way that only one variable changes (e.g. from A to $\overline{A}$ or vice versa) on going from one square to the next either horizontally or vertically. This

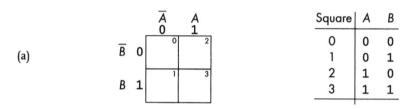

(a)

Square	A	B
0	0	0
1	0	1
2	1	0
3	1	1

(b)

Square	A	B	C
0	0	0	0
1	0	0	1
2	0	1	0
3	0	1	1
4	1	0	0
5	1	0	1
6	1	1	0
7	1	1	1

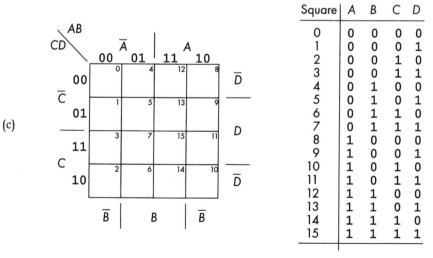

(c)

Square	A	B	C	D
0	0	0	0	0
1	0	0	0	1
2	0	0	1	0
3	0	0	1	1
4	0	1	0	0
5	0	1	0	1
6	0	1	1	0
7	0	1	1	1
8	1	0	0	0
9	1	0	0	1
10	1	0	1	0
11	1	0	1	1
12	1	1	0	0
13	1	1	0	1
14	1	1	1	0
15	1	1	1	1

Figure 3.5 K-maps for (a) two, (b) three and (c) four variables.

coding (known as a Gray code) makes the identification of terms that can be combined fairly obvious, as will now be demonstrated. Note that the square at the top left is effectively adjacent to the square at the top right: in the 4-variable map these squares are $\overline{A}.\overline{B}.\overline{C}.\overline{D}$ and $A.\overline{B}.\overline{C}.\overline{D}$, and so differ only in the variable A. In the same way, the square at the top left is also adjacent to the square at the bottom left, since only variable C differs. The map may thus be thought of as being wrapped ('around cylinders') both vertically and horizontally. It is helpful to write the shorthand number corresponding to the variable combination in each square. This enables the K-map to be filled in directly from the truth table. It should be emphasised that there is one K-map for each Boolean output variable in a design. The procedure for filling in the K-map and then using it to reduce a Boolean expression to its simplest form is as follows.

(a) Step 1

A **1** is written into each square of the map corresponding to each term in the original Boolean expression, or to each row of the truth table for which the output is a **1** value. For example, Figure 3.6 shows the 4-variable K-map for segment a of the 7-segment decoder. It contains seven **1**s corresponding to

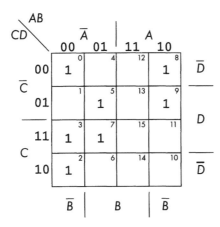

Figure 3.6   4-variable K-map for segment a of the 7-segment decoder.

the 7 product terms. Note that **0**s are represented by blank squares, and that squares labelled 10 to 15 do not have any **1**s because inputs in the range 10 to 15 do not occur.

However, these conditions can in fact be used to simplify the Boolean equation for a. If any of the input values 10 to 15 were to occur (which of course they shouldn't) then the segment values can be labelled 'don't care', meaning that each segment can either **0** or **1**. The truth table then becomes that shown in Table 3.2. These 'don't care' terms are then represented by writing a '✗' in the squares labelled 10 to 15, as shown in Figure 3.7.

Table 3.2   The truth table for the 7-segment display

Decimal number	Binary representation				Segments						
	A	B	C	D	a	b	c	d	e	f	g
0	0	0	0	0	1	1	1	1	1	1	0
1	0	0	0	1	0	1	1	0	0	0	0
2	0	0	1	0	1	1	0	1	1	0	1
3	0	0	1	1	1	1	1	1	0	0	1
4	0	1	0	0	0	1	1	0	0	1	1
5	0	1	0	1	1	0	1	1	0	1	1
6	0	1	1	0	0	0	1	1	1	1	1
7	0	1	1	1	1	1	1	0	0	0	0
8	1	0	0	0	1	1	1	1	1	1	1
9	1	0	0	1	1	1	1	0	0	1	1
10	1	0	1	0	×	×	×	×	×	×	×
11	1	0	1	1	×	×	×	×	×	×	×
12	1	1	0	0	×	×	×	×	×	×	×
13	1	1	0	1	×	×	×	×	×	×	×
14	1	1	1	0	×	×	×	×	×	×	×
15	1	1	1	1	×	×	×	×	×	×	×

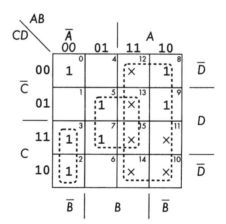

Figure 3.7   Modified K-map for a segment.

(b) Step 2

Adjacent squares containing 1s, or 1s and ×s, are then combined. Squares can only be combined in groups of powers of two, for example, 2, 4, 8, 16, etc. Each group must be a square or rectangle with sides which are a power of two. There are three basic rules that must be followed when combining squares:

1. every square containing a **1** must be included in at least one group;

2. each group should be as large as possible; and

3. **1**s must not be included in more than one group unless they increase the size of both groups.

It is usually easiest to start in the middle of the K-map. For example, in Figure 3.7 squares 5, 7, 13 and 15 can be combined. This is shown by drawing a dotted line around them. Combining these four squares means that terms 5 ($\bar{A}.B.\bar{C}.D$) and 7 ($\bar{A}.B.C.D$) are replaced by the much simpler term $B.D$. This is because the four squares cover the regions A and $\bar{A}$, C and $\bar{C}$, but only B and D (that is, the regions $\bar{B}$ and $\bar{D}$ are not covered). Without the K-map the common factor $\bar{A}.B.D$ would probably have been identified easily but it would have been more difficult to identify the 'don't care' terms that allow the removal of A. In a similar way, terms 8–15 inclusive can be combined to give A. The **1**s in squares 0, 2 and 3 are then left. A first attempt might be to combine terms 2 and 3 to give $\bar{A}.\bar{B}.C$ and to leave term 0. The expression for a then reduces to:

$$a = B.D + A + \bar{A}.\bar{B}.C + \bar{A}.\bar{B}.\bar{C}.\bar{D}$$

However, the fact that the K-map is wrapped, that is, square 0 is also adjacent to squares 8 and 2, has not been used. Using this fact, terms 0, 2, 8 and 10 can be combined to give $\bar{B}.\bar{D}$, so that a reduces to:

$$a = B.D + A + \bar{A}.\bar{B}.C + \bar{B}.\bar{D}$$

Terms 2 and 3 are adjacent to terms 10 and 11, and so can be combined to eliminate A from the third component in the equation for a. The final combination of terms in the K-map is shown in Figure 3.8, and gives:

$$a = B.D + A + \bar{B}.C + \bar{B}.\bar{D}$$

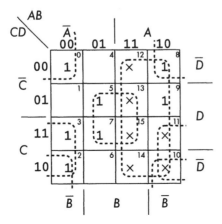

Figure 3.8 Final K-map for a segment.

This is quite startling since the original equation for a has been minimized from seven 4-variable terms to three 2-variable terms and one 1-variable term, with a consequent drastic reduction in the number and size of gates required for the implementation. Figure 3.9 shows a NAND gate implementation of this equation. There is often not a unique solution to the

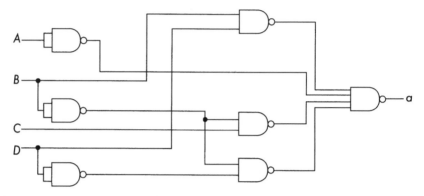

Figure 3.9 NAND gate implementation of a-segment decoder.

process of combining terms on a K-map. In the present example there is one other solution that has the same number of terms; its detection is left as an exercise for the reader. So far only the equation for the a segment has been considered. The question now arises as to what happens when multiple outputs occur, as in this example. Figure 3.10 shows the seven K-maps for the decoding required for segments a–g. Although these maps can be treated independently, using the rules discussed above to combine terms, it is better to try to identify common groupings that occur in as many of the maps as possible, since this will lead to as much common hardware in the final implementation as possible. A simple way to identify common groupings is to draw the maps on transparent film so that they can be overlapped. The K-map technique is useful and relatively easy to use for combinational designs that have a maximum of about six variables. Designs with more variables are minimized using computational methods amenable to computer solution, such as the Quine–McClusky and other methods (see Katz, for example, in the bibliography). There are also computer-aided design (CAD) tools that will minimize the amount of logic required for circuit implementation.

3.6 Medium scale integrated functions

A glance through a TTL or CMOS data handbook will show that in addition to the standard gates, such as NOT, NOR and NAND, there are a large number of special-purpose combinational circuits available. These are MSI circuits containing up to 100 gates per chip. Such circuits include arithmetic functions, binary adders and multipliers, decoders (used extensively in display functions and in address selection of memory registers within a

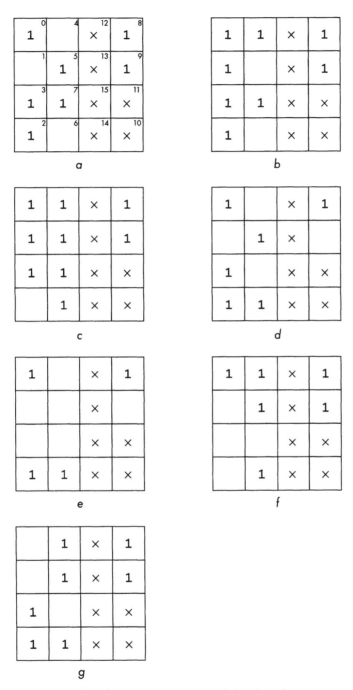

Figure 3.10 K-maps for the seven segments of the decoder.

computer), multiplexers to enable selection among a number of possible data streams, bus drivers and receivers (also used extensively in computers). In this section those MSI circuits that will be used in the construction of computer circuits in the later chapters are discussed.

3.6.1 Demultiplexers and decoders

A demultiplexer is a circuit that has one input line, and several possible output lines, N (a power of two), as shown in Figure 3.11. The input is

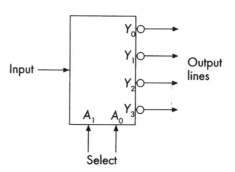

Figure 3.11 Demultiplexer (1-line to 4-line).

connected to one of the output lines, depending on the code bits that are supplied on the select lines, and so acts in exactly the same way as a switch. These select lines are often referred to as address lines, since the code word or address on them is used to select, or address, one of the output lines. M address lines are required, where $N = 2^M$. A decoder is very similar, with the exception that there is no input line. The address on the select lines is decoded to select one of the N possible output lines. An example is the 2-line to 4-line TTL decoder shown in Figure 3.12. One of the output lines, Y_0 to Y_3

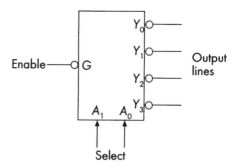

Figure 3.12 2-line to 4-line decoder.

is selected and set low, depending on the code supplied on the two select or address inputs, A_0 and A_1. The bubbles on the outputs indicate that they are active low. In addition there is an enable input G, which is also active low. The truth table for this decoder, with × representing 'don't care' values, is as shown in Table 3.3.

If $G = 1$, none of the outputs is selected, while if $G = 0$ just one of the outputs is selected, that is, taken low. Although this function could be

Table 3.3   Truth table for 2-line to 4-line decoder

Enable	Select		Outputs			
G	A_1	A_0	Y_0	Y_1	Y_2	Y_3
1	×	×	1	1	1	1
0	0	0	0	1	1	1
0	0	1	1	0	1	1
0	1	0	1	1	0	1
0	1	1	1	1	1	0

implemented easily with three 3-input NAND gates, it is required so often that it is available as a MSI chip, the TTL 74139 decoder. The 74139 contains two 2-line to 4-line decoders in a single chip. (In the data sheet of this decoder the select lines are labelled A and B, but A_0 and A_1 will be used here to avoid confusion with A and B used in the 7-segment decoder.) Decoders are available in the following sizes: 2-line to 4-line (two to a package), 3-line to 8-line, 4-line to 10-line (decimal decoder) and 4-line to 16-line. The use of a 2-line to 4-line decoder to select among different memory chips in a microcomputer system is discussed in Chapter 9.

3.6.2 Multiplexers

A multiplexer performs the opposite function to a decoder/demultiplexer switch; it connects one of a given number of input lines to a single output line. Figure 3.13 shows a 4-line to 1-line multiplexer. The input lines are D_0

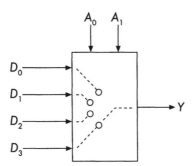

Figure 3.13 Multiplexer (4-line to 1-line).

to D_3, Y is the output line and A_0 and A_1 the select or address lines. The truth table is as shown in Table 3.4.

In addition, most multiplexers contain an enable input. The logic equation for this multiplexer is:

$$Y = \overline{A_1}.\overline{A_0}.D_0 + \overline{A_1}.A_0.D_1 + A_1.\overline{A_0}.D_2 + A_1.A_0.D_3$$

Table 3.4   Truth table for multiplexor

A_1	A_0	Y
0	0	D_0
0	1	D_1
1	0	D_2
1	1	D_3

Thus to select input D_1, for example, code $A_1 = 0$, $A_0 = 1$ is required. In addition to their use as data selectors, multiplexers are frequently used to simplify the generation of logic functions. This is most easily explained by considering the 7-segment decimal decoder discussed earlier. The equation for the a segment is:

$$a = \bar{A}.\bar{B}.\bar{C}.\bar{D} + \bar{A}.\bar{B}.C.\bar{D} + \bar{A}.\bar{B}.C.D + \bar{A}.B.\bar{C}.D +$$
$$\bar{A}.B.C.D + A.\bar{B}.\bar{C}.\bar{D} + A.\bar{B}.\bar{C}.D$$

The simplest implementation is to use a multiplexer which has the same number of select lines as variables. In this example this means a 16-line to 1-line multiplexer with four select lines, as shown in Figure 3.14a. The variables A, B, C and D are connected to the select lines A_3, A_2, A_1 and A_0 while the data lines D_0 to D_{15} are connected to either 0 or 1 as appropriate, so that the output of the multiplexer, a, is 1 for terms 0, 2, 3, 5, 7, 8 and 9, and 0 for terms 1, 4 and 6, and 'don't care', ×, for terms 10 to 15. In most implementations the 'don't care' terms will be connected to 0.

Although this solution is simple, and works, it uses a large multiplexer, so the question arises as to whether a smaller multiplexer can be used. An 8-line to 1-line multiplexer with three select lines can be used but only three of the four variables can be applied to the select lines; A, B and C are chosen arbitrarily, as shown in Figure 3.14b. The fourth variable D is now applied to the data lines, where appropriate, so that again a is generated at the multiplexer output. Consider the first term in the Boolean equation for a, $\bar{A}.\bar{B}.\bar{C}.\bar{D}$. When A, B and C are applied to the multiplexer select lines, data line D_0 is connected to the output, and so, to generate the correct logic level, $\bar{D}$ must be connected to D_0. The second and third terms of a contain the common factor $\bar{A}.\bar{B}.C$, and so reduce to:

$$\bar{A}.\bar{B}.C.(\bar{D} + D) = \bar{A}.\bar{B}.C$$

by the inverse proposition discussed in Chapter 2.

Now $\bar{A}.\bar{B}.C$ selects data line D_1, and so this must be connected to 1. Continuing in this way the data line connections required to generate a with this multiplexer are:

Data line $D_0 = \bar{D}$ for $ABC = 000$
Data line $D_1 = 1$ for $ABC = 001$

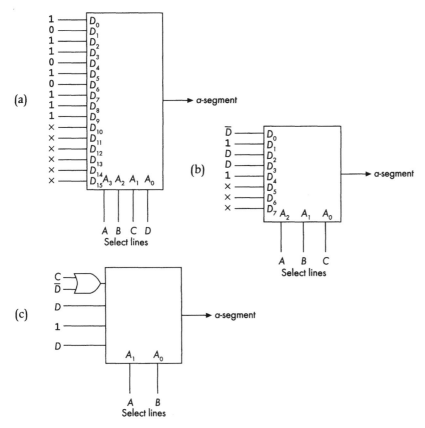

Figure 3.14 Multiplexer implementation for the a-segment of the decimal
decoder.

Data line $D_2 = D$ for $ABC = 010$
Data line $D_3 = D$ for $ABC = 011$
Data line $D_4 = 1$ for $ABC = 100$
Data lines D_5, D_6 and $D7$ are 'don't care'.

However, this is still not the minimum size of multiplexer that can be used
in this example. It turns out that a multiplexer is required which has n select
lines, where n is half the number of variables (rounded up to a power of 2
when necessary). In this case $n = 2$, so that a 4-line to 1-line multiplexer
having two select lines is the minimum size required. Two of the variables are
applied to the multiplexer select lines, while the remaining variables, known
as the residues, are applied to the data lines. The choice of which variables to
apply to the select lines is arbitrary (but see below). The data line
connections are then worked out either by following the method used above
in the 3-line to 1-line multiplexer case, or by using a modified K-map
technique, as follows. There are six possible variations of control variable,
namely AB, AC, AD, BC, BD or CD. In this example, we will arbitrarily
choose AB. The K-map for the a segment is re-drawn in Figure 3.15. The

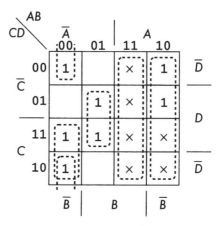

Figure 3.15 K-map for the *a* segment.

residue functions are functions of the variables C and D, and comprise the functions shown in the columns of the K-map. Because of this, terms may now only be combined in each column, as shown in Figure 3.15. The residue functions are:

$$D_0 = C + \bar{D} \quad \text{for } AB = 00$$
$$D_1 = D \qquad \text{for } AB = 01$$
$$D_2 = 1 \qquad \text{for } AB = 10$$
$$D_3 = \times \qquad \text{for } AB = 11$$

The implementation is shown in Figure 3.14c. Note its simplicity, requiring only two chips. Repeating the example with C and D as the control variables is left as an exercise for the reader. The choice of control variables should be made, by trial and error, to give the simplest residue functions. Circuits for the other segments of the decoder may be obtained in a similar manner.

3.7 Programmable logic arrays

In the text, several examples have been given of combinational functions expressed as sum-of-products equations. These equations may be implemented directly by forming the product terms of the inputs, or their complements where necessary, using AND gates, and then combining the outputs with an OR gate. A programmable logic array (PLA) is a special-purpose chip designed so that sum-of-products expressions can be implemented directly. A simple PLA is shown in Figure 3.16, having four inputs, A, B, C and D. The complement of each input is formed internally so that there are eight input signals available (A, $\bar{A}$, B, $\bar{B}$, C, $\bar{C}$, D, $\bar{D}$). In addition there are 12 AND gates, each having four inputs. These inputs are the vertical lines in Figure 3.16. The AND gates are used to form the product terms, the horizontal and vertical lines effectively forming the AND matrix.

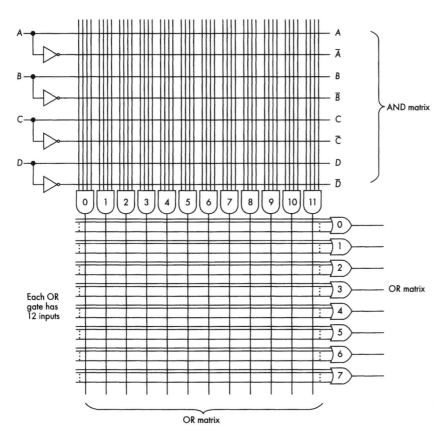

Figure 3.16 A simple PLA having four inputs, twelve product terms and eight outputs.

At each of the intersections in this matrix there is an optional link. These links are normally transistors but are thought of, and usually referred to, as 'fuses'. In this example PLA, up to 12 product terms, each having up to four inputs, may be formed. The matrix at the bottom is the OR matrix, which is connected to the output OR gates. There are eight outputs so there are eight OR gates. Each of these OR gates has 12 input lines, one from each of the AND gates. Again, connections are made where required between the vertical outputs from the AND gates and the horizontal input lines to the OR gates. Initially all the 'fuses' are intact, so all possible connections are made. The logic function required is 'placed' or programmed in the PLA by blowing those 'fuses' where links are not required. This is done either during manufacture or, in the case of a field-programmable logic array (FPLA), by using a special-purpose programmer.

As an example, consider a PLA implementation of the 7-segment decoder. The starting point is the truth table discussed in Section 3.4. There are seven outputs, a to g, so only seven of the eight PLA outputs are required. There are ten product terms corresponding to the ten possible input values 0 to 9, so ten AND gates of the PLA are used. Figure 3.17 is a slightly simplified redrawing of the PLA of Figure 3.16, in which the crosses correspond to the connections required to implement all seven decimal decoder outputs *a* to *g*.

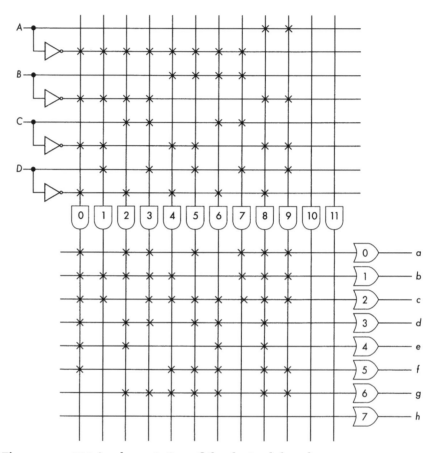

Figure 3.17 PLA implementation of the decimal decoder.

Note that the absence of a cross where a horizontal and vertical line meet means that there is no connection. In practice, PLAs are manufactured in standard sizes and the user has to choose a suitable size for the application. Minimization techniques may be unnecessary when using PLAs, unless the number of initial product terms exceeds the number of product terms in the PLA being used.

The development of PLAs led rapidly to the availability of a wide range of user-programmable electrically programmable logic devices (EPLDs). An EPLD contains a number of PLAs, as described above, and a number of user-programmable macrocells. In the earliest EPLDs, such as the EP600 from the Altera Corporation, the macrocells were directly associated with the chips' outputs. Each macrocell/output combination could be programmed into a number of different configurations, allowing both combinational and sequential circuits to be implemented with the same device. The EP600 has 20 inputs and 16 outputs (each with its own macrocell), and allows up to 160 product terms to be generated. The main advantages of EPLDs is that they are easily and quickly programmed, and can be erased using ultraviolet light in the same way as an EPROM. Some later devices are electrically erased, making them even quicker to reprogram. These devices are described more fully in the next chapter.

3.8 Read-only memories

The PLA discussed in the last section can be regarded as a memory. When a binary pattern is applied to the input lines, the output obtained on the output lines is determined by the links made in the AND and OR matrices of the PLA. The input lines are effectively address lines and the outputs are data lines on which data, which has been previously programmed into the PLA, appears. However, PLAs can only be used to form a limited number of product terms. For example, the small PLA discussed earlier with 14 inputs only has 48 product terms, so that only 48 data words may be stored in it. This is a small subset of the total number of products that can be formed from 14 variables, which is $2^{14} = 16,384$. A read-only memory (ROM) differs from a PLA in that all product terms are generated. Although functionally very similar to a PLA, a ROM is usually thought of in a rather different manner. It is a device in which sets of data called words are stored. Figure 3.18 shows a schematic diagram of a small ROM. It has five inputs, the address lines,

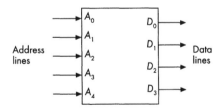

Figure 3.18 A 32 × 4 read-only memory (ROM).

labelled A_0 to A_4, and four outputs called data lines, labelled D_0 to D_3. Since five address lines can select $2^5 = 32$ different 'places', or memory locations, the ROM is said to contain 32 memory locations. In each of these, a 4-bit data word is stored. When a 5-bit address is placed on the address lines, the contents of the memory location addressed are placed on the data lines. The ROM shown is said to be of size 32 × 4 since it stores 32 words, each having a length of four bits. In general, a ROM with M address lines has $2^M \times N$ bits. Memories are one of the most important components of a computer system, and they will be discussed fully in Chapter 6.

3.9 Summary

The specification, design and implementation of combinational logic circuits has been discussed in detail in this chapter. The specification is best written down in the form of a truth table, which shows the value of each of the circuit outputs for each possible combination of the circuit inputs. This truth table must be complete, and should be thoroughly checked before the design continues. The method that is to be used for the implementation then has to be decided. Possible methods include using basic gates for relatively simple circuits, and PLAs and ROMs for more complicated circuits. If a gate implementation is to be used, a Boolean logic equation should be written down for each output in the sum-of-products form. If appropriate, these equations should be minimized using the K-map technique. The resulting equations are then converted into NAND or NOR form, using either De Morgan's theorem or the graphical 'bubble' technique, and a circuit diagram of the implementation drawn. The choice between a PLA or ROM implementation usually depends on the number of product terms of the inputs required. If this is small compared to the total number of product terms that can be generated from the inputs, then a PLA implementation will usually be the most efficient. Conversely, if most of the product terms are required, then a ROM implementation will be the obvious choice. In either case, the size of the PLA or ROM necessary for the implementation must be chosen, and the programming of the truth table into the PLA or ROM carried out.

3.10 Exercises

Exercise 3.1 Draw a Karnaugh map for:

$$F = A.B.\overline{D} + \overline{A}.B.\overline{D} + A.\overline{B}.D + \overline{A}.C.D + A.B.C.D$$

and hence minimize the logic required to implement this function.

Exercise 3.2 Minimize the logic function:

$$f = A.\overline{B}.\overline{C} + \overline{A}.B.\overline{C} + A.B.C + A.B.\overline{C}$$

using the K-map technique, and then show how it may be implemented using (a) NAND gates, and (b) a 4-line to 1-line multiplexer.

Exercise 3.3 Design a combinational circuit that has as input a decimal number in the range 0–7, represented in binary, and that outputs the binary equivalent of the square of the input. The circuit implementation should use only NAND gates.

Exercise 3.4 Design a circuit that allows a bank vault to be opened only when a key is inserted into the lock, the correct combination is set on the dial and when the vault door is closed. Assume that the key being inserted and the correct combination set are denoted by signal A and B, respectively, which are set to logic 1 to indicate completion of the required action. The closure of the vault door generates a logic 0 signal on C.

Exercise 3.5 Design a combinational logic circuit called a decoder, which has three inputs and 2^3 outputs. The output corresponding to the binary value on the input is to be set to logic 1 and all the other outputs are to be set to logic 0. The truth table for the decoder is

Input	Output
000	0
001	1
010	2
011	3
100	4
101	5
110	6
111	7

Exercise 3.6 Design a circuit to input a 3-bit value and output its 2's complement value given in the table below:

Input	Output
011	101
010	110
001	111
000	000
111	001
110	010
101	011
100	✕✕✕

where ✕✕✕ = don't care (can be 0 or 1)

Exercise 3.7 Modify the circuit designed in the previous exercise to include an extra output to determine the validity of the output. For all inputs except 100 the valid output should be true (1) and for 100, false (0).

Exercise 3.8 The majority function $M(a,b,c)$ of the three Boolean inputs a, b and c is logic-1 if two or more of the inputs are logic-1, and logic-0 otherwise. Design a circuit that implements the majority function. How would you extend it to four or more inputs?

Exercise 3.9 In Section 3.5, the implementation of the circuit required for the *a* segment of a 7-segment decoder was discussed. Design the circuits required for the other six segments (*b* to *g*). You should attempt to minimize the functions in such a way that the six circuits share as much common logic as possible, to keep the number of gates required to a minimum.

Exercise 3.10 Refer to Chapter 10 for a definition of binary coded decimal (BCD). Design a PLA circuit that has as input a decimal digit (0–9) represented in BCD, and outputs the input multiplied by 5, as two BCD digits.

4

Sequential logic design

4.1 Introduction

In the previous chapter, combinational circuits whose outputs are a function of only the inputs were discussed. However, in many digital designs there is a need for logic circuits whose outputs depend not only on the present inputs, but also on the past values of the inputs and output, of the circuit. In other words, the concept of time has to be introduced, and memory circuits are required to store information about the past history of the circuit. Such circuits are known as sequential logic circuits, because they follow a predetermined sequence. There are numerous examples of sequential circuits, one of the most widely met being the traffic light controller, which may be regarded as a black box, as shown in Figure 4.1. There are three

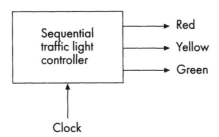

Figure 4.1 Traffic light controller.

outputs, labelled Red, Yellow and Green, to drive the three traffic lights, and a single input, labelled clock. A light will be turned on if there is a 1 on its output line. Fundamental to the design of sequential circuits is the concept of internal states, simply termed 'states'. At the beginning of the design procedure for a sequential circuit, the total number of internal states that are required must be determined. Each of these internal states is given a symbol, and it is very helpful (and usually essential) to draw a state diagram, which shows the internal states and the transitions between them. The simple traffic light controller requires four states, labelled S_0, S_1, S_2 and S_3. The state diagram is shown in Figure 4.2. Each state is shown by a circle, in which the state designation is written. The lines drawn from one state to another show the transition between states. The direction is indicated by an arrow, and the input signal (or input signal combinations) that gives rise to each transition is indicated above the arrow. In Figure 4.2 each transition between states is initiated by a clock signal, *clk*, as there are no other input signals in this simple example. Those outputs that are turned on in a given state are shown either alongside, or inside, the state circles. For example, in state S_1 Red and Yellow are on (1), while Green is off (0).

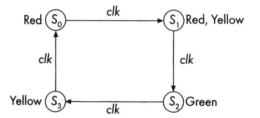

Figure 4.2   State diagram for simple traffic light controller.

4.2 Synchronous and asynchronous sequential circuits

There are two fundamentally different types of sequential circuit, namely synchronous and asynchronous. In an asynchronous (or event driven) circuit there is no clock, and transitions between states are initiated by changes in the appropriate input signals. In a synchronous circuit, transitions between states are initiated by a pulse from a single clock. It is normally assumed that any changes in the input signals occur between clock pulses, so that the input signals are stable when a clock pulse is applied. Synchronous circuits are easier to design, and so this text will be restricted to them. Figure 4.3 shows two typical clock signals. The first (Figure 4.3a) is a repetitive signal, derived from an oscillator circuit, and has a constant frequency, f, say. At any instant in time, its value is either 0 or V_H where V_H is the voltage that corresponds to a 1 for the logic family being used to implement the sequential design (typically 5 volts). The period T of this clock signal is related to its frequency by $T = 1/f$. The second clock signal (Figure 4.3b), although repetitive, does not have a constant frequency. It is often referred to as a pulsed clock, the pulses being generated in response to a change in one or more of the input signals. A synchronous circuit is designed to change state either when the clock goes from low to high, a positive edge transition,

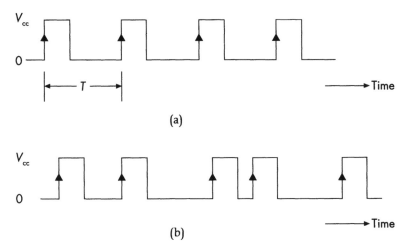

Figure 4.3 Typical clock signals used to clock synchronous logic circuits:
(a) is a repetitive clock with constant frequency $1/T$;
(b) is a pulsed clock signal.

or when the clock goes from high to low, a negative edge transition. The arrows in Figure 4.3 indicate the positive transitions of the clock.

4.3 State diagrams and state variables

The concept of the internal states of a sequential circuit will now be developed more fully using the state diagram of the simple traffic light controller shown in Figure 4.2. There are no inputs, except for the clock, which is not considered as a normal input, since all synchronous sequential circuits must have a clock, and this is not normally shown on the state diagram. Drawing the state diagram is the first stage of sequential logic design and, having checked that it agrees with the specification for the sequential logic system required, the next step is to write down a state table. The *state table* contains the same information as the state diagram but in a form that is more readily usable for the circuit implementation. For simple circuits it is possible to write down the state table directly from the specification. However, this is not advisable for the beginner since the drawing of a state diagram is a good check of the specification, and should show up any ambiguities therein.

The state table for the simple traffic light controller is given in Table 4.1. It contains a row for each state of the circuit, a column for each 'present state', and 2^n columns for the 'next state', that is, one for each possible combination of input signals. Thus if there are n input signals there are 2^n 'next state' columns. In this example there are no input signals, apart from the clock signal (that is, $n = 0$ and $2^0 = 1$) so only one column for the 'next state' is required.

Table 4.1   State table for the simple traffic light controller

Present state	Next state
S_0	S_1
S_1	S_2
S_2	S_3
S_3	S_0

The implementation of this state diagram will be considered later in the chapter.

As a second example consider a combination door lock that has three buttons, labelled a, b and c. The buttons are of the momentary type (that is, contact is made only when they are pushed). They must be pushed in the order b, a, c for the door to open. It is further assumed that a clock pulse, similar to that shown in Figure 4.3b, is generated whenever a button, or combination of buttons, is pushed. A black box diagram of the system is shown in Figure 4.4. In addition to the three input signals there is a single output, labelled Open, and the clock signal.

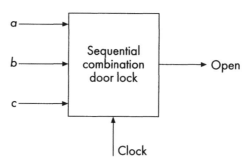

Figure 4.4   Combination door lock.

A first attempt at the state diagram for the combination door lock is shown in Figure 4.5a, and shows what happens when the buttons are pushed in the correct sequence. Initially the system is in the idle state S_0, with Open = 0, (that is, 'not open'). Pushing button b causes the transition from S_0 to S_1 on the next clock pulse. In state S_1, Open = 0. In a similar way the system goes from state S_1 to S_2 when button a is pushed, and then finally from S_2 to S_3 when button c is pushed. The value of the output Open becomes 1 when state S_3 is entered. Drawing this state diagram shows that at least four states are required. However, the state diagram is not complete, since at present it shows what happens only when the buttons are pushed in the correct order. To be complete it must also show what happens for all possible combinations of the inputs, in each state. For example, if the system is in state S_0 and button a or c is pushed, it will be assumed that the system must remain in state S_0. This is shown in Figure 4.5b by the 'arc' around the circle of state

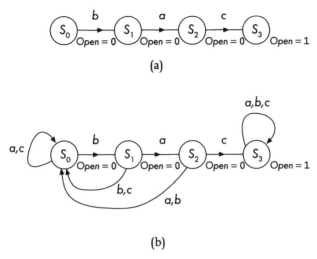

Figure 4.5   State diagrams for combination door locks.

S_0, labelled a, c. Now consider what should happen if the system is in state S_1 and either b or c is depressed. There are two possibilities: either the system remains in state S_1, or the system should return to the idle state S_0, and wait for button b to be pushed again. A similar decision must be made for state S_2, if either a or b is pushed. The customer must decide explicitly what is required so that the specification can be completed unambiguously. The state diagram of Figure 4.5b assumes that the system is to return to the idle state S_0 if the wrong buttons are pushed in any of states S_0, S_1 or S_2. This state diagram is now complete, since it shows what happens under all possible input sequences for each state.

As in the previous example the next step is to draw a state table. It will have four rows, corresponding to the four states and $2^3 = 8$ columns, corresponding to all the possible combinations of the input signals. This may seem strange at first since only three columns might be expected corresponding to the three possible inputs a, b or c. However, this is not the case since it is possible for two, or even all three, buttons to be pushed simultaneously. Each column of the state table must be filled in to show unambiguously what the next state will be for each possible combination of the inputs. Thus the specification is not complete at present; it must state what happens if buttons are pushed simultaneously. In this example it will be assumed that the system is required to return to the idle state S_0. The completed state table is shown in Table 4.2. Note that most entries in the first three rows are S_0, while in the fourth row every entry is S_3 since once the system is in this state and the door is open it is irrelevant whether any more buttons are pushed. In practice there will also be a reset signal which returns the system to state S_0 when the door is closed.

Note that every position in the state table must be completed. If this cannot be done then the specification is either incomplete or ambiguous. The

Table 4.2 State table for the combination door lock

Present state	Next state							
	abc 000	abc 001	abc 010	abc 011	abc 100	abc 101	abc 110	abc 111
S_0	S_0	S_0	S_1	S_0	S_0	S_0	S_0	S_0
S_1	S_0	S_0	S_0	S_0	S_2	S_0	S_0	S_0
S_2	S_0	S_3	S_0	S_0	S_0	S_0	S_0	S_0
S_3	S_3	S_3	S_3	S_3	S_3	S_3	S_3	S_3

major part of the system design has now been achieved. In every sequential logic system each state is defined by a set of logic signals called *state variables*. If the system can exist only in one of two states then only one state variable, A say, is required, since $A = 0$ can be used to correspond to one state, and $A = 1$ to the other state. Similarly, n state variables can be used to represent 2^n states. A sequential logic system that has m states requires n state variables such that:

$$2^n \geq m > 2^{n-1}$$

Thus in the combination lock example above, two state variables are required, that is, $n = 2$, since $2^2 = 4$ gives four states, which is exactly the number required.

For a system with five states, say, then three state variables would be necessary. However, since $2^3 = 8$ there would be $8 - 5 = 3$ unused states. These unused states must always be shown on the state table.

The final step in the design process is the implementation, which is essentially a straightforward mechanical exercise, following a simple 'recipe'. However, before considering this, storage, or memory, elements will be discussed.

4.4 Memory elements

The aim of this section is to show how a simple flip-flop, a storage element for one bit, can be built from gates.

4.4.1 The set–reset latch

Figure 4.6 shows the set-reset SR latch built from two NOR gates. There are two inputs, S and R, and two outputs, Q and Q'. Note the feedback paths from Q to the input of gate 1, and from Q' to the input of gate 2. These paths mean that the outputs Q and Q' depend not only on the inputs S and R, but also on the previous values of the outputs. Thus the circuit is not a combinational one, according to the definition given in Chapter 2, but is a

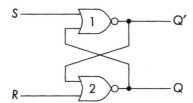

Figure 4.6 The set–reset latch implemented with NOR gates.

sequential logic element. The Boolean logic equations describing the behaviour of the SR flip-flop are:

$$Q = \overline{R + Q'}$$

$$Q' = \overline{S + Q}$$

There are four possible combinations of the input signals S and R, namely $SR = 00, 01, 10, 11$. These will now be considered in turn.

1. $S = 0, R = 0$. The logic equations reduce to:

$$Q = \overline{Q'}$$

$$\overline{Q'} = Q$$

The outputs are different and stable with either $Q = 0$ or $Q = 1$. Which of these two states the circuit is in actually depends on the previous values of S and R, that is, just before they were taken to logic 0.

2. $S = 0, R = 1$. The logic equations are:

$$Q = \overline{1 + Q'} = \overline{1} = 0$$

$$Q' = \overline{0 + Q} = \overline{Q} = 1$$

This input condition, known as reset, forces $Q = 0$ and $Q' = 1$ (that is, $Q' = \overline{Q}$)

3. $S = 1, R = 0$. The logic equations are:

$$Q' = \overline{1 + Q} = \overline{1} = 0$$

$$Q = \overline{0 + Q'} = \overline{Q'} = 1$$

This is the opposite case to 2, forcing the output to the set condition, $Q = 1$, and $Q' = 0$ (that is, $Q' = \overline{Q}$ again).

4. $S = 1, R = 1$. This case differs from the previous ones in that both outputs assume the same logic state, 0, since:

$$Q = \overline{1 + Q'} = \overline{1} = 0$$

$$Q' = \overline{1 + Q} = \overline{1} = 0$$

Although the outputs are stable, the operation of the circuit in this case becomes uncertain when S and R are changed simultaneously to 0. It is impossible to predict whether Q will remain at 0 or become 1 (and vice versa for Q'). Because of this, the case $S = R = 1$ is said to be indeterminate and is not usually allowed to occur.

Figure 4.7 shows a clocked version of the SR flip-flop in which the inputs S and R are ANDed with the clock signal. When the clock signal is 0 the

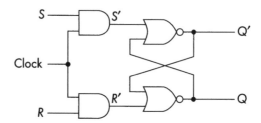

Figure 4.7 The clocked set–reset latch.

outputs of both AND gates are 0, that is, $S' = R' = 0$, corresponding to case 1 discussed above. A new value is placed in the flip-flop by first setting up the S and R inputs to the desired values and then applying a clock pulse. When this clock pulse is a 1, $S' = S$ and $R' = R$, so the latch assumes the new required state. This state is then held when the clock pulse returns to 0. Table 4.3 shows the state table for the clocked SR latch. The column labelled Q_{t+1} is the value taken by the Q output after the next clock pulse has occurred.

Table 4.3 State table for the clocked SR flip-flop

S	R	Q_{t+1}	Comments
0	0	Q_t	No change
0	1	0	Reset
1	0	1	Set
1	1	$\times$	Indeterminate

4.4.2 The D-type latch

One of the simplest but most important memory elements available as an integrated circuit is the D-type latch as shown in Figure 4.8(a). This element

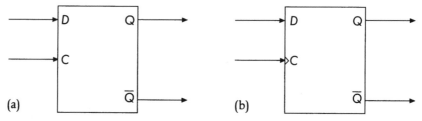

(a)   (b)

Figure 4.8 D-type (a) latch and (b) flip-flop.

is able to store a single bit of information, and so is often referred to as a 1-bit memory. It is actually a special case of the SR latch, in which the reset input is always the complement of the set input, that is, its state table is given in Table 4.4.

Table 4.4   State table of the D-type flip-flop

D	Q_{t+1}
0	0
1	1

There are two inputs, labelled data, D, and clock, C, respectively, and two outputs labelled Q and $\bar{Q}$. The $\bar{Q}$ output is always the complement of the Q output. The output Q follows the input D, so long as the clock is at **1**.

The output Q is 'frozen' with the value of D at the instant the clock is taken to **0**, that is, the latch stores the value that was on the D input. Note that in both the clocked SR latch and the D-type latch the outputs will respond to any changes in the input signals, so long as the clock signal remains at logic level **1**. This can give rise to a number of problems, which are beyond the scope of this book but which can be solved by using a modified form of edge-triggered latch. The next section discusses a D-type edge-triggered memory element, which is often referred to as a D-type flip-flop.

4.4.3 The D-type edge-triggered flip-flop

The function of the D-type flip-flop is very similar to that of the D-type latch, with the exception that the value stored is the logic level of the D input at the moment when the clock input C is taken from logic level **0** to logic level **1**. The small triangle next to the C input indicates that the device is edge-triggered. The output Q is always equal to the logic state of D when the clock transition from **0** to **1** occurs. The action of the D-type flip-flop is illustrated in Figure 4.9. The positive transitions of the clock occur at times t_1, t_2, t_3, etc., while the logic level of the D-input is changed from **0** to **1** sometime after t_1 but before t_2. However, since the next clock transition is not until t_2 the flip-flop does not store, and the outputs Q and $\bar{Q}$ do not reflect the changed state of the D-input, until time t_2. Similarly, although the D-input is changed back from **1** to **0** during the interval t_3–t_4, the flip-flop does not respond to this change until the next clock pulse at time t_4. D-type flip-flops such as this are available in both the TTL and CMOS logic families.

4.4.4 The JK-type flip-flop

The JK flip-flop is shown in Figure 4.10. It has two inputs labelled J and K as well as an edge-triggered clock input C, and two outputs Q and $\bar{Q}$. Again, $\bar{Q}$ is always the complement of Q. The operation of the JK flip-flop is summarized in the state table shown in Table 4.5.

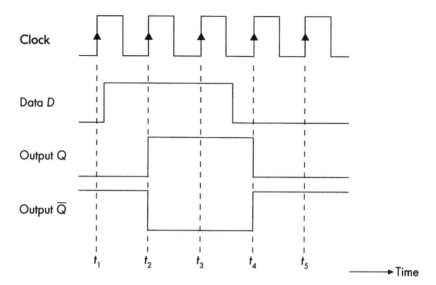

Figure 4.9 D-type flip-flop timing diagram.

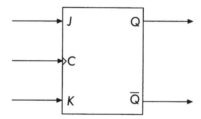

Figure 4.10 The JK flip-flop

Table 4.5 State table of a JK flip-flop

J	K	Q_{t+1}
0	0	Q_t
0	1	0
1	0	1
1	1	$\overline{Q_t}$

The column labelled Q_{t+1} is the value that the Q output assumes when the next $0{\to}1$ clock transition occurs. The JK flip-flop has four possible operations, and so is considerably more flexible than the D-type flip-flop, which has only two operations. The operations are:

1. $J = 0$, $K = 0$.   The Q output is unchanged from its present state, that is, $Q_{t+1} = Q_t$.

2. $J = 0$, $K = 1$.   This is the reset condition: the Q output is reset to 0, irrespective of the present state of the output.

3. $J = 1, K = 0.$ This is the set condition; the Q output is set to 1.

4. $J = 1, K = 1.$ The Q output assumes the opposite state to its present one, that is, $Q_{t+1} = \overline{Q_t}$. This is known as the toggle condition.

In the implementation of sequential logic using JK flip-flops the following question is asked repeatedly: what values of J and K are required for the next state to be either a 0 or a 1 given that the present state is known? The answer is given by Table 4.6. For example, suppose that the present state is 0 and

Table 4.6   JK flip-flop state change table

Original state	New state	J	K
0	0	0	×
0	1	1	×
1	0	×	1
1	1	×	0

× = don't care

the output required after the next clock transition is 1. This will be achieved either with $J = 1$ and $K = 0$ (the set condition), or with $J = 1$ and $K = 1$ (the toggle condition). Thus J must be 1 while K can be either 0 or 1, that is, it is a 'don't care' value. In this way the J and K inputs required for given output state changes may be worked out.

4.5 Sequential logic systems using D-type flip-flops

In this section, the implementation of the two examples discussed so far, namely the traffic light controller and the combination door lock, using D-type flip-flops is examined.

4.5.1 Traffic light controller

The design proceeds by referring to the state table for the traffic light controller, Table 4.1. Since there are four states, labelled S_0 to S_3, two state variables are required, X and Y, say. Each state variable is implemented with a D-type flip-flop, so in this example two flip-flops are used. Both the inputs and the outputs of the flip-flops are labelled with the suffixes X and Y, respectively, as shown in Figure 4.11. The clock inputs are connected together, and are driven from a single clock source. There are now two remaining problems, both involving combinational logic, namely the interconnections required to the D inputs of each flip-flop, and the logic required to generate the Red, Green and Yellow output signals from the state variables X and Y. The interconnections required to the D inputs of the flip-

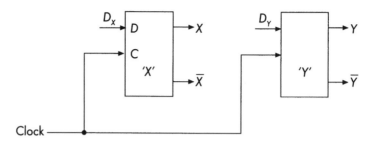

Figure 4.11 Traffic light controller.

flops are found by slightly modifying the state table. This table for the traffic light controller is shown in Table 4.7. The states are now shown by their state variables; the assignment of each variable combination to a given state is up to the designer but it is simplest, at least initially, to follow the normal binary sequence. Thus S_0 is represented by $Y = 0$, $X = 0$, S_1 by $Y = 0$, $X = 1$, S_2 by $Y = 1$, $X = 0$ and S_3 by $Y = 1$, $X = 1$. Note, however, that the choice of state variables can alter the amount of hardware required to implement the necessary combinational logic; other assignments may result in less hardware.

Table 4.7 Modified state table for the traffic light controller

Present state		Next state	
Y	X	Y'	X'
0	0	0	1
0	1	1	0
1	0	1	1
1	1	0	0

The symbols X' and Y' represent the values of X and Y at the next clock pulse, that is, the next state. Consider the first row of Table 4.7; it shows that the present state is 00, and that on the next clock pulse the state must change to 01. Thus Y does not change, while X must change from 0 to 1. The question to be answered is: what values are required for the D-type flip-flop inputs D_X and D_Y so that the state will change from 00 to 01 on the next clock pulse? The answer is to be found in Table 4.4, the state table for the D-type flip-flop. This table shows that the characteristic equation for the D-type flip-flop is:

$$Q_{t+1} = D$$

This equation shows that the next output, or state, of the flip-flop is just equal to the present value of the D input. Thus the entries in Table 4.7 for the next state are just those required for the D inputs, D_X and D_Y. Scanning down the column labelled Y' shows that there are only two 1 entries, corresponding to the present states $S_1(\bar{Y}.X)$ and $S_2(Y.\bar{X})$, so that:

$$D_Y = \bar{Y}.X + Y.\bar{X} = X \oplus Y$$

Similarly for the X' column there are also two 1 entries corresponding to states S_0 and S_2, and so:

$$D_X = \bar{Y}.\bar{X} + Y.\bar{X} = \bar{X}$$

Figure 4.12 shows the two D-type flip-flops with the logic required to generate D_X and D_Y. Finally the logic required to generate the output signals must be determined. Returning to the state diagram, it will be seen that the following output signals are required:

1. Red in state S_0 or S_1,   that is, Red $= \bar{X}.\bar{Y} + X.\bar{Y} = \bar{Y}$

2. Yellow in states S_1 or S_3,   that is, Yellow $= X.\bar{Y} + X.Y = X$

3. Green in state S_2,   that is, Green $= \bar{X}.Y$

The combinational logic to give these outputs is also shown in Figure 4.12.

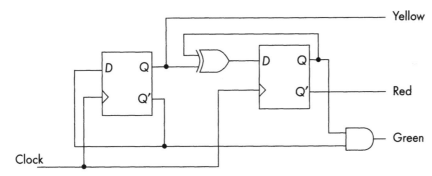

Figure 4.12 D-type flip-flop implementation of traffic light controller.

4.5.2 Combination door lock

As in the previous example, the state table of Table 4.2 is modified once the state variables for the states S_0–S_3 have been chosen. Again there are four states, so two state variables are required, labelled X and Y say. However, the excitation table is considerably more complicated since there are now three inputs to consider, a, b and c. Thus the state table will have $4 \times 2^3 = 32$ rows, one row for each unique combination of the present state and the input values. Table 4.8 shows the state table for the combination lock. Notice that many of the rows are identical. Examination of the X' and Y' columns for the 1 entries gives:

$$D_X = X' = \bar{Y}.\bar{X}.\bar{a}.b.\bar{c} + Y.\bar{X}.\bar{a}.\bar{b}.c + Y.X$$

$$D_Y = Y' = \bar{Y}.X.a.\bar{b}.\bar{c} + Y.\bar{X}.\bar{a}.\bar{b}.c + Y.X$$

Table 4.8 Combination door lock excitation table

	Present state		Inputs			Next state	
	Y	X	a	b	c	Y'	X'
	0	0	0	0	0	0	0
	0	0	0	0	1	0	0
	0	0	0	1	0	0	1
S_0	0	0	0	1	1	0	0
	0	0	1	0	0	0	0
	0	0	1	0	1	0	0
	0	0	1	1	0	0	0
	0	0	1	1	1	0	0
	0	1	0	0	0	0	0
	0	1	0	0	1	0	0
	0	1	0	1	0	0	0
S_1	0	1	0	1	1	0	0
	0	1	1	0	0	1	0
	0	1	1	0	1	0	0
	0	1	1	1	0	0	0
	0	1	1	1	1	0	0
	1	0	0	0	0	0	0
	1	0	0	0	1	1	1
	1	0	0	1	0	0	0
S_2	1	0	0	1	1	0	0
	1	0	1	0	0	0	0
	1	0	1	0	1	0	0
	1	0	1	1	0	0	0
	1	0	1	1	1	0	0
	1	1	0	0	0	1	1
	1	1	0	0	1	1	1
	1	1	0	1	0	1	1
S_3	1	1	0	1	1	1	1
	1	1	1	0	0	1	1
	1	1	1	0	1	1	1
	1	1	1	1	0	1	1
	1	1	1	1	1	1	1

Note that the last eight 1 entries in both columns correspond to state $S_3(Y.X)$ for all values of the a, b and c, and so these eight terms can be combined to give $Y.X$. The K-map technique can be used to minimize the D_X and D_Y equations, but since there are five variables (X, Y, a, b and c) 5-variable K-maps are required, which are beyond the scope of this book, so this is not attempted. The logic required to generate the output signal, Open, is very straightforward, since Open = 1 only in state S_3. Thus Open = $X.Y$ and is generated by ANDing the state variables X and Y.

4.6 Sequential logic circuits using read-only memories

The previous example, although not difficult, does show that the combinational logic of sequential logic designs that have more than a few inputs and/or outputs can quickly become very cumbersome, and result in implementations requiring many gates. One alternative approach is to use a read only memory (ROM) for the combinational logic. Figure 4.13 shows a block diagram of the general sequential digital machine (or finite state machine, FSM) in which all the combinational logic is implemented with a ROM. Note that this diagram is essentially identical to that of Figure 2.2. The

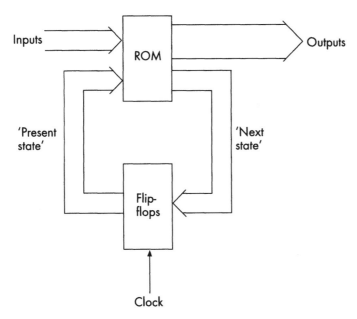

Figure 4.13 Implementing the combinatorial logic of a sequential machine with a ROM.

flip-flops hold the present values of the state variables. The outputs of these flip-flops are taken, together with the input digital lines, to the ROM address lines. Thus the ROM word that is currently being addressed is determined by the present state and the current values of the inputs. The ROM outputs must contain the next state information, that is, the next state values, and the present state outputs. In the combination door lock problem discussed in the previous section there are two state variables, three inputs and one output. To implement the door lock a ROM with five address inputs and a minimum word length of three bits is required. Five address lines gives an address range of $2^5 = 32$, so the minimum size ROM required is 32×3, as shown in Figure 4.14. In practice, a 32×4 ROM would be used, since ROMs with 3-bit

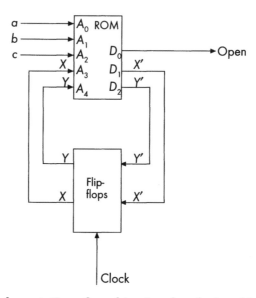

Figure 4.14 Implementation of combination door lock, with a ROM to generate the combinatorial logic.

words are not generally available. The programming information for the ROM is effectively already available in the state table, Table 4.8, with the exception of the output information. This state table has been rewritten in Table 4.9 in a form that is more suitable for the programming of the ROM. The inputs a, b and c are connected to the address lines A_0, A_1 and A_2, while the state variable outputs from the flip-flops, X and Y, are connected to A_3 and A_4. The ROM output data line D_0 is used as the open output, while data lines D_1 and D_2 hold the next state information and are connected as inputs to the state variable flip-flops. Data line D_3 is not used, and when programming the ROM it does not matter whether its value is 0 or 1.

Consider the operation of the circuit shown in Figure 4.14. Assume that it is initially in the idle or reset state. The address lines are all 0, so word 0 in the ROM is being addressed. This word contains all 0s (Table 4.9), so that Open = 0 and the next state is 00. Now suppose button b is pushed. This changes address line A_1 from 0 to 1, so that word 2 is addressed. This word contains the binary pattern 010, so that the next state is 01, while Open remains 0. The next clock pulse, generated by pushing button b, now occurs

Table 4.9 Excitation table for the combination door lock rewritten in a form suitable for implementation with a ROM

A_4	A_3	A_2	A_1	A_0	D_2	D_1	D_0
Present state			Inputs		Next state		Output
Y	X	a	b	c	Y′	X′	
0	0	0	0	0	0	0	0
0	0	0	0	1	0	0	0
0	0	0	1	0	0	1	0
0	0	0	1	1	0	0	0
0	0	1	0	0	0	0	0
0	0	1	0	1	0	0	0
0	0	1	1	0	0	0	0
0	0	1	1	1	0	0	0
0	1	0	0	0	0	0	0
0	1	0	0	1	0	0	0
0	1	0	1	0	0	0	0
0	1	0	1	1	0	0	0
0	1	1	0	0	1	0	0
0	1	1	0	1	0	0	0
0	1	1	1	0	0	0	0
0	1	1	1	1	0	0	0
1	0	0	0	0	0	0	0
1	0	0	0	1	1	1	0
1	0	0	1	0	0	0	0
1	0	0	1	1	0	0	0
1	0	1	0	0	0	0	0
1	0	1	0	1	0	0	0
1	0	1	1	0	0	0	0
1	0	1	1	1	0	0	0
1	1	0	0	0	1	1	1
1	1	0	0	1	1	1	1
1	1	0	1	0	1	1	1
1	1	0	1	1	1	1	1
1	1	1	0	0	1	1	1
1	1	1	0	1	1	1	1
1	1	1	1	0	1	1	1
1	1	1	1	1	1	1	1

and the next state information is clocked into the state flip-flops, to become the new present state, 01. Address line A_3 is now changed from 0 to 1. Thus word 8 is now being addressed. The operation of the circuit continues in this way, being entirely determined by the state table and the sequence in which the buttons are pushed. In this particular example, many of the entries in the ROM table are identical, because many of the terms in the state table are identical. When this is the case the ROM implementation is inefficient, although this will often not matter since a ROM is a standard component available at low cost. In cases where efficiency is important, and where the state table is sparsely populated with 1s, a programmable logic array may be used instead of a ROM, as discussed in the next section.

4.7 Sequential logic circuits using EPLDs

Although state machines can be implemented with read-only memories they are frequently inefficient, as discussed in Section 3.8, and a PLA implementation may be more appropriate. For example, Table 4.9 shows that in the combination door lock, the next state variables X' and Y' both contain only three different product terms:

$$X' = \bar{X}.\bar{Y}.\bar{a}.b.\bar{c} + \bar{X}.Y.\bar{a}.\bar{b}.c + X.Y$$
$$Y' = X.\bar{Y}.a.\bar{b}.\bar{c} + \bar{X}.Y.\bar{a}.\bar{b}.c + X.Y$$

that is, there are only four different terms. Similarly the output is a single term:

$$\text{Open} = X.Y$$

A PLA implementation of the combinational part of the door lock is shown in Figure 4.15. However, EPLDs are available that contain both PLAs and flip-flops, so that a complete state machine can be implemented with a single chip.

Figure 4.16 shows the pin-out diagram for an Altera EP330 EPLD, the smallest of Altera's Classic family of EPLDs. There are 10 dedicated input pins, eight input/output (I/O) pins, and eight macrocells, one associated with each I/O pin.

Figure 4.17 shows the block diagram layout of the EP330. The global bus is used to route all the input signals and their complements to each macrocell. The schematic layout of a macrocell is shown in Figure 4.18.

The PLA is able to form up to eight product terms of the input signal and their complements. These terms are then ORed together and fed to the D input of the flip-flop, and to position a of 'switch' S_1. The flip-flop is edge triggered either by the global clock from input pin 1 or by a term from the PLA. The output is either a combinational function direct from the PLA, via position a of 'switch' S_1, or a clocked, or registered, function via position b of 'switch' S_1. A signal may be fed-back to the PLA from either the output of

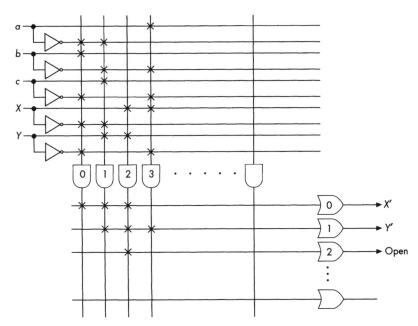

Figure 4.15 PLA implementation of the combinational logic required in the
combination door lock.

INPUT/CLK	1		20	V_{CC}
INPUT	2		19	I/O
INPUT	3		18	I/O
INPUT	4	ALTERA EP330	17	I/O
INPUT	5		16	I/O
INPUT	6		15	I/O
INPUT	7		14	I/O
INPUT	8		13	I/O
INPUT	9		12	I/O
GND	10		11	INPUT

Figure 4.16 Pin-out diagram of the Altera EP330 Classic EPLD.

the PLA, the flip-flop, or the I/O pin when it is configured as an input, via
'switch' S_2. Not shown are exclusive-OR gates, which allow the output of the
PLA or the flip-flop to be inverted if required.

These switches, of course, are actually fuses which are implemented using
what are known as floating-gate transistors. They are re-programmable,
either by using UV light or electrically (EEPLDs), as discussed in the previous
chapter.

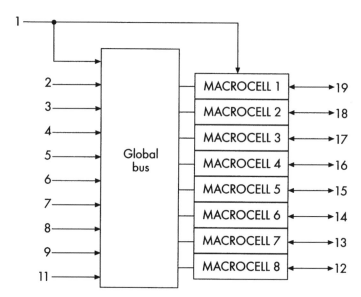

Figure 4.17 Block diagram layout of the Altera EP330 Classic EPLD.

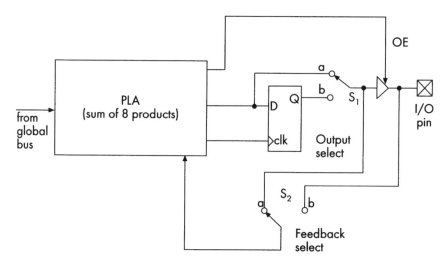

Figure 4.18 Layout of the macrocells of an EP330.

The EP330 is the smallest of the Altera devices available, having 150 so-called 'usable gates'. Although it can be used to implement small sequential logic FSMs, its main limitations are the small number of macrocells (8), and hence flip-flops, and the small number of product terms per macrocell (8). A larger member of the Classic family is the EP1810, which has 900 usable gates and 48 macrocells. Its basic architecture is the same as the EP330 and so it has the same product term limitations. There is continuing and rapid development in the EPLD market; for example, the latest Altera FLEX 10 K EPLDs have up to 250,000 usable gates and several thousand flip-flops, together with other logic elements. These devices give the user the ability to implement very complex digital logic systems onto a single EPLD.

To use EPLDs effectively it is necessary to have a sophisticated computer-aided design (CAD) system to enter the design in a user-friendly way, to simulate the design, and then to generate the programming information required. The current Altera CAD system is known as MAX+plus II and runs on both PC's and other workstations. User designs may be entered in a number of ways, including graphically, in which the computer effectively acts as a drawing board. Designs are composed of symbols from a TTL library (gates, arithmetic units, multiplexers, etc.), and input and output pads, which are joined with lines (wires). Other designs, such as state machines (FSMs) are more easily entered using a suitable textual language, or a high-level digital design language. Although these are outside the scope of this text the following is an example of the Altera state machine language for the simple traffic light controller discussed in Section 4.5.1.

```
SUBDESIGN lights
(
      clock, reset : INPUT ;
      red, yellow, green : OUTPUT ;
)

VARIABLE
      light_asm : MACHINE OF BITS (q1,q0)
                        WITH STATES (s0, s1, s2, s3) ;
BEGIN
      light_asm.clk = clock ;
      light_asm.reset=reset ;

      TABLE
      light_asm => light_asm, red, yellow, green ;

      s0 => s1, 1, 0, 0;
      s1 => s2, 1, 1, 0;
      s2 => s3, 0, 0, 1;
      s3 => s0, 0, 1, 0;

      END TABLE;
END;
```

There are two inputs, clock and reset, and three outputs, red, yellow, and green. The **VARIABLE** statement defines light_asm to be a state machine with two bits, q1 and q0, and four states s0, s1, s2 and s3. The core of the design are the statements in the **TABLE**, which is effectively a direct mapping from the state table of Table 4.1. The columns of the table are defined by the statement

```
light_asm => light_asm, red, yellow, green
```

The first two columns are the present state, and next state, and the next three columns are the three outputs. The following four rows are then the state transitions. Entering a design using a route such as this is clearly far more efficient, and less prone to errors, than the manual translation one described in a previous section. Passing this design through the Altera MAX+plus II CAD system results in a fit that uses about 50% of an EP330 device, while fitting the same design to an FLEX 8000 family device used just 2% of the smallest member of the family, the EP8282, which itself is only about 15% of the largest member of the family, the EP81500.

4.8 Counter design

Counters are a special class of finite state machine. A counter follows a pre-set sequence and repeatedly outputs the same pattern. The simplest counter is the binary-up counter in which the counter is incremented by one each time a clock pulse occurs, until the maximum count is reached. Figure 4.19 shows the state diagram for a modulo-8 counter. By convention the count

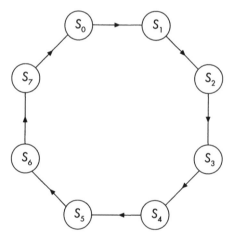

Figure 4.19 State diagrams for a modulo-8 up-counter.

begins at 0 and is then incremented by 1 on the next clock pulse until the maximum of 7 occurs. When the next clock pulse occurs the counter is reset to zero, and the sequence starts again. There are no inputs, apart from the clock. Eight states require three state variables, X, Y and Z. Where possible the state assignments are made so that the circuit outputs are just the state variables, X, Y and Z. Thus $S_0 = 000$, $S_1 = 001$, etc.

The design of a synchronous counter proceeds in exactly the same way as discussed above for any synchronous sequential circuit. For example, consider the design of a modulo-3 up/down synchronous counter. This counter has a single input labelled up/down, in addition to the normal clock. If up/down = 1 the counter is to count up in the normal way, following the sequence o, 1, 2, o, ..., while if up/down = 0 it is required to count down following the sequence o, 2, 1, o, ... There are three states, so two state variables are required, X and Y. In normal operation the fourth state, state 4, is never entered and so could be regarded as a 'don't care' state. However, if state 4 is ever entered (for example, as the random state entered when power is first switched on) then the next state should be one of the three states, state o say, so that the count sequence is properly resumed. The state table is shown in Table 4.10(a). In this example it will be assumed that each of the

Table 4.10 Modulo-3 up/down counter: (a) state table; (b) excitation table

| Present state | | Up/down | Next state | |
Y	X	U	Y'	X'
0	0	0	1	0
0	0	1	0	1
0	1	0	0	0
0	1	1	1	0
1	0	0	0	1
1	0	1	0	0
1	1	×	0	0

| Present state | | Up/down | Next state | | Flip-flop controls | | | |
Y	X	U	Y'	X'	J_Y	K_Y	J_X	K_X
0	0	0	1	0	1	×	0	×
0	0	1	0	1	0	×	1	×
0	1	0	0	0	0	×	×	1
0	1	1	1	0	1	×	×	1
1	0	0	0	1	×	1	1	×
1	0	1	0	0	×	1	0	×
1	1	×	0	0	×	1	×	1

state variables, X and Y, is stored in a JK flip-flop, as shown in Figure 4.20. As before, the problem comes down to designing the combinational logic required for the connections to the J and K inputs of the two flip-flops, and the logic to generate the output signals. The logic is determined by expanding the state table into a new modified table, called an excitation table, Table 4.10(b). Again the normal binary pattern has been assumed for the state variables. The column labelled JK flip-flop controls is filled in with the aid of the JK flip-flop state change table, Table 4.6. For example, in the first row the transition from state 00 to state 10, the state variable Y changes from 0 to 1. This requires that $J_Y = 1$ and $K_Y = ×$ (don't care). The state variable X does not change ($0 \rightarrow 0$) and so $J_X = 0$ and $K_X = ×$. Boolean

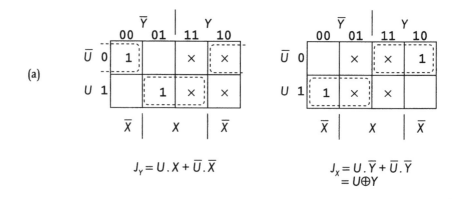

(a)

$$J_Y = U.X + \overline{U}.\overline{X}$$

$$J_X = U.\overline{Y} + \overline{U}.Y$$
$$= U \oplus Y$$

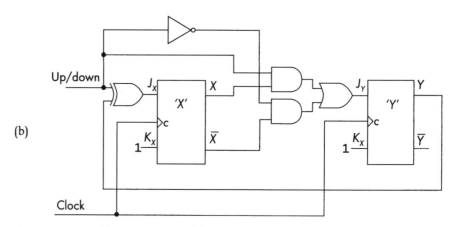

(b)

Figure 4.20 Up/down counter: (a) K-maps for J_X and J_Y flip-flop control signals; (b) implementation.

equations for the J and K values may then be written down directly by scanning each column for the **1** entries, as before, giving:

$$J_Y = \overline{Y}.\overline{X}.\overline{U} + \overline{Y}.X.U$$

$$K_Y = 1$$

$$J_X = \overline{Y}.\overline{X}.U + Y.\overline{X}.\overline{U}$$

$$K_X = 1$$

These equations can be minimized using K-maps, as shown in Figure 4.20(a). The resulting implementation is given in Figure 4.20(b).

The decision on whether to use D-type or JK flip-flops is really a matter of designer choice. A JK flip-flop implementation is slightly more difficult to design, but will often result in less hardware being required for the combinational logic, than an equivalent design using D-type flip-flops.

Another type of counter that is frequently used is the asynchronous or ripple counter. These counters use JK flip-flops connected in the toggle mode, with $J = K = 1$. Figure 4.21(a) shows a modulo-16 ripple counter. The pulses to be counted are applied to the clock input of the first JK flip-flop. The output of this flip-flop, Q_A, is applied to the clock input of the second flip-flop. Its output is applied in turn to the clock input of the third flip-flop, and so on.

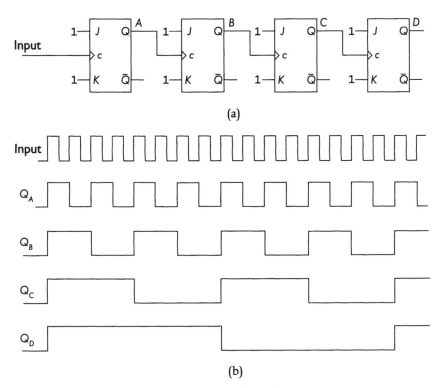

(a)

(b)

Figure 4.21 Modulo-16 ripple counter: (a) implementation using JK flip-flops; (b) input and output signals.

Figure 4.21(b) shows the input and output signals that are observed in this counter. The first flip-flop toggles, that is, changes state, on the rising edge of each of the pulses to be counted. It effectively divides the pulse frequency by 2. The second flip-flop toggles on every rising edge of Q_A, so effectively dividing the input pulse frequency by 4. The outputs of the flip-flops are thus a binary count of the input pulses, with Q_A being the least significant digit, and Q_D the most significant digit. Clearly the design can be extended to any number of stages to produce a modulo-N counter, but with the limitation that N is a power of two. It is also possible to design ripple counters where N is not a power of two, but their design is not considered here. Note also that a modulo-N counter may also be used as a divide-by-N frequency divider, dividing the input frequency by N, N^2, N^4, etc. The name 'ripple counter' comes from the fact that changes in the state of the counter ripple through the chain of flip-flops, with the result that there is a propagation delay between the outputs of the flip-flops changing. If this is important, then a synchronous counter must be used. In such a counter, all the changes occur instantaneously coincident with the clock pulse.

A variety of counters are available as MSI packages.

4.9 Design of a register bank

The basic ideas, including the design of combinational and sequential logic circuits, required for the understanding of how a computer works have now been discussed. As an introduction to the following chapters that consider the concept of a computer as a finite state machine, the evolution of a memory from a single D-type flip-flop to a register bank will now be discussed.

A register is a device in which a number of binary digits (bits) can be stored and retrieved, or read back. The use of a D-type flip-flop to store a single bit of information has been considered in Section 4.4.2 above. The data bit to be stored in, or written to, the memory (0 or 1) is placed on the D input (see Figure 4.8) and a clock pulse is then applied to the clock input. This results in the data bit being stored in the flip-flop. Its value can be ascertained at any time from the memory by reading the value of the Q output. A set of n of these D-type flip-flops, fabricated as a single unit, can be used to store n bits of information, and is known as a register. Frequently, n is a power of 2, usually 4, 8, 16, 32 or 64. Figure 4.22 is a schematic diagram of a single 4-bit register. The inputs are labelled D_0 to D_3, and the outputs Q_0 to Q_3. The pattern of bits stored in the register will be referred to as a (4-bit) word. The four clock inputs to the individual flip-flops within the register are connected to a common clock line. When a pulse is applied to this line the data on the input lines are written into the memory, over-writing the previous word stored.

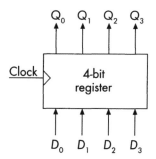

Figure 4.22 register formed from a set of four D-type flip-flops.

Clearly a set of registers is required to store a set of words; Figure 4.23 shows two 4-bit registers, R_0 and R_1. In a computer system data is transferred between the various units that make up the computer on a common data bus, which in practice is just a set of wires, or tracks on a printed circuit board, or interconnections in an integrated circuit. In

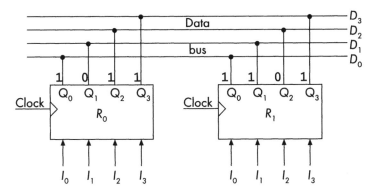

Figure 4.23 Two 4-bit registers connected to a data bus.

Figure 4.23 the outputs of the two registers are shown connected to the data bus. This bus is a 4-bit wide bus, since four bits of information are passed between the registers and computer (or other devices using the registers) at once. Note that the inputs to the registers have been re-labelled I_0 to I_3 to avoid confusion with the data bus, which is labelled according to the accepted convention D_0 to D_3. Figure 4.23 shows that each output of register R_0 is connected to the corresponding output of register R_1 via the data bus, and so breaks one of the cardinal rules of constructing logic systems. This rule states that the outputs of ordinary gates or components such as flip-flops must not be connected together. To see why, suppose the two words stored in R_0 and R_1 are **1101** and **1011**, respectively, and consider what will be the logic states of the data bus lines. D_0 and D_3 will both be **1**, since Q_0 and Q_3 are **1** for both registers. However, it is not at all clear what the states of D_1 and D_2 will be. In the case of D_1, register R_0 is trying to output a **0**, while register R_1 is trying to output a **1** (and conversely for D_2). At best, D_1 and D_2 will be indeterminate, while at worst both registers will be destroyed. This is because Q_1 of R_0 is effectively connected to the 0 volt supply line, and Q_1 of R_1 to the V_{cc} supply line. The result is a short circuit path between V_{cc} and 0 volts, leading to the probable destruction of both circuits. Moreover, logically, the device at the other end of the data bus is attempting to read from both registers at once, which is clearly not sensible.

One solution is to connect only the output lines of one register at a time to the data bus. This is achieved by inserting a special type of buffer circuit, known as a 3-state or tri-state buffer, into each output line of the registers. Figure 4.24 shows the circuit symbol and schematic circuit diagram of a tri-state buffer. Its truth table is given in Table 4.11. If the enable line is high then the tri-state buffer behaves like an ordinary buffer: the 'switch' is closed and the output logic state is the same as the input. However, if the

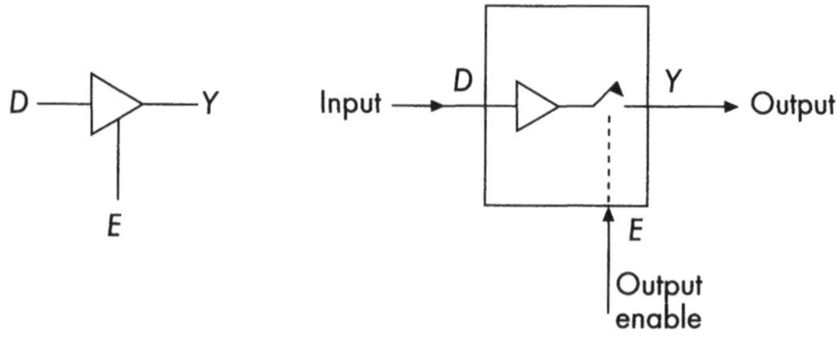

Figure 4.24 Tri-state buffer.

Table 4.11 Truth table of tri-state buffer

D	E	Y
0	1	0
1	1	1
0	0	high-Z
1	0	high-Z

enable line is low, the 'switch' is open, effectively disconnecting the output from the input. The design of a tri-state buffer is such that there is a very high impedance between the input and output, shown in the truth table by the 'high-Z' entries. Tri-state buffers are also available with an inverting action ($Y = \bar{D}$), and with active low enable. Each output line in each register has a tri-state buffer controlled by the 'output enable' control line. Clearly only one register 'output enable' must be true at any one time, or else the same problem of two registers trying to drive the data bus at the same time occurs. The next problem is how to write data into a register. Again, the data bus is used, but this time data is placed on the bus by a device such as a computer, and the task is to route the data from the data bus to the desired register. Connections can be made directly from the data bus to the register inputs (I_0 to I_3), since the data will be written into the register only when a clock pulse is applied. Figure 4.25 shows the connections between a data bus line and a single flip-flop of a register. The read, write and select control lines are common to all the cells within a register. The select line is used to select, or address, a particular register within a system. This selection is usually done with the aid of a decoder, and will be discussed in detail in Chapter 9. Read and write are control lines used to control the reading from, and writing to, the registers. These operations are as follows.

1. Read from memory cell: select and read = 1; write = 0. The output of the tri-state buffer is enabled, so the data bit stored in the cell is routed to the data bus line D.

2. Write to memory cell: select and write = 1; read = 0. The input AND gate A is enabled so the data bit present on the data bus line is routed to the

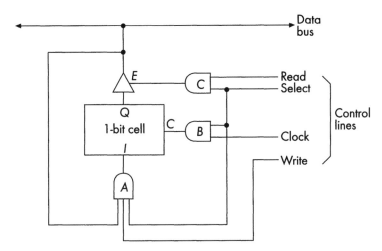

Figure 4.25 1-bit memory cell.

input of the memory flip-flop. A clock pulse is then applied, and since AND gate B is enabled, the flip-flop is clocked, so copying the data bit into the flip-flop. The output tri-state buffer is in its high-impedance state, so there is no connection between the output of the flip-flop and the data bus.

4.10 Summary

The design and implementation of synchronous sequential logic circuits has been discussed in this chapter. The normal starting point for the design of sequential logic is the drawing of a state diagram. Once this diagram is complete, and checked against the specification for the system required, the implementation process is then essentially a mechanical exercise, following a given 'recipe'. Alternatively a state machine design programme may be used. The implementations discussed in this text use both D and JK flip-flops as memory elements for the state variables, and use a simple procedure that allows the combinational logic for each of the D or J and K flip-flop inputs to be determined easily. If implementing the combinational logic using discrete gates becomes too extensive then an alternative approach is to use a read-only memory (ROM), a programmable logic array (PLA) or an EPLD. The implementation of simple counters, both synchronous and asynchronous (ripple), has also been introduced.

4.11 Exercises

Exercise 4.1 Design a synchronous circuit using D-type flip-flops to detect the sequence 0101. The circuit has a single input, x, and a single output z. The output is logic-1 whenever the input sequence 0101 is detected, logic-0 otherwise. Note that overlapping sequences are allowed.

Exercise 4.2 Design a synchronous circuit that has a single binary input, x, and a single binary output, z. The output is to be logic-1 whenever the previous three inputs contain an even number of logic-1s. For example, the input sequence `01101011...` should give rise to the output sequence `0 0 1 1 1 0 1 1 . . .`

Exercise 4.3 A synchronous circuit is to be designed to perform the serial addition of two binary numbers. These numbers are fed a bit at a time, starting with the least significant bits, to the two inputs of the circuit, X_1 and X_2. The circuit has a single output, z, which is to produce the sum of the two inputs, in serial form.

Exercise 4.4 Design a synchronous modulo-3 counter (that is, one that continually counts in the sequence 0, 1, 2, 0, 1, 2, ...) using (a) D-type and (b) JK flip-flops.

Exercise 4.5 Design a modulo-6 up/down counter using a ROM and a set of D-type flip-flops. You should specify the size and the contents of the ROM.

Exercise 4.6 A circuit has two JK flip-flops, A and B, and a single output Z. The circuit is as shown in Figure 4.26.

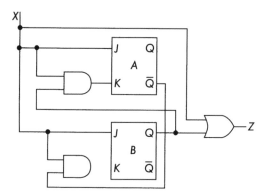

Figure 4.26 Circuit diagram for Exercise 4.6.

Obtain:

(a) the state table;

(b) the state diagram for this circuit.

Exercise 4.7 Design a sequential circuit which produces an output $Z = 1$ for any input sequence ending in `100` on the single input, A.

Exercise 4.8 What modifications would be necessary for your design for the previous circuit to make it suitable for ROM implementation?

5
The structure of a computer

5.1 Introduction

A computer, strictly a stored program computer, consists of a set of sequential and combinational logic components that act in a similar way to the sequential logic described in the previous chapter. The basic difference between a computer and a sequential logic machine is that whereas in a sequential logic machine the combinational and sequential logic defines the function performed, in a computer it is the stored instructions, the program, which determine its action. Because the program may be changed easily, the computer is much more flexible than a hardwired design. A computer can be represented in block diagram form as shown in Figure 5.1. It consists of five

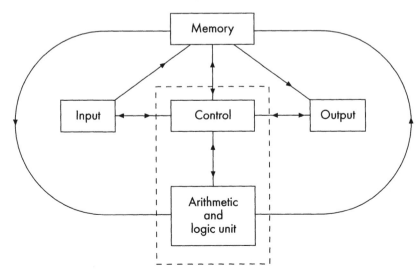

Figure 5.1 Block diagram of a computer.

functional blocks: memory, input, output, control, and the arithmetic and logic unit. The memory is used to store instructions and data, which are processed by the arithmetic and logic unit. The input and output devices, often called peripherals, are used to input and output instructions and data. The control unit coordinates the operation of the computer and most of the control resides in a central unit which, since it normally also contains the arithmetic and logic unit, is known as the central processing unit or CPU. In a simple microcomputer system, the components shown in Figure 5.1 are usually implemented using integrated circuits. Examples of Intel 80x86 and Motorola 680x0 microcomputer systems are given in Chapter 9.

5.2 The operation of a computer

The operation cycle of a computer consists of four basic steps and is illustrated in Figure 5.2.

1. Fetch the next instruction from memory to the control unit } *Fetch cycle*
2. Decode this instruction
3. Obey the instruction *Execution cycle*
4. Go to 1

Figure 5.2 The operation cycle of a computer.

Memory consists of a large number of locations, each comprising the same number of bits, the smallest group being eight bits, known as a byte. Since computers usually operate on more that eight bits at a time, a number of bytes are grouped together into a word (the size of the word will vary from one computer to another). Some of these locations contain instructions and others contain data, and each separate memory location is identified by a unique address. To write information to memory, the address of the location where the information is to reside has to be presented, together with the data. To read information already present in memory only the address of the location is required. The bit pattern representing an instruction can be considered as split into a number of fields. One of the fields specifies the operation to be carried out; other fields may specify the address in memory of operands of the instruction and the address where the results, if any, are to be put. The number and type of operand fields will depend on the operation to be performed and on the computer architecture. For example, the HALT instruction, which will halt operation of the computer, needs no operands. An ADD instruction, however, needs to know the addresses of the two operands that are to be added and the address in memory to place the result. A full discussion of instruction sets and memory addressing modes is given in Chapter 11. While the fetch cycle is identical for all instructions of a computer, the execution cycle depends on the particular instruction being executed. Hence there will be as many different execution cycles as there are instructions defined for that particular computer.

Instructions typically fall into several groups. One group, the arithmetic and logic group, includes instructions such as add, subtract, multiply and divide in the arithmetic group and ADD, OR and XOR in the logic group. A second group consists of move or copy operations, which provide a means of transferring information from memory location to memory location and between memory and input and output devices. A third group involves transfer of control. These instructions modify the instruction flow through the program, often conditionally on the result of the previous operation by forcing the next instruction to be obtained not from the next memory location but from somewhere else in memory. In addition to these groups of instructions there are usually instructions to perform specialized operations, such as halting the computer. More details of these groups of instructions are given in Chapter 11.

5.3 System packaging

Ideally the number of components in a computer system should be kept to a minimum since problems often arise at the physical interface between components because of poor contacts. Thus the ideal would be for the main electronic components to be fabricated as a single integrated circuit; a single chip. Whilst it is now possible to fabricate a mid-range microcomputer on a single chip, this is done only for high volume, simple, applications such as embedded controllers in domestic appliances. The reason for this is that for general purpose computers the system requirements are changing fast. For example, the amount of memory required in the system changes at least once a year as memory gets cheaper and software requires more memory for acceptable performance, and thus there is not a large enough market for any one particular configuration. Additionally, owners wish to upgrade their systems frequently and, if the system is a single chip, the only upgrade possible would be to replace the whole system at a relatively high cost.

Thus, most systems are assembled from a set of integrated circuit components. The simplest organization is to place all the components on a printed circuit board and to package this board, together with a power supply, in a suitable enclosure, for example, a tower cabinet. A printed circuit board consists of an insulated plastic board which has holes drilled to accept components or sockets for components. The components are wired together by having tracks of conducting material pre-formed on the board between the appropriate holes of the components. Modern circuit boards are complex as they allow many different layers of tracks to be formed on the board so that different layers can cross one another without an electrical contact being formed. The production of circuit boards is completely automated, as is the insertion of components, thus making such assemblies relatively cheap.

One of the difficulties of a simple circuit board is that it has to be drilled for a given number and type of components and is thus not very flexible. For example, if a user wants to exceed the amount of memory possible on a single board then a larger or additional board is required. This leads to the introduction of technologies for connecting printed circuit boards together. The system used to connect a number of circuit boards together is called a backplane. Each circuit board has a connector with a set of pins on an edge and these connectors plug into the backplane which provides wiring between pins on different boards. This system is used extensively in higher cost systems but typical PCs use a cheaper system. Here the main circuit board, called a motherboard, contains many of the components of the system but components which may need to be changed or upgraded – for example, memory – are placed on smaller circuit boards which slot directly into the motherboard. Thus to upgrade a component the smaller board can be removed and replaced by a board with a larger component or additional boards can be slotted into extra connectors on the motherboard. Input–output interfaces are also typically provided by boards which slot into the motherboard.

5.4 The bus

The main method of communication among the various component parts of a computer is by the use of one or more buses, each of which consists of a group of signal lines used to carry information. There are usually many different buses in a computer system, for example, inside the CPU chip, on the motherboard, in the backplane connecting circuit boards. Usually the components tap on to the bus to send and receive information as shown in Figure 5.3.

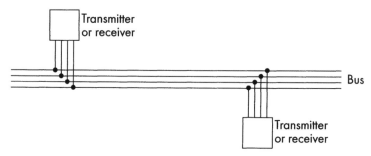

Figure 5.3   The bus.

As discussed in Section 4.8, in order to work correctly, only one sender must be active on the bus at any one time. In a simple computer this is achieved by having a single master, the central processing unit, which controls the whole system. The other devices on the bus, called slaves, respond to commands from the central processing unit which controls what information is on the bus at any one time. Any device connected to the bus may read information on it; logic has to be provided so that only the addressed device responds. Buses carry three different types of information, address, data and control, and a bus is often subdivided into these three types.

In a computer system there will be a hierarchy of groups of buses. In this text only the two lowest level buses will be considered; those between components that make up the CPU, and those between the CPU, memory and input–output interfaces on a printed circuit board.

As mentioned previously, a typical microcomputer system is made up from a number of integrated circuits providing the functions described in Figure 5.1. The CPU is normally provided as a single integrated circuit, which is connected via buses to the appropriate number of memory and input–output interfaces to produce the required computer system. This division is followed in this book with this chapter concentrating on the internal structure of the CPU.

5.5 The central processing unit

The central processing unit (CPU) consists of a control unit and an arithmetic and logic unit. In this section these two subunits are described in detail. The CPU is organized around a bus structure and although individual computers differ as to the exact organization, Figure 5.4 is typical.

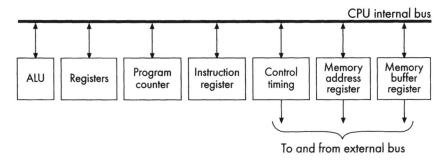

Figure 5.4 The CPU bus structure.

Not all registers have to be the same size because they hold different types of information. Those registers that hold data or instructions have to be the same size as a memory location. Registers that hold the address of a memory location, the program counter and the memory address register (MAR) of Figure 5.4, need to be large enough to contain the highest memory address. In a typical 8-bit microcomputer, the registers that hold data are 8 bits wide, whereas those that hold memory addresses are 16 bits wide to allow for a maximum memory size of 2^{16} (65,536) locations. A 16-bit microcomputer normally has a wider address range, typically megabytes. For example, the Motorola 68000 has 24 address lines giving a maximum memory size of 2^{24} (16,777,216) locations. Current processors have 32-bit words with 32-bit addressing registers, allowing a maximum addressing space of 2^{32} words although this is not all populated with memory circuits, since present day applications do not need this amount of memory. However, a 32-bit address space allows space for memory expansion as programs get increasingly larger.

5.6 The arithmetic and logic unit

The arithmetic and logic unit (ALU) is involved in the execution of arithmetic and logical operations. The operands of an arithmetic or a logical operation are to be found in memory, but to speed up the operation, many computers have several, typically 8, 16 or 32, faster memory locations, called registers, within the CPU. Some computers have a single special register, called the accumulator (ACC), which is the source of one of the operands and the destination of an arithmetic or logical operation. If this is the case, the structure of the processor can be represented as in Figure 5.5, which also shows a flag register. This register contains a number of individual bits to

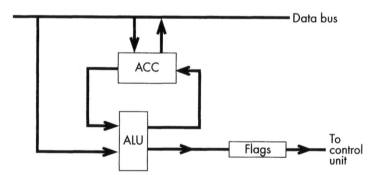

Figure 5.5 A single accumulator ALU structure.

store information about the result of the last ALU operation, for example, whether it resulted in a zero result, negative result, or produced a carry or an overflow. This information is then available for use by later instructions.

5.6.1 The structure of an arithmetic and logic unit

A simple block diagram of an ALU is shown in Figure 5.6. The inputs and the output will typically be 8, 16 or 32 bits wide, depending on the size of the ALU. The number of control signals will depend upon the number of functions that the ALU is capable of performing; as usual, n control signals are required for 2^n operations.

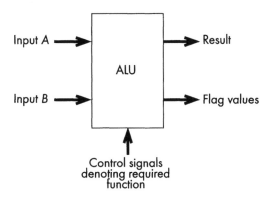

Figure 5.6 ALU structure.

5.6.2 The components of the arithmetic and logic unit

An ALU can perform a range of arithmetic and logic operations, and this section describes a few of the circuits required to perform these operations. The circuits described would not necessarily be found in this form in a modern CPU; usually they are implemented by more regular structures such as PLAs.

(a) An adder

A computer works on a pattern of bits and so the lowest level of adder is a l-bit adder, whose truth table is shown in Table 5.1.

Table 5.1   Truth table for a 1-bit adder

A	B	Carry	Sum
0	0	0	0
0	1	0	1
1	0	0	1
1	1	1	0

The circuit that implements this truth table is called a half adder, since for addition of multiple bits an additional circuit is needed which has as an extra input, the carry from the previous bit addition. This is called a full adder and its truth table is shown in Table 5.2.

For the half adder, the circuit is simple and can be produced by inspection of the truth table, as was shown in Chapter 2, that is,

$$S = A \oplus B$$
$$C = A.B$$

giving the circuit shown in Figure 5.7.

Table 5.2 Truth table for a full adder

A	B	Carry in	Carry out	Sum
0	0	0	0	0
0	0	1	0	1
0	1	0	0	1
0	1	1	1	0
1	0	0	0	1
1	0	1	1	0
1	1	0	1	0
1	1	1	1	1

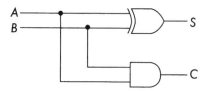

Figure 5.7 Half adder structure.

The full adder circuit is more complex. Using the combinational logic design techniques described in Chapter 3 the required logic is:

$$C_{out} = \bar{A}.B.C_{in} + A.\bar{B}.C_{in} + A.B.\bar{C}_{in} + A.B.C_{in} = C_{in}.(A \oplus B) + A.B$$

$$S = \bar{A}.\bar{B}.C_{in} + \bar{A}.B.\bar{C}_{in} + A.\bar{B}.\bar{C}_{in} + A.B.C_{in} = C_{in} \oplus (A \oplus B)$$

giving the circuit shown in Figure 5.8.

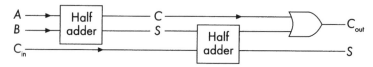

Figure 5.8 Full adder circuit.

Full adders may be cascaded together to produce multiple bit adders as shown in Figure 5.9. A point to notice here is that if one of the input values is 0, for example B_0–B_3, then, if the initial carry C_0 is set to 1, the result will be $A + 1$. This is a quick and efficient method of incrementing a value by 1.

An adder may also be used as a subtractor, using the rules of 'two's complement' arithmetic, the arithmetic normally performed by a computer. Using these rules (see Chapter 10), subtraction may be performed by one's complementing (inverting all the bits of) the value to be subtracted, incrementing the one's complement to form the two's complement, and then

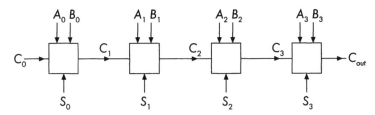

Figure 5.9 Multiple bit full adder.

adding this complemented value to the other operand. Hence for subtraction the circuit required is a set of inverters on one of the input paths to the ALU and the adder circuitry described above. The carry input to the least significant bit of the adder provides a simple incrementing mechanism.

(b) Logical tests

An ALU normally contains logic to perform a number of different logical tests, such as a test to see if the result of an operation is zero. Some of these logical tests affect the flag register used to store information regarding the result of the last operation; other logical tests produce a result used as data in further processing.

(c) Logical test for zero

All that is needed for a test for zero on a word is an OR gate with the requisite number of inputs as shown in Figure 5.10. This circuit may be used to set the zero flag on the result of an operation.

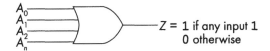

Figure 5.10 Logical test for zero.

(d) Bitwise AND of two operands

As this operation suggests, what is required is a set of AND gates that have as inputs the corresponding bits of the two operands. The outputs are the resultant AND of the bit pairs as shown by the circuit in Figure 5.11. The other bit operations, for example bitwise OR, may be implemented by similar schemes using different gates.

(e) Shifting

Most computers include some form of shift or rotate instructions in their instruction sets. These instructions move bits right or left within a word. The various shift and rotate operations differ in what is placed in the bit position left vacant by the moving of the bit pattern and by what happens to the bit that is moved out of the word by the shifting operation.

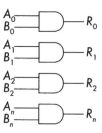

Figure 5.11 Bitwise AND of two words.

A shift register may be implemented by a series of edge-triggered flip-flops as shown in Figure 5.12. On the occurrence of a clock pulse, the external input is clocked into the first flip-flop, the output from the first flip-flop is clocked into the second one, and so on. Thus all the bits are shifted one place to the right. The output and input will be connected in the particular way required for the shift operation and initial loading of all the bits of the shift register in parallel is normally allowed.

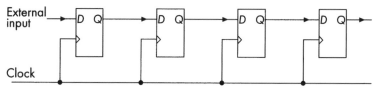

Figure 5.12 A shift register.

(f) Comparator

All computers include a number of comparison operations such as test for equality, greater than and less than. All these comparisons can be performed by subtraction, as described previously with the setting of the appropriate status flags, without the storing of the subtraction result.

(g) Multiplication and division

In most microprocessors now available, integer multiplication and division are implemented in hardware. Floating-point arithmetic is usually implemented on the CPU chip, but for some CPU families special purpose floating-point arithmetic chips, known as maths co-processors, are available, although they will not be discussed here.

5.6.3 Control

As shown earlier, to connect registers to the bus, control signals are required. They also control the function of the ALU and provide timing signals to the rest of the computer system. Most of these control signals originate in the control section of the central processing unit. All the actions of the control unit are connected with the decoding and execution of instructions, the fetch and execute cycles.

(a) The fetch cycle

The instruction cycle, as described in the beginning of this chapter, involves reading the next instruction to be obeyed from memory into an internal register in the CPU, the instruction register (IR), and then decoding and obeying the instruction.

In order to explain these actions in more detail a simple computer system will be used for illustrative purposes as shown in Figure 5.13.

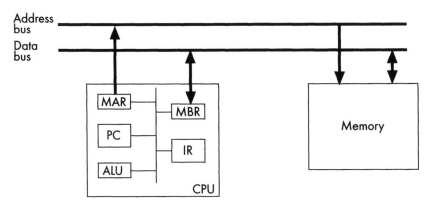

Figure 5.13 Illustrative system.

For an instruction to be fetched from memory the following sequence of operations has to be performed:

1. load the contents of the program counter into the memory address register (MAR) which is then placed on the address bus;

2. instruct the memory to perform a read operation which will result in data being placed on the data bus;

3. store the value on the data bus in the memory buffer register (MBR) in the CPU;

4. transfer the value in the MBR into the instruction register (IR);

5. increment the contents of the program counter to point to the next location in memory.

In order to carry out these operations, a number of different control signals have to be sent to the various registers within the CPU and to the memory subsystem. For example, for the first operation, the control system has to disable all the register outputs to the bus, to enable the output of the program counter on to the bus and to load the bus contents into the memory address register. The control signals required to perform these operations have to occur in the correct order and at the correct time relative to each other.

(b) The execute cycle

The set of operations described above are performed as the fetch cycle of every instruction, but the execute cycle differs from instruction to instruction, and from computer to computer as the architecture of the computer greatly influences how an operation is performed. As an example of an execution sequence, consider the architecture of Figure 5.13 where an ADD instruction is defined as adding the contents of a named register to the accumulator and leaving the result in the accumulator. Since the registers reside in the CPU the execution sequence would be:

1. transfer the accumulator contents to the ALU via the internal bus;

2. transfer the addressed register contents to the other ALU input via the internal bus;

3. signal the ALU to add;

4. store the result in the accumulator.

A much fuller discussion of control is given in Chapter 8 on microprogramming.

5.7 Examples of processors

In this section two examples of real microprocessors will be outlined, namely the Intel 80x86 and the Motorola 680x0 processor families.

5.7.1 The Intel 80x86 processor

The Intel 80x86 is a family of microprocessors that has evolved continuously from the introduction of the 16-bit 8086 in 1978, and has now progressed through x = 1, 2, 3 and 4 to the currently widely used x = 5 Pentium processor, introduced in 1993. As the series has evolved the processors have become faster, more instructions have been added, the data buses have become wider (the 80486 has a 32-bit bus, the Pentium a 64-bit bus), and more functions have been integrated onto the processor chip. All members of the family are backward compatible, so that an 80486, for example, will execute a program written for an 8086 (the reverse is not true, that is, an 8086 may not be able to execute a program written for an 80486). For simplicity, the 8086 will be used as an example in this text.

A simplified diagram of the 8086 processor is shown in Figure 5.14. It consists of an internal 16-bit bus, to which three banks of registers (general purpose, pointer, and segment registers), an instruction pointer register (IP), and an ALU are connected. The general purpose register bank is made up of four 16-bit registers (AX, BX, CX and DX), used for the temporary storage of

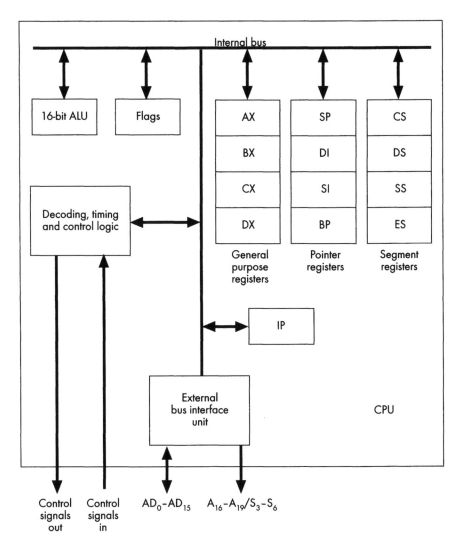

Figure 5.14 Intel 8086 CPU.

16-bit data. Each of these 16-bit registers actually comprises two 8-bit registers, known respectively as the high and low byte (for example, AX comprises AH and AL), enabling 8-bit data to be stored. The flag register containing the status bits is also connected to the internal bus. The control unit generates all the appropriate control signals both for the internal registers and for external memory and input–output device synchronization. The CPU interacts with memory and input–output devices via the bus interface unit, and the control unit.

The 8086 has the capability physically to address $2^{20} = 1{,}048{,}576$ bytes of external memory (1 Mbyte). There is a time multiplexed bi-directional 16-bit address/data (ADDR/DATA) bus, labelled AD_0 to AD_{15} in Figure 5.14. The additional four address lines required are labelled A_{16}–A_{19}/S_3–S_6, since they are also used to output status information. As the 8086 registers are only 16 bits wide the question as to how 20-bit addresses are formed arises. The answer is that a second register, called a segment register, is used, of which the 8086 has four, namely code segment (CS), data segment (DS), stack segment (SS), and extra segment (ES).

The address of the next instruction to be fetched is formed as follows. As an example, assume that the instructions are in memory, starting at address 1000_H (that is, location 1000_H). [Note: The H stands for hexadecimal, which is a number system whose base is 16. For more information on hexadecimal numbers see Chapter 10]. The code segment register, CS, is then set to this base address, but shifted four bits to the right, or 100_H, in this example (that is, CS contains the base address of the code to be executed divided by the decimal factor of 16). If the first instruction to be fetched is at address 0, relative to the base address in CS, then IP must be set to 0. The address is then calculated by adding the value in IP to that of the CS register shifted four bytes to the left (i.e. multiplied by 16), as follows:

$$CS = 100_H \text{ shifted } 4 \text{ bits left } = 01000$$
$$IP = 0 \qquad\qquad\qquad = \underline{\qquad 0}$$
$$Address \qquad\qquad\qquad = \underline{01000}$$

If this instruction occupies, say, 2 bytes of memory then IP will be automatically incremented by 2 by the CPU. The next instruction to be fetched is then at address 2 relative to CS, so the address calculation is:

$$CS = 100_H \text{ shifted } 4 \text{ bits left } = 01000$$
$$IP = 2 \qquad\qquad\qquad = \underline{\qquad 2}$$
$$Address \qquad\qquad\qquad = \underline{01002}$$

Address calculations for data and for the stack are calculated in exactly the same way, but using the data segment (DS) and the stack segment (SS) registers, respectively.

The 8086 processor is a synchronous finite-state machine, controlled by a single external clock signal, CLK. It can actually operate in one of two modes, minimum or maximum. Only the minimum mode will be considered in this text. Figure 5.15 shows the basic timing operation for the processor to perform a read operation, that is, to read a 16-bit value from memory. At least four cycles of the clock are required to read from or write to memory. These cycles are labelled T_1 to T_4. In the first cycle, T_1, the address of the location that is to be read is placed on the address and data buses, and the ALE (address latch enable) control signal is activated to indicate that the address/data bus (ADDR/DATA) contains the address. During the third cycle, T_3, the read control line, $\overline{RD}$, is activated. indicating to the external memory that the value in the location addressed should be placed on the data bus. The processor then normally assumes that the external memory responds quickly enough so that the data is available to the processor during the third and

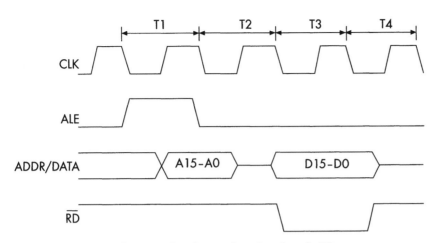

Figure 5.15 Timing diagram for the read cycle of an 8086 processor.

fourth cycles, T_3 and T_4, when $\overline{RD}$ is de-activated. The data read is then latched into the appropriate processor register during T_4. If the external memory, or input device, is slow, then it must signal that it is not ready to the CPU, which then automatically inserts wait states, TW, between T_3 and T_4. This is achieved by using the READY input control signal to the processor. This type of data transfer is known as asynchronous, since the processor has the capability of waiting for memory or input/output devices that are slower than the CPU. The minimum cycle time is four clock cycles. Given that the maximum clock rate that may be used in the 8086 is 10 MHz this corresponds to 2.5 MHz. Much higher clock frequencies are used in Pentium processors, typically several hundred MHz.

The write operation proceeds in a similar way, except that the write control signal $\overline{WR}$ is used instead of $\overline{RD}$.

The processor also has a number of control signals, which allow for hardware interrupts to be generated, and for a number of 8086 processors to be combined together in a multi-processor system. Full details of all the signals and the timing relationships can be found in the *Intel 8086 Microprocessor Manual*.

The 8086 processor described above is one of the simpler members of the family and the versions on sale today are much more complex. Later family processors, such as the Pentium, have a greatly extended addressing capability so that several gigabytes (Gbytes, where 1 Gbyte = 2^{30} bytes) of memory can be used. Most Pentium-based PCs are now supplied with at least 64 Mbytes of random access memory (RAM) as standard and a hard disk with a capacity of many Gbytes. The basic difference between the later members of the family and the earlier members is that later members – from the 80386 onwards – are 32-bit machines, all based on the same basic architecture. There are many detailed differences from the 8086 but the major ones are the introduction of new 32-bit processor registers, the introduction of a virtual machine architecture so that programs running at the same time can be protected from one another and the MMX – multimedia – extension to the instruction set. The instruction set of the processors has been extended to cope with the 32-bit architecture but the instruction set remains irregular and complex since it is still based on the original design.

5.7.2 The Motorola 68000 processor

The Motorola 68000 processor was actually the first member of a family of compatible processors, ranging from the 8-bit 68008 to the later 64-bit 68050. All the processors are object code compatible, which means that they all execute the same base-level instructions. The 68000 is available in a number of different packages; Figure 5.16 shows the logical layout of the pins. The data bus is 16 bits wide, and the address bus is effectively 24 bits

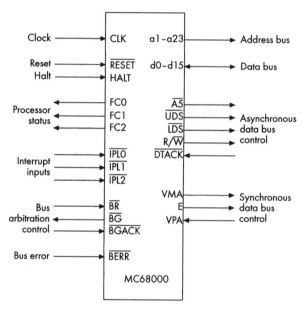

Figure 5.16 Motorola 86000 processor.

wide, so that 2^{24} or 16 Mbytes of memory can be addressed. The remainder of the pins are for power and control signals, some of which will be discussed below. The processor contains seventeen registers: eight data registers, D_0–D_7, seven address registers, A_0–A_6, two stack pointers and a status register. With the exception of the status register, all the other registers are 32 bits wide, so that 32 bit values can be stored and operated upon. The 68000 allows operations on bytes (8 bits), words (16 bits), and long words (32 bits). The registers are connected via internal buses, which are 32 bits wide.

The main difference between the members of the 68000 family of processors is the number of read-write operations to fetch-store a value from-to memory. For example, the 68008 requires four read operations to fetch a

32-bit value from memory, the 68030 just one operation. The 68000 has a full 32-bit ALU. As well as the normal logical and arithmetic operations, it also supports hardware multiplication and division of integer values. For the arithmetic operations one of the operands must be in a register (usually a data register), while the second operand can be in another register or in memory. A description of some of the 68000's addressing modes and instructions is given in Chapter 11.

Consider now a read operation from memory to a 68000 internal register. Figure 5.17 shows a slightly simplified timing diagram. The read operation

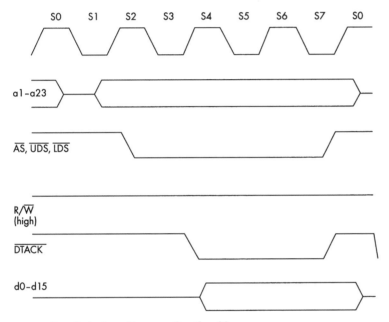

Figure 5.17 Read timing diagram for the 68000 processor.

takes a minimum of four clock cycles, or eight states which are labelled S_0–S_7. Note that two states make up one clock cycle. The read operation starts in state S_0. Unlike the Intel 8086, the 68000 has a single signal $R/\overline{W}$ to tell the memory whether it is doing a read operation $(R/\overline{W} = 1)$, or a write operation $(R/\overline{W} = 0)$. During S_0 $R/\overline{W}$ is set high to indicate a read operation. In state S_1 the address of the memory location to be read is output onto the address bus, while in state S_2 the address strobe signal $\overline{AS}$ is activated, that is, goes to 0. This signal is used by the memory to detect that there is a valid address on the address bus. It has already been noted that the 68000 has a 16-bits wide data bus, so that it can transfer 16-bit values (words) at a time. If this is required then the two control lines labelled $\overline{UDS}$ and $\overline{LDS}$, upper and lower data strobes respectively, are activated. However, if the processor is to read a single byte, then only one of the two strobes is activated, depending on whether the processor is to read a byte from the upper or lower half of the data bus. All control signals are now set for the read to proceed. The processor waits for the external memory to place the value stored in the location addressed onto the data bus, and then to signal back to the processor that it has done so, and that there is valid data on the data bus. This is achieved via the data acknowledge signal $\overline{\text{DTACK}}$. If $\overline{\text{DTACK}}$ is activated before the end of state S_4 then the read operation is completed by the end of state S_7. During S_7 the address and data strobes ($\overline{\text{AS}}$, $\overline{\text{UDS}}$ and $\overline{\text{LDS}}$) are negated and the data are latched internally into the appropriate 68000 register. If $\overline{\text{DTACK}}$ does not go low by the end of S_4 then wait states are automatically inserted between S_4 and S_5, until the external memory does respond. This data transfer scheme between processor and memory is fundamentally the same as in the Intel 8086.

A write operation occurs in a very similar way, with the processor again waiting until $\overline{\text{DTACK}}$ is asserted.

Examination of Figure 5.16 shows that there are a number of other groups of control signals. The synchronous bus control signals ($\overline{\text{VPA}}$, valid peripheral address, $\overline{\text{VMA}}$, valid memory address, and E, enable) allow older 8-bit peripheral input–output devices, originally developed for the Motorola 6800 processor to be used by the 68000. The interrupt control signals and the bus arbitration control signals are generally used by peripheral devices to transfer data quickly between the 'real world' and the processor; they will be discussed in Chapter 7. Finally, the three processor status lines are used to output a code to indicate the processing state of the 68000 processor. Full details of all the signals and the timing relationships can be found in the *Motorola 68000 Microprocessor Data Manual*.

5.8 Input and output

Clearly a computer is useless unless information can be input from the 'real world', and the results of information processed passed back to the 'real world'. As the subject of input/output is so important a separate chapter (Chapter 7) is devoted to it. At this point it is necessary to realize only that a wide range of devices exist for input and output for most computer systems. These devices usually contain registers, which then appear as normal memory to the CPU, and can be manipulated in the same way as memory. Thus an input device assembles information from the real world and places it in a register; the computer can then read this information from the register. The converse is true for output. The computer places information to be output in a register in the selected output device; the device then presents this information to the outside world.

5.9 Summary

The hardware of a computer consists of combinational and sequential logic. This logic is organized around a central bus structure, which provides the communication between the memory, processor and input/output devices.

The processor consists of a control and timing section, together with a set of registers and the arithmetic and logic unit (ALU). The ALU consists of a set of circuits that implement the arithmetic and logical operations provided by the instruction set of the computer.

5.10 Exercises

Exercise 5.1 Why can only a single device transmit on a bus at one time? How is this condition satisfied in a system comprising of several transmitters?

Exercise 5.2 Why is two's complement arithmetic used in a computer? How is subtraction performed on a system using the two's complement notation?

Exercise 5.3 What is the operation cycle of a processor? How does this limit the amount of concurrency which can be obtained in the implementation?

Exercise 5.4 What is the purpose of the instruction register in the processor?

Exercise 5.5 Why aren't all processor registers the same size?

Exercise 5.6 Why do modern processors contain several data registers rather then just a single accumulator?

Exercise 5.7 In the timing diagrams given in this chapter, why is there a delay between the read signal becoming active and the data becoming available?

Exercise 5.8 The Motorola 68000 outputs the current state of the processor on to a set of output lines from the processor. Why do you think it does this?

Exercise 5.9 A 4-bit arithmetic and logic unit (ALU) is to be designed for a 4-bit microprocessor. The ALU has two 4-bit wide inputs, labelled i_1 and i_2 and a 4-bit output labelled *out*. In addition there is a carry out bit. Design the ALU so that it implements the following functions:

add:	$out = i_1 + i_2$
subtract:	$out = i_1 - i_2$
shift-left:	$out = i_1$ shifted-left by 1-bit
shift-right:	$out = i_1$ shifted-right by 1-bit
transfer:	$out = i_1$

Exercise 5.10 A 4-bit microprocessor is to be designed. The processor is to use the ALU designed in Exercise 5.1, and in addition should have four general-purpose registers, a program counter (PC), an instruction register (IR), a memory address register (MAR) and a memory buffer register (MBR). Investigate a possible architecture for the organization of these registers and the ALU, and consider how the registers are to be connected to the various internal buses of the processor. Finally consider how the data flow between the registers, the ALU and external memory should be controlled, and in particular consider what control signals are necessary. (Although the control unit for a processor will be discussed in detail in Chapter 8, it is interesting at this stage to consider what it has to do, and what control signals are necessary.)

6
Memory systems

6.1 Introduction

In the previous chapter the structure of processors was considered, together with two examples of microprocessors, namely the 8086 and the Motorola 68000. To make a usable computer system the processor requires a memory system to store programs and data, and input–output interfaces to connect it to the 'real world'. Memory systems will be considered in detail in this chapter, and input–output interfaces in Chapter 7.

6.2 Memory

Chapter 4 showed some simple memory circuits such as flip-flops and registers. The central processing unit contains a number of registers used for special purposes, such as the program counter and the accumulator, but the main directly accessible storage of the computer is concentrated in a separate unit, the memory subsystem. Memory can be thought of as a set of registers, all the same length, the word length of the computer. Each memory location has a unique address, which is used by other devices within the computer to access that location. Two memory parameters of interest are the size of each memory location (normally the word length of the computer) and the number of memory locations. The number of memory cells is usually a power of two, since an n-bit pattern, used to store an address of a memory cell, may contain 2^n separate values. The size of a memory is normally quoted in multiples of 1024 (i.e. 2^{10}) called K, multiples of 2^{20} called M and 2^{30} called G. A 64 Kbyte memory contains $64 \times 1024 = 65,536$ bytes, a 4 Mbyte memory contains $4 \times 1024 \times 1024 = 4,194,304$ bytes and a memory of 2 Gbytes contains $2 \times 1024 \times 1024 \times 1024 = 2,147,483,648$ bytes.

One complication of memory structure concerns the way in which smaller units are put together to form larger units. As a simple example, consider a word of memory. Is bit 0 the most significant bit in the word or the least significant bit in the word? If you never address bits then this is of no interest as long as the internal machine operations always treat the bit ordering in the same way. The same problem arises when a large data item has to be stored. The large data item is stored as a sequence of bytes in memory and the problem is whether the most significant or least significant byte of the data occupies the highest or lowest address. Again, if only the large data item is accessed, the ordering is immaterial as long as the machine is consistent. Different manufacturers have adopted different approaches. Intel processors have adopted the little endian approach whereby the numbering of the units starts at the low order end. Conversely, the Motorola 68000 processors have adopted the big endian approach where the numbering starts at the high order end. Problems arise if you design a system containing both big endian and little endian processors as they require data from memory to be delivered in a different order!

6.2.1 The basic memory structure

The basic operations on a memory location are read and write. Since basic memory operations are concerned with one word, the address of this word must be presented to the memory with the read/write control signals. The operations read and write operate on one word of data and hence a data route one word wide must be provided to the memory. This gives the basic memory structure as shown in Figure 6.1. There is typically a delay of several tens of

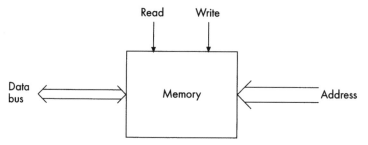

Figure 6.1   Basic memory structure.

nanoseconds between the start and finish of an operation in memory. In Chapter 3 the operation of a decoder was shown and this can be used to decode the address of a register in a register bank. In a similar manner a decoder is used in the memory subsystem to convert from an n-bit address stored in the address register to a control line to a single memory location, and will be shown in more detail later.

6.2.2 The operation of memory

Consider the state of memory as shown in Figure 6.2. In this example it has been assumed that the word length is only four bits and the memory size 256 words, requiring an address register that is eight bits wide (since $2^8 = 256$).

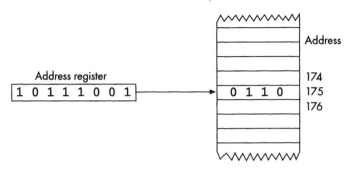

Figure 6.2 Memory addressing.

To read the contents of word 175 from the memory it is necessary to perform the following operations:

1. load the address register with 175;

2. set the read control signal.

At some time later, determined by the propagation time of the memory, the contents of word 175, 6 in the example, will be available at the data outputs of the memory.

To perform a write operation the following sequence is required:

1. load the address register with 175;

2. load the data buffer register with the required new contents of word 175;

3. set the write control signal.

At some time later, again depending on the characteristics of the memory, the contents of word 175 will reflect the new value.

6.2.3 Properties of memories

Having described the basic operation of memory, the properties of different types of memories are considered.

(a) Random access

The type of memory described above is known as random access (RAM) since it takes the same time, the access time, to access any memory location. In most computer systems there are several forms of memory and not all of them have this random-access property. For example, it is usual to store programs on some form of magnetic medium such as tapes, disk or CD ROM, and access to these memories is not random. In the case of magnetic tape the access is sequential since each item is read in sequence from the tape, starting at the beginning. A magnetic disk, on the other hand, provides a quicker access mechanism, somewhere between random and sequential access, depending on the type of disk and organization of the information. Random-access memory is often used as a synonym for read-write memory (RWM) as opposed to read-only memory (ROM). Strictly, both RWM and ROM are random-access memories since access to any memory location takes the same time.

(b) Cycle time

This is the minimum time required between two successive read or write operations to memory. It is a basic physical property of the memory, as is the access time, defined above. Because of the need for circuits to stabilize, there is often a significant difference between the access time and the cycle time. This leads to some of the techniques, described later, which attempt not to access the same memory circuit on consecutive accesses in order not to encounter this extra delay.

(c) Volatility

A memory that loses its information when power is removed is said to be volatile. Semiconductor read-write memories are volatile because they rely on external power to maintain the information stored. Magnetic disks and tapes, however, are non-volatile and can keep their information almost indefinitely. It is because of the volatility of semiconductor memory (RAM) that most processors have power-fail circuitry. If power is lost, there is a small amount of time for the processor to store away vital information in non-volatile memory. One method of saving information in volatile memory is to provide battery backup so that battery power take over if mains power fails.

(d) Static and dynamic memory

The memory described above is known as a static memory (SRAM). Once a value has been stored in the memory, no action is required to keep it other than to maintain the power supply. In contrast to this, there is a type of memory known as dynamic memory (DRAM) where the information is stored as charge on a capacitor. Since a capacitor will gradually discharge itself with time, this type of memory has to be continually recharged (refreshed) in order to avoid loss of information. The read operation in dynamic memory is destructive so the cell includes circuitry to rewrite the contents after a read operation. Thus a read operation may be used to refresh the memory. Dynamic memory systems normally include some means to refresh memory by periodic read operations. The refresh may be performed by software but, since memory has to be refreshed every 1 or 2 milliseconds, this imposes a high burden on the processor. A more satisfactory solution is to use some of the period when the processor is not accessing memory to perform the refresh, or to use an independent refresh controller. Because of the need for this extra circuitry, the use of dynamic memory may seem undesirable, but a dynamic memory uses only about one-quarter of the silicon area of the equivalent static memory and hence the extra density on an integrated circuit makes its use attractive. For the same area a dynamic memory will contain about four times as many memory cells as the corresponding static memory chip. Since system costs are directly related to the number of integrated circuits used in their production, the reduction in chip count using dynamic memories outweighs the complication of adding refresh circuitry in large memory system. Also, with the ever-increasing amount of logic which can be put on a chip, dynamic memories with internal refresh have been available for several years.

There are many different types of static and dynamic memory. Extended data output (EDO) is a form of dynamic memory that allows pipelined access to memory, that is, a second memory reference can start before the first one is complete. This allows faster access to memory at the expense of more complex control. Synchronous DRAM (SDRAM) is a hybrid of static and dynamic memory which is driven by a single clock.

(e) Read-only memory

Some types of memory may be both read from and written to, read-write memory (RWM), whilst others may only be read, read-only memory (ROM). This latter type appears to be less useful but has the additional property that it is non-volatile, that is, the contents of the memory are not lost when power is removed from the circuit. This means that by using ROMs to store programs, equipment can be produced that will function immediately it is switched on without having to be loaded with programs from media such as floppy disks. For embedded systems, such as microcomputers in washing machines, cars or general laboratory instruments, this is essential. There are several types of ROM available, the differences being in the method initially used to write the information into memory. In mask programmed ROMs the program is inserted during the manufacturing process and cannot be changed. This type of memory is used for standard programs which are produced in large quantities. Erasable programmable ROMs (EPROM) can be programmed by the user using special programming equipment and may be erased for reuse by exposure to ultraviolet light. Electrically erasable ROMs (EEPROM or E2PROM) are also available. These devices allow programming in situ and individual bytes can be erased electrically.

(f) Flash memory

Recently a new type of non-volatile memory called flash memory has become available that is now often used in portable computers and hand-held devices. These memories can be read and written to many times – up to 10,000 – before the memory becomes unusable. They are similar in operation to EEPROMs except that memory contents can be erased by the low voltages available on a PC rather than requiring the high voltages provided by an EEPROM programmer. Flash memory requires much less power than storage peripherals – see Chapter 7 – such as a hard disk, and are much faster, which are reasons why such devices are popular for portable computers.

6.2.4 An integrated circuit random-access memory

The basic binary storage cell, which is the building block for static memory, is shown in Figure 6.3. The select signal is generated by the address decoder

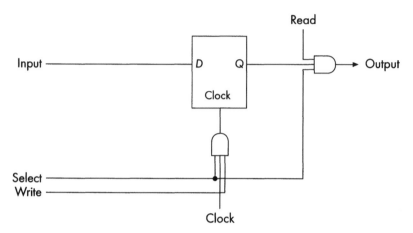

Figure 6.3   Memory storage cell.

and applied to all the bits of the selected word. The read and write inputs determine the cell operation and the 1-bit input and output are the data interfaces to the rest of the computer system. A slightly different form of the basic cell, incorporating a tristate buffer, is shown in Figure 4.25. A clock signal is shown in the cell in Figure 6.3. This is not strictly necessary as one of the other control signals, such as read or write, could be used to gate the input and output to and from a non-clocked flip-flop. However, many memories operate with a clock signal to synchronize their operation with the rest of the computer. The circuit in Figure 6.3 contains storage for one bit. Memories are normally organized as a number of bytes or words. Since the basic memory operations work on these larger quantities, usually bytes, the organization of a byte of memory is shown in Figure 6.4. All the basic cells

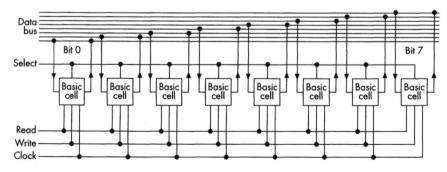

Figure 6.4   Organization of a byte of memory.

in the byte are accessed in parallel and operate on different bits. The select signal is produced from the address decoder and only one select signal will be active at any one time, limiting access to one byte. The data bus is attached to all the bytes of memory, for example, bit o of all the bytes of memory will be attached to bit o of the data bus. The memory can be thought of as an array of basic cells n bits wide, where n is the word length, and m bits long, where m is the number of words in memory. Each bit in the row of this matrix is connected by the select line, and equivalent bits in different words are connected by the data lines for input and output. All the cells are connected to the same read, write and clock lines. This structure is shown in outline in Figure 6.5.

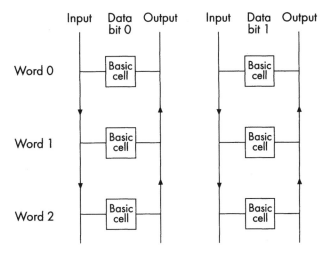

Figure 6.5 The memory matrix.

6.2.5 The structure of a typical integrated circuit memory

In this section some typical memory chips are considered and their mode of action explained.

(a) Static memory

The Hitachi HM6264 RAM chip shown (slightly simplified) in Figure 6.6 corresponds closely to the logical structure described before. Since there are 8192 (2^{13}) words of memory, thirteen address lines (A_0-A_{12}) are required. Each word is 8 bits wide and hence eight lines ($I/O_1-I/O_8$) are required for data input/output.

The chip requires a standard power supply of 5 V. Since this chip will be one of many that have to be interfaced to the data bus of the computer, it must be active only when it is being addressed; the active-low chip select ($\overline{CS}$) signal is used for this purpose. External decoding circuitry is necessary to generate from bits $A_{13} \dots A_n$ of the address bus, which is used to control

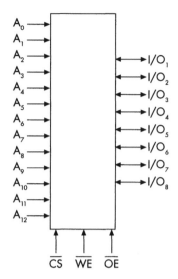

Figure 6.6 The Hitachi HM6264 8192 × 8 static RAM.

the tristate buffers on to the data bus. The other two control lines are output enable $\overline{OE}$ and write enable $\overline{WE}$, also active-low.

To write a word into the HM6264, the CPU must first output the appropriate RAM address and the data onto the address and data buses, respectively, and then activate the chip select and write enable signals. To read a word from RAM the processor must first output the required RAM address and activate the chip select and output enable signals. This will cause the RAM to output the addressed word onto I/O_1–I/O_8 which is connected to the processor's data bus.

(b) Dynamic memory

In order to address 262,144 locations, 18 address bits are required. The chip shown in Figure 6.7 has only nine address lines. The 18 bits required are

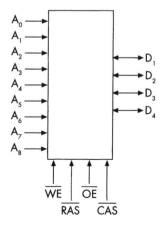

Figure 6.7 The Intel 21014 256K × 4-bit dynamic memory.

multiplexed on these nine pins, that is, the address is given in two halves. The memory is organized as a 512×512 cell array and this is accessed by row and column addresses, each of nine bits. The control signals $\overline{RAS}$, row address strobe, and $\overline{CAS}$, column address strobe, replacing the single address select of the static RAM chip, are used to latch the appropriate address into an internal register. These control signals indicate which nine address bits are currently being accessed via the address lines. The internal register is needed in this case to assemble the 18-bit address from the two 9-bit values presented. The read and write signals are multiplexed onto a single pin, $\overline{WE}$. Since dynamic memory gradually loses its information with time, refreshing of this information is periodically necessary. It may be performed by cycling through all the rows of memory with $\overline{RAS}$ low and $\overline{CAS}$ high. This refreshes the memory a row at a time. Alternatively, normal read operations or hidden refresh cycles can be used. This latter technique allows data to be read from the memory as well as performing a refresh operation.

(c) Read-only memory

A read-only memory circuit looks very similar to the equivalent static RAM circuit. Figure 6.8 shows a Hitatchi 2764 8K $\times$ 8 EPROM. The complete

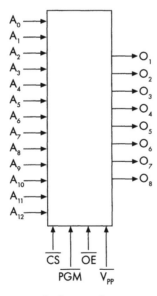

Figure 6.8 The Hitachi HN2764 8192 $\times$ 8 EPROM.

memory may be erased by exposure to ultraviolet radiation of the correct wavelength. The main difference between the RAM and the EPROM is that the EPROM has a program control pin $\overline{PGM}$, and a V_{PP} supply of $+25$ V needed to program the memory. To program the EPROM the V_{PP} pin has to be kept at $+25$ V, the address and data lines set to the required values and a 50 ms pulse applied to the $\overline{PGM}$ pin. This operation has to be carried out for every memory address that requires new data. The output enable signal is provided for the same purpose as chip select on a static RAM, that is, to turn the tristate drivers on the data lines on and off. Chip select is provided because the ROM can operate in stand-by mode when not in use, consuming less power than normal, and the chip select signal is used to determine whether the chip is in use or in stand-by mode. The appropriate combination of chip select and output enable should be used to obtain maximum benefit from the device.

6.2.6 Memory modules

In present day computers, memory is normally present in the form of modules rather than single chips. One organization is called a single in-line memory module (SIMM) which is a small printed circuit board that fits into slots in the motherboard. A number of memory chips are placed on the SIMM and several SIMMs are usually required to provide the system memory requirements since their data width is smaller than the 64 bits required by current Pentium processors.

There are several other types of module organization using the same principle of placing several memory chips on a small printed circuit board. Module organization is used to provide a simple way of upgrading the amount of memory in a system.

6.3 Architectural considerations and memory

In the system described in the last chapter, there was a single composite bus, carrying address, data and control between processor and memory. This is the most common architecture in small computer systems. In this section, options for increasing performance and producing cost-effective memory subsystems are investigated.

6.3.1 The memory hierarchy

One of the objectives of the computer architect is to produce a computer that is fast, bearing in mind the technology used. Since much of a processor's time is spent reading and writing to memory, one critical area of attention for the architect is the processor-memory interface. It would appear, at first sight, that the ideal solution would be to have the maximum amount of fast, directly accessible memory placed as close to the processor as possible. This is not feasible, both on space and economic grounds, but, perhaps surprisingly, memory systems can be built with almost the same performance. This is possible because programs typically exhibit a property called locality. This phenomenon concerns the way in which references to instructions and data are grouped in a program. Analysis of programs has shown that references to the address space of a program, instructions and data, tend to become confined to a few localized areas over a period of time. The crucial fact is that membership of these small, localized areas changes only slowly with time, owing to the way in which programs are normally structured. This means that if the members of these areas are kept in fast memory, the program will execute quickly even if the rest of the instructions and data are stored in slower memory. Using this scheme, there has to be some method of transferring instructions and data between memories when this becomes necessary. Since memory cost is proportional to memory speed (the higher the speed required the greater the cost), architects need to use the least amount of fast memory without sacrificing performance.

There are several levels in the memory hierarchy. The first level, the fastest, is a set of registers, typically 8, 16 or 32, which resides within the CPU. This level of the hierarchy is found in virtually all computer systems. The next level is cache memory, typically 2K to 20K words, which is not as fast as the internal registers but faster than main memory, the third level. The fourth level is backing storage such as disks and tapes, and this has the property of not being directly accessible. In order for the CPU to process information from backing store, the information must first be read into directly accessible memory, modified and then written back. In order to relieve the programmer of this chore, some systems implement virtual memory, where the programmer is given access to a large address space, only part of which resides in directly accessible memory at any one time. Transfer to and from the directly accessible memory is transparent to the programmer who can assume that any information that is required is directly accessible. From the programmer's point of view, virtual memory systems are very convenient, hence the current trend for an increase in their use. Not all computer systems have all the levels of the memory hierarchy; those levels present will be determined by the cost and the use of the computer.

In the following sections some of the techniques used to speed access to memory, while being transparent to the programmer, are discussed.

6.3.2 Interleaving

In a normal memory subsystem there is a time lapse, called the access time, between the time when the address is presented to memory and the time when the operation, read or write, is complete. One way of using this 'dead time' on the bus is to split the memory into a number of memory banks, each containing a subset of the memory space. Assuming that each of these memories has its own address and data buffers, operations to access memory may be overlapped as shown in Figure 6.9. There are, however, a number of problems with this technique. For example, for maximum efficiency, memory references have to be distributed so that consecutive accesses are to different memory banks. Since instruction flow through a program is normally sequential, memory banks are usually divided using the lower address bits as the bank number. This means that sequential access will cycle through all the memory banks in order. Interleaving also assumes a more

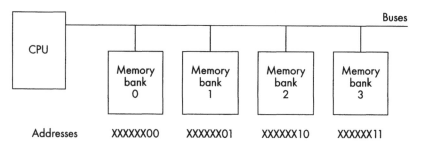

Figure 6.9 Interleaved memory.

complicated processor, which can control several concurrent memory activities.

6.3.3 Cache memory

Normally, fast devices are more expensive than slow ones and this is true for memory; the faster the memory, the more expensive. Thus the use of large amounts of fast memory is precluded on economic grounds for even the most expensive computer system. Fortunately, using the property of program locality, only a small proportion of the program address space need be kept in fast memory and yet the program will run nearly as quickly as if it were all in fast memory. This is the basis of the use of cache memory; small, fast memory placed between the CPU and main memory. The basic operation of the cache is as follows. An access to memory is made to the cache. If the required address (or data) resides there then it is used, but if it is absent then a block of memory is transferred from main memory to the cache typically consisting of 32 bytes containing the addressed word. This block of words will displace some other information in the cache if it is already full. The reason for fetching a block rather than just the required word is to take advantage of spatial locality, that is, the property of programs that access will be made in the near future to addresses close to a recently accessed address.

The performance of the cache is measured by the hit ratio, which is the ratio of the number of successful accesses to the cache compared with the total number of accesses to memory. The hit ratio measures the locality of reference of the program being executed and so should be measured experimentally. The hit ratio obviously depends upon the size of the cache as well as the degree of locality in the program. Typical cache memories are of the order of 32K words and studies of their use have shown a number of programs to exhibit hit ratios between 0.9 and 1.0, that is, almost all references to the cache were successful. There are two ways in which memory can respond to a write request to memory. The first method is the write through method where main memory is updated on every write, in addition to the cache if the information is stored there. This method ensures that main memory always contains up-to-date information and that its contents are always synchronized with the cache contents. The second method, called write back, only updates the cache copy of the information on a write. A flag, associated with each word of cache, is set so that when the information is removed from the cache it is written back to main memory. The fact that main memory is not always up-to-date does not matter, since access will always be to the cache until the information is updated in main memory. Each word of cache has a bit associated with it called the valid bit. On initialization, all the valid bits are set to zero, indicating that the associated words do not contain valid data. The valid bit of a word is set to 1 the first time a valid data item is copied into the word. The write back method is faster than write through since cache memory is faster than main memory.

Some of the problems that need to be solved for efficient operation include:

- Cache memory is smaller than main memory so several main memory locations must map on to the same cache address. Is it better to have memory locations close to one another or further away from one another map on to the same cache address? (Remember the order in which instructions in programs are executed.)

- If two or more memory locations map on to the same cache address, how do you tell which memory location is mapped at any time? For example, supposing that memory locations 0 and 1000 mapped to cache address 0, how would you tell if you read cache address 0 whether you were reading the contents of memory address 0 or memory address 1000?

- If a cache address can hold the contents of two or more memory locations, how do you decide which one to replace if space is needed to hold another value? For example, each cache address can hold the contents of two memory locations and memory locations 0, 1000 and 2000 all map to cache location 0. If cache location 0 holds the contents of memory locations 1000 and 2000 what happens when the contents of memory location 0 needs to be held in cache? Is the copy of location 1000 or 2000 removed?

Solutions to these questions are discussed in the next sections.

6.3.4 Cache organization

Important features of a cache include the internal organization and that part involved with the transfer of information to and from main memory (Figure 6.10). One form of cache organization uses an associative memory, which stores both the memory address and the contents (Figure 6.11). Access to information in the cache requires a search for the required address among all the stored addresses. In an associative memory, the comparisons between the required address and the table of stored addresses can be performed in parallel, thus making them fast. If a match is found, the data associated with

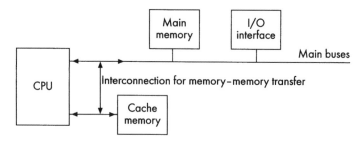

Figure 6.10 Typical cache memory structure.

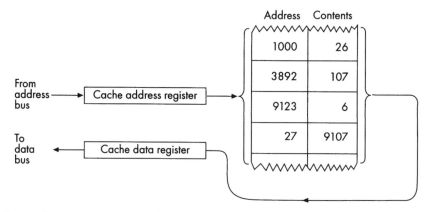

Figure 6.11 Associative cache memory.

the required address may be read or written to but if no match is found then access to main memory is initiated. If there is no free space in the cache then a block of address/data pairs from main memory has to overwrite pairs already in the cache. Typically this will be done in a round robin fashion, that is, first-in first-out (FIFO).

Another form of cache organization is direct mapping (Figure 6.12), which may be used where associative memory is considered too costly. It is presently the most common form of cache organization. In this case, normal random-access memory (RAM) may be used for the cache. Concurrently with main memory access, the cache is addressed using the n least significant bits of the memory address. In the cache are stored the remaining memory address bits, called the tag bits, and the data. Since the cache is addressed using only some of the memory address bits, several main memory addresses map onto the same cache address. The tag bits in the cache will match only one of the possible mapped addresses – the one presently stored in the cache – and this allows the processor to determine whether the required information is in the cache.

Inefficiencies can occur with this cache organization since only one of the mapped main memory addresses can reside in the cache at any one time. To overcome this, a method called set associative mapping has been developed, which allows each word of cache to store multiple values, thus allowing

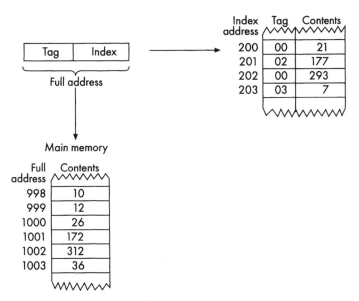

Figure 6.12 Direct mapping cache.

several main memory locations mapping onto the same cache address to be stored concurrently, as shown in Figure 6.13. An *n*-way set associative cache allows up to *n* entries in each cache position. Typical values of *n* are 2 and 4. A new problem that is introduced with this organization is that of determining which entry to replace when a new entry is to be loaded. Without knowledge of future accesses to memory it is impossible to determine the optimum replacement strategy. An algorithm that gives good results without needing to know the pattern of future accesses is the least recently used algorithm (LRU) which replaces the entry that has been in that cache position without being used for the longest time.

It should be noted that cache organization can become very complex. It is possible to have a separate cache for instructions and data or to combine the two as a single cache. Additionally it is possible to have several levels of

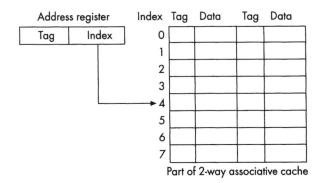

Figure 6.13 Set associative cache organization.

cache between main memory and the processor. The reason for putting cache memory in the system is to improve the bandwidth and latency of memory access and the size and type of cache memory is optimized by the architect for the expected workload for that machine.

6.3.5 Virtual memory systems

The instruction set of a computer allows the user to access a range of addresses known as the address space. In many computers the address space is identical to the main memory address space. In a virtual memory system, however, the address space is very much larger than the main memory address space and the virtual memory subsystem, software and hardware, is responsible for mapping virtual memory references to main memory addresses. Thus main memory, at any one time, only contains a subset of the total virtual memory contents as shown in Figure 6.14. In order to make the

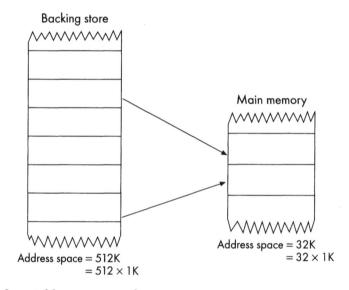

Figure 6.14 Address space and memory space.

transfers between main memory and backing store relatively simple, transfers are normally restricted to fixed size blocks. These blocks, typically 4K words, are known as blocks of main memory or pages of virtual address space. This gives rise to the term 'paging' because a page is the unit of transfer between main memory and backing store. For example, if the size of backing store used for paging was 1024K words, it could hold 256 pages of 4096 words, and a main memory of 128K words could hold 32 pages and would be divided into 32 blocks. Modern computers contain very much more memory but the same principles apply. In this example, the main memory could hold one-sixteenth of the information on backing store. The reason for pages being of size 2^N is that any address in the page can be represented by N bits. Thus a virtual memory address can be subdivided into two fields; the top M bits representing the page number and the bottom N bits the address within the page. To produce the real memory address from the virtual address, the translation mechanism has to replace the page number by the appropriate memory block address. This is the task of the virtual memory architecture. Since the addressing mechanism is used frequently, address translation from virtual to real has to be performed by hardware. The moving of pages between main memory and backing store is not so critical because it happens less frequently and almost all virtual memory computers are multi-programmed so that the time needed to move a page can usefully be used by another program. The moving of pages is controlled by software. A block diagram of the memory mapping hardware required – often called the memory management unit (MMU) – is shown in Figure 6.15 and an example showing the translation for a small address space is given in Figure 6.16. The blank entries in the page table would cause a

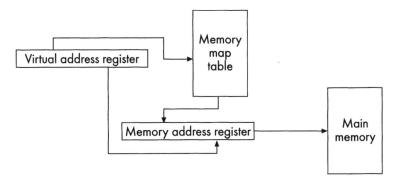

Figure 6.15 Memory mapping hardware.

page fault if they are accessed. Because this address translation scheme is applied to every memory access, it must be fast. The time-consuming operation is the page table look-up and in many computers associative memory is used to perform a parallel search of all the entries. Because of the locality of programs, as mentioned previously, most accesses to the virtual address space will result in accesses to main memory, but a small proportion will result in a page fault if the page requested is not in main memory. If this is the case, software is activated to initiate the transfer of the referenced page from backing store to main memory. The software has to decide which page to remove from main memory, assuming that it is full, and when to replace a page. The scheme outlined above is known as demand paging – a scheme in which a page is placed in main memory when demanded (referenced). There are several different types of replacement policy which are used; the most common being first-in-first-out (FIFO) and least recently used (LRU). The FIFO method is implemented by the system keeping a queue of the page numbers

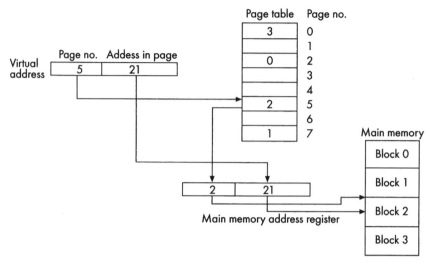

Figure 6.16 Example of address translation scheme.

in the order in which they are placed in memory. If a page has to be replaced the one whose identification number is at the head of the queue is chosen. In the LRU method a counter is kept with each page in main memory and incremented at fixed time intervals. When a page is referenced the counter is reset to zero. When a page has to be replaced the page with the highest associated counter is selected to be overwritten. There are other techniques similar to paging used in virtual memory systems. The most important one is segmentation where segments are equivalent to pages but are of variable length. This causes problems for the management system since both the mapping and page management policies become more complex. For this reason, segmentation is often used in conjunction with paging to get the best of both techniques; paging for hardware simplicity and segmentation for ease of use by the programmer. The importance of segmentation is that access control can be applied to segments; one may be read-only for program code, another read-only for data and another read-write for data. An attempt to access a segment for the wrong usage leads to an immediate hardware-generated interrupt.

Paging is based on the working set model of memory use. This model is based on the observation that programs exhibit locality in accessing memory, that is, memory references tend to cluster in a small number of pages over a small interval of time and membership of this set of pages changes relatively slowly with time. Thus it is possible to make a program run quickly if only the currently required pages are held in main memory. The set of pages required at any one time is known as the working set and main memory needs to be large enough so that a program can have its working set of pages resident in main memory at all times. If main memory is not large enough, thrashing occurs; pages are continually interchanged between main memory and disk with the consequent loss of processing throughput.

6.4 The 80x86 memory organization

The architect who designs a computer organization has a difficult job, especially when it comes to defining memory organization since, on the one hand, the cost of memory has fallen dramatically over the past 20 years and on the other, many programs have become very much larger. The problem concerns the amount of memory the processor can address and the way in which this memory can be addressed. In order to show how memory organization has evolved, the organization used in a number of different generations of 80x86 systems is considered.

Initially the designers of the first operating system, DOS, for the 8086 and 8088 decided to allow for an addressing space of 1 Mbyte. This requires an address of 20 bits, which is what these processors generated. This address space has to contain space for application programs and for operating system functions such as the BIOS – basic input–output system. The designers decided to limit the program space to 640 Kbytes with the remaining 360 Kbytes dedicated to operating system functions. Even some of the program space is used by the operating system so the maximum size of a user program was considerably less than 640 Kbytes. In fact most machines bought at that time – the late 80s – had considerably less than 1 Mbyte of memory, typically only 128 Kbytes. The designers failed to predict that future systems would require very much larger address spaces. The limit of what can be done with this memory organization was reached with the 80286 which allowed the parts of the operating system which previously occupied part of the 640 Kbytes to be moved to memory above the 1 Mbyte limit, thus giving the programmer access to almost 640 Kbytes as shown in Figure 6.17. This was possible because the 80286 has 24 address lines allowing 16 Mbytes to be accessed. The 80286 and later members of the family all had larger address spaces but these could be accessed only in so called protected mode, which is incompatible with DOS. To be able to use the DOS operating system, real mode has to be used which limits addressing to 1 Mbyte. How then can these later members of the 80x86 family have programs larger than 640 Kbytes in size? The technique used by the Windows operating system, which operates on top of DOS, is to switch between real and protected modes to allow access to memory above 1 Mbyte. There are other techniques that can be used to access more than 1 Mbyte and every operating system that relies on DOS has to use one of these techniques to access more than 1 Mbyte of memory.

The Pentium processor can operate in one of three modes, real, virtual 8086 mode and protected mode. In real mode it can address only 1 Mbyte of memory. In virtual 8086 mode, an operating system can provide a program with an environment that mimics real address mode, that is, the program can still address only one Mbyte of memory but errors will be caught by the operating system instead of crashing the machine. In protected mode the processor can access the full range of facilities in the real machine. Memory is divided into 16,384 segments each of size $2^{32}-1$, that is 32-bit addressing

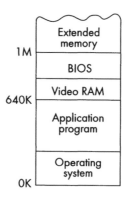

Figure 6.17 Memory organization in DOS.

within segments is used. Most present day operating systems use only one segment and hence the processor has a single 32-bit address space with each byte having an address. As stated earlier, all of the 80x86 family, including the Pentium, use little endian addressing. The designers have tried to cope with future memory expansion by the inclusion of the 16384 segments, which appears at present to be overkill but only time will tell if this is sufficient.

6.5 Summary

Memory is an integral part of a computer system; it is used to store programs and data. There is a hierarchy of memory types, ranging from the on-chip registers of a processor, through high-speed semiconductor memory (both ROM and RAM), to low-speed magnetic backing store, such as magnetic tape and floppy disks. The cost of memory depends on its speed – fast memory is more expensive than slow memory – so that while the amount of semiconductor memory that a computer system has is usually limited, the amount of backing-store available is unlimited, or at least very large (typically thousands of megabytes compared to a few megabytes of semiconductor memory). This fact has led to the development of memory management schemes that automatically transfer program fragments and data from backing store to main memory when they are required by an executing program, and out again when they are no longer needed if they have been changed. In addition, many processors contain a cache memory, which may be either a part of the processor chip itself, or a separate set of chips. This cache memory is used to store the instructions that are currently being executed. Cache memory is faster than the main semiconductor memory, but smaller in size. The efficiency of a cache memory depends on a factor called the 'hit rate', which is the effective probability that the next instruction to be executed is in the cache memory. If it is not, then the cache has to be re-loaded from the main semiconductor memory, which reduces performance.

Virtual memory was developed to allow programmers to ignore the physical structure of the memory subsystem and concentrate on the logical structure. Memory is split into pages, which are moved between main memory and backing storage on programmer demand so that information required is always in main memory and immediately accessible. The virtual memory subsystem is responsible for managing the transfer of information between main memory and backing store and has to decide where to put the information in main memory and what to replace. Systems that use virtual memory have to ensure that they have sufficient main memory, otherwise the system is liable to experience thrashing, which drastically reduces efficiency.

6.6 Exercises

Exercise 6.1 How many address lines are required to access 64K words of memory? How many words of memory can be accessed using 20 address lines?

Exercise 6.2 The Intel 8086 microprocessor has the lower part of the address bus $(A_0 - A_{15})$ multiplexed onto the data bus. Does this impose a time penalty? If so, estimate the penalty for a processor operating with a 10 MHz clock frequency.

Exercise 6.3 In a Motorola 68020 microprocessor (an enhanced version of the 68000) an instruction fetch takes a minimum of three clock cycles. However, with most semiconductor memories at least two extra cycles are required for the memory to respond. These extra cycles are called 'wait states'. No such wait states are necessary for instruction fetches from the cache memory. Given that the hit rate to the cache memory for a particular program is 0.9, calculate the percentage by which the program is speeded-up by the use of a cache memory over a similar processor with no cache memory.

Exercise 6.4 Interleaving is a simple way of reducing memory access time by attempting to direct consecutive memory accesses to different memory modules. Why does the mapping function normally take the bottom n bits of the memory address as the bank select signal rather than a more random selection of address bits?

Exercise 6.5 A cache memory has an access time of 10 nanoseconds and main memory has an access time of 50 nanoseconds. Assuming a hit ratio of 0.4, what is the average access time?

Exercise 6.6 A computer has a main memory of 8 Mbytes and a cache of 512K words. The cache memory starts off empty and uses a write-back policy; the following sequence of memory access are made by the processor.

Assuming that it takes 1000 nanoseconds to read information in main memory, 500 nanoseconds to read information in cache and 1200 nanoseconds to copy a word from main memory to cache or vice versa, what is the difference between set associative organization of the cache and direct access mapping?

Read	location 1000
Write	location 1000
Read	location 525288
Read	location 1049576
Write	location 66536
Write	location 1573864
Read	location 1000
Read	location 1573864

Exercise 6.7 A computer has a 48-bit virtual address space and uses 32 Kbyte pages. How many pages are there on this computer?

Exercise 6.8 A computer architecture uses virtual memory and the computer system comprises main memory of 2K words and a virtual address space of 2^{12}. A page is 1024 words. How many pages are there in this system and how many blocks in main memory?

Assuming that initially memory block 0 contains page 1 and memory block 1 contains page 2, explain what happens when access is made to the following sequence of virtual memory addresses: 500, 1500, 2500, 500, 2500. If a page needs to replace a page in main memory assume that the least recently used (LRU) algorithm is used.

Exercise 6.9 In many respects cache and virtual memory are similar. Why do they not use the same policies and techniques for implementation?

Exercise 6.10 There are arguments for and against considering processor registers as another level of the memory hierarchy. What do you think these arguments are?

7

Input–output

This chapter considers how to interface devices in the 'real world', such as printers and keyboards, to a computer. Such devices are known as input–output devices or peripherals. A later section of the chapter describes the properties and mode of action of a number of common input–output devices.

7.1 Input–output interfaces

The standard method of transferring data inside a computer is along parallel n-bit buses, where n is the word size. Input–output devices interface to this parallel bus on one side and to the 'real world' on the other. Inside the computer, information is coded in a particular manner, for example, the 7-bit ASCII code for characters, and its physical realization has particular properties, for example, logic 0 and 1 are represented by 0 and 5 V approximately. The large numbers of interface circuits, which exist within a computer, are there to make signals from the 'real world' compatible with the internal representation. 'Real world' signals can take a variety of different forms and to convert them to the internal representation required, some of the following functions may be needed:

1. serial to parallel conversion and vice versa;

2. analogue to digital conversion and vice versa;

3. encoding and decoding;

4. changing the current drive capability;

5. changing voltage levels.

There are integrated circuits available to perform many of these tasks, for example, a USART, universal synchronous/asynchronous receiver transmitter, performs serial-parallel conversion and vice versa, a function required to interface a standard computer terminal, a visual display unit (VDU), to a computer. This book is concerned with basic architectural principles rather than detailed interfacing, so only simple interfaces are considered here. The interested reader is referred to the books by Stone and Artwick in the bibliography for more information on interfacing techniques.

7.1.1 The logical structure of an input–output interface

In order for the processor to communicate with the input–output device, the interface must provide registers both to buffer the data and to control and monitor the input–output device. Buffers are required since the 'real world' operates asynchronously with the processor clock. The logical structure of the input–output interface is shown in Figure 7.1.

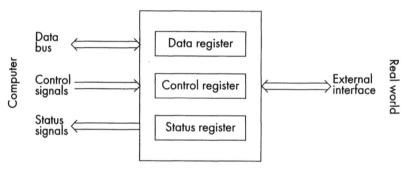

Figure 7.1 Logical I/O port structure.

There may be several registers of each of the three types shown, depending on the complexity of the external device. For the interfaces considered in the following sections, a single control and status register suffices, but for more complicated interfaces, for example to a disk, several control and status registers would be present.

There are two different methods of implementing addressing of the interface. The first method, called memory mapping, places the registers of the interface in the normal address space of the processor. This permits access by any memory reference instruction at the expense of address space for real memory. The alternative scheme, called I/O mapping, involves creating a separate address space specifically for input–output registers and a special instruction set to address this space. This involves special instructions such as IN and OUT, which transfer information between a known place in memory, usually a register, and the input–output device. This scheme implies less flexibility but a larger total address space, which is useful when the addressing range is limited, as it was in the early 4- and 8-bit microcomputers. The Intel 80x86 series is an example of processors that have separate input–output mapping, while the Motorola 680x0 is an example of processors with memory-mapped input–output.

The connection from an interface circuit to an I/O device is known as a port, several of which may be provided by a single interface circuit.

7.1.2 Parallel port

Even if a device has a bus-compatible parallel interface some interfacing circuitry is required to link it to a computer. In simple cases this may be only to provide buffering and control of the gating of input signals or output signals to and from the bus at the correct time, that is, to synchronize the 'real world' to the computer. The structure of a parallel interface is shown in Figure 7.2.

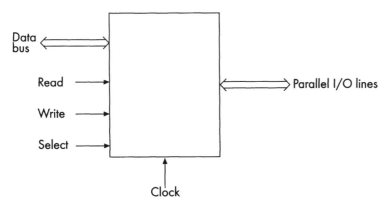

Figure 7.2 Structure of a parallel port.

In order for the processor to read and write from the port, it must first be selected, and this selection is carried out by some external decoding logic connected to the 'select' input. Because the computer has no control over the actions of the external world, it is important that the direction of transfer of information between the port and the external world be determined at all times. In order to do this, each port has a data direction register associated with it which is programmable for input or output mode. Furthermore, since the outside world needs to be synchronized to the computer for the transfer of data, it is usual to associate some control signals, used for handshaking, with each port and also to provide some data buffering.

(a) The Intel 8255 programmable peripheral interface (PPI) (Figure 7.3)

This is a circuit that was designed many years ago and has been superseded by more complex, 16-bit chips. However, it is a simple circuit whose mode of action is simple to explain. The three ports of eight bits provided by this parallel industry-standard interface can be configured as two groups of 12 bits and can operate in one of three modes. In the simplest mode, mode 0, each of the two groups may be programmed, in sets of four bits, to be either input or output. Mode 1 allows each group to have eight data bits and four control and status bits for handshaking. Mode 2 is used to configure an 8-bit bi-directional bus with five control lines. The modes are set up under program control, normally at the beginning of the program.

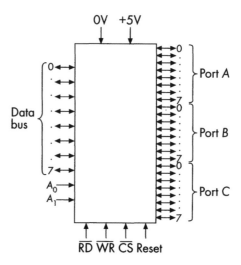

Figure 7.3 Intel 8255 programmable peripheral interface.

The address lines A_0 and A_1, so called because they are normally connected to the least significant bits of the address bus, are used in conjunction with the processor's $\overline{RD}$ and $\overline{WR}$ control signals to select one of the 8-bit data registers associated with each port or the internal control register. The reset control signal clears the control register and sets all the ports to input mode.

The eight bits of the control word specify the mode of each group of 12 bits and whether the ports are in input or output mode. The details of the use of mode 1 and mode 2 are complex and are not dealt with here. To use all the ports in input mode, no programming is required on power-up or reset, otherwise a control word has to be sent to the control register before any data transfer commences.

Figure 7.4 shows the schematic diagram of the logic for one bit of the PPI (programmable peripheral interface), P_0. Both the data direction register and the output register are D-type latches connected to d_0 of the internal data bus of the PPI. If the port has been set up in output mode, by writing a logic 1 into the data direction register, then the tri-state buffer between the output latch and the P_0 pin is enabled, so that the output of the latch is connected to pin P_0. For the port to act as an input, logic 0 is written into the data direction register, so that the P_0 pin is isolated from the output latch. The input tri-state buffer is then activated, enabling the logic level on P_0 to be read.

(b) A simple example of the use of a programmable peripheral interface

One simple use of a programmable peripheral interface (PPI) is to connect a keyboard to the computer system as shown in Figure 7.5. Each key is connected to one input line and one output line as shown. When no key is depressed the pattern **1111** in binary will be read at the input port. If zeros

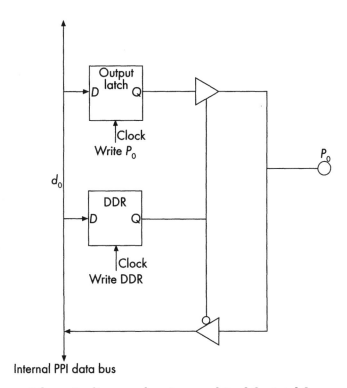

Figure 7.4 Schematic diagram showing one bit of the Intel 8255 programmable peripheral interface.

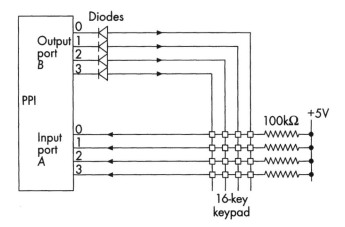

Figure 7.5 Interfacing a keyboard to a PPI.

are output from the output port, then any key depression will result in one of the input lines going to zero. (The diodes are needed to stop multiple key depressions shorting the input port.) By changing the output pattern so that only one zero is output at any one time, both the row and column of the depressed key may be determined. This keyboard-scanning algorithm has to be run in software on the host computer, and becomes quite complex when multiple key depressions and contact bounce have to be taken into account. Such a scheme might be used for a small special-purpose keypad. Because of this complexity and because control of a full keyboard is frequently required, special keyboard controller integrated circuits have been developed, providing a convenient way of connecting a keyboard and display to a microcomputer-based system.

7.1.3 Serial port

With the simplicity of the parallel port it is not obvious why a large number of slow to medium speed peripherals do not use this method. Two of the reasons are cost and standardization.

1. Cost. A parallel interface requires n wires, where n is the word length, between interface and device, whereas a serial device, for the same purpose, uses only three, one for the signal in each direction and one for ground (reference). For long distances, the cost of the extra cable for a parallel interface is considerable.

2. Standardization. Because the original teletypes used over the telephone network worked serially, the telecommunications authority (CCITT) published a standard to allow networking across the world. The presence of a standard and the potentially large market in telecommunications motivated the industry to invest heavily in this method of communication.

The structure of a serial interface is shown Figure 7.6. Internally the interface consists of a number of registers, one for transmitted data, one for received data and one or more for control and status information.

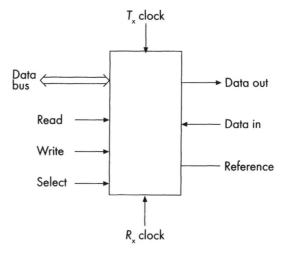

Figure 7.6 Serial interface structure.

An interesting difference between this logical structure and the parallel port is the need for two different clock signals. The clock signal shown is used for the same purpose as in the parallel port, namely to synchronize the interface to the processor. The clock signal labelled T_x/R_x clock (in reality two signals, one for data in and one for data out) is used to determine the speed of the serial transmission. Both transmitter and receiver have to agree on the transmission speed, usually between 300 and 57,600 bits s^{-1}. Because the transmitter and receiver cannot be driven by the same clock, owing to the distances between the sending and receiving devices, the problem of keeping the transmitter and receiver in synchronization, vis-à-vis the characters that are transmitted, arises. There are two different solutions to this problem:

1. asynchronous, where each character contains it's own synchronising information, namely a start bit and one or more stop bits;

2. synchronous, where characters are always transmitted on the line even when there is no information to send. This keeps both ends permanently in synchronism.

Normally, low-speed transmission uses the asynchronous method and higher speeds use the synchronous method.

(a) The standard

An older standard for serial transmission is CCITT V24, also known by the American equivalent RS232C, is still in use widely across the world. This standard defines all the details of a serial connection including voltage levels, pin connections and plug types, as follows:

Logic levels	logic 1 between −3 V and −25 V
	logic 0 between +3 V and +25 V
	(typically −12 and +12 V are used)
Plug type	25-way D-type connector
Bit order	least significant bit first
Idle state	logic 1
Pin connections	defined for data and control lines

Hence a typical character, such as the letter A (41 hexadecimal in the ASCII code), would be sent as shown in Figure 7.7. The penalty, which has to be paid for serial transmission, apart from the slowness of transmission, is the translation from parallel to serial form and vice versa in the interface. Fortunately, this is relatively simple using a shift register. Using serial interfaces is not always as simple as presented here, since the V24 standard defines a large number of control signals associated with a serial connection. The reason for this is that the CCITT standard was defined for use over telephone lines where a pair of modems (modulator-demodulators – see Chapter 14) is required between the transmitter and receiver. Many of the

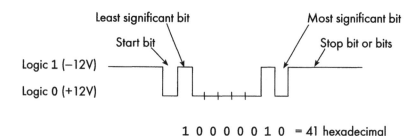

Figure 7.7   Transmission of the letter A.

control signals are provided for signalling between the modem and transmitter or receiver. Where direct connection between transmitter and receiver is possible these additional control signals are not required, but there is no standard for this so V24 is still used. In this case only the three signal lines defined above are required and the use of most of the control signals are undefined. This leads to confusion as some systems use the extra control signals whilst others do not. The reader is referred to the interfacing books in the bibliography for more details.

(b) The Intel 8251 USART

It is possible to get all the logic required for serial-parallel conversion on a single integrated circuit, normally called a UART or USART, which microcomputer manufacturers produce. An early USART circuit from Intel is the 8251A shown in Figure 7.8.

The transmitter and receiver have separate clocks, T_xC and R_xC, and data lines, T_x and R_x, to allow full duplex operation, at different speeds if required. The T_xRDY and R_xRDY signals are status lines indicating that the transmitter is ready to accept the next character to be output from the processor, and that the receiver has a character for the processor, respectively.

In addition the status register has two bits that correspond to these conditions. The command register, which must be set-up before the USART is used, sets the number of bits that are to be transmitted/received for each character, the number of stop-bits required, and whether a parity bit is to be added to a transmitted character, and checked for an incoming character. The four registers (transmit, receive, command and status) are selected by the use of the three control signals, $C/\overline{D}$ (control/NOT data), $\overline{RD}$ and $\overline{WR}$ together with the chip select signal $\overline{CS}$.

The clock signals for the transmitter and receiver are normally generated by the use of a timer chip, which is programmed to give a clock signal of the required frequency.

The extra control and status signals indicated in the diagram are needed when the device is used over a telephone line with a modem. The control signals are for controlling and sensing the state of the modem. For direct

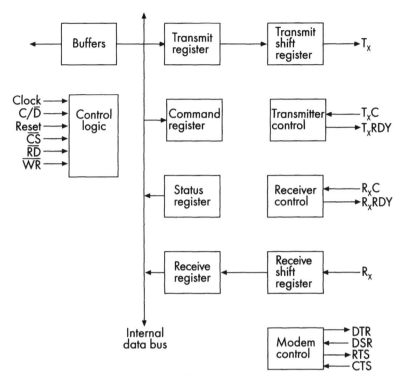

Figure 7.8 Schematic diagram of Intel 8251A USART.

connection to another serial interface these control signals are not required but have to be connected to the correct voltage levels.

(c) The universal serial bus

Recently the universal serial bus (USB) has become a popular way of attaching input–output devices to personal computers. As implied by its name, this bus allows the processor to communicate to a number of devices using a serial interface. There were a number of design goals specified for this bus including the ability to be able to add connections whilst the computer was running, the so-called plug-and-play, and the necessity of keeping the implementation of the interface simple to keep the cost down. The latter resulted in a relatively slow bus by today's standards with a maximum throughput of 1.5 M bytes s^{-1}. For this reason only slow peripherals are connected to this type of bus. The bus is implemented as a tree structure as shown in Figure 7.9. The root of the tree, called a hub, is connected to the main bus in the computer and provides up to 16 connections, either to input–output devices or to expansion hubs which in turn can provide extra connections.

The connections between hub and input–output device are provided by a cable containing four wires, two for data, one for 5 volts power and one for 0 volts reference (ground). The two data lines allow data to be sent

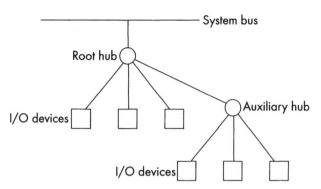

Figure 7.9 Universal serial bus (USB) architecture.

bidirectionally along the cable. The encoding of signals is different from RS232C in that a logic 0 signals that a logic transition has taken place since the last bit time, that is, if the last bit was a 1 this bit is a 0 or vice versa. A logic 1 signals that no logic transition has taken place since the last bit time, that is, the signal at this time is the same as the last signal.

In order to make plug-and-play work satisfactorily, the root hub has to detect when a new device is added to the configuration and inform the operating system inside the computer. The operating system determines whether it has the bandwidth to cope with this new device on the bus. If so it sends information to the device to configure it so that its communications will not conflict with other devices on the bus, for example, by giving the device a unique address.

Communications between the central processor and the attached device are quite complex and follow a scheme similar to the protocols described in Chapters 14 and 15. The root hub broadcasts a frame of information to every attached device every millisecond. If there is no data to send it still sends a frame as this allows all devices to keep in synchronization.

7.2 Controlling input–output devices

Input–output devices transfer data between the 'real world' and the processor. However, because they are interacting with the real world they must operate at a speed at which the real world can present and accept information to and from the computer. This speed is almost always different, and usually slower, than the speed at which the processor can transfer data to an I/O device, so it is necessary to synchronize the computer to the 'real world'. There are three main ways in which this can be achieved, namely polling, interrupts and direct memory access; these will now be discussed.

7.2.1 Polling

Consider the transmission of a character string using the USART discussed in Section 7.1.3. If the transmission rate is set at 9600 bits per second, then 960 characters can be transmitted per second, assuming that there are 10 bits per character (1 start bit, 8 data bits, and 1 stop bit). Thus it takes 1/960 s, or approximately 1 ms, to transmit each character. This is slow compared with the time that the processor will take to fetch the next character of the string from memory and transfer it to the USART (typically 1 μs to 10 μs). Thus, it is necessary to synchronize the transfer of characters to the USART to the speed at which the USART communicates with the real world. One way to do this is for the processor continually to check, or *poll*, the transmitter ready bit in the USART's status register. When this bit is set to 1, the transmitter register is empty, and so the processor can transfer the next character to the transmitter register. This automatically clears the transmitter ready bit in the status register, so that the next time it is polled it will indicate that the transmit register is not yet ready to be loaded with the next character. Figure 7.10 shows the algorithm of the program fragment for outputting a character. This technique is known as *polling* since the transmitter ready bit

```
while more characters to transfer
begin
    get next char from memory
    while transmitter not ready
    begin
        read transmitter status bit
    end
    transfer char
end
```

Figure 7.10 Algorithm to output a character.

is continually sampled, or polled, until it is set to indicate that the transmitter register is empty. The processor spends the majority of its time polling since, as was said above, it will take only a few μs to execute the transfer of a character to the USART, while output to the USART's transmit register can occur only about every 1 ms.

The receiver operation is very similar. When a character is received by the USART into its receiving register the receiver ready bit in the status register is set. Thus to read a character, the processor must continually poll this receiver ready bit until it is set, and then transfer the received character from the receive register to memory. Reading from the receive register automatically clears the receiver ready bit in the status register.

7.2.2 Interrupts

Although the polling scheme for I/O, discussed in the previous section, is simple to understand and to implement, it is inefficient with slow I/O devices, as the processor can spend a lot of time waiting for an I/O device to become ready. Consider the following fragment of a program:

calculate	x
print	x
calculate	y
print	y

If the printer interface is operated by a polling technique, then the processor will have to wait after the calculation of x, while x is being printed, before the calculation of y can begin. For example, if the speed at which the characters can be printed is 10 s^{-1}, say, then the processor will have to wait for 1/10 s, or 100 ms, while each character is being printed. If the character string corresponding to x is just five characters say (for example, 1.234) then the processor will have to wait for 500 ms while the string is being printed. This greatly exceeds the execution time of a processor instruction and is wasted time that might have been usefully used performing the next calculation. What is required is a system that allows the calculation of y to be started immediately the calculation of x is completed, and for x to be printed when the printer is ready.

One way in which this can be done is as follows. If the calculation of y contains a number of intermediate steps then the printer interface can be polled at the end of each intermediate step to see if it is ready and, as soon as it is, x can be output. However, this solution is clearly cumbersome and is impractical to use generally. Moreover, it also wastes time, as the processor has to keep having to poll the interface. A more practical solution is for the program that is calculating x and y to store these values in a buffer, and then for the printer interface to take a character from the buffer when it is ready to print the next character. This is achieved by stopping the main program when the printer interface is ready, and running a second program which takes a character from the buffer, transfers it to the printer interface, and then finally returns to the main program. A scheme that works in this way is known as an *interrupt scheme*.

When a peripheral device such as the printer interface discussed above requires servicing, it outputs a special signal known as an interrupt signal. This signal goes from the peripheral to a pin on the processor, often labelled INTR for interrupt request, as on the 80x86 processor. When such an interrupt signal occurs the processor has three basic actions to carry out:

1. It must recognize that an interrupt has occurred and, if there is more than one interrupt possible, it must determine which of the peripheral devices generated the interrupt.

2. It must stop the program that is currently being executed, and start running the program that is associated with the interrupt. This program is usually known as an *interrupt handler*, or an *interrupt service routine*.

Each peripheral device that is able to generate an interrupt has its own interrupt handler associated with it.

3. When the interrupt handler has finished, it must re-start the execution of the main program at the point at which it was interrupted.

In Section 5.1 it was shown that a processor continually repeats the actions of fetching, decoding and then executing an instruction from memory, the fetch-execute cycle. To cope with an interrupt, this cycle is modified to:

1. Fetch and decode the next instruction from memory

2. Execute the instruction

3. If an interrupt request has occurred start executing the interrupt handler, else go to step 1.

The fetch and execute phases are executed as before, but at the end of the execute phase the processor checks to see if an interrupt request has occurred, that is, if INTR = 1. If it is, then the processor must store some information about the main program, so that it knows where to return when the interrupt handler has finished. The minimum information that must be saved is the current value of the program counter (PC), which points to the next instruction of the main program to be executed, and the status bits, or flags, stored in the status register (SR). These values are stored in memory, and the PC is then loaded with the address of the first instruction of the interrupt handler. In the simplest systems the interrupt handler starts at a fixed address in memory. The first instruction of the interrupt handler is fetched and executed, the PC incremented to point to the next instruction, which is then fetched and executed, and so on. A special instruction, called return from interrupt (RTI), must be placed at the end of the interrupt handler. This instruction causes the execution of the interrupted program to be restarted. It is accomplished by re-loading the saved PC and the status register. The values of these registers are usually saved in a special area of memory, called a stack, which is discussed in detail in Chapter 11. The flow of control of interrupts is shown in Figure 7.11.

(a) Saving and restoring registers

When a program is executing, some, or all, of the processor's registers will be used to store temporary values, pointers to tables in memory, etc. Now consider what happens when an interrupt occurs. The interrupt service routine starts executing and it will almost certainly also want to use the processor's registers. In doing so it will overwrite values stored there by the main program. However, when the interrupt service routine finishes and control returns to the main program, this program assumes that the appropriate values in the registers are still there; it is unaware that the registers may have been changed by the interrupt service routine. To prevent such corruption the interrupt service routine must save the contents of those

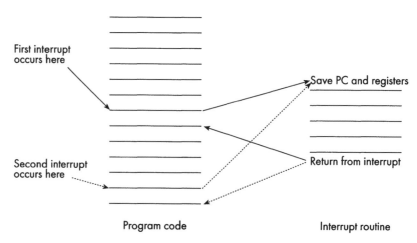

First interrupt
occurs here

Save PC and registers

Second interrupt
occurs here

Return from interrupt

Program code

Interrupt routine

Figure 7.11 Flow of control of interrupts.

registers that it is going to use before their use, and then restore their contents at its completion, just before the RTI instruction is executed. The contents of the registers are most easily saved on the stack, and most processors have special instructions for saving and restoring registers to and from the stack. The basic structure of an interrupt service routine is then:

Save registers on the stack

. . . . . .

Process body of the interrupt service routine, which must contain instructions to clear the interrupt

. . . . . .

Restore registers from the stack
Return from interrupt

7.2.3 Multiple interrupts

In many situations there are likely to be several I/O devices that require servicing by the processor and that are capable of producing an interrupt. For example, in the USART discussed earlier, both the transmitter and the receiver sections will have separate interrupts. The transmitter produces an interrupt when it is ready to accept the next character for transmission, while the receiver will generate an interrupt when it has received a character. Each of the possible interrupts will have an interrupt handler associated with it. The interrupt situation is now more complicated. When an interrupt occurs, the processor must identify which of the possible interrupting devices has generated the interrupt and then execute the appropriate interrupt handler. When an I/O device generates an interrupt it also sets a bit (or flag) in its own status register to indicate that it is the device that has produced the interrupt and so requires to be serviced. The processor has to respond to the interrupt by polling the I/O devices to see which one produced the interrupt. As an alternative to polling, a scheme that is frequently used is one in which the interrupting I/O device automatically places the address of its interrupt handler onto the data bus. This scheme gives a faster response to an interrupt, although the I/O device is more complicated. Indeed many special-purpose I/O devices, such as floppy disk controllers are more complex than the processor, but their availability greatly simplifies the task of designing a computer system. In a system with interrupts, there will be occasions when the processor does not want to respond immediately to a given interrupt, such as when it is dealing with another higher-priority time-critical interrupt. All processors contain a facility for enabling and disabling interrupts under program control. Modern processors contain a number of different levels of interrupt priority, which may be selectively enabled and disabled.

7.2.4 Direct memory access

Transfers of data between a peripheral and memory frequently involve blocks of characters and take place on a character-by-character basis. Each character transfer involves the intervention of the processor to control and monitor the transfer. This is a waste of processor time, even using interrupts. An improvement on this technique is to use direct memory access (DMA). In this scheme, the peripheral interface includes a controller, which is able to act as a bus master and to transfer information between memory and the peripheral without the intervention of the central processor. The CPU initiates the transfer by writing the starting address of memory involved in the transfer into a register in the controller, together with the direction and number of transfers. The controller then manages the transfer of information, incrementing the memory address and decrementing the count after each individual transfer.

In a system with only one bus or where the path between peripheral and memory is shared with the central processor, there is potential conflict on the bus. In order to avoid this, the processor and controller have to synchronize their use of the bus. On simple systems the processor idles whilst the DMA transfers take place, but on more complex systems the DMA device 'cycle steals', that is, it uses the bus in preference to the processor when there is contention. This requires more complex arbitration logic but is more efficient. On the Intel 80x86 system, a DMA controller will gain access to the bus by asserting the CPU HOLD signal and awaiting HLDA, the signal that the processor has released the bus. On completion of the DMA operation, the controller de-asserts the HOLD signal. The CPU idles until DMA finishes and HOLD is de-asserted.

There are a number of DMA controllers available for the 680x0 processor, including the Motorola standard MC68450 four-channel controller. Although these devices are complex, often with many features, they are all functionally similar. DMA data transfers between a peripheral device and memory, or vice versa, are initiated by the DMA controller in response to an external request (usually from a peripheral device). The DMA signals the processor that it requires use of the 680x0's address, data and control buses by asserting the bus request signal $\overline{BR}$ (see Figure 5.16). The DMA controller then waits for the bus grant signal, $\overline{BG}$, from the processor to be activated, indicating that the processor has released the use of the buses, and acknowledges by asserting the bus grant acknowledge signal, $\overline{BGACK}$. Data transfer between a peripheral device and memory now proceeds under the control of the DMA controller. This data transfer may be programmed to take place either in 'burst mode', where several data words may be transferred, or in 'cycle stealing mode', where only a single data word is transferred at a time. In the cycle stealing mode, DMA data transfers are shared, or interleaved, with normal processing, that is, the processor and the DMA controller share the processor's buses.

In order to lower the system cost, a DMA controller may be shared among a group of peripherals. This type of facility is called a channel by IBM. The DMA controller is a small processor and the programming of this controller becomes very complex when the channel is shared among many peripherals.

7.3 Peripheral devices

Clearly a computer is of no use unless information and data can be input in a convenient way, and the results of information processed presented back to the user, for example via a visual display unit (VDU) or a printer. Earlier in this chapter the main principles of both parallel and serial input between the 'real world' and a computer were discussed. This section introduces the main peripheral devices that are used for input and output, namely the computer keyboard, the VDU and the printer. In addition, magnetic media storage devices, both floppy disk and hard disk, are discussed.

7.3.1 Input devices

(a) Computer keyboards

Despite the huge and productive research effort into direct voice input, the 'QWERTY' keyboard remains the principle device for inputting data into a computer. This keyboard is based historically on the typewriter, QWERTY being the order of the keys on the top row of the keyboard. Although there have been many attempts to produce different key layouts that are perhaps more suited to the frequencies at which individual keys are used, the QWERTY keyboard is so well established that it is difficult to see it ever being replaced, at least until and unless voice input becomes the norm.

The standard keyboard contains the full alphanumeric key set (A–Z and 0–9), shift keys to generate capitals as well as special codes, and 12 or 15 special function keys (F1 to F15). Most keyboards also contain a separate numeric (0–9) keyboard, with special arrow keys for moving the cursor around on a visual display unit (VDU) when editing a document.

The operation of a keyboard is straightforward in principle, although, as with most peripheral devices, complicated in detail. When a key is depressed a mechanical contact in a switch is made, which causes a code to be transmitted to a buffer in the computer; an interrupt or a polling request informs the computer that a key has been depressed on the keyboard, and the code is read from the buffer.

Figure 7.12 shows how keys are encoded using a demonstration keyboard of four keys, S_0, S_1, S_2 and $S3$, arranged in a 2×2 matrix between the horizontal wires x_0 and x_1, and the vertical wires y_0 and y_1. Switch S_0 is

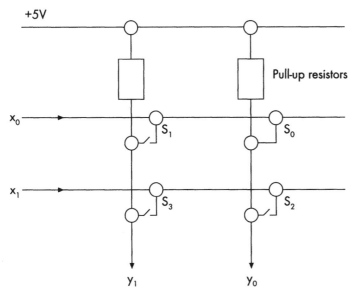

Figure 7.12 Simple keyboard organization.

shown depressed, so making a connection between the horizontal wire x_0 and the vertical wire y_0. Normally x_0 and x_1 are maintained at 5 V, so that y_0 and y_1 are also at 5 V since they are pulled up by the two resistors (to logic 1). Thus $y_1y_0 = 11$ despite the switch S_0 being depressed. However if x_0 is taken to 0 V, y_0 will now be pulled down to 0 V as S_0 is depressed. Thus y_1y_0 will now be 10, i.e. the combination of $x_0 = 0$, and S_0 depressed, takes y_0 to 0. The algorithm for finding which key is depressed is clear. Each of the horizontal rows is taken low in turn, and if a vertical line is low it indicates that the key at the intersection of the horizontal and vertical lines is depressed.

In a keyboard the horizontal lines are driven from an output port of a single-chip microcomputer, for example, the Intel 8048, while the vertical lines are taken to an input port. The algorithm for scanning the keys is implemented in software, which also carries out key debouncing. Debouncing is necessary since the mechanical action of the switch means that the contacts 'bounce' rather than going from open to closed, or vice-versa, in a single action. If the state of the switch is sampled during this bouncing action the incorrect state may be obtained. When a key, or a key combination, is found to have been depressed the code corresponding to that key, or key combination, is stored in a small internal buffer in the 8048. If a key, or key combination, is depressed for more than 0.5 s the code is stored again once every 100 ms. When the 8048's buffer contains a character, an interrupt signal is generated from the 8048 to the computer to indicate that a key has been depressed and that action should be taken by the computer. The operating system of the computer then runs a software process known as a keyboard driver (or handler) which reads the key code(s) from the 8048, performs simple editing such as removing backspace characters, and buffers the input for the appropriate computation process. Key codes are transmitted serially from the 8048 to the computer, in an analogous way to the UART discussed earlier in this chapter.

Interpretation of multiple key sequences is performed in software, for example, SHIFT and an alphabetic key combination to give an upper case character or CNTRL, ALT and DEL depressed together to reboot a PC.

(b) The mouse

The mouse has become the most common pointing device used for input on personal computers. It consists of small plastic case with, typically, one or two buttons on the top and a roller ball underneath. The cursor displayed on the VDU or LCD screen is controlled by software which senses the movement of the roller ball under the mouse and translates it into movement of the screen cursor. The buttons on the mouse activate functions in the program being used on the computer. For example, if a word processor such as Microsoft Word is being used, double clicking, that is, clicking the mouse button twice in a short period of time causes the word over which the cursor is positioned to be selected.

The internal operation of a mouse is simple. The buttons are switches and the roller ball connects via friction couplings, to two devices at right angles, whose output is proportional to the movement of the ball. The information from these components is encoded and sent to the computer via a serial interface.

There are three different types of mouse. The most common, and cheapest type, is the mechanical mouse as described above, where a ball is connected to potentiometers via friction devices and the mechanical motion of the mouse, and therefore the ball, is converted into an electrical signal. A second type is the optical mouse which contains a light emitting diode (LED) instead of a ball. This uses a special reflective mouse mat, which is covered with a large number of closely spaced lines. A detector in the mouse detects line crossings by the change in the reflectance of the light from the LED. The number of line crossings is counted and this determines the movement of the cursor. This type of mouse has been largely superseded by the mechanical mouse. The third type of mouse is an optomechanical mouse which uses a rolling ball like the mechanical mouse but the rotation is measured optically rather than electrically.

Typically the mouse sends information to the computer every time it moves more than a set amount. Low level software on the computer collects this information and converts it into a screen movement. When the user clicks one of the mouse buttons the computer knows where the mouse is from the cursor position on the screen.

A trackball is similar to a mouse except that the roller ball is larger and sits on top of the mouse. The device is kept stationary and a user operates the device by moving the ball and operating the buttons with one or more fingers. The internal operation is identical to that of a mouse.

(c) Scanners

A scanner is a device that reads text or graphics printed on paper and translates the information into a bit map which may be further processed by software. There are several different types of scanners. Firstly, there is the flat-bed scanner, which is similar to a photocopying machine except that the output is a file containing a bit map of the information placed on the scanner rather than a copy of it on paper. Flat-bed scanners are often used with optical character recognition (OCR) software to translate the bit pattern images into formatted text and such techniques provide an easy method of importing paper information into a computer. Scanners are also used in fax machines to scan paper images into bitmaps for transmission over a telephone line to a remote site. Handheld scanners are used for some applications where portability is important. Such scanners work by the user sweeping or rolling the scanner over the required image. This is less accurate than the fixed automatic scanning in a flat bed scanner and also suffers from errors due to an uneven rate of scan and stray reflections. Thus input from such devices often needs more processing to remove errors.

A second type of scanner is the bar-code reader widely used in supermarkets. Special line patterns, known as bars, represent codes and are read by a laser beam. The lines of the bar-code are of different widths and spacing to represent different characters. The reader converts the bar-code pattern into a code, which can be used to identify the item. A standard code, called the universal product code (UPC), is widely used for bar-codes.

There are also drum scanners used for print-quality scanning and film scanners for slides and negatives, but these are outside the scope of this book.

(d) Magnetic input

Credit and charge cards use magnetic strips on the back of the cards to encode information about the owner. Card readers at a point of sale read the information on the strip and use this to log the transaction. The technology is very similar to the tape technology used for digital tapes; a read head senses the magnetic encoding on the magnetic area of the card and translates it into a set of digital values. An error checking code is added to the data so that errors in reading are detected.

Another magnetic input technique is magnetic ink character recognition (MICR) which is used in the encoding of details on cheques. The process uses ink containing iron oxide, which can be magnetized. The pattern of magnetization is used to distinguish between characters. The advantage of magnetic characters is that they can be read by humans as well as easily read by computers.

Magnetic encoded cards are being replaced by smart cards, which are cards with an embedded microchip instead of a magnetic strip. The information in the memory of the chip can be read and written by appropriate equipment and thus the cards can be used in a way similar to cards with a magnetic strip. The main advantage of smart cards over traditional cards is that they are difficult to forge and hence are more secure and that they can contain more information.

7.3.2 Display devices

(a) Video displays

The standard peripheral for output for desktop computers is the ubiquitous video display unit (VDU), which is based on cathode ray tube (CRT) technology, as used in televisions. Laptop computers have displays that use liquid crystal display (LCD) technology which, although currently more expensive than VDUs, may completely replace the standard CRT display in the future. As with computer keyboards, the detail of displaying text and graphical information is complex, and this section focuses on fundamentals.

Figure 7.13 shows a schematic diagram of a CRT tube. At the left is an electron gun, which emits a steady stream of electrons, a control grid, and a focusing system, which focuses the electrons into a narrow beam. The beam then passes between magnetic coils to deflect the beam vertically, and further coils to deflect the beam horizontally. These deflection coils continuously move the beam in 'lines', referred to as a raster scan, from top-left to bottom right across the phosphor coating at the viewable end of the CRT, causing the phosphor to emit light. In practice a voltage is applied to the control grid and this varies the intensity of the light generated, so that a combination of this grid with the vertical and horizontal sweeps allows any pattern of text and graphics, or a combination, to be drawn on the screen. The screen is refreshed every 1/60th of a second or less, which is sufficient for the pattern on the screen to appear to be flicker free.

In the now standard colour VDU the screen is coated with a series of phosphor dots, in groups of the three colours, red, blue and green, and there are three electron guns. A metal mask is incorporated behind the screen so that each of these electron guns illuminates one colour only, so the electron guns can be labelled red, blue and green. If all three guns illuminate a group

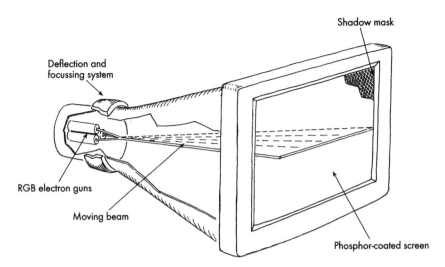

Figure 7.13 Schematic of a CRT.

then the dot will appear white, while adjusting the intensities of the three electron guns can generate any intermediate colour.

VDU systems are defined in terms of the number of pixels (a group of three red, blue and green dots) that can be displayed, and the effective number of colours. Evolving sets of standards have been developed since the IBM PC was introduced, with the most common today being the *super video graphics array* (SVGA). This standard covers a number of resolutions from 800 horizontal pixels by 600 vertical pixels (800×600), to 1600×1200. In theory the standard supports 16 million colours, but in practice the number depends on the video graphics adapter used. This adapter contains the electronics that goes between the computer and the VDU. Its main components are a video RAM, which contains a bit map of the image to be displayed, and the complex electronics that generates the signals to drive the electron guns, together with the necessary timing and synchronization signals. In a black and white display the bit map contains a single bit to represent each pixel, so that an 800×600 display requires a video RAM of 800×600 bits, or about 0.5 Mbit. In a colour display able to display 256 colours say, then each pixel requires 8 bits (or one byte) to represent the range of 256 colours, so the amount of video RAM increases to about 0.5 Mbytes. This triples if the full range of 16 million colours is used. The bit map is generated by the computer's processor and then written to the video RAM. Most adapters also contain a specialized video processor so that they are able to carry out some processing of the image, thus relieving the computer's main processor enabling it to get on with other tasks. The video RAM must be very high-speed memory since, for example, in the colour example above, the memory is accessed 480,000 times every 1/60 of a second, or every 34.7 ns.

When text is displayed each character is represented by an array of pixels. Each font defines the array of pixels required for each character in a character set and thus the amount of text displayed depends on the size of the screen, its resolution, the font and the size of the font.

(b) Liquid crystal displays

The liquid crystal display (LCD) is used mainly in portable (laptop) computers at present. A liquid crystal is an organic molecule which can flow like a liquid but can also behave as a crystal, that is, it can fix its shape. An LCD display consists of two plates placed close together with liquid crystal sealed in the gap between them. The display is lit from behind, either with natural or – more commonly – artificial light. The display is controlled by sending different electrical voltages to the pixels' positions on the screen. The advantage of LCDs over VDUs is that they use considerably less power (about 10 watts), are flicker free, emit little radiation and are compact, features that are paramount in a portable computer.

Vertical and horizontal grids of lines are used to turn pixels on and off. The switching at the crossover points of the grids is provided by an electric field in passive displays. The contrast ratio of such passive displays is low because the electric field has to be kept low to avoid unwanted electrical effects. Active matrix displays have transistors located at the crossover points and the transistors act as amplifiers allowing smaller currents to give better contrast ratios of up to five times better than passive displays. Active matrices are also faster in operation and are becoming the standard for portable computer screens.

Colour LCD displays are now the norm in portable computers. Their operation is complex and outside the scope of this book.

7.3.3 Printers

Printers are electromechanical devices that produce hard copy of computer text and graphics on paper. The criteria that are used to evaluate a printer are mainly how well is the text and graphics produced, speed, that is, how many pages of output can a printer deliver per minute, and price. As with other peripheral devices there has been a rapid development of printer technology, including the daisy-wheel, dot matrix, line, thermal, ink-jet and laser printer. The first three of these are normally used to produce only text, while the thermal, ink-jet and laser are used for both text and graphics. The quality of text output is usually judged against that of a high quality typewriter, while graphics are rated in terms of the number of dots per inch (dpi) that can be produced. The greater the dpi the higher the resolution; for example, laser printers typically have resolutions of 600 dpi or greater, so that there are $600 \times 600 = 360,000$ dots per square inch of paper, which is generally sufficient to produce high quality images. The most popular printers for PCs are ink-jet and laser, and they will be briefly described.

(a) Ink-Jet printer

The ink-jet printer has probably become the most widely used as a personal printer for PCs. Such printers give high quality text and high resolution graphics, approaching the quality of the laser printer, can produce colour as easily as black and white, and are both portable and relatively inexpensive. Resolution is typically 600 dpi or better.

Figure 7.14 shows a schematic diagram of an ink-jet printer. The ink is

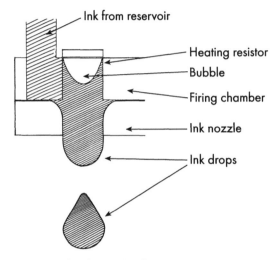

Figure 7.14 Principles of a thermal ink-jet printer.

emitted from small nozzles as high-speed streams of ink drops at a rate of about 10^5 s^{-1}. This may be achieved by the use of a piezoelectric crystal, mounted at the end of the nozzle, vibrating at a high frequency or alternatively by heating the ink to boiling point so that it explodes out of the front of the nozzle. The drops are only about 0.05 mm diameter, with a spacing of about 0.1 mm. The nozzle is held in a cartridge unit, which is moved by a stepper motor across the paper, so providing movement in the y-direction. The combined movements of the ink stream and the nozzle head allows an image to be generated on the paper, which is itself moved at right angles to the nozzle head. Colour ink-jet printers usually contain two ink cartridges, a black ink cartridge for black and white printing, and a colour cartridge containing three colour inks for colour printing, cyan, magenta, and yellow. Combinations of these four inks in different proportions allow a wide range of colours to be generated.

The ink-jet printer is controlled by complex electronics contained within the printer. The interaction from a computer is via a printer driver, which accepts text and graphics images and generates the appropriate control signals for the printer.

(b) Laser printer

Laser printers are the ideal choice if a combination of high quality, approaching that of offset printers, high speed, and quietness are required. They are, however, generally more expensive than ink-jet printers, and less portable, and so they tend to be fixed items in offices, often shared by a number of users over a network. Colour laser printers are available but relatively expensive, so most laser printers produce output in black, white and shades of grey and are used for printing text and simple images where colour is not necessary. For current models resolutions are typically 600 dpi up to 1200 dpi, and the number of pages printed per minute ranges from about four to twenty.

The technology is similar to that of a photocopier, and is based on the electrophotographic printing technique originally developed by Xerox. The major component of a laser printer is a revolving drum, which is coated with selenium. This is a material that is normally an insulator but becomes conducting when illuminated by light. The principle is illustrated in Figure 7.15. As the drum rotates the selenium coating is initially given an

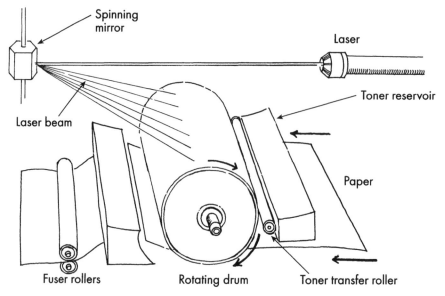

Figure 7.15 Schematic of a laser printer.

electrical charge. At the next part of the revolution a laser beam scans the drum in lines parallel to the drum's axis. The action of a light spot hitting the selenium coating causes the corresponding selenium spot to be discharged. The beam intensity is turned on and off, driven by the bit map that is to be printed. The result is that the selenium coating contains discharged areas equivalent to an image required on the paper. Toner is then applied to the drum where it adheres to the discharged areas of the drum. Finally this image is transferred to the sheet of paper and the excess toner is removed from the drum.

The software required to drive a laser printer is complicated because the encoded form of the output has to be transformed into the equivalent bit map before it can be printed. In cheaper printers the transformation is performed in the attached computer and the bit map sent to the printer but in more expensive printers the transformation is performed in the printer by an embedded computer. Some of the more expensive laser printers accept as input files encoded in Postscript, a page description language developed by Adobe Systems, which has become the standard for desktop publishing.

7.3.4 Data storage devices

The main semiconductor memory of a computer was discussed in Chapter 6, and reference made to the need for backing (or secondary) memory, where programs and data that are currently not being used can be stored for future retrieval into main memory. This function is normally realized with a combination of hard disk and floppy disks. A hard disk is normally permanently resident within a computer, although some computers have removable hard disk packs, while floppy disks are portable. Floppy disks have much less capacity than hard disks and are slower to access, but are inexpensive and provide a convenient means to transfer programs and data from one computer to another.

The mechanism used for all magnetic storage devices is very similar. A write head is a small piece of material in which a magnetic field can be induced via an electric current through a coil. The magnetic field is large enough to affect the small magnetic particles in the magnetic recording material which lie directly under the head. By moving the recording medium it is possible to record areas magnetized to represent 0 and 1. The values are usually stored in encoded form rather than directly. A read head, which may or may not be combined with the write head, works in the opposite manner. The motion of the magnetized recording medium under the read head generates a small electric current in the coil and this current is sensed to recover the data.

(a) Floppy disks

As with all computer peripherals the evolution of floppy disks has been very rapid, from the original large 8 inch disk, through the 5.25 inch disk, to the present much smaller 3.5 inch disk. However the continuous improvements in recording technology means that current 3.5 inch disks store more information than the obsolete 8 inch disks. Figure 7.16 shows the schematic of a floppy disk. It consists of a circular sheet of plastic, coated with a magnetic material, which is free to rotate within a rectangular plastic envelope. There is a central hole which allows the disk to be located on the

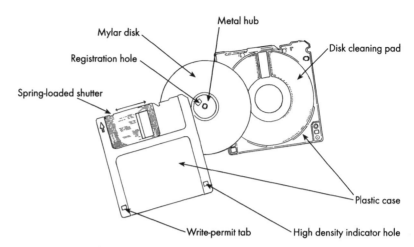

Figure 7.16 A floppy disk.

drive spindle of the disk unit which rotates the disk, and a rectangular hole with a sprung metal cover through which the read/write head of the unit makes contact with the disk. Floppy disks are rotated at a relatively low speed of 300 revolutions/minute. Information is written to the disk by magnetising a small area with one of two different patterns, one which represents logic 0 and the other logic 1, and read by retrieving the magnetization state. A floppy disk is logically divided into a number of tracks with each track being a 'ring' of magnetization around the disk. Each track is divided into a number of sectors which correspond to an arc of the circular track. A complete sector of information is written or read at a time. A sector contains a preamble which allows the head to be synchronized before reading and writing and an error correcting code at the end to allow for error correction. There is a small gap – called the intersector gap – between adjacent sectors. As an example the standard for the 3.5 inch PC high-density disk is 80 tracks on each side of the disk, with 18 sectors per track. There are 512 bytes of control and data per sector, so that this disk has a capacity of $2 \times 80 \times 18 \times 512 = 1.44$ Mbytes.

Figure 7.17 shows schematically a floppy disk, the drive motor and the read/write head. The head is moved across the disk by the worm drive that is driven in steps by the stepper motor. To read or write a sector the read/write head is moved to the required track by the stepper motor. This is done by the stepper motor control unit issuing the correct number of pulses together with a signal indicating which direction the head should move. The drive waits for the start of the track (which it knows because the disk is located on the drive spindle by means of the rectangular locating hole in the hub) and information is then read from, or written to, the appropriate sector of this track. A directory of information is maintained on track 0 of a floppy disk, maintaining a record of both the used and free sectors. This is used by a software process, known as a floppy-disk handler, in the computer's

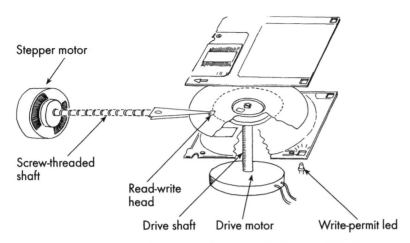

Stepper motor

Screw-threaded
shaft

Read-write
head

Drive shaft   Drive motor   Write-permit led

Figure 7.17 Read-write and drive mechanism of a floppy disk drive.

operating system to decide where to write new information, and where the
disk needs to be positioned to retrieve previously written information.

The complex electronics associated with controlling a floppy disk is
contained within a single chip known as a floppy disk controller. The
controller also contains an internal memory, which is used as a temporary
store for information to be transferred to or from the disk. When reading a
file the floppy-disk handler sends the track and sector numbers that contain
the file information to the controller. The controller then retrieves the next
file sector, buffers it in its internal memory, and passes it to the computer.
The reverse process happens when writing to a file.

Wear is a particular problem in floppy disk drives since the head is in
contact with the disk when reading or writing takes place. To reduce wear
the heads are retracted and the disk rotation stopped when the disk is not
being accessed.

(b) Hard disks

The term 'hard disk' is used to refer to the permanent disk drive(s) within a
computer, differentiating it from the floppy disk. In principle hard disks are
very similar to floppy disks, storing information magnetically on disks in
sectors within tracks. However they hold more data and are faster than
floppy disks. For example, modern hard disks can store anywhere from many
megabytes to several gigabytes, whereas most floppies have a maximum
storage capacity of about a megabyte. Hard disks rotate at speeds in excess of
ten times those of floppy disks.

A hard disk consists of between one and eight rotating disks, known as
platters (see Figure 7.18). Unlike floppy disks these platters are rigid, usually
made of magnetically coated aluminium a mm or so thick. Each platter has
two read/write heads, one for each side. These heads are attached to a single
access arm so that they move together. Each platter has the same number of

tracks, and a track location that is common to all platters is called a cylinder. For example, a typical 3.8 Gbyte hard disk might have three platters (six sides), rotating at 4500 rpm, and six heads. Notice that since tracks are of different lengths – those closer to the centre are smaller – the density of information is higher on the tracks nearer the centre, since the disks revolve at a constant speed. On older drives this applied across the whole disk but on newer drives the disk surface is divided into zones that comprise a number of adjacent tracks. The density of information in each zone decreases with distance from the centre of the disk but zones further away from the centre contain more sectors, thereby increasing the density at the expense of complexity of information management.

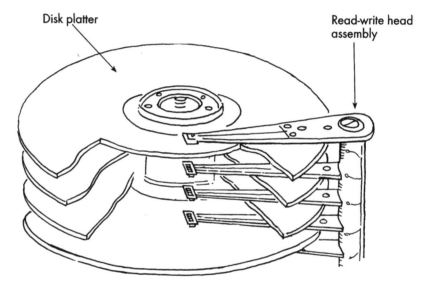

Disk platter

Read-write head assembly

Figure 7.18 A hard disk drive.

The performance criteria for hard disks include the speed of rotation, the diameter of the platters, the packing density of the information and the speed of the disk interface. A frequently stated parameter is the average access time, which is the time taken to position a head over a sector, and is typically 10 ms. Additional heads can be used per side to decrease this access time. The read/write heads are usually moved by a voice coil magnetic system, which is analogous to a loudspeaker drive mechanism, being faster, quieter and more reliable than a stepper motor drive.

The read/write heads in hard disk drives float on a cushion of air above the disk surface. They travel very close to the surface and any imperfections in the surface, such as a piece of dirt, can cause the head to come into contact with the disk surface in what is known as a 'head crash'. Such actions can lead to loss of data and, in extreme cases, terminal damage to the disk drive.

Many disk drives are known as Winchester disks, which are fixed drives, sealed at the factory to stop dirt entering. They are named after the location of the first IBM factory that made these type of drives.

There are many types of drive interfaces but the most common at the present are IDE (Integrated drive electronics) – or EIDE (Extended IDE) – and SCSI (Small computer systems interface). IDE controllers are integrated with the drive instead of being separate. The addressing format of these controllers allows four bits for the head (up to 16), six for the sector (max 63 sectors) and 10 for the cylinder (max 1024) which gives a maximum drive capacity of 528 Mbytes, which is small by current standards. This has led to the extended IDE (EIDE) controller which allows 24 bits for sector number only, giving a maximum of $2^{24}-1$ sectors. In this system the controller has to convert sector number to head, sector and cylinder address.

SCSI disks have a different interface and a faster transfer rate than IDE disks. Because of the higher transfer rate, SCSI disks are standard on high performance workstations, Macintoshes and higher performance PCs such as servers. An important feature of a SCSI interface is that up to seven devices can be connected in series to such an interface. The last device in the chain has to be terminated to prevent reflections and interference. Thus a SCSI based system can be expanded by adding another disk sub-system to the interface whereas an IDE drive either has to be replaced with a larger drive or a separate bus slot is required for another drive.

(c) CD-ROM drives

The principle of optical storage devices is that tiny bumps, called pits, in the surface of the recording medium can be detected by measuring the reflection of a beam of light aimed at the medium. In practice the beam of light is provided by a laser, which is focused via a lens system into a small dot of light. The pits on the surface of the medium scatter the beam of light and this can be detected. Resolution is determined by the wavelength of the laser used and the optics of the lens system.

Phillips developed the original CD-ROM in 1980 to replace LP records. The size of platter they used has become standard at 120 mm diameter and 1.2 mm thick. The master is made by burning holes in a glass disc with a laser and a mould is made from this with bumps where the pits in the glass were. The CDs are made by injecting polycarbonate resin into the mould generated from the glass master.

The data stored on a CD-ROM is stored in a single spiral track and is encoded to reduce errors and maximize storage density. Many errors occur because of the way CD-ROMs are manufactured and used and complex error correction codes have to be used. The surface of the CD has to be streamed by the read head at a constant rate, which means that the speed of rotation has to vary with the distance of the head from the centre of the disc. Partly because of this and partly to reduce costs, the speed of a CD is much slower than a hard disk.

CD-ROMs are removable optical disks for reading data that has been recorded as part of the manufacturing process of the disc, and look identical to music CDs. With a storage capacity of about 650 Mbytes (equivalent to about 470 floppy disks) they are the ideal medium for the distribution of software, since the reproduction costs are very small for large quantities. The main disadvantage of the CD-ROM is the slow access speed, currently about 100 ms, and the inability to write. The reading speed of the devices is given in terms of the transfer rate of an audio drive, which is 150 KBytes so a 20× drive will read at a rate of 3 Mbytes/sec. In older drives the speed of the drive was adjusted to make the speed of transfer the same no matter where the information was being read from on the disc whereas on newer drives the information is read faster when it is closer to the middle of the disc. CD changers are available to allow the system to hold larger amounts of data. Disc changing takes approximately 3 to 10 seconds. Like integrated circuits, single CD-ROMs are expensive to produce but mass production reduces the cost to the order of pence.

Initially CDs were intended for music, but in 1984 the potential for data storage was recognized and Phillips and Sony collaborated in defining the standard format. The standard unit of storage on a CD is a 588-bit frame which holds 24 bytes of data with error correction. A sector on a CD consists of 98 frames which holds 2048 bytes of data together with a sector preamble and error correcting code. Single speed CDs operate at about 150,000 bytes/sec whereas typical drives today operate at 30 times this speed, approximately 5 Mbytes/sec. A file system called High Sierra, now standardized as ISO9660, has been devised so that CDs can be read on computers using different operating systems.

Writeable CD-ROMs (CD-R) are now available. Using a laser beam these discs can be written to just once, but the information cannot be changed once written. Rewritable CD-ROMs are also now available (CD-RW), and they allow discs to be written to up to 3000 times, although such discs cannot be read by standard CD-ROM readers. The surface contains a layer of an alloy of silver, indium, antimony and tellurium which is used for recording. This alloy can be in one of two states; crystalline, which is used to represent a **0** bit and amorphous, which is used as the pits and represents a **1** bit. The drive uses three lasers, one of high power which converts a spot of alloy from the crystalline to the amorphous state, one of medium power which converts the spot to crystalline state and one of low power which just reads the state using the different reflectance.

Videotape has been around for many years and many companies would like to replace it with a higher quality, cheaper medium taking up less space. Developments in technology have meant that it is now possible to manufacture a disc similar to a CD-ROM which can hold much more information but which is still relatively cheap to manufacture. This is the digital versatile disc (DVD) which is an optical technology allowing up to 4.7 Gbyte to be stored on the disc. The differences between a DVD disc and a CD-

ROM are that the pits are smaller – half the size – the information is packed more tightly and a different laser is used to read the information. Because of the use of the different laser a DVD drive cannot read normal CDs without the incorporation of a second laser. For compatibility, present DVD drives are built with two lasers so that the same drive can read DVDs and CDs. The capacity of a DVD disc is only just sufficient for holding the types of multimedia material for which it is intended. Using compression technology it is possible to squeeze 133 minutes of high resolution video and soundtrack on to a single disc but there are several applications for which this is not sufficient. Four different formats have been defined, partly because the industry cannot agree which is the best format. The formats differ in the number of recording layers and the number of sides of the disc which are used; details are outside the scope of this book. The reader is referred to one of the references in the bibliography for more details. It is as yet unclear whether DVD drives will be successful; they are only now – at the time of writing – starting to appear as part of hi-fi systems and substitutes for CD drives in PCs.

(d) Magnetic tapes

Magnetic tape technology has been used for many years in computers but disks have largely superseded its use because it is relatively slow and access is sequential, even though it is cheap. One current use of magnetic tapes is to back up information stored on hard disks. Backup is essential because disks are liable to head crashes with the resultant loss of data. To reduce the possibility of loss, the information on a hard disk is copied on a regular basis to tape backup, which is stored in a safe location. Backup software is available to allow incremental backup, that is, to backup only the information changed since the last backup. The relatively low speed of tape is not a problem in this application since it should rarely be required to restore the hard disk contents.

7.4 Summary

'Real world' digital data exists in either parallel or serial form. In this chapter, input–output devices that allow the computer to receive and send such data have been considered, including examples of both Intel and Motorola interfaces. Important techniques that allow the synchronization of 'real world' events with the computer have been discussed.

Peripheral devices are attached to a computer for the input and output of data and for intermediate storage of data and programs. The most common form of input is the keyboard which is normally attached to the serial port. Other forms of input are a mouse, a scanner and magnetic input media such as magnetic characters and magnetic tape strips on credit cards. The most common form of output is the VDU. The second most common output device is a printer of which there are several types, including laser printers and bubble jet printers. Several devices can be used for intermediate storage of data and programs including floppy disks, hard disks and magnetic tape in several forms. CD-ROMs can be used for distributing programs and data.

7.5 Exercises

Exercise 7.1 Discuss the advantages and disadvantages of memory-mapped I/O versus separate I/O memory.

Exercise 7.2 Data is transferred between computers as 8-bit ASCII code with one start bit, one stop bit and no parity at a baud rate of 9600. What is the effective data rate?

Exercise 7.3 The ASCII character B (42 hexadecimal) is transmitted across a serial link using the RS232C protocol. Draw a timing diagram showing the waveform that would be seen at any point of the transmission path.

Exercise 7.4 Discuss the advantages and disadvantages of using interrupt-driven rather than polled input–output.

Exercise 7.5 Why do you need to store register values on entry to an interrupt procedure and restore them on exit?

Exercise 7.6 Estimate the time taken to transfer 10 Kbytes of data between a peripheral device and a processor's memory using (a) a polled I/O system and (b) a DMA system. Why are DMA devices usually given a higher priority for using the system bus than the processor?

Exercise 7.7 In a given microcomputer system, the time taken for the processor to recognize and acknowledge an interrupt is 4 μs, while the time taken to save or restore the program counter and status registers is 10 μs. If the execution time of an interrupt handler associated with a peripheral device is 70 μs, estimate the highest interrupt frequency that may be used. Assume that there are no other interrupts.

Exercise 7.8 A disk contains 2 Gigabytes of information stored on two surfaces, each containing 200 tracks, each of which contains 500 sectors. How much information is stored in each sector?

Exercise 7.9 Multimedia information has to be compressed in order to be able to get more than two hours of material on to a single DVD disc. Calculate how much compression is necessary assuming that the image data is stored as pictures, each of 640×480 pixels, with each pixel requiring 24 bits, and that 25 frames a second are required in order to produce a realistic image on the screen. Assume that 3 Gigabytes are available for data storage on the disc.

Exercise 7.10 What is the difference between a mechanical mouse and a trackball input device?

Exercise 7.11 What software and hardware would you need to be able to edit a document that was only available as a paper copy if you did not wish modify the paper copy?

Exercise 7.12 What medium would you use to back up the data from the hard disk on your personal computer? Justify your choice.

Exercise 7.13 A company wishes to buy a new printer for each of its departments. It has asked you as the data processing manager to recommend suitable devices. Outline the choices available and suggest questions that you would need to ask each department head in order to decide what type to supply.

8

Control & microprogramming

Earlier it was shown that a computer is effectively a collection of registers, an ALU, and a connection to external memory, all of which are interconnected by buses. Data is transferred from one register to another, possibly undergoing a transformation on the way via the ALU, by connecting the registers onto the appropriate buses with control signals. The control unit, the most complex part of the CPU design, controls this flow of information. All the actions of the control unit are concerned with the decoding and execution of instructions, that is, the fetch and execute cycles. In this chapter, the design of a control unit will be considered, and the concept of microprogramming will be introduced.

8.1 The fetch cycle

The fetch cycle involves the reading of the next instruction to be obeyed, from memory into an internal register of the CPU, the instruction register. The instruction is then decoded so that it is ready to be executed. To explain these actions in more detail, a simple computer system will be used for illustrative purposes, as shown in Figure 8.1. This computer consists of a number of registers, three internal buses, and an ALU.

For simplicity, all registers and buses will be assumed to be 16 bits wide. The three buses marked bus1, bus2 and bus3 are internal to the CPU and are used to route data between registers and the ALU. The memory address register (MAR) acts as a buffer between the CPU and the external address bus. The memory buffer register (MBR) acts in the same way between the CPU and the external data bus, and is bi-directional, that is, data can be transferred to and from external devices. Each register contains 16 D-type flip-flops with tristate outputs and control lines similar to the register bank design discussed in Section 4.8. The ALU has two inputs, bus1 and bus2, and a

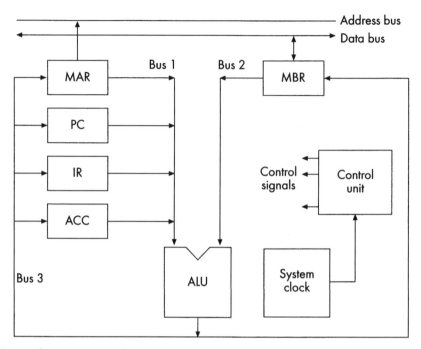

Figure 8.1 A minimal processor architecture.

single output connected to bus3. The only input to bus2 in this design is the output from the MBR register.

For an instruction to be fetched from memory the following sequence of operations has to be performed:

1. Load the contents of the program counter register (PC) into MAR, which results in the value appearing on the address bus.

2. Instruct the memory to perform a read operation by asserting the read control signal. This results in data being placed on the data bus.

3. Store the value on the data bus in the MBR, and transfer this value from the MBR to the instruction register (IR).

4. Increment the contents of the PC so that it points to the next instruction in memory.

For operation 1, transfer of the contents of the PC to the MAR, there must be a path between the two registers. In this architecture the only such path is via the ALU, so the ALU must have a transfer operation, which directly connects bus1 to bus3.

The five steps listed above are a description, or specification, of the register transfer operations that correspond to the fetch cycle. It is very useful to have a language that can be used to describe such operations, partly so that such operations can be described concisely, and partly to prevent ambiguities. There are many high-level hardware-description languages in use (for example, the industry-standard VHDL) but a simple register-transfer notation will be used here. It is best described by examples. The fetch cycle, described above, written in a register transfer notation is:

1. PC → MAR

2. READ

3. MBR → IR

4. PC + 1 → PC

The notation is self-explanatory. In (1) the contents of the PC are transferred to the MAR. A READ cycle is then initiated in (2) which will result in the contents of the addressed memory being placed in the MBR, and so on. What we have written is a sequence of actions or a program. We will assume that each program statement takes the same fixed time to execute. This time will be called a *minor cycle*. Thus the fetch cycle consists of four minor cycles. During each minor cycle, one or more control signals is asserted at the start of the cycle, and de-asserted at the end of the cycle. The minor cycles for the fetch cycle will now be considered in more detail.

Minor cycle 1; PC → MAR
Since the only connection between the output of the PC and the input to the MAR is from bus1 to bus3 via the ALU, the ALU requires a transfer operation to transfer its input from bus1 to the output on bus3. Two control signals are required, one to enable the tristate outputs of the PC to connect the contents of the PC onto bus1 at the beginning of the minor cycle, and the other to latch bus3 into the MAR at the end of the minor cycle. In addition the operation code for 'transfer' must be sent to the ALU.

Minor cycle 2; READ
The only control signal required is READ which tells the external memory to perform the read cycle. This signal is also used by the MBR to latch data from the external data bus at the end of the minor cycle.

Minor cycle 3; MBR → IR
Again the only data pathway between the MBR and the IR is from bus2 to bus3 via the ALU. Two control signals are required, one to enable the tristate outputs of the MBR onto bus1, and the other to latch the contents of bus3 into the IR. In addition, an ALU operation is required to transfer the contents of bus2 to bus3.

Minor cycle 4; PC + 1 → PC
The contents of the PC must be routed onto bus1, the value 1 placed onto bus2, the operation code for 'add' sent to the ALU, and finally the contents of bus3 latched into the PC. The value 1 is most easily organized by having a special read-only register, which can be connected to bus2, containing the binary pattern 00 . . . 1.

Each minor cycle must last long enough for the actions required to be completed. For example, in minor cycle 1, PC → MAR, this cycle time must be at least equal to the time taken for the contents of the PC to be output onto bus1, and for the contents of bus1 then to be transferred by the ALU onto bus3. Minor cycle 2 will take the longest time since it involves a read from external memory, whereas the other minor cycles involve only register-to-register transfers within the CPU. In a simple computer, it is usual to make all minor cycle periods the same, and equal to that of the longest minor cycle. However, if speed of execution is important then a more complicated clocking scheme can be used in which each minor cycle is given a variable time just sufficient for its required actions to complete.

8.2 The execute cycle

Although the fetch cycle is the same for every instruction, the execute cycle will differ from instruction to instruction. Execute cycles also differ among computers as the architecture of a computer greatly influences how an operation is performed. As an example of an execution sequence, consider the minor cycles required to perform an 'add immediate' instruction with the simple architecture shown in Figure 8.1. With this architecture, an 'add immediate' instruction is defined as adding the contents of the next location in memory to the contents of the accumulator register (ACC), and leaving the result in the ACC. In a typical assembly programming language this instruction might be written as

ADD #*x*

where *x* stands for a number, and # means use immediate addressing mode (see Chapter 11 for a fuller explanation of assembly code). It is assumed that the ADD instruction is stored in one word, and the value *x* in the next word.

In the fetch cycle just completed, the instruction 'add immediate' has been fetched from memory, and is in the IR. Before the addition can be carried out, a second modified fetch cycle must be performed to fetch the value *x* from memory into the MBR. The addition can now be carried out; using the simple register transfer language it is

1. MBR → ALU
   ACC → ALU

2. ADD

3. ALU → ACC.

In step 2, the control signals necessary to get the ALU to perform the add operation must be sent to the ALU. The minor cycles are then:

Minor cycle 1; Issue control signals, which output the contents of ACC to bus1 and MBR to bus2.

Minor cycle 2; Send ADD command to the ALU.

Minor cycle 3; Issue a control signal that latches the contents of bus3 into the ACC.

8.3 The control unit

The task of the control unit, which is the most complex part of the CPU, is to issue the appropriate control signals for the minor cycles of both the fetch cycle and the various execute cycles. There are two design implementation techniques, namely hardwiring and microprogramming. The first, the hardware approach, treats the control unit as sequential logic, implemented using standard logic components, with each minor cycle being a state. The design method closely follows that discussed in Chapter 4.

The second solution is to use a technique known as microprogramming. Using this technique, the register transfer programs for the fetch and execute cycles are actually the instructions for a simpler processor. These instructions are known as micro-instructions, to differentiate them from the instructions of the higher-level machine. The outline structure of a simplified microprogrammable control unit is shown in Figure 8.2. It is explainable in terms similar to those used to define the higher-level machine. It consists of a set of registers and a memory (usually called the control or microprogram memory) in which the sequences of micro-instructions that correspond to the fetch and execute cycles of the higher-level machine are stored. This ROM has n address lines so that 2^n words are addressed, and each word is m bits long. The output from the ROM is latched into the m-bit wide micro-instruction register. Some of the bits are used as control bits, controlling individual signals, while others are grouped into fields for particular actions (see below).

Consider the fetch cycle:

1. PC $\rightarrow$ MAR

2. READ

3. MBR $\rightarrow$ IR

4. PC $+ 1 \rightarrow$ PC

These four register transfer statements translate directly to four micro-instructions, stored within the microprogram ROM, as follows.

PC $\rightarrow$ MAR
Two control signals are required: PC-to-bus1 and bus3-to-MAR as described earlier. These control signals are shown as bits 5 and 10 of the micro-instruction word in Figure 8.2. In addition a code to transfer bus1 to bus3 has to be sent to the ALU. A control field assumed to be four bits, labelled

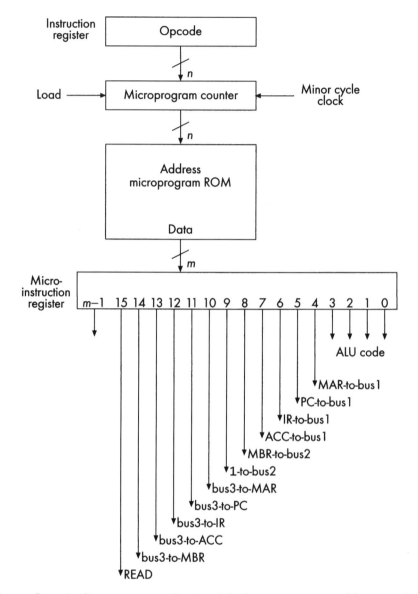

Figure 8.2 Outline structure of a simplified microprogrammable control
unit.

wwww, is set aside for this function, and occupies the least significant four
bits of the micro-instruction word. Thus the micro-instruction is

$$0 \ 0 \ . \ . \ . \ 0 \ 0 \ 0 \ 0 \ 0 \ 1 \ 0 \ 0 \ 0 \ 0 \ 1 \ 0 \text{w w w w}$$

It is assumed here that the contents of bus3 are latched into the MAR on
the falling edge of the control signal, at the end of the micro-instruction (or
minor) cycle.

READ

Bit 15 of the control field is used as the READ signal to external memory, so the micro-instruction is

$$0 \ 0 \ . \ . \ . \ 1 \ 0 \ 0 \ 0 \ 0 \ 0 \ 0 \ 0 \ 0 \ 0 \ 0 \ 0 \ 0 \ 0 \ 0 \ 0 \ 0$$

Note that all other bits must be set to zero.

MBR → IR

This is very similar to PC → MAR. Two control signals are required: MBR-to-bus2 and bus3-to-IR, so the micro-instruction required is

$$0 \ 0 \ . \ . \ . \ 0 \ 0 \ 0 \ 1 \ 0 \ 0 \ 0 \ 1 \ 0 \ 0 \ 0 \ 0 \ \text{w w w w.}$$

Again **wwww** is the code required to transfer bus1 to bus3.

PC + 1 → PC

This is the most complicated micro-instruction in the fetch cycle. It requires a control bit in the control field to output the contents of the PC to bus1 (PC-to-bus1), a control bit to output the register containing 1 to bus2 (1-to-bus2), the code for ADD to be sent to the ALU, and a control bit to latch the result of the addition from bus3 into the PC. The micro-instruction is

$$0 \ 0 \ . \ . \ . \ 0 \ 0 \ 0 \ 0 \ 1 \ 0 \ 0 \ 0 \ 0 \ 0 \ 1 \ 0 \ \text{w w w w}$$

where **wwww** is the four-bit pattern code for ADD.

This set of four micro-instructions completes the microcode for the instruction fetch cycle.

Note that at the completion of the fetch cycle, the opcode for the present high-level machine instruction is in the instruction register. This opcode is then transferred into the microprogram counter by activating the *load* control signal. The microprogram counter is an ordinary binary counter, with its output acting as the address into the control ROM. Thus the opcode is actually the starting address of the micro-instruction sequence in ROM that corresponds to that opcode. The ROM acts in the usual way: the word corresponding to that address is output from the ROM to the micro-instruction register. This word is made up of the m bits of the control field, and consists of the register control bits and the ALU operation code.

At the start of the next minor clock cycle the microprogram counter is incremented to point to the next micro-instruction. In this way a sequence of micro-instructions is executed, in an analogous way to the execution of a sequence of machine code instructions. When the micro-instruction sequence for an execute cycle has finished, the microprogram counter must then be set to the start of the fetch sequence again. This cannot be done with the present simple architecture, as there is no means for the microprogram counter to branch to an address that is out of sequence. In addition there is no control path for the load signal.

These deficiencies are corrected with the modified architecture shown in Figure 8.3. An extra bit, known as the *load control* bit, is allocated in the

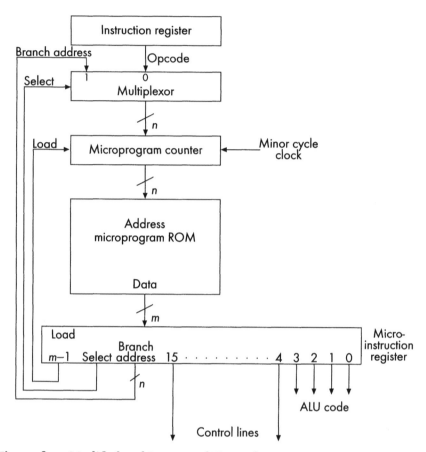

Figure 8.3 Modified architecture of Figure 8.2.

micro-instruction register and is connected to the load signal. In Figure 8.3 this bit is the most significant bit, that is, bit $m-1$. When this bit is 1 the microprogram counter is loaded with a new address; when it is 0 the microprogram counter is incremented on each minor clock cycle to point to the next micro-instruction in a sequence. The last micro-instruction of the fetch cycle will be to load the microprogram counter, so this micro-instruction will have the load control bit set to 1, and all other bits to 0.

The ability to branch to an arbitrary address in the microprogram ROM is achieved by adding a multiplexer in front of the microprogram counter, together with an address select bit and a branch address field in the instruction register. When the address select is 0, the microprogram counter is loaded from the instruction register when load is activated as before. However, when the address select bit is set to 1 the microprogram counter is loaded, via the multiplexer, with the branch address contained in the current micro-instruction. This causes execution to continue at that address. The micro-instruction register has now become very wide. In the architecture of Figure 8.1 each register was assumed to be 16 bits wide. If this is the case, the n in Figures 8.2 and 8.3 is also 16, so that the microprogram ROM has 2^{16} (that is, 64K) registers each with a word width of at least 32 bits (four for the ALU code, 16 for the branch address, and 12 control bits). However, this ROM size is much too large, since a typical CPU will probably have only of the order of 100–200 separate instructions, and each instruction will require no more than 10–20 micro-instructions. These figures lead to a maximum microprogram ROM size of about 4K words. Moreover, the size of the opcode need only be sufficient to give a unique binary pattern for each instruction, which for 200 instructions is eight bits. Consequently in a 16-bit machine only eight bits will be used for the opcode, leaving eight bits available for address information. This topic is covered further in Chapter 11.

Now a 4K ROM requires an address of 12 bits, so if an 8-bit opcode is used a further four bits are required completely to specify an address within the ROM. In the simplest system, each micro-instruction sequence will start on a 256-word boundary. The starting address of a sequence is then given by concatenating the eight bits of the opcode with four least significant bits which are all zero. However, the branch address field in the micro-instruction register must contain all 12 bits if a jump to any arbitrary address within the ROM is required.

8.4 Horizontal and vertical microcoding

In the scheme discussed above, each bit in the micro-instruction register is used to control a single register control line, either to gate data from a bus into a register, or to output data from a register onto a bus. The micro-instruction register rapidly becomes very wide; even in the simple example discussed, there are 32 bits. In a more realistic design, the number of bits may easily exceed 100. This method of coding is simple, and is known as horizontal microcoding. An alternative scheme is to group control signals into fields, and then to use additional decoding circuits to generate the control signals. For example, examination of Figure 8.1 shows that only one register can output at a time onto bus1, so that only one of the four control signals ACC-to-bus1, IR-to-bus1, PC-to-bus1 and MAR-to-bus1 can be active at one time. Consequently these four signals could be grouped together, and controlled by just two bits from the instruction register, i and j, say. The truth table for the decoding circuits is then given in Table 8.1.

Note that with this simple scheme one register is always connected to bus1. This is acceptable for output onto a bus, but not for input, since there will be many minor cycles when no input from a bus is required. In a more realistic scheme, more control signals will be grouped together. For example, three micro-instruction register bits can control seven control signals; when all three bits are 0 none of the registers is active.

Table 8.1   Truth table for decoding circuit

i	j	ACC-to-bus1	IR-to-bus1	PC-to-bus1	MAR-to-bus1
0	0	1	0	0	0
0	1	0	1	0	0
1	0	0	0	1	0
1	1	0	0	0	1

This second scheme is known as vertical microcoding. There is a trade-off between the width of the micro-instruction register, and the amount of additional decoding circuitry required. A horizontal encoding scheme will give the fastest speed of operation, while a vertical scheme may well give more compact hardware with a smaller microcode ROM, but will be slower due to the additional propagation delays through the decoding circuits. In most real microcoded computers, a mixture of the two encoding schemes is used.

8.5 Emulation

One advantage of the microprogramming approach to control unit design is that because it is programmable it is always possible to add additional micro-instruction sequences by reprogramming the ROM. This means, for example, that users can be given a limited ability to add new micro-instructions tailored to a particular task. Another advantage is that standard software development techniques can be used.

An interesting feature of microprogrammed control is the ability to emulate another computer's instruction set. Suppose, for example, that we have a program written for a computer X, say, but we want to run it on a different computer Y, say (that is, Y has a different instruction set to X). One possibility, of course, is to re-write the program using Y's instruction set. However this may well be a time-consuming and error-prone process, and must be repeated for every program. Another possibility is to re-write the micro-instruction program for Y, so that it 'understands' the original instructions of computer X. This technique is known as emulation, in this case Y is said to emulate X. Emulation is a widely used technique in the computer industry. Clearly once an emulator has been written for Y to emulate X, then it can be used for any program that runs on computer X.

8.6 Microcoded versus hardwired implementation

Initially, in the 1950s and 1960s, computers were hardwired, that is, the control units in the CPU were designed using standard sequential logic techniques. In the 1970s microprogramming became more widespread as processors became more complex, making control design more difficult. From the second half of the 1980s the trend was to make processors much simpler – described in Chapter 17 – which resulted in the hardwiring for control unit implementation. At present, many processors use hardwiring although many designs based on old architectures use microprogramming techniques for control unit implementation.

8.7 Summary

The design of the control system for a processor has been discussed. A processor is a complex synchronous finite-state machine, and the job of the control unit is to generate all the control signals required in the correct timing sequence. The control system may be implemented in hardware, or using microprogramming techniques.

8.8 Exercises

Exercise 8.1 Why did microprogramming and microprogram control become popular? Recent RISC computers use hardwired rather than microprogram control. Suggest why this is so.

Exercise 8.2 What is the difference between vertical and horizontal microprogramming?

Exercise 8.3 In general, microprogramming is much more difficult than programming at a higher level. Suggest reasons why this is so.

Exercise 8.4 Write out the micro-instruction sequences for the following assembler instructions, using the architecture given in Figure 8.1 and the controller scheme of Figure 8.2:

(a) CLR
   (clear the accumulator);

(b) LDA #10
   (load the accumulator with the number that immediately follows the load instruction);

(c) ADD 20
   (add to the accumulator the number whose address (20 in this case) immediately follows the add instruction, and leave the result in the accumulator).

Exercise 8.5 The controller scheme shown in Figure 8.3 is very simple. In particular there is no means for executing different micro-instruction sequences depending on the value of the accumulator flags (zero, carry, etc.). Investigate how you would add this facility to the controller scheme of Figure 8.3.

Exercise 8.6 As an extension to the previous question, investigate how you would add a subroutine facility to the microprogrammable controller.

Exercise 8.7 The microprogramming level of control can be thought of as implementing higher level control with a lower level computer – the input is the instruction and the outputs are the control signals to drive the higher level machine. Using this notion, a computer can be designed as a multilevel machine with the control of the higher level machine being implemented by a computer at the next level down. Can you suggest reasons why architects usually use only one or two levels of this hierarchy? What are the problems of implementing successively lower level control via this technique?

9

Design of a small computer system

In previous chapters, the principal components of a computer system have been discussed, namely the CPU, memory and input–output devices. This chapter shows how these components are connected together to make a computer system, and discusses the design of two simple microcomputer systems, one Intel and the other Motorola, built up from the type of components already described. Present day designs are similar but more complex.

9.1 Connecting the components together

The interfacing of memory and input–output interfaces to a processor requires that the address, control and data lines from all the components be connected together. When connecting circuits from the same family, interfacing the control signals is usually simple, since the circuits are designed so that they are compatible. Connecting circuits from different families can be more complex, since not only may the sense of the signals be inverted, but also the control signals may not be used for exactly the same purpose. However, for the sake of the discussion here, compatible circuits are assumed. Interfacing the data and address buses together is less straightforward, especially in the case of memory, because the size of the address and data buses from the processor almost certainly will not match those of the other components.

9.1.1 Decoding

In typical processors, the address bus is at least 20 bits wide, giving an address space of 1M words or greater. This address space is usually populated by several memory chips, some being ROM and some RAM. In addition, the address space is frequently not fully populated since a particular installation might not need the maximum amount of memory. Individual memory circuits usually contain less memory than the total memory space and so will have fewer address pins than the processor. In this case, the memory circuits are connected to the lower-order address lines from the processor and the higher order address lines are decoded to generate the chip select signals.

Example 9.1

To connect a 2K word ROM at address 0–2047 and two 256 word RAMs at addresses 2048–2303 and 4096–4351 to a processor that has a 16-bit address bus. The memory map required is shown in Figure 9.1.

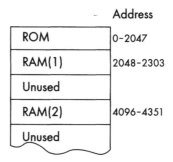

Figure 9.1 Memory map.

The 2K ROM requires 11 address lines to address the individual words within it, while each RAM requires eight address lines. A memory map may then be drawn, as shown in Table 9.1.

Table 9.1 A memory map for the example circuit

A_{12}	A_{11}	A_{10}	A_9	A_8	A_7	A_6	A_5	A_4	A_3	A_2	A_1	A_0	
0	0	—	—	—	—	—	—	—	—	—	—	—	ROM
0	1				—	—	—	—	—	—	—	—	RAM(1)
1	0				—	—	—	—	—	—	—	—	RAM(2)

Note that '—' here means either 0 or 1, and not don't care. To implement this memory system, A_0–A_{10} from the processor are connected to the address lines on the ROM chip and A_0–A_7 to both the RAM chips. The memory chip enable (or select) lines have to be driven from a decoding of address lines, and A_{11} and A_{12} are used in this example to specify which chip is being addressed. Note that A_{13}, A_{14} and A_{15} are not used. The simplest method is to use a decoder as described in Chapter 2. In this case, a 2-to-4 line decoder is required with the inputs connected to A_{11} and A_{12} and the first three outputs connected respectively to the enable inputs of the ROM chip, the first

RAM chip and the second RAM chip, with the fourth left unconnected. The required circuit is then as given in Figure 9.2.

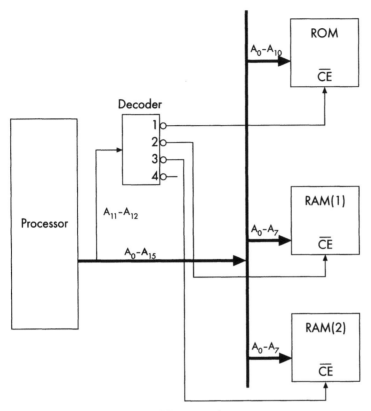

Figure 9.2 Decoding memory addresses.

The chip enable equations are:

$$\overline{CE}_{ROM} = \overline{\overline{A_{12}}.\overline{A_{11}}}$$

$$\overline{CE}_{RAM(1)} = \overline{\overline{A_{12}}.A_{11}}$$

$$\overline{CE}_{RAM(2)} = \overline{A_{12}.\overline{A_{11}}}$$

Note that these enable signals are active low, and are generated with a 2-to-4 line decoder that has active low outputs. Address lines A_{13}, A_{14} and A_{15} are not used in this simple example.

Example 9.2

In the example above, if the ROM were not required, then the circuit could be modified simply by removing the ROM and leaving the chip enable signal unconnected. However, decoding of the chip enable signals to the RAMs could be provided much more simply in this case by connecting the appropriate address line directly to the RAM chip. Since RAM chips normally have a $\overline{CE}$ input, RAM 1 could be connected to A_{11} and RAM(2) to A_{12}.

The decoding described in Example 9.1 can lead to a number of problems. Address lines A_{13}–A_{15} are not used at all. For any address generated by the processor, only the bottom 13 bits are significant, which means that eight different addresses generated by the processor will all map to a single memory address. For example, 0, 8192, 16384, 24576, 32768, 40960, 49152 and 57344 will all map to memory address 0. Since the system is configured with the given memory map, presumably the addresses, other than 0, should never be generated except in error. However, this does mean that finding errors in programs can be difficult. In Example 9.1 above, to be completely safe, a 5-to-32 line decoder should be used with inputs A_{11}–A_{15} and only the three required outputs connected. Any address other than 0 would not then access a memory location. Another problem that can occur is in the use of the partial decoding of address bits as used in the second example. As well as suffering from the same problems as Example 9.1, this circuit also suffers from the fact that it is difficult to expand since the addition of more memory may involve the addition of a decoder.

The problem of decoding does not occur with data lines but it is frequently the case that memory chips have a smaller number of data inputs and outputs than that of the processor. To overcome this, it is necessary to group the memories together and connect them in parallel to provide the necessary data width. For example, to produce an 8K memory system to connect to the 16-bit data bus of a processor using 8K × 1-bit memory chips, requires sixteen memory chips to be connected in parallel, one to each bit of the data bus. This would produce a memory system 8K in size. All the control signals, for example $\overline{RD}$, $\overline{WR}$, $\overline{CE}$, would be connected in parallel to all the memory chips.

The problem of matching the size of the address and data lines between memory and processor can give rise to interesting trade-offs when designing a complete system. For example, if an 8K × 16 memory system were required, then two 8K × 8 memory chips would be ideal. However, if a large memory system is required, which is not available as a single integrated circuit, the designer may have the choice between circuits with the required number of address bits but fewer data bits and circuits with the required number of data bits but fewer address bits. The circuit with the required number of address bits is often preferred because it requires no address decoding. For example, to produce a 64K × 16-bit memory system the designer might have the choice of using sixteen 64K × 1 or sixteen 8K × 8-bit memory chips. In the former case, the address lines could be routed to all the memory chips without decoding, while in the latter case, a 3-to-8-line decoder would be required. The former would be preferable since it uses fewer components and so needs less space to implement.

The discussion above, although using memory as the example, also applies to input–output. In this case, the data route is usually the same size as the processor, but decoding is normally required on the address lines since the interface contains only a few registers, which may be memory mapped or part of a separate input–output address space. The exact method of decoding required depends on how the input–output system is to be operated.

The examples given above have used very small memory circuits. Current circuits are much larger but the same principles apply; the processor address space is larger than the capacity of a single memory circuit and a typical memory system comprises many memory circuits of varying capacities and properties.

Two small processor systems will now be considered, the first using the Intel 8088 processor and the second the Motorola 68000 processor. The Intel 8088 is a 'cut-down' version of the 16-bit Intel 80x86 processor, with an 8-bit data bus. This leads to a slightly simplified hardware system without any loss of functionality. It executes a subset of the instruction set of the Intel 80x86 processors.

9.2 A minimal Intel 8088 system

Figure 9.3 shows a simple microcomputer system using the Intel 8088 processor, with 8K bytes of EPROM and 8K bytes of RAM. Input/output

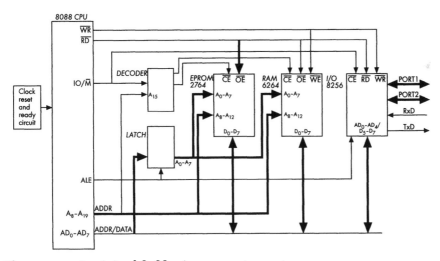

Figure 9.3 A minimal 8088 microcomputer system.

capabilities are provided with a single multifunction device, the Intel 8256, which contains two parallel ports, a programmable serial interface (UART) with integral baud rate generator, and five counter/timers (not shown). The parallel ports are similar to those of the Intel 8255 discussed in Section 7.1.2, while the UART is similar in functionality to the Intel 8251 discussed in Section 7.1.3.

The memory chips used, namely the 2764 EPROM and 6264 RAM have been discussed previously in Chapter 6. In this minimal system only address lines A_0–A_{12} and A_{15} are used, so that the memory is limited to the two devices used, that is, 16 Kbytes, and there is no memory extension capability. To address the individual locations within these memories, 13 address lines are required. The EPROM memory is placed at the top of this address space, the RAM at the bottom. Address line A_{15} is used to select between the EPROM and the RAM, as shown in the address map in Table 9.2.

Table 9.2   A memory map for the 8088 system

A_{15} A_{14} A_{13} A_{12} A_{11} A_{10} A_9 A_8 A_7 A_6 A_5 A_4 A_3 A_2 A_1 A_0	
1 — — — — — — — — — — — — — — —	EPROM
0 — — — — — — — — — — — — — — —	RAM

As discussed previously, the Intel family uses a separate address space for input–output devices, called I/O mapping. The IO/$\overline{\text{M}}$ (IO/NOT memory) control signal from the 8088 (and 80x86) selects between input/output devices and memory. When IO/$\overline{\text{M}}$ is 1 the processor is executing an input or output instruction and the address generated on the address bus refers to an input or output port. When IO/$\overline{\text{M}}$ is 0, the processor is accessing normal memory (EPROM or RAM). The equations for the EPROM and RAM chip enable signals, which are active low, are then:

$$\overline{\text{CE}}_{\text{ROM}} = \overline{A_{15} . \overline{\text{IO}/\overline{\text{M}}}}$$

$$\overline{\text{CE}}_{\text{RAM}} = \overline{\overline{A_{15}} . \overline{\text{IO}/\overline{\text{M}}}}$$

Thus the EPROM is selected when A_{15} is 1 and the RAM when A_{15} is 0, and IO/$\overline{\text{M}}$ is 0 in both cases. The least significant eight address lines of both the EPROM and the RAM are connected to the 8088's multiplexed address/data bus via the latch, while address lines A_8 to A_{12} are connected directly to the address outputs of the 8088, labelled ADDR. The EPROM and RAM data lines are connected directly to the 8088's address/data bus. The 8088's $\overline{\text{RD}}$ signal is connected directly to the $\overline{\text{OE}}$ pins of the EPROM and the RAM, while the $\overline{\text{WR}}$ signal is connected to the $\overline{\text{WE}}$ pin of the RAM.

Five address lines are used to select among the 8256's 32 registers. These lines are connected directly to the address/data bus, as the device uses the address latch enable signal, ALE, from the processor directly. As there is only one I/O device in this simple design, the decoding of the 8256 is achieved by connecting the IO/$\overline{\text{M}}$ signal directly to the 8256's chip select pin.

The enable signals for the EPROM and RAM are easily generated with gates or a simple EPLD, such as the Altera EP610 device.

9.3 A Motorola 68000-based microcomputer

Figure 9.4 shows a simple microcomputer consisting of a Motorola 68000 processor, 8K words of ROM, 8K words of RAM, and a Motorola 68901 multi-function peripheral. This peripheral is similar to the Intel 8256 discussed in

Section 9.2, but comprises eight general-purpose input/output bits (pins), four timers, and a USART. It is designed to interface directly to a 68000 system. The 68000 has a 23-bit address bus, labelled A_1-A_{23} so that it can address 2^{23} or 8M words of data. However, memory is actually byte addressable. As discussed in Chapter 5, the 68000 has two control lines labelled $\overline{\text{UDS}}$, upper data strobe, and $\overline{\text{LDS}}$, lower data strobe, to facilitate byte addressing. When a word is being accessed, both $\overline{\text{UDS}}$ and $\overline{\text{LDS}}$ are asserted (that is, taken low); when a byte is being accessed, $\overline{\text{UDS}}$ is asserted if the byte is on the upper half of the data bus (D_8-D_{15}), and $\overline{\text{LDS}}$ if it is on the lower half of the data bus (D_0-D_7). In order to provide 8K words of RAM, two 6264 RAM chips are required, connected to the upper and lower halves of the data bus, respectively. Similarly, the 8K words of ROM are provided by two 2764 EPROMs. No multiplexing is used on the buses of the 68000, so the connections between the memory chips and the processor are more straightforward than with the Intel 8088 discussed in Section 9.2. The memory chips require 13 address lines (to select among their internal memory locations) and so the low-order address lines A_1-A_{13} are connected directly to the chips. Address lines $A_{14}-A_{16}$ are then used to select among the various memory and input–output devices (the Motorola processors use the normal address space of the processor for the input–output registers), and, in this example, to allow for future expansion. Note that address lines $A_{17}-A_{23}$ are not used in this simple design. The address map for the system is then as shown in Table 9.3 (where '—' stands for 0 or 1).

Table 9.3 A memory map for the 68000 system

A_{16}	A_{15}	A_{14}	A_{13}	A_{12}	A_{11}	A_{10}	A_9	A_8	A_7	A_6	A_5	A_4	A_3	A_2	A_1	
0	0	0	—	—	—	—	—	—	—	—	—	—	—	—	—	EPROM
0	0	1	—	—	—	—	—	—	—	—	—	—	—	—	—	RAM
1	0	0									—	—	—	—	—	68901

The EPROM is placed at the bottom of the address range because when the system is started, or a reset performed, the processor expects to find initialising information in the bottom 1K bytes of memory. This information is most easily placed in the EPROM. The RAM is then placed immediately above the EPROM's address space. The chip select signals for the four EPROM and RAM chips are generated by combining A_{16}, A_{15} and A_{14} with the address strobe signal $\overline{\text{AS}}$, and the $\overline{\text{UDS}}$ and $\overline{\text{LDS}}$ data-strobe signals. The address strobe signal is used so that the memory chips are selected only when there is a valid address on the address bus. The address decoder circuit generates the following active-low chip enable signals:

$$\text{ROMh} = \overline{\overline{A_{16}}.\overline{A_{15}}.\overline{A_{14}}.\overline{\text{AS}}.\overline{\text{UDS}}}$$

$$\text{ROMl} = \overline{\overline{A_{16}}.\overline{A_{15}}.\overline{A_{14}}.\overline{\text{AS}}.\overline{\text{LDS}}}$$

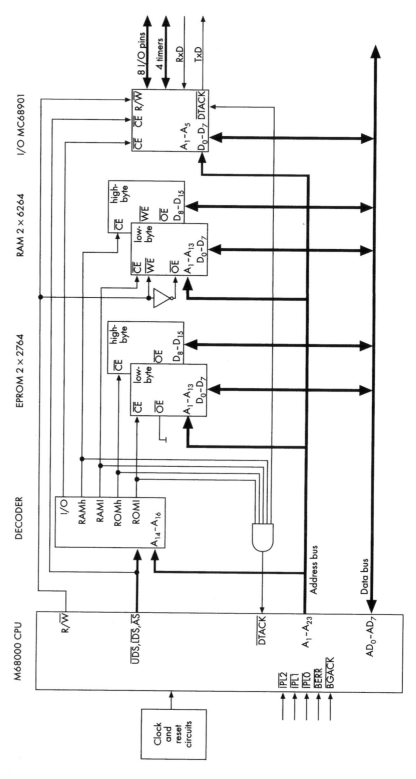

Figure 9.4 Small Motorola 68000 microcomputer system.

$$\text{ROMh} = \overline{\overline{A_{16}.A_{15}.A_{14}}.\overline{AS}.\overline{UDS}}$$

$$\text{ROMl} = \overline{\overline{A_{16}.A_{15}.A_{14}}.\overline{AS}.\overline{UDS}}$$

$$68901 = \overline{\overline{A_{16}.A_{15}.A_{14}}.\overline{AS}}$$

Again the address decoder can be built either from discrete gates and a decoder chip, or from a simple EPLD. The only 'novel' part of the circuit is the data acknowledge $\overline{\text{DTACK}}$ (data acknowledge) generator. In this design the four memory chip enable signals from the address decoder are ANDed together with the $\overline{\text{DTACK}}$ signal from the 68901, to form the input to give a ready signal which is connected directly to the 68000 $\overline{\text{DTACK}}$ input. When neither the memory nor the 68901 is being addressed, the input to the 68000's $\overline{\text{DTACK}}$ signal is high. Whenever one of the memory select signals, or the 68901's $\overline{\text{DTACK}}$ signal, goes low, the input to the 68000's $\overline{\text{DTACK}}$ signal goes low, signalling to the 68000 that the memory or the 68901 is ready. This is the simplest possible data acknowledge scheme for EPROM and RAM, but it has two disadvantages. First, fast EPROM and RAM must be used, and secondly the generator cannot cope with the case, frequently met in practice, in which a mix of devices having widely different access speeds are used. Referring back to the 68000 read timing diagram (Figure 5.17), it can be seen that the memory devices must have access times of less than two clock cycles (that is, they have to respond between the end of state S_2 and the beginning of state S_7). With a clock frequency of 8 MHz this is just $2 \times 125 = 250$ ns. RAMs with these access times are available; for example, the Hitachi HM6264 has a quoted access time of 150 ns, and faster devices are available. EPROM's are generally slower than RAMs, with access times typically in the region of 300–500 ns. However, there is a fast Hitachi 8K EPROM available, the HN482764G-2, with an access time of 200 ns. Clearly, if a faster clock speed is used, then either faster memories or a more complicated data acknowledge generator that introduces a suitable delay must be used. The output enable, $\overline{\text{OE}}$, pins of the memory chips are tied low, and the R/$\overline{\text{W}}$ control signal is taken from the 68000 to the write enable, $\overline{\text{WE}}$, pins of the RAMs.

Finally, note that all unused inputs on the 68000, such as the external bus request input $\overline{\text{BR}}$, need to be tied high using pull-up resistors. This section has given only a very brief introduction to a simple 68000-microcomputer system; readers requiring further information on how to design and build 68000 systems are referred to the book by A. Clements in the bibliography.

9.4 Summary

The design of a small microcomputer system involves the connection of the processor to memory and to input–output devices. This requires the connection of appropriate signals, such as the data and address buses, and the generation of extra control signals such as the chip-enable signals. The design of systems based on 16-bit processors is no more difficult than 8-bit systems, except that the data and address buses are wider.

9.5 Exercises

Exercise 9.1 A system has to be built with 16K of RAM at address 0 to 16383 and 16K of ROM at address 16384 to 32767. Assuming a 16-bit address bus, explain the decoding necessary to connect the memories to the address bus,

(a) using partial decoding

(b) using full decoding.

Exercise 9.2 A 16-bit computer system consists of RAM and ROM connected to the processor bus as shown in Figure 9.5.

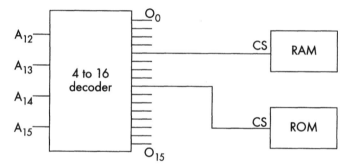

Figure 9.5 A 16-bit computer system.

(a) What addresses do the RAM and ROM respond to?

(b) If you needed to add a 1K EPROM at address 11K, suggest how you would modify the decoding scheme to do this.

Exercise 9.3 Modify the Intel 8088 system design given in Figure 9.3 to use 4K bytes of RAM and 8K bytes of ROM.

Exercise 9.4 Modify the 8088 system design given in this chapter for full decoding of the addresses for RAM access.

Exercise 9.5 Modify the Motorola 68000-system design of Figure 9.4 to change the RAM size to 4K words.

10

Data representation & manipulation

10.1 Introduction

All information in the memory of a computer is represented by a bit pattern of 0s and 1s. There is no distinction in the memory between instructions and data; they are all bit patterns. The difference manifests itself only in the way the bit patterns are used, that is, a bit pattern fetched as an instruction is assumed to be an instruction and a bit pattern operated on as data is assumed to be data. In fact the same bit pattern can represent different types of data or an instruction, depending on the context.

It is possible to represent a maximum of 2^n different bit patterns using n bits and thus the size of the bit pattern determines the number of different instructions or data which can be stored. In most computers the basic storage unit is a byte (eight bits) and instructions and data are normally stored in units comprising multiple bytes.

Since much of the data stored in computers is numeric we will examine number systems first before considering how other data is represented and manipulated. Instruction representation will be considered in Chapter 11.

10.2 Number systems

In the decimal number system, ten different symbols, the digits 0 to 9, are used to represent numbers and each digit in a number is ten times more significant than the digit to its right and ten times less significant than the digit to its left. This figure of ten is known as the radix, or base, of the number system. Thus a number such as 1372 is shorthand for $1 \times 1000 + 3 \times 100 + 7 \times 10 + 2 \times 1$ or $1 \times 10^3 + 3 \times 10^2 + 7 \times 10^1 + 2 \times 10^0$.

Other number systems use different values for the base; the binary system uses a base of two, the octal system a base of eight and the hexadecimal system a base of 16. The radix or base defines the number of symbols needed to represent all possible numbers in the number system, for example, two for binary. The decimal values of numbers in these different number systems can be calculated as in the decimal example above but substituting the appropriate radix. For example, 1372 in the hexadecimal number system (base 16) is equivalent to $1 \times 16^3 + 3 \times 16^2 + 7 \times 16^1 + 2 \times 16^0 = 1 \times 4096 + 3 \times 256 + 7 \times 16 + 2 \times 1 = 4978$ in the decimal system.

10.2.1 The binary system

Computers use the binary number system, which has a radix of two, and thus two symbols, normally 0 and 1, are sufficient to represent any number. Each binary digit in a number is twice as significant as the digit on its right and half as significant as the digit on its left. Using the notation $(...)_n$ to represent a number in the radix n number system, some examples of positive binary integers – whole numbers – and their corresponding decimal equivalents are given below.

$$(1011)_2 = (1 \times 2^3 + 0 \times 2^2 + 1 \times 2^1 + 1 \times 2^0)_{10} \qquad\qquad = (11)_{10}$$

$$(011)_2 = (0 \times 2^2 + 1 \times 2^1 + 1 \times 2^0)_{10} \qquad\qquad = (3)_{10}$$

$$(101010)_2 = (1 \times 2^5 + 0 \times 2^4 + 1 \times 2^3 + 0 \times 2^2 + 1 \times 2^1 + 0 \times 2^0)_{10} = (42)_{10}$$

(a) Decimal to binary conversion

One method of converting a decimal number to binary is continually to divide the number by two until the quotient is zero. The remainders, in reverse order, give the binary representation of the number, as illustrated by the example using the number 23 below.

	remainder
2)23	1
2)11	1
2) 5	1
2) 2	0
2) 1	1
0	

$$\text{so } (23)_{10} = (10111)_2$$

(b) Binary to decimal conversion

To convert from binary to decimal the scheme outlined previously could be used, that is, multiply the binary digits by the correct power of two and sum them. An alternative method is the reverse of the decimal to binary conversion outlined above, that is, starting with the most significant bit - the leftmost one - multiply by two and add the next most significant bit, multiply this result by two and add the next bit and so on for all the bits, as shown in the example of $(111001)_2$ below:

$$2 \times 1 + 1 = 3$$

$$2 \times 3 + 1 = 7$$

$$2 \times 7 + 0 = 14$$

$$2 \times 14 + 0 = 28$$

$$2 \times 28 + 1 = 57$$

so $(111001)_2 = (57)_{10}$

10.2.2 Octal and hexadecimal numbers

It is very tedious and error-prone to write out a long string of binary digits so binary numbers are often written as an octal (radix eight) or hexadecimal (radix 16) number. The eight symbols used to represent the octal digits are 0, 1, 2, 3, 4, 5, 6, 7. The sixteen symbols used to represent hexadecimal numbers are 0, 1, 2, 3, 4, 5, 6, 7, 8, 9, A, B, C, D, E, F.

Conversion between binary, octal and hexadecimal is easy. The radix of the binary system is two and that of octal is eight and, since $8 = 2^3$, to convert from binary to octal the binary digits are grouped into threes starting from the right hand end of the bit pattern and padding the leftmost group with zeros to make a pattern of three, if necessary. Each group of three is coded as a single octal digit using the table below.

binary pattern	octal digit
000	0
001	1
010	2
011	3
100	4
101	5
110	6
111	7

Notice that the octal digit is the same as the decimal value of the equivalent bit pattern. To convert from octal to binary the reverse operation is carried out, that is, each octal digit is expanded into the equivalent three binary digits.

Conversion between binary and hexadecimal values is similar except that the binary digits are grouped into sets of four, since $16 = 2^4$. The conversion table between binary patterns and hexadecimal digits is given below.

binary pattern	hexadecimal digit
0000	0
0001	1
0010	2
0011	3
0100	4
0101	5
0110	6
0111	7
1000	8
1001	9
1010	A
1011	B
1100	C
1101	D
1110	E
1111	F

An example of the conversion of binary to octal and hexadecimal is given below.

1 0 1 1 0 1 1 0 0 1 1 1 0 0 1 1	16-bit binary number
|0 0 1|0 1 1|0 1 1|0 0 1|1 1 0|0 1 1|	grouped into threes
1 3 3 1 6 3	octal equivalent
|1 0 1 1|0 1 1 0|0 1 1 1|0 0 1 1|	grouped into fours
B 6 7 3	hexadecimal equivalent

so $(1011011001110011)_2 = (133163)_8 = (B673)_{16}$

The reverse conversion is simply to write the binary equivalent of each octal or hexadecimal digit and concatenate the resulting bit patterns, for example:

3 7 C F	hexadecimal number
|0 0 1 1|0 1 1 1|1 1 0 0|1 1 1 1|	binary groups

so $(37CF)_{16} = (0011011111001111)_2$

Conversion between octal and hexadecimal numbers and decimal numbers can be performed as outlined above for binary to decimal conversion except for the replacement of two by eight or 16 as appropriate. For example, $(7A2)_{16}$ is converted as follows:

$$1 \times 7 = 7$$

$$7 \times 16 + 10 = 122 \text{ (since } A_{16} = 10_{10})$$

$$122 \times 16 + 2 = 1954$$

so $(7A2)_{16} = (1954)_{10}$

10.3 Binary arithmetic

Binary arithmetic can be performed in a way similar to decimal arithmetic except that it is much simpler since there are only two binary digits, 0 and 1.

The basic rules for addition, subtraction, multiplication and division are given below:

$0 + 0 = 0$	$0 - 0 = 0$
$0 + 1 = 1$	$0 - 1 = 1$ borrow 1
$1 + 0 = 1$	$1 - 0 = 1$
$1 + 1 = 0$ carry 1	$1 - 1 = 0$
Addition rules	Subtraction rules
$0 \times 0 = 0$	$0/0 = $ error
$0 \times 1 = 0$	$0/1 = 0$
$1 \times 0 = 0$	$1/0 = $ error
$1 \times 1 = 1$	$1/1 = 1$
Multiplication rules	Division rules

Using these rules, an example of binary addition and multiplication is given below.

```
    0010          2
    0101 +        5 +
   ─────         ───
    0111          7


    0011          3
    0010 ×        2 ×
   ─────         ───
    0011
    0000
   ─────
    0110          6
```

These rules become more complex when the number representation includes negative values as described later in this chapter.

10.4 Representation and manipulation of data in a computer

All information stored in the memory of a computer is stored as a bit pattern which can represent both instructions and data.

The instructions of a computer are designed to operate on a small number of data types, typically characters, integers and real numbers. For each of these types a coding has to be defined so that all values can be stored as binary representations. As explained in the following sections, there are several different coding schemes used for each data type but any computer will support only a small subset.

10.4.1 Characters

Computers often have to manipulate textual information, the basic unit of which is the character. The most widely used character code is the American standard code for information interchange (ASCII). This is a 7-bit code allowing 2^7 or 128 different characters to be represented. Among the characters represented are upper and lower case letters, the digits 0 to 9 and the standard punctuation characters such as ';' and ':'; in other words, all the characters that can be typed on a standard keyboard. There are fewer than 128 of these characters and the extra codes available are used for special control purposes that we will not discuss here. A character is normally stored in a byte (eight bits) of memory and the corresponding ASCII code for the character is stored in the bottom seven bits with the most significant bit often being ignored but sometimes being used as a parity check. When parity is being used, the eighth bit is set to 0 or 1 to make the number of 1 bits in the byte odd, for odd parity, or even, for even parity. The parity of a character is used to detect single bit errors on inputting characters from external devices which are prone to error.

Much input and output from computers is in the form of streams of characters, for example, from keyboards and to printers. This communication uses the ASCII code. Thus any key depressed on a keyboard causes the corresponding ASCII code to be sent to the computer and similarly any ASCII code sent to a printer causes the corresponding character to be printed. The ASCII code is given in Table 10.1.

10.4.2 Integers

Integers are whole numbers; numbers without a decimal point. Integers may be signed, positive or negative, or may be unsigned when they are assumed positive. Sometimes these two types of integer are treated differently in a computer because unsigned do not have to store the sign, which makes arithmetic simpler.

The range of integers that needs to be stored defines the number of bits required. A computer memory is normally organized in bytes, so integers are

Table 10.1 The ASCII code

Decimal	Hexadecimal	Character
0–31	0–1F	CONTROL CODES
32	20	SPACE
33	21	!
34	22	"
35	23	#
36	24	$
37	25	%
38	26	&
39	27	'
40	28	(
41	29	)
42	2A	*
43	2B	+
44	2C	,
45	2D	–
46	2E	.
47	2F	/
48–57	30–39	0 TO 9
58	3A	:
59	3B	;
60	3C	<
61	3D	=
62	3E	>
63	3F	?
64	40	@
65–90	41–5A	UPPER CASE A–Z
91	5B	[
92	5C	\
93	5D	]
94	5E	^
95	5F	_
96	60	`
97–122	61–7A	LOWER CASE A TO Z
123	7B	{
124	7C	|
125	7D	}
126	7E	~
127	7F	DELETE

stored in memory in an integral number of bytes. Thus 8, 16 and 32 bits allows 256, 65,536 and 4,294,967,296 different unsigned integers to be represented, respectively.

There are several different ways of encoding integers, that is, of allocating bit patterns to decimal integers.

Unsigned integers Unsigned integers are normally encoded as the equivalent binary value with leading zeros added to pad the binary value to whatever size is required. For example, the value $(2)_{10}$ would be encoded as $(10)_2$ and fourteen leading zeros added if the representation used 16 bits. Thus the range of integers that can be stored is from 0 to 2^n-1, where n is the number of bits in the representation.

Signed integers: sign-magnitude In this representation one bit, normally the leftmost bit, represents the sign of the number and the rest of the bits are the binary equivalent of the absolute value of the integer, as shown in Figure 10.1.

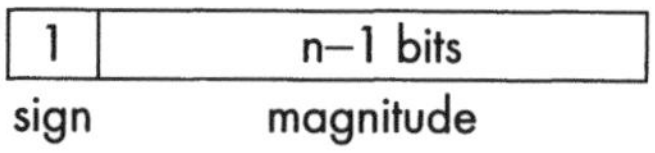

Figure 10.1 Sign-magnitude representation.

An example of this format is shown in Table 10.2 where it is assumed that 0 represents + and 1 represents −. Note that this choice is arbitrary and does not matter as long as it is consistent. The range of numbers which can be represented in this format is from $-2^{n-1}-1$ to $+2^{n-1}-1$. Note that there are two representations of zero, +0 and −0.

This representation has fallen into disuse because it requires more hardware to perform arithmetic on numbers stored this way than the schemes outlined below.

Signed integers: one's complement This coding scheme uses the binary encoding for positive integers and the one's complement of the positive value for negative integers. The one's complement is formed by subtracting the positive encoding from the same length bit pattern comprising of all 1s or by simply inverting each bit, that is, by changing 1s to 0s and vice versa. For example the binary code for 5 is 0101 and the one's complement of 5, which represents −5, is 1010. The range of values which can be represented in this format is exactly the same as the sign-magnitude representation, that is, from $-2^{n-1}-1$ to $+2^{n-1}-1$.

This coding scheme is no longer used because it has the drawback of two encodings for 0, a bit pattern of all 0s and one of all 1s. Thus hardware for manipulating such a representation has to take these two representations of the same value into account and is more expensive than hardware for the method described below.

Table 10.2 Sign-magnitude representation using four bits

Sign/magnitude	Decimal equivalent
0111	+7
0110	+6
0101	+5
0100	+4
0011	+3
0010	+2
0001	+1
0000	+0
1000	−0
1001	−1
1010	−2
1011	−3
1100	−4
1101	−5
1110	−6
1111	−7

Signed integers: two's complement   This coding scheme is very similar
to the one's complement scheme described above but it has only a single
representation of zero, all 0s. Negative values are represented by the two's
complement of the positive value which can be computed by adding one to
the one's complement described earlier. Thus the representation of −5 is
1010 + 1 = 1011. The range of values which can be stored in two's
complement form is from -2^{n-1} to $+2^{n-1}-1$.

In both the one's complement and two's complement coding scheme it is
possible to represent only 2^n different values in n bits and these
representations have to be shared between positive and negative values.
Representations of positive values have a leading zero and representations of
negative values have a leading one. Table 10.3 shows how integers are
allocated to 4-bit patterns for one's and two's complement notation.

Notice that the one's complement form has two representations for 0 but
the two's complement notation has only one and so can represent an extra
negative value.

Another reason for using two's complement representation is that
subtraction can be performed more cheaply than sign-magnitude
representation. To perform subtraction using the two's complement system,
the subtrahend is first complemented, that is, all the bits are inverted, and
one is added to the value. The result of adding this value to the other operand

Table 10.3 Correspondence between 1's and 2's complement
representations

Decimal equivalent	1's complement	2's complement
+7	0111	0111
+6	0110	0110
+5	0101	0101
+4	0100	0100
+3	0011	0011
+2	0010	0010
+1	0001	0001
+0	0000	0000
	1111	—
−1	1110	1111
−2	1101	1110
−3	1100	1101
−4	1011	1100
−5	1010	1011
−6	1001	1010
−7	1000	1001
−8	—	1000

is exactly the same as would have been obtained by subtracting the original
value, see the example below.

```
   0101            0101
   0011 −          1100 +
   0010            0001 +
                  10010
```

Since it is four-bit arithmetic which is being performed here the result can
only be four bits long and hence the highest order bit is ignored in the two's
complement sum. Thus subtraction can be performed by the use of an adder
and inverter. The circuit to invert a bit pattern is required for other purposes
and is cheaper and less complex than a subtraction circuit.

10.4.3 Binary coded decimal

Virtually all computers use the two's complement representation described
above but this representation is not very efficient for some applications like
cash registers or digital watches. To understand why requires an analysis of
the task of processing data. Data has to be input into the computer, processed
and then output. As stated above, data is usually presented to the computer

in ASCII code which then has to be converted to, in the case of numeric data, integer or real number format before processing can proceed. The result then has to be converted back into ASCII code before it can be output. The reason for the code conversion is that it is simpler to perform arithmetic on the internal code representation rather than direct manipulation of the ASCII codes. When only simple arithmetic processing is required, for example, only addition and subtraction of integers, the conversions can be simplified by using an internal code called binary coded decimal (BCD).

In BCD each separate decimal digit is regarded as a separate 4-bit number, for example,

$$2 \quad\quad 4 \quad\quad 8 \quad\quad 1 \quad\quad \text{in decimal}$$

$$\text{is} \quad |0\ 0\ 1\ 0|0\ 1\ 0\ 0|1\ 0\ 0\ 0|0\ 0\ 0\ 1| \quad \text{in BCD}$$

Since the BCD code takes four bits per digit, two BCD digits can be stored in a byte. The conversion from the ASCII code for a digit to the equivalent BCD code is very simple; the bottom four bits of the ASCII code have to be extracted. Similarly, the reverse transformation is also very simple.

Table 10.4 gives examples of the different representations discussed so far.

10.5 Arithmetic using integer representations

Once an integer value has been input and converted to an internal representation, it is normally used in computation. Only two's complement and BCD arithmetic will be considered here since these are the two representations used today.

Overflow   Consider two's complement representation and the addition of the values 5 and 4 where the result has to be stored in four bits:

$$\begin{array}{r} 0101 \\ 0100\ + \\ \hline 1001 \end{array}$$

The result of the computation, as shown above, is **1001** which is the representation of −7 and is obviously incorrect. The problem here is that not enough bits have been allocated to store the result. For example, consider the same example but using five bits:

$$\begin{array}{r} 00101 \\ 00100\ + \\ \hline 01001 \end{array}$$

Table 10.4 Table of code comparisons

Decimal	Binary	Octal	Hexadecimal	BCD	
0	00000	0	0	0000	0000
1	00001	1	1	0000	0001
2	00010	2	2	0000	0010
3	00011	3	3	0000	0011
4	00100	4	4	0000	0100
5	00101	5	5	0000	0101
6	00110	6	6	0000	0110
7	00111	7	7	0000	0111
8	01000	10	8	0000	1000
9	01001	11	9	0000	1001
10	01010	12	A	0001	0000
11	01011	13	B	0001	0001
12	01100	14	C	0001	0010
13	01101	15	D	0001	0011
14	01110	16	E	0001	0100
15	01111	17	F	0001	0101
16	10000	20	10	0001	0110
17	10001	21	11	0001	0111
18	10010	22	12	0001	1000
19	10011	23	13	0001	1001
20	10100	24	14	0010	0000

which works correctly. The original example exhibits overflow. In the two's complement system, overflow can be detected by checking the most significant bits of the operands and the result. If the most significant bits of the operands are the same and the most significant bit of the result is different then overflow has occurred. Overflow can occur only after arithmetic operations on signed values.

Carry A carry occurs when the result of the operation is one bit longer than the operands, for example,

$$
\begin{array}{rr}
1111 & -1 \\
\underline{1010} \ + & -6 \\
11001 & -7
\end{array}
$$

The extra, most significant bit, is called the carry bit. Notice in the example here the result is correct if the carry bit is ignored and in two's complement arithmetic the carry bit is often ignored.

It is possible for both carry and overflow to occur in the same computation, for example,

$$
\begin{array}{ll}
\text{1111} & -1 \\
\underline{\text{1000}} + & \underline{-8} \\
\text{10111} & 7 \text{ in four bits}
\end{array}
$$

Conditions such as overflow and carry are stored so that the following instruction can test whether the previous instruction caused a particular condition to occur. In many computers this information is stored in the processor status word (PSW) or condition code register (CCR), which is a special storage location in the processor holding several bits, each of which denotes whether the particular condition associated with that bit occurred during execution of the previous instruction. This register is also sometimes known as the flag register as it contains a set of flags each denoting part of the state of the processor. In newer processors these condition code bits are sometimes stored in a general register rather than the condition code register to facilitate concurrency.

10.5.1 Two's complement arithmetic

Addition   Numbers can be added together in the two's complement number system using the rules of binary arithmetic given at the beginning of this chapter, for example,

$$
\begin{array}{ll}
\text{0101} & +5 \\
\underline{\text{0001}} + & +1 \\
\text{00110} & +6
\end{array}
$$

$$
\begin{array}{ll}
\text{0101} & +5 \\
\underline{\text{1110}} + & -2 \\
\text{10011} & +3
\end{array}
$$

Notice that the carry bit is ignored in the second example. Overflow can occur as indicated above and carries set the appropriate bit in the condition code register but are otherwise ignored.

Subtraction   In two's complement arithmetic subtraction is performed by adding the two's complement of the subtrahend to the minuend, for example,

To subtract 1101 from 1111 we first complement the subtrahend giving 0011, and then add to the minuend:

$$
\begin{array}{ll}
\text{1111} & \\
\underline{\text{0011}} + & \\
\text{10010} & \text{which is 0010 to four bits.}
\end{array}
$$

Multiplication Multiplication of two integers is more difficult. Consider the standard long multiplication algorithm applied to the two's complement representation of positive integers

```
            0111              +7
            0011  ×           +3
        ──────────
        00000111
        00001110
        ──────────
        00010101              +21
```

Notice that the result requires up to twice as much space as the numbers being multiplied together. This method works for positive values as shown above but it does not work for negative values:

```
            0111              +7
            1101  ×           −3
        ──────────
        00000111
        00011100
        00111000
        ──────────
        01011011
```

which is not the correct answer, 11101011 (−21).

The reason why this does not work is that in the negative number representation the bit pattern does not correspond to the powers of 2 required to generate the number. A similar problem arises in the case of the multiplicand being negative and when both multiplier and multiplicand are negative but for different reasons.

There are several algorithms for multiplying two two's complement integers together but the one most commonly quoted is Booth's algorithm. In this algorithm two memory locations – registers – are used which eventually hold the result. Another one bit register is required which conceptually sits to the least significant side of the least significant result register. A further register holds the multiplicand.

Booth's algorithm is

set result register to multiplier
set 1-bit register to zero
set count to zero
repeat
      if the l.s.b. of the result register is zero and the one
         bit register holds 1 then add the multiplicand to
         the most significant half of the result register.
      otherwise if the l.s.b. of the result register is 1 and
         the one bit register contains 0 then subtract the

multiplicand from the most significant half of the result register.
add 1 to the count
shift the contents of the result register and the one
bit register one bit right losing the bottom bit
and duplicating the top bit
until the count equals the number of bits in the multiplicand.
[Note: l.s.b. means 'least significant bit']

An example will show how this algorithm works. Consider the multiplication of 7 and −3

	Result register	1-bit register	Multiplicand
Initially	0000 1101	0	0111
After 1 iteration	1100 1110	1	0111
After 2 iterations	0001 1111	0	0111
After 3 iterations	1101 0111	1	0111
After 3 iterations	1110 1011	1	0111

and the result is **11101011**.

The first line in the table shows the initial state with the result register containing the multiplier, the multiplicand register the multiplicand and the one bit register 0. On the first iteration the l.s.b. of the result register contains 1 and the one bit register contains 0 and so the contents of the multiplicand register (0111) are subtracted from the four most significant bits of the result register giving 1001. One is then added to the count and the contents of the result register and the one bit register − 1001 1101 0 − are shifted one bit right with the most significant bit being duplicated and the least significant bit being lost giving 1100 1110 1 as shown in the second line of the table. This process is repeated until the count is equal to four when the answer − 1110 1011 − is in the result register.

Booth's algorithm works by using the fact that multiplication by any block of 1's in a bit pattern is equivalent to multiplication by the result of subtracting two numbers. Consider the example

$$00110 \times \text{multiplicand}$$
$$(6)$$

This is equivalent to

$$(2^3-2^1) \times \text{multiplicand},$$

that is, $(2^{\text{highest 1-bit position} + 1}) - (2^{\text{lowest 1-bit position}})$ and this is true for multiplication by any string of 1s. Similarly, multiple strings of 1s separated by 0s can be treated in the same way. Thus any string of 1s, delineated by the patterns **01** and **10**, can be multiplied by another number simply by shifting the second number and performing an add and a subtract, for example,

$$0110 \times 1110 = 1110 \times (2^3-2^1)$$

$$= 1110000 - 11100$$

This is the basis of Booth's algorithm.

Division   Division is similar but more complicated and will not be discussed here; interested readers are referred to the book by Scott in the bibliography for details of the algorithm.

10.5.2 Binary coded decimal

The arithmetic used with BCD is usually addition and subtraction, for example, in cash tills and digital watches, and we will consider only these two operations here.

Addition   There are two differences between BCD and two's complement addition. The main difference is that when the result of adding two BCD digits is greater than 9, ten has to be subtracted from the result and one added to the next significant digit, as in normal decimal arithmetic. For example,

```
      0010          0110           2    6
      0011          0100  +        3    4 +
      ────          ────          ─────────
      0101          1010              10
    + 0001        − 1010          +1  −10
      ────          ────          ─────────
      0110          0000           6    0
```

An additional problem concerns the treatment of negative values. Usually signed values are represented as above but with a preceding four bit pattern denoting the sign, which is treated separately in the computation.

Subtraction   Subtraction is performed by methods similar to addition except that the opposite correction has to be made if the result of subtracting two BCD digits is greater than 9, that is, 10 has to be added to the result and one subtracted from the next most significant BCD digit.

```
      0011          0100           3    4
      0010          0110  −        2    6
      ────          ────          ─────────
      0001          1110           1   14
    − 0001        + 1010          −1  +10
      ────          ────          ─────────
      0000          1000                8
```

Again, negative numbers are treated differently by having a separate four-bit pattern for the sign.

BCD suffers from a number of problems. Firstly, arithmetic operations are more complicated than the equivalent binary ones. Secondly, BCD encoding requires more storage than the equivalent binary representation, for example, 65536 requires 16 bits using standard binary representation but 20 bits using BCD and the disparity grows as the size of the number to be represented increases. The advantage of BCD is that conversion between external representation and BCD is quick and thus simple applications can save time by using BCD instead of pure binary. Processors that support BCD typically have special instructions to help perform the arithmetic as described above.

There are other coding schemes possible for BCD but they are outside the scope of this text.

10.6 Real numbers

Real numbers are numbers which, unlike integers, have a decimal point. The representation and manipulation of real numbers is complex and hence some processors do not provide instructions to manipulate such values. For such processors, software is provided for these operations and sometimes extra processors, called floating point arithmetic units, can be attached to the main processor to provide this facility.

10.6.1 Fixed point representation

The simplest form of representation is to store the real number encoded as a binary value with the decimal point. This gives rise to inefficiency in arithmetic computation because different numbers have the decimal point in different places and the position has to be determined when any arithmetic computation is performed. The solution is to fix the position of the decimal point in the bit string stored and this representation is called fixed point representation. An example will illustrate the representation:

$$27.75 = (2^4 + 2^3 + 2^1 + 2^0) \cdot (2^{-1} + 2^{-2})$$

$$= 11011.11$$

which can be represented in 16 bits as:

$$0000001101111000$$

assuming that the decimal point occurs between the 6th and 5th least significant digits.

Using this representation it is possible to perform binary arithmetic as discussed above. The main limitation with this approach is that very large or very small numbers cannot be represented accurately in a reasonable sized representation. It is for this reason that floating point representation is the normal method used to store real numbers.

10.6.2 Floating point representation

Large numbers are often written using scientific notation, for example, six million is written as 6×10^6. This is the basis of floating point representation except that the numbers are stored in base two rather than base 10. Real numbers can be written in the form

$$\pm M \times 2^E$$

where $\pm$ is the sign of the number, M is the mantissa and E is the exponent.

Since the base is two for all numbers stored the two does not need to be stored. One possible representation for these values is shown in Figure 10.2.

$\pm$	exponent	mantissa

Figure 10.2 A representation of a floating point number.

There are many different ways of representing the same number, for example, all those below are representations of 48:

$$11.00 \times 2^4$$

$$1.10 \times 2^5$$

$$0.110 \times 2^6$$

$$0.0110 \times 2^7$$

To simplify arithmetic, floating point numbers are usually stored in normalized form, that is, of the form

$$0.1 bbbbb \times 2^{\pm E} \qquad \text{where } b = 0 \text{ or } 1$$

Thus the value of the mantissa is greater than or equal to 0.5_{10} but less than 1.0. Since all numbers have this form the 0.1 need not be stored and is implied in any computation.

A signed exponent is required to enable small and large numbers to be represented. In most schemes, the exponent is stored as an unsigned binary number but a value is subtracted from this before any arithmetic is performed. An example that illustrates this is given below.

Assume six bits for the exponent which gives a range of 0–63 in unsigned binary. By subtracting 32 from this, exponents between −32 and +31 can be represented. In this case the representation is known as excess-32 code or as having a bias of 32.

Using the example above the range of numbers that can be represented is:

$$\text{from } -1.0 \times 2^{31} \text{ to } -0.5 \times 2^{-32}$$

$$\text{and from } +1.0 \times 2^{31} \text{ to } +0.5 \times 2^{-32}$$

which graphically gives the mapping shown in Figure 10.3.

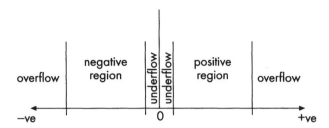

Figure 10.3 Overflow/underflow of floating point numbers.

If any computation generates a result more negative than the largest negative number that can be represented *negative overflow* occurs. Similarly if a negative number is generated which is smaller than the smallest negative number that can be represented *negative underflow* occurs. Similarly, positive underflow and overflow can occur.

One problem with this scheme is that there is no representation for zero, so a special bit pattern – all zeros – is used for this value. This is the value approximated to if positive or negative underflow occurs. Notice that the special representation of zero complicates arithmetic as this value has to be checked for explicitly rather than using the general arithmetic algorithms which work with other values.

A difficulty with this representation concerns the decision on how many bits are needed to represent the exponent and how many bits are required for the mantissa. If a number is represented in n bits there are 2^n different numbers that can be represented and this is true whatever value is being represented. Thus representing a floating point number in a fixed number of bits requires the designer to trade off the number of bits allocated to the mantissa with those allocated to the exponent. Since the exponent size determines the range and the mantissa size the accuracy the designer can trade range against accuracy.

This interplay among range, accuracy and size of representation has led to a number of different representations of floating point numbers. Many computer systems have two formats for floating point numbers, known as single precision and double precision. Typically, double precision values take twice as much storage as single precision values and, as the name suggests, the values are stored to approximately double the accuracy. Some computers make provision for even higher accuracy representation and manipulation, especially those machines aimed at scientific computation.

IEEE **Standard**   Until quite recently it was the case that each computer manufacturer had its own floating point format and thus the same computations on different manufacturers equipment could lead to different results due the differences in accuracy and range in their representations. In 1985, the Institution of Electrical and Electronic Engineers (IEEE) developed a standard for floating point representation called the IEEE 754 standard and this has now been adopted by all major manufacturers. This aids the portability of programs and encourages the development of sophisticated numerical programming libraries.

The IEEE standard defines both single precision (32-bit) and double precision (64-bit) formats. In the single precision format the exponent occupies eight bits and the mantissa 23 bits (as in Figure 10.4) whilst in the double precision format the exponent occupies 12 bits and the mantissa 51 bits. The standard defines the bit patterns for 0 and infinity and the bias used in single precision form is 126 and, in double precision form, 1022. One value is also reserved for a number of error conditions. More details can be found in references in the bibliography.

1 bit	8 bits	23 bits
sign	exponent	mantissa

sign = 0 for positive and 1 for negative;
exponent is an unsigned 8-bit integer;
mantissa is the 23 bits after the initial 1.
Thus number = $(-1)^{sign} \, 2^{(exp-127)} \, (1.mantissa)_2$

Figure 10.4 IEEE single precision standard for floating point numbers.

Examples

(a) 1.0 is represented as

0	01111111	00000000000000000000000

that is, $(-1)^0 \times 2^{(127-127)} \times (1.0000)_2 = 1 \times 1 \times 1.0000 = 1.0$

(b) 0.5 is represented as

0	01111110	00000000000000000000000

that is, $(-1)^0 \times 2^{(126-127)} \times (1.0000)_2 = 1 \times 2^{-1} \times 1.0000 = 0.5$

(c) 2.0 is represented as

0	10000000	00000000000000000000000

that is, $(-1)^0 \times 2^{(128-127)} \times (1.0000)_2 = 1 \times 2 \times 1.0000 = 2.0$

(d) −2.5 is represented as

1	10000000	01000000000000000000000

that is, $(-1)^1 \times 2^{(128-127)} \times (1.0100)_2 = -1 \times 2 \times (1.0100)_2 = -2 \times 1.25 = -2.50$

10.6.3 Floating point arithmetic

As stated previously, floating point arithmetic is complex and many advanced computers use a separate floating point processor to provide this capability; thus we will outline only the algorithms here.

Addition and subtraction   Remembering that zero is a special value, both operands of an addition or subtraction have to be checked first to see if one is zero and, if so, to take special action, for example, to make the other value the result in the case of addition.

Having checked for zero, the exponents of the two operands have to be equalized. This is performed by shifting the mantissa of the smaller value right, one bit at a time, and adding one to the exponent until both the exponents have the same value. When this is complete the mantissas can be added or subtracted. Finally, the result has to be normalized to bring the value of the mantissa between 0.5 and 1.0 by shifting the mantissa and adjusting the exponent. Note that this adjustment can involve shifting the mantissa left or right and therefore incrementing or decrementing the exponent. The example below, which assumes an accuracy of three binary places, illustrates the computation required.

$$0.101 \times 2^7 + 0.110 \times 2^5 = 0.101 \times 2^7 + 0.00110 \times 2^7$$
$$= 0.11010 \times 2^7$$
$$= 0.110 \times 2^7$$

$$0.101 \times 2^7 + 0.110 \times 2^6 = 0.101 \times 2^7 + 0.0110 \times 2^7$$
$$= 1.000 \times 2^7$$
$$= 0.100 \times 2^8$$

$$0.101 \times 2^7 - 0.110 \times 2^6 = 0.101 \times 2^7 - 0.0110 \times 2^7$$
$$= 0.010 \times 2^7$$
$$= 0.100 \times 2^6$$

The implementation of this algorithm is rather more complex as there are problems of rounding, underflow and overflow, which have to be considered for the general case. We will not deal with these problems here; the interested reader is referred to one of the books in the bibliography for more information.

Multiplication and division   Contrary to expectation, multiplication and division are less complex than addition and subtraction. Again the first check is to see if either of the operands is zero and, if so, to set the result to zero or set a flag denoting that overflow has occurred. If neither of the operands is zero then the two exponents are added for multiplication or subtracted for division. Note that the actual value of the two exponents has to be used and thus it may be necessary to adjust the result by subtracting (for multiplication) or adding (for division) the bias value. This arithmetic may give rise to overflow or underflow, which has to be signalled as an error condition and the computation terminated. If no error occurs, then the two mantissas are multiplied or divided and the result normalized as before.

One complication of floating point arithmetic concerns the precision of the result. Real numbers are not stored exactly but to a given accuracy, depending on the size of the mantissa. Hence it may not be possible to store the result of a computation exactly. Two methods are used for dealing with this, truncation and rounding. Truncation involves simply losing the excess least significant bits whereas rounding uses the bits that will be lost to influence the least significant bit stored. The simplest rounding scheme is to add one to the least significant bit of the stored value if the most significant bit of the discarded bits is a 1 and to do nothing if the most significant bit is a 0.

10.7 Summary

Information - instructions and data – has to be encoded into a bit pattern to be stored in the memory of a computer. The size of bit pattern required is determined by the number of different values possible for the type of information, for example, an eight bit pattern can store one of 256 (2^8) different patterns, each of which can represent a different value. Information is normally stored in units whose size is a multiple of a byte and the most common sizes are 8, 16, 32 and 64 bits.

Internally a computer stores and manipulates values as binary values. Long strings of binary digits are difficult to remember and they are usually quoted in computer output as octal or hexadecimal values since these are simple to convert to and from binary and they are much shorter and easier to remember and manipulate.

Most computers use two's complement representation for signed integers. BCD representation is reserved for those computers intended for simple arithmetic computation in devices such as cash registers and digital watches.

Characters are normally represented using the ASCII code and integers using two's complement representation. Floating point numbers are represented following the IEEE 754 standard. Some computers also provide for the representation of values in binary coded decimal (BCD); normally those that are intended for performing simple arithmetic in embedded systems such as cash registers.

Arithmetic computations can give rise to errors such as overflow, underflow and carry. All these conditions can occur when the storage space allocated for the result of an arithmetic operation is not large enough. Checks for these errors have to be made on most arithmetic operations.

Division and multiplication is more complex than addition and subtraction for integers whereas the reverse is true for floating point numbers. Booth's algorithm is one common algorithm for performing integer multiplication and a similar algorithm can be used for integer division.

10.8 Exercises

Exercise 10.1 Convert the following decimal values to binary, octal and hexadecimal.

(a) 27

(b) 96

(c) 1032

(d) 1111

Exercise 10.2 Convert the following decimal numbers to six-bit two's complement form in binary.

(a) 27

(b) −27

(c) 0

(d) −32

Exercise 10.3 Perform the following decimal arithmetic in binary. Indicate any computations that give rise to overflow or underflow if the computations are performed to six bits accuracy. Can you suggest any way of avoiding overflow or underflow in any of the cases without increasing the number of bits required?

(a) 5 + 7

(b) 12 − 3

(c) 20 + 16 − 5

(d) −30 + 7 −12

(e) 12 × 5

Exercise 10.4 Perform the computations given in Exercise 10.3 in BCD arithmetic.

Exercise 10.5 Multiply 14 by 6 using Booth's algorithm. Repeat using 14 and −6.

Exercise 10.6 Show the conversions required in a program to input the characters 1 4 3 from a keyboard, convert them to two's complement form in eight bits, subtract from 52 using binary arithmetic and convert to character form to output to a printer.

Exercise 10.7 Convert the following decimal values into the IEEE standard single precision floating point representation.

(A) 0.0

(b) 1.0

(c) −10.0

(d) 123.4375

Exercise 10.8 Show in detail how the following floating point operations would be performed, assuming that the values were stored in IEEE 754 standard single precision format.

(a) 0.0 + 4.0

(b) 4.0 + 0.4375

(c) 2.0 − 2.4375

(d) 4.0 × 4.0

(e) 4.0 ÷ 4.0

Exercise 10.9 Write a program that can input an integer and convert it into the corresponding floating point representation assuming the IEEE 754 standard single precision format.

Exercise 10.10 A machine holds floating point numbers in a format that uses 32 bits for the mantissa. What is the accuracy to which numbers can be stored? Give your answer in decimal.

11

Instruction sets & addressing modes

11.1 Instruction sets

A computer executes instructions that have been preloaded into its memory. Each instruction consists of an operation code (or opcode) which defines the function that the operation performs and usually one or more operands which define the location of the values that are to be manipulated by the opcode (see Figure 11.1). One of the operands is defined as the destination operand and specifies the address where the result of the instruction is to be placed and the remainder of the operands are called source operands and specify the addresses of the other operands involved in the instruction.

The set of different instructions provided on a particular processor is called its instruction set and the different ways in which the operands can be specified are known as the addressing modes.

An instruction is represented by a bit pattern. Although the length of an instruction could be any number of bits, most systems represent instructions in one or more words since a word is the unit of transfer of information between memory and CPU. Different instructions may have different lengths and formats because they have different numbers of operands or because the operands are represented differently. The ramifications of this are explored later in this chapter.

Operation code	Operands	
	Source(s)	Destination

Figure 11.1 Structure of an instruction.

A program comprises a set of instructions and is represented in memory as a set of bit patterns. This is the machine code for the program. It is inconvenient to write programs as bit patterns since it is easy to make mistakes. Instead some form of symbolic representation is used to specify the program (see Figure 11.2) and a translator is used to translate this symbolic form into the equivalent bit patterns which is the only form the computer can directly execute. The simplest form of symbolic language used is called assembly code which is a simple mnemonic encoding of the bit pattern. The binary code resulting from the translation of an assembly code program is loaded into the main memory of the computer by means of a program called a loader. More details of translators and loaders are given in Chapter 12.

In this chapter, the type and format of instructions both at the assembly and machine code levels are explained together with examples of small programs for the Motorola 680x0 and Intel 80x86 processors. The chapter is intended to give a flavour of these typical computers at this architectural level. Readers who require more detailed information to program either of these processors should consult the manufacturers' literature or one of the books cited in the bibliography.

There are two differing styles of architecture common today, one called complex instruction set computer (CISC) and the other called reduced instruction set computer (RISC). The former, to which the Intel 80x86 and the Motorola 680x0 belong, are characterized as having a large instruction set, whereas the latter are characterized as having a small instruction set. The CISC have relatively large slow, complex processors whereas those of the RISC are small, fast and relatively simple. The discussion in this chapter concentrates on the CISC architectures since the two examples used for illustrative purposes are both CISC architectures. RISC architectures are considered in outline in Chapter 17.

The Motorola 680x0 and the Intel 80x86 are not single processors but a family of processors. Later members of the families have faster execution speeds, more instructions and more addressing modes than the earlier members. Most of the discussion in this chapter refers to features of all the members of each family. Current versions of these processors have additional features not described here.

11.1.1 Opcodes

The instruction set defines the combinations of operations of the ALU and operands which can be activated by the control unit as a single operation at this level of the architecture. Restrictions on the number of different operations and the combinations of operations and operands are imposed by the designer, since the size and complexity of the processor has to be limited because this affects the price and speed of the device. The objective of the designer is to optimize the processor so that it provides the most cost-effective device for a range of application areas.

One of the tasks of the computer designer is to decide how to encode the operation code of each instruction. The simplest method is to encode the

```
        ADD     CX,BX      ;add the contents of register BX to register CX

        move.b  #1,d2      ;move 1 into the contents of register d2

L3:     JMP     L2         ;jump to the statement labelled L2
```

Figure 11.2   Examples of assembly code instructions.

opcode in the minimum number of bits, with n bits being able to represent 2^n different instructions. However this may not be the best way to encode the opcode. The designer will usually decide how many words are needed to store an instruction, calculate how many bits are required to store the operands and use the remainder of the bits to encode the opcode. If there are more than $\log_2 n$ bits available to represent the opcode then a less dense encoding can be adopted which makes decoding easier.

A processor provides operations on a range of different data types. The range of types supported by a processor will depend on the complexity of the instruction set but even the simplest general purpose processors will support operations on characters (represented in eight bits) and integers (represented in 16, 32 or 64 bits) as part of the instruction set. Processors intended for numerical computation will also include operations on floating point numbers (see Chapter 10). The two processors examined in this chapter – the Motorola 680x0 and the Intel 80x86 – are available in a number of different versions but all current versions provide operations on 8-, 16- and 32-bit quantities. In general, floating point operations were often provided by means of an extra chip attached to the CPU by a dedicated bus. The CPU dispatched floating point operations to the attached co-processor which processed them and returned the result to the CPU. A major difference between the Intel Pentium processor and its family predecessors is that it implements floating point operations on the processor chip rather than using a separate floating point processor.

For each of the data types supported, different instructions are required to perform the same function since different internal operations are required in the processor to manipulate different numbers of bits. For example, the ADD operation to add two 16-bit quantities together will require two 16-bit values to be sent to the ALU and a 16-bit value to be stored as the result, whereas an equivalent ADD for 32-bit quantities will manipulate 32-bit values. A simple way to differentiate between the same operations on different data types is to allocate one or more bits in the instruction to denote the data type involved.

11.2 The programmer's models

Before considering instructions in more detail, the programmer's model of the system needs to be elaborated. Simplified models for the Motorola 680x0 and the Intel 80x86 are shown in Figure 11.3 and Figure 11.4. The programmer's model in both cases consists of the registers that reside in the CPU together with the way in which these registers are structured.

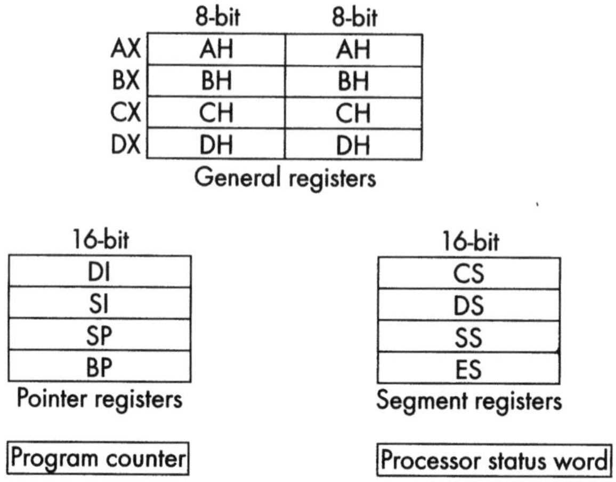

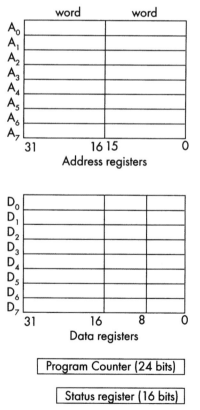

Figure 11.3   Programmer's model of the 80x86.

Figure 11.4   Programmers model of the 680x0.

11.2.1 The 80x86

The 80x86 has four 16-bit registers that are used in general purpose computations called AX, BX, CX and DX. Each of these registers is comprised of two 8-bit registers giving a set of 8-bit registers AH, AL, BH, BL, CH, CL, DH, DL, where the H registers correspond to the most significant (highest) 8 bits of the corresponding X register and the L registers correspond to the least significant (lowest) 8 bits. Thus the registers can be used to hold either 16-bit or 8-bit data, but not both at the same time. Some instructions use registers implicitly whereas others use registers explicitly and thus allow any of these registers to be used as operands. In addition to this there are four 16-bit registers that are used to hold addresses for data pointing, DI, SI, SP and BP. DI is the destination index register, SI the source index register, SP the stack pointer register and BP is the base pointer register. These registers are used in indexed addressing as explained below under addressing modes. They may also be used as temporary 16-bit working registers.

In addition to these registers, there are four segment registers called code segment (CS), data segment (DS), stack segment (SS) and extra segment (ES). These 16-bit registers are used in memory addressing. Their use is quite complicated and is not relevant to the discussion in this chapter and so the topic is omitted. Suffice to say that the registers were introduced into the architecture to extend the addressing range. The architecture is fundamentally 16-bit and thus memory addresses are 16 bits in length giving an addressing range of $2^{16} = 65536$ bytes. This is insufficient for many applications and a segment based addressing scheme using the registers described above was devised to extend the addressing to 20 bits. The programs described in this section are very small and do not need to alter the contents of the segment registers.

11.2.2 The 680x0

The 680x0 has 16 general purpose registers, each 32 bits wide, called A_0 to A_7 and D_0 to D_7. The set D_0 to D_7 are known as data registers and are generally used for storing the intermediate results of calculations. They are completely general in that any instruction that can use a register of one type can use any register of that type; there are no restrictions. Each register may be operated on by three groups of instructions; longword instructions which operate on all 32 bits in the register, word instructions which operate on 16-bit quantities in the lower 16 bits of the register and byte instructions which operate on the least significant eight bits in the register. Any bits not specifically operated on by an instruction are unaffected by that operation, for example, a word instruction writing to the lower 16 bits of a register does not affect the contents of the top 16 bits.

Registers A_0 to A_7 are known as the address registers because they normally hold values that are addresses of locations in main memory. They may also hold data, but both word and longword operations on these registers affect all 32 bits and byte operations are not allowed. A_7 is a special register called the stack pointer which is used for subroutine linkage. In fact there are two registers called A_7 and which one is being referenced depends on the context but this complication will be ignored here.

In addition there are two special registers. One of these registers is the processor status register (PSW) which contains condition codes reflecting the result of the last instruction executed, for example, whether the result was zero or non-zero and whether the operation resulted in arithmetic overflow as discussed in the previous chapter. The upper byte of the status register contains bits that specify the current processor priority whose use is explained in Chapter 7. The other special register is the program counter (PC) which holds the address in main memory of the next instruction to be obeyed. This register, just as in the 80x86, cannot be explicitly addressed by the programmer.

11.2.3 Memory structure

In both architectures, memory is organized as a sequence of bytes and larger data items have to be mapped to a sequence of bytes. To make memory accessing efficient, larger units, such as words and longwords, have to be aligned on particular byte boundaries, for example, words have to have an even address. Even with this restriction there are two ways of mapping word to bytes as shown in Figure 11.5. In one case byte 0 is the least significant

word	byte	byte
0	0	1
2	2	3
4	4	5
6	6	7

680x0 memory addressing (big endian)

word	byte	byte
0	1	0
2	3	2
4	5	4
6	7	6

80x86 memory addressing (little endian)

Figure 11.5   Memory addressing.

byte of the word and in the other case it is the most significant byte. The former case is known as 'little endian' addressing and the latter as 'big endian' addressing. This difference usually is of no concern to a programmer unless one wishes to access the same data as two different data types or unless one wishes to transfer a binary program from one architecture to another. The Motorola 680x0 adopts the big endian convention whereas the Intel 80x86 uses the little endian convention.

11.3 Assembly code

Assembly code is a mnemonic form of machine code or bit patterns; symbols in assembly code represent bit patterns in machine code. An instruction is represented in assembly code by one or more symbols which represent the opcode and operands of that instruction, for example, the instruction on the 80x86 to move the contents of the DX register to the AX register can be written in assembly code as:

```
MOV AX, DX
```

In this instruction MOV represents the opcode for move and DX and AX are the symbols representing their respective registers. The standard symbolic names for the opcodes are defined by the original manufacturer of the processor and hence the names change from architecture to architecture. A move instruction for the 680x0 is normally represented by the symbol MOVE in its assembly language whereas it is represented by the symbol MOV for the 80x86. Note that upper case is used for the opcodes for the 80x86 in this text and lower case for the 680x0. This convention is solely so that the reader can easily distinguish between the two different assembly codes; either code can normally be written in either upper or lower case. The names for the operand fields can be register names, as defined in Figures 11.3 and 11.4, constants or memory locations. Constants, which have to be preceded by a # sign in 680x0 assembly code, or memory locations are usually given symbolic names by the programmer as shown in later examples in this chapter. User defined symbols consist of letters and digits and usually have a maximum length and start with a letter.

An assembly code instruction is split into a number of fields; a label field, an opcode field, zero, one or more operand fields and a comment field. The label is optional and is necessary only if the instruction has to be referred to symbolically by another instruction in the program. Labels are mostly attached to instructions that are the target of transfer of control instructions or are definitions of variables or constants. The label is typically separated from the opcode by a colon or one or more spaces. The opcode is separated from the operands by one or more spaces. Operands are normally separated by commas. Notice that the 80x86 assembler gives the destination operands first, followed by the source, whereas the 680x0 uses the opposite order. The final field is the optional comment field which is for the programmer to add explanatory information. It is normally separated from the operands by a separator character such as ';'. Thus the structure of a typical assembly code statement or instruction is:

label: *opcode*   *operand1, operand2*   *; comment*

for example,

```
SORTED:   MOV     DX, AX      ;START OF SORTING CODE
```

The exact format of the statements for a particular assembler is defined by the producer of the *assembler* which is the translator program that converts assembly code to machine code. The particular producer's manual has to be consulted to discover the conventions used as different assemblers for the same processor may have different formats.

As discussed in a previous section, processors support several data types and the data type has to be specified in the instruction. In typical assemblers for the 680x0 the opcode has a code attached to it, .1 for longword, .w for word and .b for byte, to define the data type of the operand. Thus the instruction to transfer 32 bits, a longword, between register D_0 and D_1 on this processor is represented in assembly code by

move.1   d0, d1

whereas the same instruction operating on 16 bits is represented by

move.w   d0, d1

The 80x86 uses a different scheme. It uses generic opcodes which work on all data types, for example, MOV. To differentiate between access to a byte and a word where it is not obvious from the context of the instruction, the 80x86 assembler uses byte and word on operands, which can be abbreviated to b and w.

MOV DX, AX

is unambiguous since DX and AX are 16-bit registers and hence the move operation moves 16-bit values. If the 8-bit move is required the programmer uses the names of the 8-bit registers, for example,

MOV DL, AL

For cases where it is not obvious what the data type is, for example, when an even address is used which could refer to a 16- or 8-bit quantity, the prefix word ptr or byte ptr (or w or b) can be used with the appropriate operand, for example,

NOT b[1234]

which inverts all the bits – the logical NOT operator – in the byte at address 1234.

In addition to assembly code, assembly code programs also contain statements called assembler directives. These directives are commands to the assembler causing some action to be taken when the code is translated. In the examples later in this chapter four directives are used, equate, define, end and origin. The equate directive, EQU, associates a user defined symbol with a value, thus

X EQU 7

equates the symbol X with the value 7, that is, wherever X appears in the program it stands for 7. The define directive allows the user to allocate and store values in storage. This directive is usually labelled so that the program can refer to the values using the label. The directives are different for the 680x0 and 80x86 assemblers. The 680x0 uses the dc.1, dc.w and dc.b directives to define lists of constants of size 32 bits, 16 bits and 8 bits, respectively. Thus

```
table: dc.w 1,2,3
```

defines three consecutive storage locations for the three word values 1, 2 and 3 and the first location can be referred to as table, the next as table+2 and the final one as table+4, since word values require two bytes of storage.

The 80x86 assembler uses the directives DW and DB for define word and define byte and these have actions identical to the dc.w and dc.b directives on the 680x0.

The END directive is used to signal to the assembler that this is the last statement of the assembly code program. The origin statement, .= or ORG, is used to specify the starting address in memory for the program and hence usually occurs at the beginning of the program.

More details of the operation of assemblers is given in the following chapter.

11.4 Instruction types

Each type of processor provides its own unique set of instructions which can be classified into one of a number of classes.

11.4.1 Data movement instructions

Probably the most extensive class of instructions provided on all present day processors are data movement instructions. These instructions allow the programmer to move data between registers, between registers and memory and between memory locations.

The instructions on the 80x86 to perform data movement are called move (MOV) instructions. The name move is something of a misnomer since it actually performs a copy operation, that is, the source operand still retains the original value after the completion of the operation. The size of the operands is either implied by the operands or explicitly stated by use of the byte ptr or word ptr prefix.

The 680x0 has a large number of move instructions (move and its derivatives such as moveq – move quick) to accomplish transfers between any pair of registers, between any register and a memory address and to load a constant embedded in the instruction to a register or memory address. Many of the move instructions operate on the three sizes of data types which the 680x0 can manipulate; bytes (8 bits), words (16 bits) and longwords (32 bits).

The 680x0 is also able to move data between memory locations directly since it has multiple address registers. There are a large number of move derivatives on the 680x0 concerned with moving the contents of special registers, moving multiple registers and the like.

Examples

```
80x86   MOV  DX, AX   ; move the 16-bit contents of AX to DX
        MOV  CL, DL   ; move the 8-bit contents of DL to CL
        MOV  DX, 26   ; move the decimal constant 26 to DX.

680x0   move.b  d0, d1  ; move the bottom 8 bits of d0 to d1
        move.l  d0, d1  ; move the 32 bits in d0 to d1
        moveq   #3, d0  ; move (quick) constant 3 to the 32 bits of d0
```

11.4.2 Arithmetic and logical operations

Another class of instructions are the arithmetic and logical operations. The main arithmetic and logical operations available on the 80x86 and the 680x0 are shown in Table 11.1.

Table 11.1   Arithmetic and logical operations

80x86	Operations	680x0
ADD	add	add
SUB	subtract and variants	sub
INC	increment (add 1)	
DEC	decrement (subtract 1)	
	negate	neg
AND	logical AND	and
XOR	logical exclusive OR	eor
OR	logical OR	or
ROL	rotate left	rol
ROR	rotate right	ror
	arithmetic shift left	asl
	arithmetic shift right	asr
IMUL	integer multiply	muls
IDIV	integer divide	divs

The 80x86 has a full set of logical and arithmetic operations which operate on both bytes and words. The 80x86 includes increment (add 1) and decrement (subtract 1) operations, unlike the 680x0 which has to use **add** or subtract instructions to perform the same operations. It includes integer multiply and divide and instructions to manipulate BCD values. It does not support floating point arithmetic.

The 680x0 has a conventional set of arithmetic and logical operations. It has a full set of addition and subtraction operations which operate on 8, 16 and 32-bit operands. In addition, it has integer multiply and divide operations. It also has a separate set of operations to facilitate BCD arithmetic, but has no operations to manipulate floating point values. Its logical operations include **and**, **or** and **eor**.

Examples

```
80x86    ADD DX, 3 ; add the decimal constant 3 to the contents of the DX
                   ; register and store the result in the DX register.
         INC AX   ; add 1 to the contents of the AX register

680x0    add.w d0, d1 ; add the least significant 16 bits of d0 to the
                      ; least significant 16 bits of d1, store the result
                      ; in the least significant 16 bits of d1.
         add.l d0, d1 ; as above but with 32 bit operands
```

11.4.3 Bit manipulation operations

The 80x86 does not provide separate bit manipulation operations; bit manipulations have to be performed using the logical operators AND, OR, XOR and NOT which perform logical operation on each bit of the data type separately. This has equal power to the 680x0 operations described below but the individual operations are not so transparent.

The 680x0 provides four instructions which operate on single bits in an operand. There are operations to test the value of a single bit, to set the value of a single bit to 1 or 0 and to change the value of a bit from 0 to 1 or vice versa, as shown in Table 11.2. These operations are very useful if a set of Boolean values is packed into a single location since they allow each bit to be manipulated individually.

Table 11.2 Bit manipulation instructions provided by the 680x0

bset	set the nth bit in the destination to 1 where n is the value of the source operand.
bclear	set the nth bit in the destination to 0 where n is the value of the source operand.
bchng	complement the nth bit of the destination, that is, changes it from 0 to 1 or vice versa. n is the value of the source operand.
btst	test the nth bit of the destination and sets the z condition code appropriately. n is the value of the source operand.

Examples

```
80x86   AND DX, 4 ; all the bits of DX are set to 0 except for bit 2
                  ; which is left in its initial state
         OR  DX, 4 ; all the bits of DX are unaltered except for bit 2
                  ; which is set to 1

680x0   bset.1 d1, d5 ; the value of d1 modulus 32 is taken as the number
                      ; of the bit in d5 which is to be set to 1.
         btst.1 d3, d6 ; the value of d3 modulus 32 is taken as the number
                      ; of the bit in d6 which is to be tested. If this
                      ; bit is 1 the Z condition code is set, otherwise
                      ; it is cleared.
```

11.4.4 Program control instructions

By default a processor executes a set of instructions in sequential order. The address of the next instruction to be executed is kept in the program counter which is automatically incremented to point to the next instruction in sequence. To deviate from this order, program control instructions have to be used. Program control instructions cause control to transfer to an instruction other than the next one in sequence by writing a value directly to the program counter. The simplest form of control instruction is the branch instruction which replaces the current contents of the program counter with the operand value of the branch instruction, for example, an instruction of the general form

```
branch   2000
```

which is represented by

```
JMP 2000
```

in 80x86 assembly code and

```
bra 2000
```

in 680x0 assembly code would cause the next instruction to be obtained from memory address 2000. More generally, control instructions can be data dependent, that is, a condition is tested which determines whether or not the transfer of control takes place. The condition which is tested is normally one or more of the condition codes in the processor status word (PSW) which hold information about the result of the previous instruction. Thus a combination of an arithmetic or logical operation and a conditional test can be used to implement data dependent control transfer. For example, if a piece of code has to be executed once for every data item input and the number of data items is stored in a register, an instruction to subtract 1 from the count of the number of data items followed by an instruction to branch back to the start of that piece of code if the result of the last operation was non-zero would be placed at the end of the code. In 680x0 assembler this could be coded as:

```
       move.w #10,d2 ; initialize loop count to 10
start: .....
       .....
       sub.w  #1, d2
       bne    start ; branch back to start if d2 is not equal to 0
```

Conditional branches are very commonly used in programming and processors usually have instructions to transfer control on a variety of different conditions. In most instruction sets not all instructions affect all the condition codes and so it is often necessary to add a specific test instruction to set the required condition codes before a conditional branch.

Transfer of control instructions contain the address of the instruction to which control is to be transferred. The simplest way for the programmer to state the address in assembly code is to label the target instruction and use the label as the operand of the transfer of control instruction. The assembler calculates the address of the target instruction and places the correct value in the address field of the transfer of control instruction. This is described in Chapter 12.

Although most processors provide similar condition codes, they are rarely identical, for example, the 80x86 includes flags for carry, direction, overflow, parity, sign and zero whilst the 680x0 provides flags for carry, overflow, zero and extend.

(a) Condition tests

Both the 80x86 and the 680x0 provide compare instructions whose only result is to set the condition codes depending on a comparison of the two operands of the instruction as shown below. The 680x0 has the two operand instruction, CMP, which sets the condition codes on the result of subtracting the source operand from the destination operand. It also has a single operand instruction, TST, which sets the condition codes on the value of its operand. The 80x86 has a similar compare instruction, CMP, and a TEST instruction which takes two operands and sets the condition codes as a result of ANDing the two operands together. See Table 11.3.

Examples

```
80x86  CMP   DX, 4 ; subtract the decimal constant 4 from DX and sets
                   ; the condition codes depending on the result. The
                   ; contents of DX are not changed.
       TEST  DX, CX ; set the condition codes depending on the result
                    ; of performing the bitwise AND of the two operands.
                    ; The contents of both registers are unchanged.
```

```
680x0   cmp.l  d0, d4 ; subtract the 32-bit value stored in d0 from that
                      ; in d4 and set the condition codes depending on the
                      ; result. Neither the contents of d0 or d4 are
                      ; changed.
        cmpi.b #7, d5 ; subtract the integer 7 from the least significant
                      ; 8 bits of d5 and set the condition codes from the
                      ; value computed. The contents of  d5 is not
                      ; altered.
        tst.w  d1     ; set the condition codes depending on the value
                      ; stored in the least significant 16 bits of d1.
```

Table 11.3   Conditional test instructions

80x86	CMP	set the condition flags on the result of subtracting the source operand from the destination operand
	CMPS	set the condition flags as the result of comparing two strings of bytes or words
	TST	the two operands are ANDed together and the result affects the condition flags
680x0	cmp	set the condition flags on the result of subtracting the source operand from the destination operand
	tst	compare the destination operand with zero and sets the condition flags accordingly

(b) Branch instructions

Both the 80x86 and the 680x0 have an extensive set of conditional branch instructions as shown in Table 11.4. Each of these instructions uses the value of one or more of the condition codes or flags to determine whether the next instruction to be obeyed is the next one in sequence or the one supplied as the operand of the conditional jump instruction. Both architectures include unconditional branch instructions.

Examples

```
80x86   JZ A ; go to the instruction labelled A if the result of the
             ; previous instruction was zero, that is, the Z condition
             ; code is set
        JGE B ; go to the instruction labelled B if the result of the
              ; previous instruction was greater than or equal to 0, that
              ; is, the C condition code is clear.
```

```
680x0   beq lab    ; jump to the instruction labelled lab if the result of
                   ; the last instruction was equal to zero, that is, the Z
                   ; condition code was set, otherwise take no action.
        bpl there  ; jump to the instruction labelled there if the result
                   ; of the last instruction was positive, otherwise take
                   ; no action
```

Table 11.4 Some jump and branch instructions

Branch condition	Condition code tested	80x86	680x0
zero bit clear	$z = 0$	JNZ	bne
zero bit set	$z = 1$	JZ	beq
negative bit clear	$n = 0$	JNS	bpl
negative bit set	$n = 1$	JS	bmi
last result ≥ 0	z, n, v	JGE	bge
last result less than 0	n, v	JL	blt
parity odd		JPO	
parity even		JPE	
always branch		JMP	jmp
			bra

(c) Subroutine call and return

Another class of transfer of control instructions is the subroutine entry and exit instructions, often called call and return instructions, respectively. There are frequent cases in programming where the same sequence of instructions is required at more than one place in a program. Instead of writing the code in both places, it may be written once as a subroutine and call instructions inserted in the code at the appropriate place to cause transfer of control to the subroutine. At the end of the subroutine, control has to be returned to the instruction following the call and this is performed by the return instruction which is the final instruction executed in the subroutine. This is illustrated in Figure 11.6.

In order for this action to be possible the return address has to be stored when the subroutine is called and this address restored to the program counter by the return instruction. Subroutines often call other subroutines and hence the storage structure used to store the return addresses must be able to store several addresses and retrieve them in the correct order. The most common way of doing this is by the use of a data structure called a stack which acts as a last-in first-out store. Stacks are explained in more details later in this chapter. On the 80x86 the instructions for subroutine entry and

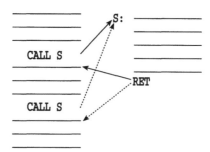

Figure 11.6   Subroutine call and return.

exit are called CALL and RET whereas on the 680xo they are JSR and RTS although they have similar actions.

Examples

```
80x86   CALL SUB ; go to the instruction labelled SUB and store the return
                 ; address on the stack
        RET      ; return from the current subroutine by replacing the
                 ; program with that on the top of the stack

680xo   jsr sub  ; jump to the instruction labelled sub having stored the
        rts      ; address on the stack
```

11.4.5 Input–output instructions

Input and output devices are interfaced to the system by one or more registers and these registers are normally accessed by one of two different mechanisms. One method, called memory-mapped input–output, maps the input–output registers into the normal memory address space of the processor, thus allowing standard data movement instructions to be used to perform input–output operations. This is the mechanism used on the 680xo. The other technique is to provide special instructions, called IN and OUT on the 80x86, which are used solely to perform input–output, usually to/from a special register. The IN and OUT instructions take a port address as a parameter to identify the particular input–output device involved in the transfer. There are advantages and disadvantages to both techniques, for example, the use of special input–output instructions complicates the instruction set and the implementation but the use of memory mapping reduces the address space for real memory. Memory mapping has become dominant in newer architectures which have large memory address spaces and hence have no problems in losing a small amount of this space to input–output registers.

Examples

```
80x86   IN 20  ; input a byte into AL from port 20
        OUT 10 ; output the byte in AL to port 10
```

```
68oxo   move.b d0, ad  ; output the least significant 8 bits of d0 to the
                        ; peripheral which is memory mapped to memory
                        ; address ad
        move.b ad, d3  ; input the 8-bit value from the peripheral memory
                        ; mapped at address ad to the least significant 8
                        ; bits of d3
```

11.4.6 Other instructions

As well as the classes of instructions mentioned above, most processors provide additional instructions. All processors include an instruction to halt the processor and most processors, including the 68oxo and the 80x86, include an instruction which has no effect, a no-operation. This latter type of instruction can be useful when debugging or programming a timing loop. Most processors also provide some form of arithmetic shift operation which provides a quick means of division or multiplication by two. Readers requiring a detailed knowledge of the instruction set of a particular processor are encouraged to look at the manufacturer's processor handbook or to consult some of the references in the bibliography.

11.5 Operands

Consider an ADD instruction. The information required when the instruction is obeyed is:

1. the address of the two values to be added;

2. the address in memory where the result is to be placed;

3. the address of the next instruction to be obeyed.

This information may be given explicitly in the instruction or it may be implied. The task of the designer of the processor is to decide how this information is to be represented for that particular processor.

If an operand can reside anywhere in the address space of the processor then the address fields in an instruction must be the same size as the address bus. For a typical 16-bit microcomputer, the address bus is 16 bits wide, implying that an ADD instruction, which requires four addresses (the address of the two source operands, the destination address and the address of the next instruction), would require about 9 bytes of memory if all this address information were given explicitly. For 32-bit architectures the storage requirements would be approximately 17 bytes. This leads to excessive memory requirements so the designer has to find some way of reducing the storage required for each instruction. This can be done by reducing the number or size of operand fields.

11.5.1 Reducing the number of operand fields

The information required on instruction execution cannot be reduced, hence the only scope for the designer is either to make one or more operands implicit or to combine some of the operand fields.

The 80x86 and 680x0 instructions given previously had fewer than four operands. These architectures, together with many others, reduce the number of operands by using the following architectural modifications. If instructions are stored in sequence in memory the address of the next instruction will, most frequently, be a few words further on in memory, the exact number of words depending on the length of each instruction. This being so, a register, the program counter, can be used to store the address of the next instruction. The addition of a small constant to the program counter will give the address of the next instruction in most cases. In fact the operation of updating the program counter is not as complex as it might appear. The requirement is simply that the program counter be incremented after each word of an instruction has been fetched. The inclusion of a program counter removes the need for a next instruction address field, but means that the branch class of instructions have to be provided to change the value of the program counter when the next instruction to be executed is not the next one in sequence.

With the above modification an ADD instruction still requires three operand fields. A common method of reducing this still further is to amalgamate one of the source fields with the destination field, so that the result of the operation overwrites one of the source operands. This reduces the number of operand fields to two, at the expense of providing a copy operation to save the overwritten source operand before it is overwritten, if necessary.

To reduce the number of operands still further, one or more of the operands must be implied. A common technique, employed on older architectures, is to provide a special register called an accumulator, to and from which all ALU operations take place. Hence an ADD instruction requires only a single operand on such an architecture since, by implication, one operand will be found in, and the result placed back in, the accumulator.

This technique can be taken to its logical conclusion and all the operands implied so that the ADD instruction would require no explicit operands. It would be possible to do this assuming that the operands and results were always in fixed registers or memory locations, but this creates problems since information has to be moved from place to place to satisfy the requirements of different instructions. A better solution is to use a stack architecture. A stack may be thought of as a last-in-first-out (LIFO) memory structure. The two operands of the ADD instruction have to be loaded onto the stack by previous instructions. The ADD instruction removes these two operands from the stack, computes the result and places it back on the stack. All instructions in this type of architecture obtain their operands from and put the results back on the stack. Hence the stack acts as a communication area between instructions. For this type of architecture extra instructions are required to load data on to the stack and to store information from the stack at particular positions in main memory. The possible options for the designer in reducing the number of address fields are shown in Table 11.5.

Table 11.5   Instruction variations using ADD as an example

Instruction type	Example	Result
4 address	ADD A, B, C, xxx	operands in A and B result in C next instruction at address xxx
3 address	ADD A, B, C	operands in A and B result in C next instruction next in sequence
2 address	ADD A, B	operands in A and B result overwrites B next instruction next in sequence
1 address	ADD A	operands in A and accumulator result overwrites accumulator next instruction next in sequence
0 address	ADD	both operands on top two stack positions result put back on top of stack next instruction next in sequence

Although the techniques outlined above greatly reduce the size of an instruction the computer designer is also concerned with the size of the program and the speed at which it operates. There is no simple correlation among all these factors, hence the range of different processor architectures. In fact many computers designed ten to twenty years ago cannot be classified as falling into any one of these categories; they encode different instructions using a mixture of zero, one and two addressing forms. The Motorola 680x0 and Intel 80x86 are examples of such processor architectures. The Intel 80x86 has some instructions that can use one of a number of registers as operands whereas other instructions do not allow choice and use specified registers. The 680x0 is more regular and orthogonal, that is, many instructions can use any register and addressing mode. More modern reduced instruction set computers (RISC) tend to favour simpler coding schemes and are often 3-address architectures. RISC architectures are described in Chapter 17.

11.5.2 Reducing the size of operand fields

As well as reducing the number of operand fields, the computer designer can also consider reducing the size of operand fields. The problem here is that to address 2^n words of memory a minimum of n bits are required. This suggests that there is a limit to the reduction in the size of the operand fields if the complete addressing range of the processor is to be supported. However, there is a method that designers use specifying the address indirectly rather than directly. If a register can hold any address in main memory then instead of quoting the memory address required for an operand the instruction could contain the address of a register that has been preloaded with the required memory address. Since the number of registers in a processor is generally very much smaller than the number of words in main memory, typically 16 or 32 as opposed to 2^{16} or 2^{32}, the size of the operand field in an instruction can be reduced, from 16 or 32 bits to four or five bits in the example quoted. There is, of course, a penalty for doing this. Instead of the operand address being obtained from the instruction the address required has to be fetched from the register specified in the instruction and this imposes a time penalty as an extra read operation has to be performed. Also the address has to be placed in the register before the instruction is executed and this might require the use of an extra instruction. However, in spite of these time penalties, this technique of indirect addressing is frequently used and examples are given later.

11.6 Addressing modes

The method by which an operand is encoded into an instruction is known as its addressing mode. There are many different modes and many of the common ones are described below. The address required to access an operand is known as the effective address of the operand and it is this value that has to be calculated from the addressing mode information contained in the instruction.

11.6.1 Direct or absolute addressing mode

The simplest way of encoding the address information is directly to encode the address as a bit pattern in the opcode field. This is known as direct or absolute addressing, see Figure 11.7. For example, the address 1020 decimal would be encoded in a 16-bit field as the bit pattern 0000001111111100. The size of the address field determines the largest address that can be stored and hence the amount of memory that can be addressed by this addressing mode for that instruction.

Examples

```
80x86   MOV   DX, w[1234] ; move the contents of word address 1234 to DX

680x0   move.w 122, d5   ; move the 16-bit contents of memory location 122
                         ; to register d5
```

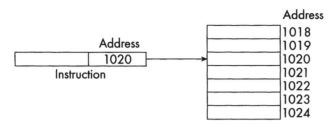

Figure 11.7   Direct addressing.

11.6.2 Indirect addressing mode

The designer may wish to use indirect addressing mode to reduce the number of bits required to specify an operand or to improve the access to programmers data structures. In indirect addressing, shown in Figure 11.8, the address quoted in the operand field of the instruction is not the address of the required operand but the address of a location holding the required address. For indirect addressing the effective address is obtained by performing a read operation on the address specified in the operand field. The address quoted in an instruction is usually a register address rather than a memory address as this requires fewer bits.

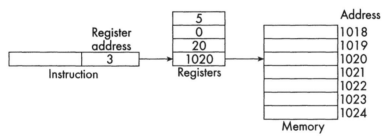

Figure 11.8   Indirect addressing.

To differentiate between direct and indirect addressing, the operand field has to contain information which specifies the addressing mode used as well as the address. To do this, most computers split the operand field into two subfields; the addressing mode, defining the addressing scheme to be used to calculate the effective address of the operand and the address to be used in the effective address calculation, that is, a register address. If only two addressing schemes, or modes, as discussed so far, were allowed, then only a single bit would be required to differentiate among them. However, many computers in widespread use today support a range of addressing modes and hence several bits are required to differentiate between them. The 80x86, with its roots in an old design, only supports a limited number of addressing modes. The Motorola 680x0, a more modern design, contains a large number of addressing modes. More modern RISC processors tend to have fewer addressing modes, sometimes only one.

The two addressing modes discussed above, direct and indirect, are sufficient to enable the programmer to specify any type of addressing required. However, some more complex addressing occur so frequently that it is more convenient for the programmer and more efficient for the implementation if extra addressing modes are provided in the architecture. Some of these additional addressing modes, available on the 680x0 but not the 80x86, are described below.

11.6.3 Autoincrement mode

This addressing mode is the same as indirect addressing except that the register used is incremented after the effective address has been calculated as shown in Figure 11.9.

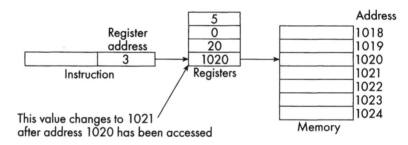

Figure 11.9   Autoincrement addressing.

Identical behaviour can be produced by using the required opcode with indirect addressing plus an extra instruction to increment the register contents if autoincrement is not supported on a particular processor. Note that the register contents are incremented by a constant which depends on the size of the data item being accessed. On the 680x0, which supports this form of addressing, the increment is one for byte operands, two for word operands and four for longword operands. The reason for this is because the register may be used as a pointer to a vector of such data items. Incrementing the register contents by these amounts means that the register points to the next byte, word or longword in the vector.

Examples

```
680x0   move.w  (a0)+, d2    ; move the contents of the memory word whose
                             ; address is in a0 to d2 and then increment
                             ; thecontents of a0 by 2
        move.b  d1,   (a1)+  ; move the least significant 8 bits of d1 to
                             ; the memory location whose address is in a1
                             ; and then increment the contents of a1 by 1
```

11.6.4 Autodecrement mode

This mode has the same action as indirect addressing except that the register used is decremented before the effective address is calculated as shown in Figure 11.10.

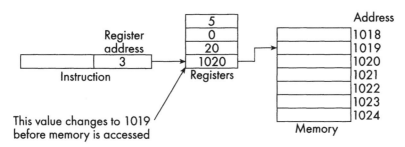

Figure 11.10 Autodecrement addressing.

The amount by which the register is decremented is determined in exactly the same way as for autoincrement addressing. This mode can also be simulated by two instructions, one to decrement the register contents and another indirectly to access the register used.

Examples

```
680xo   move.l -(a2), d3 ; subtract 4 from the contents of a2 and then
                         ; move the contents of the longword whose memory
                         ; address is in a2 to d3
```

11.6.5 Index mode

Both a register and a small integer called an offset are specified for this mode. The effective address is calculated as the sum of the contents of the register and the offset as shown in Figure 11.11.

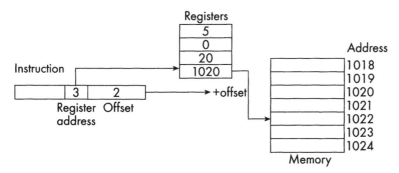

Figure 11.11 Indexed addressing.

The offset value is normally stored as part of the instruction, thus making instructions using this addressing mode longer than instructions using any of the previously discussed addressing modes.

Examples

```
680x0   move.w 4(a2), d1       ; move the word whose address is
                               ; (contents of a2)+ 4 to d1
        move.b 3(a0, d0.b),d1  ; this is a more general mode available on
                               ; the 680x0. Move the byte whose address is
                               ; the sum of 3, the 32-bit contents of a0
                               ; and the contents of the least significant
                               ; 8 bits of d0 to the least significant 8
                               ; bits of d1
```

11.6.6 Relative mode

Using this mode, the address in the operand field is an address relative to the position of the instruction. The effective address is the sum of the content of the address field and the current contents of the program counter as shown in Figure 11.12.

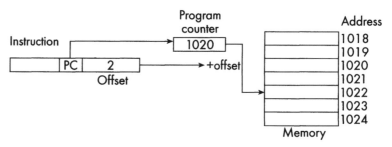

Figure 11.12 Relative addressing.

Examples

```
680x0   move.w 1000(pc), d1  ; move the word whose address is the sum of
                             ; 1000 and the contents of the program counter
                             ; to d1
```

11.6.7 Immediate mode

The contents of the address part of the operand field are regarded as a constant to be used as the operand. The effective address is the operand field itself, that is, part of the current instruction. This is the addressing mode used to include constants in a program.

Examples

80x86   MOV DX, 3 ; load the register DX with the decimal constant 3

680x0   move.b #2, d2 ; move the constant 2 to the least significant 8
                       ; bits of d2

11.6.8 Other addressing modes

In addition to the addressing modes described above, there are many more modes possible, although they are not common. For example, there are indirect forms of many of the modes described above, such as indirect autoincrement, where the effective address is the content of the location whose address is the content of the location whose address is given in the operand field of the instruction; it is simply one level of indirection more than autoincrement mode. As stated above, additional modes are not strictly necessary as they can all be formed by combinations of other modes. The more complicated the addressing mode the longer the execution time of the instruction, but it is usually quicker to use a complicated addressing mode rather than to use simpler modes and extra instructions.

11.7 Instruction encoding

The opcodes and operands of an instruction have to be encoded as a bit pattern and stored in the memory of the computer. In most computers, including the 80x86 and the 680x0, instructions occupy one or more words. Often these words are divided into fields, each of which represents a separate feature of the instruction, for example, the opcode or the mode of an operand. The fields are encoded to make decoding by the processor as simple as possible within the space constraint of the field.

Examples

		Binary	*Hexadecimal*
80x86	AH, 7	1011010000000111	B407

where the bottom eight bits represent the constant (seven in this case) and the top eight bits represent the opcode and destination register.

		Binary	*Hexadecimal*
680x0	move.w d0, d1	0011001000000000	3200

with the bit encoding partitioned into fields as

00	11	000001	000000
size	destination	source	

	Binary	*Hexadecimal*
moveq #3, d2	0111010000000011	7403

with the bit encoding partitioned into fields as

0111	010	0	00000011
	register		data

	Binary	*Hexadecimal*
bra L1	01100000xxxxxxxx	60yy

where yy is the address offset.

Notice that the 680x0 has the more regular structure in so far as the opcode field is distinct from the operand addressing fields.

11.8 Use of addressing modes

The reader might be wondering why a computer designer would provide such a wide range of addressing modes. The range of addressing modes is necessitated by the types of data structure found in high level programming languages and how these structures are accessed. There are two basic types of operand, constants and variables. As the name implies, constants are values that remain constant during the execution of a program. They are also known as literals and examples are the number 2 and the character string abc. Operands that change during execution are called variables and instances of these are given symbolic names, called identifiers, to differentiate them. Thus the identifier A could represent a variable whose value could change from, say, 0 to 5 and then 8 during the execution of a program.

11.8.1 Table

Constants and variables can be organized into structures where each item in the structure bears a relationship to other items in the structure. The simplest type of structure is a table or vector and the simplest form is a list of items of the same type, for example, integers.

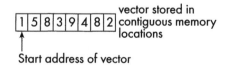

Figure 11.13 A vector of integers.

A table is normally stored in memory in consecutive memory locations. The table is characterized by a start address, sometimes called the base address and each item is characterized by an index or offset from this base address. The address of any item may then be obtained by adding its index into the table to the base address of the table in memory, assuming that each data item occupies a single memory location. This arithmetic is exactly that which is performed in indexed addressing. In present 16- and 32-bit microcomputers indexed addressing modes are provided. These take into account the number of words occupied by each data item, since characters typically take eight bits each whilst integers take 16 or 32 bits.

Frequently, a table structure has to be searched to see if it contains a particular item. The simplest form of search is a linear search in which each item in the table is examined, starting at the beginning. This form of search can use autoincrement addressing where the base address of the vector is placed in a register. When the first item is accessed using autoincrement mode the register contents are automatically incremented to point to the next data item in the table. Two dimensional table structures, matrices, are very common in mathematical applications and these are normally stored in memory either by row or by column. Accessing an individual item now requires two indices, one for the row address and one for the column address, and the address calculation is slightly more complex although indexed addressing is still required. Since this structure is so common in many applications, some processors have extra addressing modes to simplify the address calculation. This is the purpose of the register indirect with index addressing mode on the 680x0.

A table also has length and this is sometimes used to check that access to the table is within the limits of the table size. Each address calculation then additionally has to check the calculated address against a predefined constant. Some architectures have an instruction to allow this checking to be performed.

11.8.2 Lists

Another method of storing a set of items is in a data structure called a list. In this structure the separate items are stored anywhere in memory and each item includes a pointer which contains the address of the next item in the list, (see Figure 11.14).

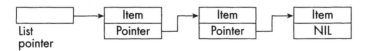

Figure 11.14 Representation of a list.

The start of the list is pointed to by a standard header and the end of the list is signified by a special marker called nil. The main difference between a list and vector or table is in the method of access. Whereas in a table, access to any item takes the same amount of time, since the address of any item is obtained by adding its offset to the base address, in a list, access to any item is only via the list header and a chain of pointers thus the access time depends on the position of the item in the list. The standard operations allowed on a list rely on the ability to manipulate the address pointers and hence on indirect addressing.

11.8.3 Stacks

A stack is a form of data structure with the property that the last item written is the first item to be read, that is, the stack acts as a last-in first-out (LIFO) structure already referred to. The operations allowed include adding another item to the stack (pushing), taking the top item from the stack (popping) and testing whether there are any items on the stack. A stack may be represented by a contiguous block of memory with a pointer indicating the current top, see Figure 11.15.

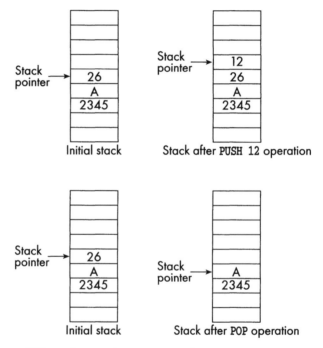

Figure 11.15 Effect of operations on a stack.

The operation of pushing a value on to the stack involves moving the stack pointer upwards and writing the value to the top of the stack using indirect addressing via the stack pointer. Similarly the operation of popping a value off the stack involves reading the top value indirectly via the stack pointer and then moving the stack pointer value downwards. Notice that the operations of adjusting the value of the pointer occur before the stack access in one operation and after the access in the other operation. The operations of push and pop may be accomplished by the use of the autoincrement and autodecrement addressing modes. Note that the way in which the autoincrement and autodecrement addressing modes were defined previously means that the stack has to work downwards in memory, that is, pushing a value is performed using autodecrement mode and popping uses autoincrement mode. The definitions of autoincrement and autodecrement mode given above, that is, pre-increment autoincrement and post-decrement autodecrement, are those most frequently found on current processors. Post-increment autoincrement and pre-decrement autodecrement are occasionally used and they result in a stack which works upwards. The 80x86 provides PUSH and POP operations for stack manipulation whereas the 680x0 has autoincrement and autodecrement addressing modes which can be used with many instructions for stack manipulation.

The stack provides an orderly method for storing procedure or subroutine return addresses as described previously. This is another reason why autoincrement and autodecrement modes are common on many computers.

11.8.4 Queues

A queue is a similar to a stack except that access for reading and writing is to opposite ends of the structure and hence it acts as a first-in first-out structure (FIFO), and so corresponds to the normal notion of a queue. A queue is represented by a contiguous block of memory with two pointers, one pointing to the head of the queue and the other to the tail. Access to the head and tail of the queue uses the same addressing mode, either autoincrement or autodecrement depending on the direction in which the queue grows. As data is added and removed from the queue the data structure moves through memory since both types of access move the pointers in the same direction. This is obviously inconvenient so a queue is normally mapped on to a fixed block of memory and the pointers wrap around when they reach the block boundary (see Figure 11.16). Checking is required to detect the pointers reaching the boundary and also for the conditions of underflow, trying to read a value when the structure is empty, and overflow, trying to write a value when the structure is full.

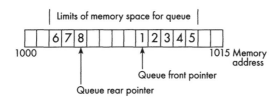

Figure 11.16 Circular queue containing 1,2,3,4,5,6,7,8.

Both stacks and queues may also be implemented as linked lists as described earlier, in which case they require indirect addressing to access the structures.

These are just some of the data structures found in high-level programming languages and used by assembly code programmers. As can be seen from the foregoing discussion, the implementation of these structures requires a number of different addressing schemes and this is why many modern processors support a range of addressing modes. As has been shown, the only addressing modes that are strictly necessary are the direct and indirect modes; the other modes can be simulated by just these two modes and more instructions. However, the provision of the extra addressing modes makes for more efficient implementation in terms of memory use.

11.9 Examples to illustrate assembly code and addressing modes

The previous sections have described some of the features of machine code instructions and assembly languages. In this section, a number of small assembly code programs are presented with the equivalent machine code for illustrative purposes. The examples are extensively documented so that they should be understandable even though not all the instructions have been explained in detail previously. Readers who experience any difficulty or require more information should consult one of the relevant texts mentioned in the bibliography. The code can be downloaded from the website.

The code below contains some software interrupt or trap instructions – trap on the 680x0 and INT on the 80x86. These instructions are calls to routines available in the operating system of the computer used to assemble the code. They result in input–output operations being performed as specified in the comments. Reading from the computer keyboard and writing information to the screen involves several instructions and it is easier and less error prone if these are provided with the system and they are used here to simplify the code. They act in a similar way to CALL and JSR instructions. More details of interrupts and software interrupts are given in Chapter 7.

11.9.1 Program to count the number of occurrences in a vector

These programs count the number of times a given item, identified by the symbol 'lookup', occurs in the table and leaves the result in a register. The algorithm used is to scan the vector from beginning to end, incrementing a count whenever the desired item is found. The code is not the most efficient that could be written for this problem; it is written to be easy to comprehend and to illustrate the use of instructions and addressing modes.

80x86 code

Addr (hex)	Code (hex)	Label	Opcode	Operands	Comments
0100	B006	START:	MOV	AL,LOOKUP	; store search item in ; AL
0102	B100		MOV	CL,0	; initialize count to 0
0104	BB0000		MOV	BX,0	; initial table offset
0107	BF2D01		MOV	DI,LENGTH	; move address of ; length to DI

Addr (hex)	Code (hex)	Label	Opcode	Operands	Comments
010A	3A872F01	LOOPL:	CMP	AL,TABLE[BX]	; compare item and ; current table posn
010E	7502		JNE	EOL	; if different don't ; increment count
0110	FEC1		INC	CL	; increment count
0112	43	EOL:	INC	BX	; increment table ; pointer
0113	3B1D		CMP	BX,[DI]	; compare table pointer ; table length
0115	75F3		JNE	LOOPL	; if not equal compare ; next items
0117	88C8		MOV	AL,CL	; else move count to AL ; for output
0119	0430		ADD	AL,'0'	; convert to char code
011B	50		PUSH	AX	; put AX onto the stack
011C	8BD4		MOV	DX,SP	; MS-DOS memory-pointer ; now points to the ; AL-value
011E	B90100		MOV	CX,1	; we will output 1 byte
0121	BB0100		MOV	BX,1	; open-file handle for ; standard output 1
0124	B440		MOV	AH,040	; function number for ; MS-DOS write
0126	CD21		INT	33	; write the AL-value to ; standard output
0128	B8004C		MOV	AX, 04C00	; exit back to DOS
012B	CD21		INT	33	
	0006	LOOKUP:	EQU	6	
012D	0500	LENGTH:	DW	5	
012F	0703090706	TABLE:	DB	7,3,9,7,6	

68oxo code

Addr (hex)	Code (hex)	Label	Opcode	Operands	Comments
		lookup:	equ	2	; the symbol 'lookup' ; is equivalent to 2
0000	05	length:	dc.b	5	; length contains 5, ; the table length
0001	0703090106	table:	dc.b	7,3,9,1,6	; table holds 7,3,9,1,6
0006	207c	start:	move.l	#table,a0	; puts address of table
	0000				; to address register 0
	0001				; base address of table ; vector

Addr (hex)	Code (hex)	Label	Opcode	Operands	Comments
000c	1239 0000 0000		move.b	length,d1	; puts length of table ; in data register 1
0012	303c 0000		move.w	#0,d0	; initialize d0, to ; hold result, to 0
0016	0c18 0002	loop:	cmp.b	#lookup,(a0)+	; compare next table ; entry with required ; value
001a	6602		bne	eol	; if the two operands ; compared in the last ; two instructions were ; unequal, go to the ; statement labelled ; eol
001c	5240		addq	#1,d0	; increment the count ; by 1
001e	5341	eol:	subq	#1,d1	; decrease count of the ; number of items in ; the table left to ; search
0020	66f4		bne	loop	; if not at the end of ; the table go back to ; the statement ; labelled loop
0022	4e72			stop end	; halt execution ; end of program

11.9.2 Program to add two single-digit integers

These programs illustrate the conversion required between internal and external representations when values are input and output. The 680x0 code also illustrates the use of subroutines.

80x86

Addr (hex)	Code (hex)	Label	Opcode	Operands	Comments
0100	B407	START:	MOV	AH,7	; code for DOS input ; char function
0102	CD21		INT	33	; input char code ; returned into AL
0104	2C30		SUB	AL,'0'	; convert from char ; code to int
0106	8AD8		MOV	BL,AL	; store in BL

Examples to illustrate assembly code and addressing modes

Addr (hex)	Code (hex)	Label	Opcode	Operands	Comments
0108	B407		MOV	AH,7	; code for DOS input ; char function
010A	CD21		INT	33	; input char code ; returned in AL
010C	2C30		SUB	AL,'0'	; convert to char code ; in AL
010E	00D8		ADD	AL,BL	; add two ints input, ; store in AL
0110	3C0A		CMP	AL,10	; compare sum with 10 ; decimal
0112	7D0A		JGE	MTO	; if >10 go to ; statement labelled ; MTO
0114	0430		ADD	AL,'0'	; convert to char code
0116	E81A00		CALL	OUT_VALUE	; output value
0119	B8004C		MOV	AX,04C00	; return to DOS
011C	CD21		INT	33	
011E	2C0A	MTO:	SUB	AL,10	
0120	88C4		MOV	AH,AL	; store in AH
0122	B031		MOV	AL,'1'	; put this into another ; register
0124	E80C00		CALL	OUT_VALUE	; output value
0127	88E0		MOV	AL,AH	; restore AL to ; original value
0129	0430		ADD	AL,'0'	; convert to char code
012B	E80500		CALL	OUT_VALUE	; output value
012E	B8004C		MOV	AX,04C00	; return to DOS
0131	CD21		INT	33	
		OUT_VALUE:			
0133	50		PUSH	AX	; push AL value onto ; the stack
0134	8BD4		MOV	DX,SP	; MS-DOS memory-pointer ; now ; points to the AL ; value
0136	B90100		MOV	CX,1	; we will output 1 byte
0139	BB 01 00		MOV	BX,1	; open-file handle for ; standard output 1
013C	B440		MOV	AH,040	; function number for ; MS-DOS write
013E	CD21		INT	33	; write the AL-value to ; standard output

Addr (hex)	Code (hex)	Label	Opcode	Operands	Comments
0140	58		POP	AX	; pop AL back off the ; stack
0141	C3		RET		; return from ; subroutine

68oxo

Addr (hex)	Code (hex)	Label	Opcode	Operands	Comments
0000	2e7c 0000 0bb8	start:	move.1	#3000,a7	; initialize stack ; pointer to 3000
0006	7000		moveq	#0,d0	; set d0 to 0
0008	7200		moveq	#0,d1	; set d1 to 0
000a	6218		jsr	input	; jump to subroutine ; labelled input
000c	1200		move.b	d0, d1	; copy the value input ; into d1
000e	611e		jsr	input	; jump to subroutine ; input
0010	d041		add.w	d1,d0	; add the two values ; input together into ; d0
0012	b07c 000a		cmp.w	#10,d0	; is total greater than ; 10?
0016	6a04		bpl	mto	; if so go to statement ; labelled mto
0018	6120		jsr	output	; else output result by ; calling subroutine ; output
001a	4e72		stop		; and stop execution
001c	90bc 0000 000a	mto:	sub.1	#10,d0	; gets lowest digit of ; total
0022	2200		move.1	d0,d1	; and save in d1
0024	7001		moveq	#1,d0	; first digit to output
0026	6112		jsr	output	; and output it
0028	2001		move.1	d1,d0	; restore second digit
002a	610e		jsr	output	; to d0 and output it
002c	4e72		stop		; halt execution
002e	4e4f	input:	trap	#15	; software interrupt
0030	0011		dc.w	$11	; parameter to ; interrupt meaning ; input

Addr (hex)	Code (hex)	Label	Opcode	Operands	Comments
0032	90bc 0000 0030		sub.l	#48, d0	; convert character ; input to integer code
0038	4e75		rts		; return from ; subroutine
003a	d0bc 0000 0030	output:	add.l	#48,d0	; convert integer value ; in d0 to character ; code
0040	4e4f		trap	#15	; software interrupt
0042	0012		dc.w	$12	; meaning output
0044	4e75		rts		; return from ; subroutine
			end		; end of program

11.9.3 Program to search a vector for a given input value

The algorithm used here is a sequential search through the vector, comparing each value with the given input value. If a match is found then the code for 'found' is output otherwise 'notfound' is output at the end of the program.

8o x86

Addr (hex)	Code (hex)	Label	Opcode	Operands	Comments
0100	BF3A01	START:	MOV	DI, LENGTH	; put address of length ; of table in D1
0103	8A1D		MOV	BL, [DI]	; put length of table ; in BL
0105	B407		MOV	AH, 7	; input into AL
0107	CD21		INT	33	; software interrupt
0109	2C30		SUB	AL, '0'	; make char input into ; int code
010B	BF3B01		MOV	DI, TABLE	; put table address ; into DI
010E	3A05	LOOP1:	CMP	AL, [DI]	; compare int to table ; value
0110	740F		JZ	MATCH	; if the same go to ; match
0112	47		INC	DI	; if not increment ; table value
0113	FECB		DEC	BL	; decrement length of ; table to be searched
0115	75F7		JNZ	LOOP1	; if more table to be ; searched go back

Addr (hex)	Code (hex)	Label	Opcode	Operands	Comments
0117	B030		MOV	AL, NOTFOUND	; code for notfound to ; AL
0119	E80F00		CALL	OUT_VALUE	; and output
011C	B8004C		MOV	AX, 04C00	; exit to DOS
011F	CD21		INT	33	
0121	B031	MATCH:	MOV	AL, FOUND	; code for found to AL
0123	E80500		CALL	OUT_VALUE	; and output
0126	B8004C		MOV	AX, 04C00	; exit to DOS
0129	CD21		INT	33	
		OUT_VALUE:			
012B	50		PUSH	AX	; push AL value onto ; the stack
012C	8BD4		MOV	DX, SP	; MS-DOS memory-pointer ; now points to the AL ; value
012E	B90100		MOV	CX, 1	; we will output 1 byte
0131	BB0100		MOV	BX, 1	; open-file handle for ; standard output is 1
0134	B440		MOV	AH, 040	; function number for ; MS-DOS write is 040
0136	CD21		INT	33	; write the AL-value to ; standard output
0138	58		POP	AX	; pop AL back off the ; stack
0139	C3		RET		
	0031	FOUND:	EQU	49	
	0030	NOTFOUND:	EQU	48	
013A	05	LENGTH:	DB	5	
013B	0703090106	TABLE:	DB	7,3,9,1,6	

68oxo

Addr (hex)	Code (hex)	Label	Opcode	Operands	Comments
		found:	equ	49	; found represented by ; character code 49
		notfnd:	equ	48	; notfound represented ; by code 48
0000	05	length:	dc.b	5	; location length ; contains constant 5
0001	0703090106	table:	dc.b	7,3,9,1,6	; table is that address ; of table of bytes

Addr (hex)	Code (hex)	Label	Opcode	Operands	Comments
0006	307c	start:	move.w	#table, a0	; start is the first
	0001				; instruction the
					; address of table
					; moved to register a0
000a	7000		moveq	#0, d0	; clear register d0
					; which will contain
					; the input value
000c	7200		moveq	#0, d1	; d1 contains offset of
					; current table value
000e	1239		move.b	length,d1	; initialize offset to
	0000				; the length of the
	0000				; table
0014	4e4f		trap	#15	; software interrupt
0016	0011		dc.w	$11	; parameter to
					; interrupt meaning
					; input
0018	903c		sub.b	#48, d0	; convert character
	0030				; input to integer code
001c	b018	loop:	cmp.b	(a0)+, d0	; compare the current
					; table value with the
					; required value and
					; point to the next
					; table position
001e	670e		beq	match	; if the values were
					; equal go the
					; statement labelled
					; match
0020	5341		subq.b	#1,d1	; reduce the count of
					; the number of table
					; items to check by 1
0022	66f8		bne	loop	; and jump if still
					; entries to check
0024	103c		mov.b	#notfnd,d0	; put the code for
	0030				; notfound into d0
0028	4e4f		trap	#15	; software interrupt
002a	0012		dc.w	$12	; parameter to
					; interrupt meaning
					; output
002c	4e72		stop		; terminate execution
002e	103c	match:	move.b	#found, d0	; put the code for
					; found into d0
0032	4e4f		trap	#15	; software interrupt

Addr (hex)	Code (hex)	Label	Opcode	Operands	Comments
0034	0012		dc.w	$12	; parameter to
					; interrupt meaning
					; output
0036	4e72		stop		; terminate execution
			end		; end of program

11.10 Summary

An instruction consists of an operation code (function) and, usually, one or more operands. The operands define addresses of memory locations containing data for the instruction and the addresses where results are to be deposited. Both the operation code and the operands are stored in memory as sets of bits and the operands are frequently represented as two separate fields called mode and register. The mode field specifies the way in which the effective address is calculated from the register field.

Most processors, including the 80x86 and the 680x0, have a number of different classes of instructions – data movement, arithmetical and logical, bit manipulation, program control, input–output and miscellaneous. The two basic forms of addressing mode are direct addressing and indirect addressing. Indirect addressing specifies the address of a location containing the required address. Many other addressing modes are possible and are included in some architectures, for example, the Motorola 680x0, in order to reduce the number of instructions necessary to manipulate the data structures typically found in programming. The use of these modes reduces memory requirement but complicates the processor architecture and implementation.

11.11 Exercises

Exercise 11.1 How many general purpose registers are available to the programmer and what length are they:

(a) on the 8086;

(b) on the 680x0?

Exercise 11.2 In each of the following cases, state which addressing mode would be used and give example code:

(a) to write a value to a given position in a table or vector;

(b) to push a value on to a stack;

(c) to add an item to a queue;

(d) to access an item in a list.

Exercise 11.3 Would you expect the results of the following two Motorola 680x0 instructions to give the same result? Why?

```
Add.b #1,  d0
Sub.b #-1, d0
```

Exercise 11.4 Write instructions or sequences of instructions for the following English descriptions.

(a) 8086
   i) Add the contents of register AX to register BX;
   ii) Add the contents of register BH to the contents of register CL;
   iii) Put the contents of location 2000 into register AX;
   iv) Put the contents of word 4 of the byte table whose address is in register DI into register BX;
   v) Put a zero in register BX if the AX contains 6, otherwise put a 1 in register BX;
   vi) Jump to the subroutine labelled SUB if register BX contains 2. The subroutine should put zero into register BX and return.

(B) 680x0
   i) Add the longword contents of register D_1 to register D_0;
   ii) Add the contents of word 2000 to the contents of register D_0;
   iii) Add the contents of byte 2000 to register D_0;
   iv) If D_1 contains 3 move zero to register D_1, otherwise move 1 to D_1;
   v) Jump to the subroutine labelled SUB if register D_1 contains 6. The subroutine should set the contents of D_1 to zero and return.

Exercise 11.5 Write a program fragment for the 80x86 to put 0 into register AX if register BX contains an even value and 1 if it contains an odd value. Repeat the program for the 680x0 assuming that the value to be tested is in D_1 and that the result is to be placed in D_0.

Exercise 11.6 It is possible to exchange the values in two registers without using an additional register or a memory location. Can you think of any way of doing this? [Note: there are at least two ways of doing this.]

Exercise 11.7 Write a program to sort a table of integers, each occupying a word of memory, into ascending order, in either 80x86 assembly language or 680x0 assembly language. [Hint: one algorithm to sort a table of items is to search for the smallest item and interchange that item with the first one in the table. This process is repeated, omitting the new item placed at the front of the table, until the complete table has been ordered.]

Exercise 11.8 Write a program in a high level language to simulate a queue as described in Section 11.8.4.

Exercise 11.9 In threaded code a sequence of subroutine calls is replaced by the address of the calls and code to call each one in turn, as shown below.

Non-threaded code			_Threaded code_		
Start:	jsr	first	Start:	movea.1	#List,a0
	jsr	second		movea.1	(a0)+,a1
	jsr	third		jmp	(a1)
			List:	dc.1	first
				dc.1	second
				dc.1	third

Why do you think threaded code was invented? Why is it to be preferred over the non-threaded alternative?

12

Introduction to system software

12.1 Introduction

In the previous chapter some computer architectures were described together with the way in which their features were reflected in the assembly and machine codes of some example processors. Processors can directly 'understand' only their own machine code; any other description of the program has to be transformed into machine code before it can be executed by the processor. In this chapter the software involved in this transformation and the relationship between languages and machines is discussed.

12.2 Assembly language and assemblers

An assembly language is one in which there is normally a small ratio, typically 1:1, between statements in the language and the equivalent machine code instructions. As we have seen in the previous chapter, an instruction at the machine code level consists of a bit pattern, some of the bits representing an operation code and some representing operands or addresses of operands. It is not convenient for the programmer to program at this level because it is easy to make mistakes and there is little correspondence between the bit patterns and the objects and operations of the application being programmed. Higher level languages were invented so that the programmer's job was easier and so that there was a closer correspondence between the objects and operations of the language and of the application. There is a hierarchy of higher level languages from those close to machine code to those close to a particular type of application. At the level of language immediately above machine code is assembly language. This language is very close to machine code, the main difference being the use of symbols instead of bit patterns. We have already seen the use of this type of language in the previous chapter, for instance, the use of ADD to specify the add instruction and A to represent an operand rather than bit patterns. These symbols are called mnemonics, as they are an aid to memory. The use of a higher level language means that the program cannot be directly executed by the computer since it 'understands' only bit patterns; the machine code defined by the designer. Hence the program in the higher level language has to be translated into the equivalent machine code before it can be executed. This translation can be performed by a computer, given a suitable program. The program that translates from assembly code to machine code is called an assembler and, since the machine code for different computers is different, a different assembler is required for each different type of computer. The translation process is relatively simple, since assembly code is so close to machine code. The major operation is one of changing mnemonics to the bit patterns they represent, as discussed later in this chapter. The advantage of using an assembler rather than a higher level language is that the programmer has available the complete range of machine facilities. A higher level language abstracts further away from the machine architecture and in many higher level languages some features of the machine are not accessible. It requires an experienced programmer to make efficient use of assembly code and it is relatively easy to make mistakes. The chances of producing an error free program decrease exponentially with the length and complexity of the program; assembly code is therefore not suitable for producing large programs, especially with inexperienced programmers. Typical figures for debugged code production are between five and 10 instructions/programmer/day for assembly code in a large-scale project, depending on the application.

Examples of assembly code were given in the previous chapter. As shown there, different assembly codes have different syntax but most assemblers have many common features. An assembly code instruction or statement typically consists of an opcode and zero, one or more operands, just like machine code, except that each of these quantities is represented by a symbol rather than a bit pattern. The symbols representing the opcodes are usually defined by the processor manufacturer whilst those used for the operands are defined by the programmer. The fields of the instruction are delimited by special characters which are specific to the particular assembly code, but a typical code might use the following scheme

label: opcode operand1, operand2 ; comments

which is close to that used by many Motorola 680x0 assemblers. Operand fields may be expressions rather than single symbols but these expressions are often limited in the operators they allow, for example, only allowing the use of plus, minus and some logical operators.

All assembly codes allow a label to be attached to an instruction or data item in the language so that reference may be made to that item symbolically from elsewhere in the program. One common use of a label on a statement is to enable a jump or call instruction elsewhere in the program to specify the labelled statement as the operand of the jump.

All assembly codes allow the programmer to intersperse assembly directives or pseudo operations with the code to be translated. These assembly directives allow the programmer to give information and to control the operation of the assembler. Two of the most common pseudo-operations are those to tell the assembler the starting address of the assembled code (or subsection of code) and those that tell the assembler that the end of the code to be assembled has been reached. Neither of these directives generates any code; they just control the assembler. Other types of directives do generate code. A typical example is the 'data' directive (dc.b for the Motorola 68000 examples in the previous chapter) which allows the user to place a vector of constants or expressions into the code. This directive is normally labelled so that its associated data can be referred to symbolically by instructions in the program. Another type of directive (equ for the Motorola 68000 examples in the previous chapter) allows the user to associate a symbol with a value. Table 12.1 shows some typical directives.

Table 12.1   Some assembler directives for typical 80x86 and 680x0 assemblers.

Meaning		80x86	680x0
Define position of code or data		ORG addr	.=addr
Define constant	byte	DB val,val,...	DC.B val,val,...
	word	DW val,val,...	DC.W val,val,...
	longword		DC.L val,val,...
Define storage block		DS size	DS.B size
			DS.W size
			DS.L size
Equate symbol with constant		sym: EQU const	sym: EQU const
End of assembly code		END	END

12.3 Translating from assembly code to machine code

A processor is able to execute only machine code, so any programs written in assembly code have to be translated into machine code before they can be executed. The translation task is relatively easy since the two codes differ only in syntax and not in semantic level, that is, different symbols are used to represent the same items in assembly and machine code. A program, called an assembler, converts programs written in assembly code to machine code.

The central task of an assembler is to parse – split up – assembly code statements into their constituent symbols and rewrite them as the equivalent machine code. The simplest way of storing the equivalence between symbols in assembly code and bit strings in machine code is to use a symbol table. The permanent symbol table (PST) stores all the possible opcodes defined for the assembly code together with their machine code equivalents. This table is fixed and built into the assembler so that the information is always available. The user symbol table (UST) stores the user defined symbols in an assembly code program with their machine code equivalents. This table will be different for different programs since no two programs, in general, use exactly the same set of symbols. The user symbol table is initially empty and entries are gradually added as definitions of user symbols are encountered in processing a program. As well as storing the values of symbols the symbol tables usually hold a number of other attributes of the symbols. For example, many architectures have several different classes of instructions each with its own different machine code format and content. This information is coded into the permanent symbol table so that the machine code for each instruction can be generated from its constituent parts.

Before describing the algorithm normally used by an assembler in detail it is worth considering why a simple approach will not suffice. The obvious algorithm for the translation is for the assembler to read in an assembly code statement, split it up into its constituent symbols, look up each symbol in a symbol table and write out the corresponding machine code in the correct position. The problem with this simple algorithm is that not all user symbols are defined before they are used, so the assembler may find a symbol that is used before it is defined, hence it will not exist in the symbol table. A simple example of this is a forward reference:

```
         bra      output
         . . . . . . . . . .
         . . . . . . . . . .
         . . . . . . . . . .
output:  move.b   d1,d0
```

In this example output is defined as the address of the move statement by being attached to that statement as a label, but it is used in the bra statement, which occurs before it in the code. When the assembler attempts to replace the symbol 'output' in the bra instruction with the corresponding machine code value it will discover that the symbol 'output' is not in the user symbol table and hence it does not know what value to put for 'output' in the bra statement. This is known as the forward reference problem.

How can this problem be overcome? There are two solutions:

(a) A two pass system

In this solution the assembler reads the assembly code twice, firstly to collect all the user symbol definitions into the user symbol table and the secondly to translate the assembly code into machine code.

(b) A one pass system

In this solution the assembler reads the assembly code only once. When it encounters a symbol whose definition is not in the user symbol table it leaves a 'hole' in the machine code and remembers in another table – the branch ahead table – where the 'hole' is and what assembly code symbol value has to be placed there. At the end of the assembly process the generated code may have 'holes' in it which have to be filled in by other software which uses the branch ahead table and the final user symbol table.

As can be seen from the description above the two pass system is much simpler and this approach is now used by all assemblers so the one pass system is not considered further here.

12.3.1 The two pass assembler

As the assembler translates assembly code into machine code it maps the machine code generated to addresses in memory where the code will be placed when it is executed. In order to do this it uses an assembly location counter, which keeps track of the next location in memory into which code can be placed. This counter is initially set to zero and incremented as statements are processed. An assembly code will have a pseudo-code or assembler directive which can be used directly to alter the value of this counter. This directive is often called . (that is, a dot) or ORG.

The first pass of a two pass assembler reads in the assembly code statements, statement by statement. Each statement is examined to see if it contains the definition of a user symbol which takes the form of a particular assembler directive such as equ or by the symbol appearing as a label. If it does, the symbol will be entered into the user symbol table with its value. The value of a symbol used as a label is the address of the instruction to which it is attached. The assembly location counter (ALC) keeps track of the address in memory into which the current instruction will be placed and thus it is the contents of this counter that will be inserted into the symbol table as the value of a label. The ALC is updated by the size of the equivalent machine code each time a new assembly code statement is processed. With some assembly codes, the computation of the size of the equivalent machine code is simple but with others it is more complex. For example, the size of the equivalent machine code for most Motorola 68oxo assembly code instructions depends on the addressing modes used for the operands and hence the mode of the operands has to be decoded to determine the increment to the ALC for each statement in such an assembly code program. If the assembly code statement is an assembler directive rather than an executable statement the assembler has to calculate the amount of memory, if any, the information associated with this directive will take in the final code produced. In some cases, for example, the definition of the value of a symbol, no code is generated so the ALC does not have to be updated, but with an assembly code directive such as .db each successive item takes up a byte of memory so the action required in pass one of the assembler is to calculate the number of items in the list after the dc.b and update the ALC by that amount. When the end of the assembly code program is reached, normally denoted by an assembly code directive such as end, pass one terminates and pass two commences. The pseudo code for pass 1 is

> set ALC to 0
> for all statements
>> parse the statement
>> if the statement is the END directive exit
>> if the statement contains an opcode
>> if a label is present
>>> put label and ALC value in UST
>>> calculate the space requirements from
>>>> the permanent symbol table and
>>>> the addressing modes of the operands
>> if the statement contains an assembler directive
>>> call the function to perform the action for the directive
>>>> including calculating the space requirements
>> update the ALC

In pass two of the assembler the code is translated into machine code using the symbol definitions in the permanent and user symbol tables. The code produced is usually buffered in an internal buffer before being output to a file on disc. The assembly code is read, statement by statement, and the opcode is translated using the information in the permanent symbol table. The operands are translated taking into account the addressing modes and using the symbol values stored in the user symbol table. The ALC is updated as described for pass one. Labels are ignored in this pass and the action taken on encountering an assembly code directive is specific to that assembly code directive. For example, for .db the items in the list following are translated, item by item and placed in successive bytes in the output buffer. The pseudo code corresponding to the pass 2 algorithm is

> set ALC to 0
> for all statements
>> parse the statement
>> if the statement is the END directive exit
>> if the statement contains an opcode
>>> get code template from PST
>>> decode operands, add to code
>>> output code and ALC value to buffer
>> if the statement contains a directive
>>> call the appropriate function to deal with the particular directive

It is worth noting here that the major problem with the design of any translator, including an assembler, is deciding how to deal with all possible errors in the input. If a user makes an error in the code input to the translator it should normally attempt to recover so that it can check for errors in succeeding statements. The problem is that the user may make errors anywhere in the code and designing a translator to cope with any possible error is difficult.

12.4 Relocation

A major question which has to be resolved in the translation of programs into machine code is when the decision is made to determine where in memory the machine code equivalent of the program will be placed when the program is executed. In the discussion above, it was assumed that the decision was made by the programmer, either by using the default value for the ALC or by setting the ALC to the desired value using the appropriate assembler directive. If the programmer has sole use of the computer and generates all the code required as a single module then this is a suitable method for defining the position of the code in memory. However, consider:

1. The programmer writes code as a set of modules. If one module is changed all the modules have to be retranslated because the code is generated in successive memory locations and any change to one module can change the position of all the following code.

2. The programmer wishes to include library modules in the code. Since the size of the library modules is unknown they have to be included as source code in the users program. This is wasteful, since library code is fixed and needs to be translated only once rather than for each use of the code.

3. The computer is a large timesharing machine which runs several users programs concurrently. If the programmer is allowed to decide where in memory the program resides it will not be possible to run several programs concurrently if they use the same memory locations.

These are some of the reasons why it is preferable to defer the decision as to where to place a program's code and data in memory to as late as possible and not to let the programmer specify it in the code. The problem with deferring the decision is that, in general, machine code will run correctly only at the place where the translator assumed it would run. Consider the assembly code statement:

```
bra    output
```

where 'output' is a label on a statement defined somewhere else in the program. Some assemblers will generate code with the absolute address of the instruction labelled 'output' in the operand field of the branch instruction so that, on execution, the next instruction to be executed after the branch instruction will be the one labelled output. Assuming that output has the value 2000 and that the code starts at location 0, if the code is now moved to start at 5000 then the program will not work correctly since when the branch instruction is executed it will still jump to location 2000 which does not now contain the correct code. The jump should have been to location 7000 to work correctly. One way on ensuring that it does work correctly in such circumstances is to use relative addressing rather than absolute addressing, that is, to store the distance between the labelled statement and the current one, rather than the labelled statement's address. Thus the example above would not store 2000 in the operand field of the bra instruction but would store the difference between the address of the instruction labelled output and the bra instruction. If the code is now moved in memory the program will work correctly since it will jump to an instruction a given distance from the bra instruction. Code that will work identically wherever it is placed in memory is known as position independent code. Some assemblers can be configured to generate this type of code but it does require the computer to have the requisite addressing modes and not all architectures do (for example, the Intel 80x86). If an architecture does not allow position independent code to be generated then the alternative is to relocate the code when it is moved or loaded at a different location from which it was assembled. Relocation of the code implies adjusting values of fields in the machine code of a program. In order to know which fields have to be adjusted the assembler has to generate a table, called the relocation directory, indicating which locations in the code have to be changed if the code is relocated. The table also contains some extra information since operands may be expressions, not just single symbols, and in this general case the adjustment to the field might not be as simple as presented here. Assembly code programming systems that allow the programmer to write programs as sets of modules include directives so that the programmer can specify which symbols are relocatable and the assembler can generate the appropriate relocation table.

12.5 Linking

If the programmer is allowed to specify a program as a set of modules or segments that can be separately assembled then there is a further problem with the definition and use of symbols. Symbols may be defined in one module and used in another and this can give rise to another instance of the forward reference problem described above.

The solution to this problem used for the multi-module case is to use a separate program called a linker or link editor to link the assembler output of the modules together, that is, to fill in the values of symbols used in one module and defined in another. The linker also relocates the code since the programmer cannot tell when writing a module where it will reside in memory; that depends on the size of the preceding modules and the start address of the complete program. The advantage of being able to use multiple assembly code modules rather than just a single one is that it makes the whole translation process more efficient. If the programmer makes an error in a module only that module has to be reassembled and then linked with the other modules. For a large program this can save considerable time over reassembling all the code. Library modules can be provided already assembled and just linked with the user program as required.

The linker normally outputs relocatable code since it does not know where the final program will be loaded into memory.

12.5.1 The linker algorithm

In the previous section on the assembler algorithm the output was assumed to be a continuous stream of code with a start address. For the multiple module case, there is more information and structure to the assembler output. A typical relocatable loader would generate a block of output consisting of four sections:

Header
Code
External symbol directory
Relocation directory

The header section consists of management information such as the name of the module, the time and date of creation and the size of the code section. The code section consists of a string of bytes representing the translated code. The external symbol directory (ESD) contains symbols and their associated values defined in this module which can be referred to from other modules and symbols used but not defined in this module. The relocation directory (RLD) consists of the addresses of fields in the code which need to be adjusted if the code is relocated.

The input to the linker is a set of blocks, each one the result of assembling the code from a module. The linker uses a two pass algorithm to perform the linking and relocation. In the first pass the linker allocates space to the segments and calculates the relocation constant for each module by reading the segment sizes from the header sections. It assumes that the program will start at location o and thus the relocation constant for the first module is o, that for the second module is the size of the first module, that of the third module the combined length of the first and second modules and so on. It also builds a global symbol directory(GSD) by concatenating the symbols defined in the external symbol directories from each module. At the end of pass one this global directory contains all the symbols that can be accessed from any of the modules. During the second pass, the code is linked by filling in the references in the code to symbols that have been defined elsewhere.

This is done by correlating symbols in the external symbol table for the module which have been used but not defined in the module with the value of the same symbol in the global external symbol directory. The code is relocated by adding the relocation constant calculated in pass one to the code addresses specified in the relocation directory for each module.

Pass 1

> set relocation constant for first block to 0
> clear global symbol table
> for each module
>> read size of module from header section
>> store relocation constant for this block
>> compute relocation constant for next block to previous
>>> relocation constant + block size
>> read in symbols defined in ESD into GSD. Value is value in
>>> ESD + block relocation constant

Pass 2

> set relocation constant to value for first block
> output header section to buffer
> for each module
>> read in code from code section
>> read undefined symbols from ESD, look up in GSD and update
>>> code in specified position with symbol value
>> read in RLD and add relocation constant to code position given
>> output code and RLD

12.6 Loading

The output of the link editor will be a file containing the code to be run, together with relocation information, so that the code can be placed in any set of memory locations to be executed. The program that loads the output of the linker, usually called the object file, into memory is called a loader. An absolute loader will assume that the code does not have to be relocated and will just load the code at the address specified in the object file and transfer control to the start address to execute the program. A relocating loader, given the address from which to start loading the code, will load the object code, relocating it as necessary. On completion, it will transfer control to the loaded program at the given start address.

There is a different type of loader called a bootstrap loader. Consider the case of a computer that has just been switched on. How is a program loaded into the memory to be executed? The normal mechanism is for a small program – called a bootstrap loader, resident in non-volatile memory, to be automatically executed when the computer is powered up. This loader is very simple and normally only loads a more complex loader, usually from a fixed position on a hard disk, to which it passes control. This larger loader then loads more information from disk and the process is continued until all the information necessary to run the computer has been loaded. This process of a small program loading a larger program which loads a larger program is known as bootstrapping.

12.7 High-level languages

The level of the language used in developing software depends on a number of factors. The higher the level of language that can be used to develop software the cheaper the total development costs. The reason why lower level languages are used is because either the facilities needed are not available in a high-level language or the high-level language implementation is not efficient enough for the particular requirement. High-level languages are more application oriented and necessarily further away from the machine architecture and therefore more portable than lower level languages. Since much of today's programming is concerned with re-implementing a given application on a different computer, portability has a high priority.

Conventional high-level languages provide the user with a set of control and data structures. The control structures typically include assignment, conditional and repetition statements. An assignment statement allows the user to assign the value of an expression to a variable. In C, a common higher level language, an assignment statement would look like

$$total = item1 + item2;$$

where total is an identifier representing a variable that will hold the sum of the contents of the variables identified by item1 and item2. The symbol = is the assignment and the expression on the right hand side of this can be formed from variables, constants and arithmetic operators. A typical conditional statement is the IF statement which specifies the actions to be taken if a condition is true or false. An example in C is

$$if(x<2) \; x=x-y; \; else \; x=x+y;$$

On execution the conditional expression is evaluated, in this case the value of the variable named x is compared with the constant 2, and one of two actions taken. If the condition is true then the statement following the condition is executed, otherwise the statement following the else is executed. An example of a repetitive statement is the while statement which specifies that the following statement is to be executed while the condition is true. An example of a while construct in C is given below.

$$while \; (x<y) \; x=x+7;$$

On execution the condition is tested and, if it is true, the statement following is executed and control returns to the condition which is re-evaluated and so on. If the condition is false, control passes to the next instruction after the while construct. High-level languages usually have several different forms of conditional and repetitive statements.

Just as at the machine code level high-level languages have mechanisms for procedure call and return. These mechanisms are more elaborate than those at the machine level, allowing the programmer to specify parameters to the call. These parameters allow the programmer to tailor a particular call, that is, to give values that are specific to the particular call, and hence make it possible to write more general procedures.

High-level languages provide the programmer with a range of data structures. Some of the data structures provided in high-level languages have been described in Chapter 7. C, for example, supports all the data structures described here and more. The structures supported in any language depend on the use to which the language is intended to be put and hence different languages will support different data structures.

The question of which high-level language to use to develop software for a given application is a difficult question to answer since it depends on a large number of factors. The reason why there are so many different high-level languages in existence is that different applications require different features in a language; there is really no general purpose high-level language that is suitable for all applications. Also, with more knowledge, language designers have produced languages that are more efficient to execute and that contain more application oriented features. However, languages that were designed several decades ago are still in very frequent use simply because of the amount of investment made in programs in those languages. One classification of high-level languages is to divide them into scientific, commercial data processing and non numeric classes. An example in the first category is Fortran. Fortran was first designed in the 1950s but has been modified a number of times since. The main data structure required in numerical work is the vector and matrix and these are the only data structures provided in the language. The control structures provided in the language are very standard and mirror those available at the machine code level. In effect Fortran acts as a high-level assembler although later modifications have tried to raise the level of the language.

For commercial data processing, COBOL was the main language for many years. It originated in 1960 and has been updated many times. The main requirements of data processing applications are to handle structured files efficiently. COBOL therefore devotes a great deal of effort to file processing and allows the user to manipulate record structures which contain related items of different type and size, for example, address lists.

Non numeric applications cover a broad spectrum. Generally these languages require a larger set of data structures and a more extensive set of control structures. No one language is suitable for all types of application so we shall consider some subsets here. On small computers the efficiency of the language becomes important and it is for this reason that languages such as C and Java have become popular on these computers. Another class of languages is the so called string processing languages, typified by SNOBOL. These languages, as the name implies, are intended to manipulate string of characters very easily so that operations such as concatenating two strings and searching a string for a given substring are provided. Another class of applications concerns artificial intelligence. The leading language in this field is the logic programming language PROLOG which is of a completely different type to the other languages described above. Whereas the other languages, called imperative languages, require the programmer to describe how to solve the problem, PROLOG allows the programmer to describe the problem and let the system decide how, or whether, the problem can be solved with the information given. The implementation depends on the mathematical technique of theorem proving. Whilst this approach is attractive for applications other than artificial intelligence it is not applicable, at the present time, to all applications.

Currently there are two trends which are noticeable in high-level language programming. Firstly, much of the programming which is done today uses the C programming language or one of its derivatives. C was designed about 25 years ago to write the Unix operating system and has become very popular in the past ten years for a number of reasons. Firstly, the language is quite low level and hence it is relatively easy to produce efficient machine code. Secondly, since the language is low level, the programmer has access to all the features of the machine through the language. Finally, the language is relatively small and easy to learn. To give a flavour of the language a small program to sort a set of integers is given below.

```c
#define        TRUE    1
#define        FALSE   0

int main()
{
        int i, temp, sorted;
        int list[10];

        printf("\nType in number of integers followed by integers");
        scanf("%d",&n);
        for (i=0;i<n;i++)
                scanf("%d",&list[i]);

        do {    sorted = TRUE;
                for (i=0;i<n-1;i++)
                    if (list[i]>list[i+1])
                        {   temp = list[i];
                            list[i] = list[i+1];
                            list[i+1] = temp;
                            sorted = FALSE;
                        }
```

```
        } while (!sorted);

    printf("\nSorted list is ");
    for (i=0;i<n;i++)
        printf("%d ",list[i]);
    printf("\n\n");
}
```

The other trend is in the use of object oriented languages. In an object oriented language the model of computation is a set of objects comprising of data and associated access functions called methods which communicate with each other by sending messages. Inheritance is also a common feature of object oriented languages. An object is an instance of a class which defines its data and behaviour. Classes can be specialized by inheriting data and behaviour from other classes and then modifying them to produce the specialized behaviour required. Thus applications can be produced from a small number of base classes which are specialized for the particular application under development. This allows developers to reuse code easily, one of the major benefits claimed for object oriented programming. The best known true object oriented languages are Smalltalk and Eiffel, which were designed as object oriented languages from the outset. Other approaches to object orientation have been to take an existing language and modify it by adding some object orientation. C++ is the best known example of this and is probably the most widely used language with object orientation. However, C++ is based on the language C, which is not object oriented so it is really a hybrid language and programmers can write programs in C++ that are not object oriented. Java is currently the language favoured for object-based application.

The language to be used for programming the solution to a problem depends on many factors, not only the technical question of which is the best language to code the application. For example, translators must be available for the target computer and the library functions required must be available.

12.7.1 Implementation

There are two basic methods of implementing a high-level language; interpretation and compilation. The process of compilation translates a high-level language program into an equivalent set of machine code instructions which may then be directly executed (see Figure 12.1). Interpretation, on the other hand, simulates the action of the abstract machine defined by the high-level language (see Figures 12.2, 12.3 and 12.4). The abstract machine simulator, or interpreter, then 'understands' statements in the high-level language and can execute them. Another way of considering this is to remember that the machine designer has built a machine to interpret the machine code; an interpreter is simply a machine built in software to interpret another language at a higher level.

The basic differences between compilation and interpretation is that an interpreter is relatively simple to construct, is slow to execute and contains good error detecting facilities, whilst a compiler is more complex but produces a program that runs faster than an interpreted version. Interpreter code is more compact than compiled code and this is one reason why the original languages for microcomputers, such as BASIC, were often interpreted rather than compiled. Now memory is relatively cheap and thus the amount of memory required for applications is of only secondary importance; speed of execution is the overriding consideration and thus compilation is the method by which most languages are implemented. Some languages are implemented in several stages, by a mixture of compilation and interpretation because of their different properties.

```
IF X > Y THEN X := X + 1


MOV   DX,[X]   Load DX with contents of memory location X
CMP   DX,[Y]   Compare contents of X and Y
JLE   L1       Jump if X less than or equal to Y
INC   w[X]     Increment X
L1
```

Figure 12.1 Typical high-level language statement and equivalent assembly code for 8085 produced by a compiler.

1. Fetch next instruction from memory to register using simulated program counter

2. Increment simulated program counter.

3. Go to subroutine for that instruction indirectly via an address table.

4. Return to step 1.

Figure 12.2 Typical structure of an interpreter

12.8 The translation environment

The way in which assembly code programs are translated and then linked and loaded was described in a previous section of this chapter. There are two ways in which the compilation of a high-level language can be incorporated into this system:

1. The compiler can generate assembly code which can be dealt with in the same way as described previously.

```
                                          simulated program counter = BC
START    MOV      DI,[BX]                  get next instruction
         INC      BX                       increment simulated program counter
         JMP      TABLE[DI]                jump on table address
INS1     .

         .

         JMP      START
INS2     .

         .

         JMP      START


INSn     .

         .

         JMP      START


TABLE    DW       INS1,INS2,INS3...        address table
```

Figure 12.3 Typical interpreter structure for Intel 80x86.

```
start    move.l   (a0)+, a1                get next instruction
         jmp      table(a1)                jump on table address


ins1     .

         .

         jmp      start
ins2     .

         .

         jmp      start
insn     .

         .

         jmp      start


table    dc.l     ins1,ins2,ins3.....  address table
```

Figure 12.4 Typical interpreter structure for Motorola 680x0.

2. The compiler can generate the same form of output as the assembler and
   this output can be fed into the linker to bind in any necessary library
   functions.

Most compilers generate the semi-compiled output necessary to feed into
a linker thus giving rise to the translation structure shown in Figure 12.5.

This system has the useful feature that programs can be generated using
modules in mixed languages and joined together into a single program via
the linker. It is also possible to mix the level of the languages used so that if

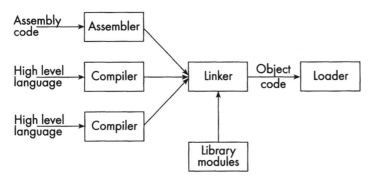

Figure 12.5 Typical language translation process.

a high-level language does not allow the programmer access to the required machine features it is possible to add a module in a lower level language for this purpose.

In order for the programmer to implement a program he/she requires access to a number of tools, for example, an editor to generate the program code, compilers and assemblers to translate the code into semi-compiled form, a linker to link the modules together and a loader to load the linked code into memory. In addition to this, he or she needs tools to help manage the development process and tools to help test the program to ensure that it solves the user's requirements. In order to help with the organization of this development process, many manufacturers of software systems now provide a complete environment with which the programmer can develop code. Examples of such systems for the C programming language are the Borland C/C++ Development System and the Microsoft Visual C/C++ Development System. Such systems include sophisticated facilities to help with all aspects of the development of programs, for example, all the tools mentioned above are integrated into the environment and a common interface, visual in the case of the two environments mentioned, is provided to access all the tools. As an example, the programmer sets up a project in the environment when starting to work on a new application. The project is the container for all the code concerned with the application and the system keeps track of the state of all the modules in the development. For example, if the programmer changes the code of two modules and requests the system to run the application code again, the system will detect that two modules have been updated and therefore need to be recompiled but that the other modules do not. The environments contain a number of debugging tools to help the programmer find errors in the code. For example, the programmer can breakpoint the code by stopping execution at any high-level language statement and examine the contents of any variable, or can execute the program a single statement in the language at a time. Such environments improve programmer productivity and hence reduce the cost of program development.

12.9 Summary

A processor can directly execute only machine code so programs written in any other languages have to be translated to machine code before they can be executed. The translator from assembly code to machine code is called an assembler, which performs the translation using a two stage process. In pass one the definitions of user symbols are collected into a user symbol table and this table is used, together with the permanent symbol table, in pass two to perform the translation. For large programs, it is convenient for the programmer to be able to split the code into modules, each of which can be separately translated. The separately assembled modules have to be linked together into a single contiguous block of code using a program called a linker or link editor which also uses a two pass process. The linked code is loaded into memory for execution via a loader.

Some architectures allow the translators to produce position independent code which can be loaded anywhere in memory and still execute correctly. For architectures that do not have the requisite addressing modes, code has to be modified if it is to be executed anywhere in memory other than the position at which the translator assumed it would run. This modification process is known as relocation. In a typical system the code translators and the linker assume that the code starts at memory location 0. The linker has to relocate modules other than the first and the loader will have to relocate the linker output to the position required to run the program.

High-level languages are used to write programs whenever possible because of higher programmer productivity. There are many different types of high-level language but the most common today are C/C++ and Java. C++ is an object oriented programming language where the computation model is of a set of objects which are instances of classes which communicate by passing messages to one another. These types of languages are popular at present because they increase programmer productivity by increasing the reusability of code.

Most modern systems use a program development environment which provides the programmer with sophisticated management facilities to make the development process easier and less error prone. Current environments are language and hardware specific.

12.10 Exercises

Exercise 12.1 Give an outline of the linking process indicating the actions that occur in pass 1 and pass 2.

Exercise 12.2 Show the assembler symbol table contents after the end of pass 1 for the fragment of code given below assuming the default value of the assembly location counter is 0.

```
Start:    move.b    #1, d0       (4 bytes)
          trap      #15          (2 bytes)
          dc.w      $10          (2 bytes)
L1:       move.w    d0, d1       (4 bytes)
          end
```

Exercise 12.3 Indicate what would need to be changed in the code for the 680x0 processor shown below if it were to be relocated to location 400016 onwards. What would be the difference if the data, length and table, were located at 200016 and the code at 400016?

```
          .=0                   ; code and data start at location 0
table:    dc.b    1,3,4    ; data table
endtable:

start:    move.1   #table,A0    ; address of table to A0
          clr.w    D0           ; clear found indicator
          cmpi.b   #1,(A0)+     ; current table value 1?
          beq      found        ; yes
          cmpa.1   #endtable,A0 ; at end of table?
          beq      notfound     ; yes
          bra      start        ; no
found:    move.b   #3,-(A0)     ; replace 1 by 3
          move.w   #1,D0        ; indicate 1 found
          stop
          end
```

Exercise 12.4 Translate into the equivalent 680x0 or 80x86 assembly code the following section of high-level language code to find the largest value in an array. Note any assumptions you make.

```
LARGEST = 0;
INDEX = 0;
WHILE (INDEX<LIMIT)
    {
    IF (NUMBER[INDEX]>LARGEST)
    LARGEST = NUMBER[INDEX];
    INDEX = INDEX + 1;
    }
```

Exercise 12.5 What is wrong with the following piece of 680x0 assembly code to count the number of 3s in the table called X and put the result into D_0? Modify it to make it understandable.

```
X:    dc.w    2,3,5,7,3
ABC:  move.w  #0,D1
      move.w  #0,D2
```

```
Q:    cmp.w   #5, D2
      hlt
      cmp.w   #3,X[D2]
      bne     Z
      addi.w  #1,D1
Z:    addi.w  #1,D2
      jmp     Q
      end     abc
```

Exercise 12.6 Is it possible to generate an assembler for a given architecture? If so, outline how it can be done.

Exercise 12.7 Explain the difference between a program counter and an assembly location counter.

Exercise 12.8 Will a typical assembler allow you to use the same symbol for an opcode and a label? Explain your answer.

12.11 Longer programming exercises

All the following exercises use the simple architecture described below.

A very simple computer (VSC) is a 12-bit machine which has a single accumulator, an instruction register, a program counter and a single ALU. Memory is limited to 4096 words but only 256 words can be directly addressed.

Instructions occupy a single word and have the following format:

Opcode	D/I	Address
11 9	8 7	0	bits

Since the address field is eight bits wide the maximum memory that can be directly addressed is $2^8 = 256$ bytes, although 2^{12} bytes can be addressed indirectly as explained below. The opcode field is three bits wide and hence eight instructions are supported as defined below:

Opcode	Mnemonic	Action
000	LDA	load the accumulator with the contents of the effective address
001	STA	store the accumulator in the effective address
010	TCA	replace the contents of the accumulator with its two's complement
011	ADD	add the contents of the effective address to the accumulator

Address			Assembly code		Machine code (decimal)
100		JLE		replace the contents of the program counter with the effective address if the result of the last instruction was less than or equal to zero	
101		HLT		halt the computer	
110		IN		input a character from an input device into the accumulator	
111		OUT		output the contents of the accumulator to an output device	

Note that both the IN and OUT instructions have to convert between internal binary format and ASCII code. The computer has two addressing modes – direct addressing and indirect addressing – and each instruction denotes which mode is to be used by the value of the D/I bit. D/I is 0 for direct addressing and 1 otherwise. The effective address for an instruction is computed using the value of the D/I field and the address field:

If D/I = 0 then EA = Address else EA = Memory[Address]

Sample program
Here is a simple program for VSC which sums the contents of locations 12 to 15 inclusive and leaves the result in location 19.

Address		Assembly code		Machine code (decimal)
0	L2:	LDA	(11)	267
1		ADD	19	1555
2		STA	19	531
3		LDA	11	11
4		ADD	(17)	1809
5		STA	11	523
6		ADD	(18)	1810
7		JLE	L1	2058
8		LDA	(16)	272
9		JLE	L2	2048
10	L1:	HLT		2560
11		12	; address of start of data	12
12		1	; first data item	1
13		2	; second data item	2
14		3	; third data item	3
15		4	; fourth data item	4
16		0	; constant 0	0
17		1	; constant 1	1
18		-15	; 2's comp of addr of last data	-15
19		0	; sum location	0
		END		

The notation in the assembly code is that labels are separated from an instruction by a colon. Brackets around an operand denote indirect addressing and lack of brackets denotes direct addressing. Comments are separated by semicolons.

Exercise 12.9 Write a simulator for the VSC machine in a high-level language of your choice. Test your simulator on the sample test program given.

Hints To simulate this computer in a high-level language requires the following design steps to be taken:

1. Decide how to represent the storage locations of the target architecture. For this machine use appropriately named variables for the accumulator, program counter, instruction register etc. Use a vector or array – called memory – to simulate the main memory of the target architecture.

2. The overall structure of the simulation program should be

   Load test machine code into simulation memory

   Set program counter to zero

   Set going to true

   While (going)

       Fetch next instruction to instruction register

       Decode instruction in instruction register

           separate fields

           calculate effective address

       Execute instruction in instruction register

   Endwhile

Note that the format of the execute action should be a case or switch statement using the value of the opcode field to select which piece of code should be executed. To separate the fields in the decoding phase use bit manipulation operators in the high-level language or integer arithmetic. Execution of the HLT instruction should set going to false.

Exercise 12.10 Write a program in VSC assembly code to input two single digit integers, add them together and output the result. Test your code on your simulator.

Exercise 12.11 Write an assembler in a high-level language for the VSC machine. Assume that data is represented in assembly code by a decimal value, one per line, as given in the test program.

13

Concurrency

13.1 Introduction

Two actions are concurrent if they overlap in time, that is, at some instant in time both actions are in progress. For example, at any instant in time there are many computers being used concurrently across the world. There are many reasons for using concurrency in computer systems, for example, fault tolerance, but in most cases the overriding one is to increase the performance of the overall system. If many tasks are performed at the same time the overall time needed to complete them will be less than if they were performed one at a time, so that the throughput, the amount of work done per unit time, is potentially greater in a concurrent system. Note the use of the word potentially here. Tasks can truly be performed concurrently only if they are independent, that is, if there is no interaction between them. Any interaction will reduce the amount of concurrency and, in the worst case, the tasks will have to be performed sequentially. Consider the input of a single character. The code to perform this action, described in Chapter 7, consists of code to initiate the transfer by setting a bit in the interface and then a loop that the processor has to cycle around waiting for another bit to be set in the interface indicating that the input action is complete. Thus the processor is active concurrently with the input–output action but the processor is not performing useful work; it is waiting for the input action to be completed. Thus this is an example where the throughput of the system is not improved by the use of concurrency. Interrupts, described in Chapter 7, were invented to enable input–output and CPU processing to proceed concurrently with the CPU performing useful work.

In a computer system, concurrency can be exhibited at all the architectural levels. For example, components of a combinational circuit, such as AND and OR gates, react to changing circuit inputs concurrently. At a higher level still, some high level languages, for example, ADA, allows the programmer to specify that statements in the language may be executed concurrently. Additionally, one of the main functions of an operating system is to provide mechanisms to control the concurrency of multiple tasks executing at the same time.

In this book we are primarily interested in concurrency at the level of the basic machine architecture. At this level there appears, at first sight, to be relatively little concurrency, since the assembly code of the machine specifies the sequential execution of a set of instructions and the basic instruction cycle of the processor is sequential. However, there are ways in which concurrency can be used; some, such as the use of interrupts, have already been covered in earlier chapters whilst others will be discussed in this chapter and in Chapter 17.

13.2 Multiple processor systems

If more than one operation is to be performed at one time, more than one processor is required. Thus if it is required to execute two programs at the same time, the system must have an architecture including at least two CPUs. But what is the difference between a single computer system with two processors and two computer systems, each with a separate processor? The only reason for using a single machine with two CPUs is because the two programs share some resources; if they do not, it would be better to use two separate computers. The feature of all concurrent systems of interest is that they share some resources, for example, data.

If resources are shared, then some control of the shared resources is required if more than one of the devices that have access to the same shared resource can write information to that resource. For example, if two processors can write data to the same area of memory then there has to be some control over the writing, otherwise interference can occur and the value stored can be a combination of the two write operations. The simplest form of control is called mutual exclusion where only one device can write to a shared resource at a time.

In the context of concurrent systems a processor is any device which can manipulate or transfer information in the system. In a typical single CPU computer system there are many processors; the CPU and each I/O device is a processor. Thus even a single processor CPU system has the potential for concurrency which is explored in this chapter.

In a system with multiple processors there are two main methods of organising the control. The simplest method is to designate one of the processors to be the master controller and only that processor may initiate actions; the other processors are slaves and may only respond to commands from the master controller. This organization is the one normally adopted for single CPU systems where the CPU is the master controller and the other processors – the I/O devices – take their commands from the CPU. The other organization, which is often used in systems with multiple CPUs, is for the control to reside in one of a number of possible processors and these processors communicate among themselves to decide who is the master at any one time. This is the organization typically used in a local area network as discussed in the following three chapters.

13.3 Hardware controlled interrupts and input–output

In Chapter 7 the role of interrupts in input–output processing was explained. In effect interrupts allow the CPU, the shared resource, to be shared between two tasks, one of which is the input–output task and the other is a compute task. Interrupts are more general than this; they provide a general mechanism for sharing resources. The CPU can be shared among any number of tasks using interrupts to signal requests for the CPU from each of the tasks. This is the mechanism used by an operating system to share the processor among a large number of tasks.

In the discussion in Chapter 7, hardware interrupts were generated by a device in response to a particular condition, for example, completion of a DMA transfer, but the model of interrupts can be extended to software generated interrupts thus generalising the interrupt model.

13.4 Software interrupts

Just as hardware devices can generate interrupts to signal to the processor that they require service, so software tasks can signal to the processor that they require service by the use of software interrupts which are often called traps to distinguish them from hardware interrupts. The action that the processor takes on receiving a software trap, which is normally generated by a special type of instruction, TRAP in the case of the Motorola 680x0, is exactly the same as with a hardware interrupt except that the identity of the interrupt service routine (ISR) is encoded as part of the trap instruction.

Software traps may be generated by system software in response to hardware and software errors and exception conditions, such as division by zero. They are a mechanism by which the processor can be shared among a number of different tasks. They are also are very useful for user program communication with an operating system, not just because they are usually faster than standard subroutine calls but also because they do not require the user to know the address of the operating system utility.

13.5 Types of concurrency

There are many different ways in which two or more actions can occur concurrently. Two forms that are of particular interest to computer architects are parallelism and concurrency. In general, it is relatively easy to build a hardware system with multiple resources so that multiple activities can be active simultaneously; the difficult task is to organize one or more programming tasks so that they can make concurrent use of the hardware resources.

13.5.1 Parallelism

Parallelism strictly applies to two or more tasks that start simultaneously and end simultaneously, that is, tasks that take the same time to complete and that are concurrent throughout their whole lifetime. However, many authors used the term in a much looser sense, often implying just that several tasks are active concurrently at some time. Here we use the stricter definition since this is more widely applicable to hardware, for example, if a system contains two processors they are presumably switched on at the same time when the system power is applied and shut down simultaneously when the power is removed.

Parallelism is used in computing systems to speed up execution. If a task can be split into a parallel set of independent subtasks then it is possible to use parallelism in the hardware to speed up the execution. Figure 13.1 shows five tasks of which three may run in parallel. Figure 13.2 shows the execution profile of this set of tasks. Note that not all the tasks to be performed in parallel take the same execution time but that the specification of parallelism implies that all the parallel tasks start at the same time and the succeeding task cannot start until all the parallel tasks have completed execution. In effect this extends the execution time of all the parallel tasks to that of the longest one.

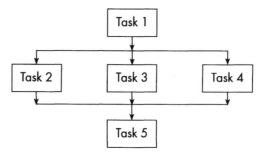

Figure 13.1 Program structure showing three tasks to be run in parallel.

```
Task 5                          ————————
Task 4                 ————————
Task 3                 ——————————
Task 2                 ——————
Task 1    ——————————

          |————————————————————————————————————————▶
                                                Time
```

Figure 13.2 Execution profile of program of Figure 13.1.

If a task can be split into n parallel tasks then, provided the hardware has the required parallelism, execution will take $1/n$ of the time of the sequential version, providing all the parallel tasks are the same size. Typically a speed-up of this magnitude cannot be obtained, even for equal sized partitions, since the information required by the parallel tasks has to be distributed to them before the parallel action and recovered afterwards, but substantial speed-ups can be obtained, especially for specialized applications.

13.5.2 Pipelining

Pipelining is used when there is a repetitive task to be performed on a sequence of data items and the task can be split into a number of separate, independent subtasks. This is the type of concurrency used in assembly line techniques for manufacturing.

The basic idea behind pipelining is that a series of tasks can be completed in a shorter time by splitting the tasks into a series of smaller subtasks which can be arranged so that subtasks of different tasks are performed at the same time as shown in Figure 13.3.

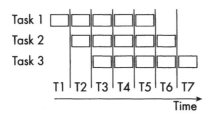

Figure 13.3 Pipelining three tasks, each comprised of five subtasks.

As can be seen in this figure, the subtasks of each task are performed sequentially by three processors. In the steady state, subtask n of task x is being processed, together with subtask $n+1$ of task $x-1$ and subtask $n-1$ of task $x+1$. Thus, in the steady state in this example, three different subtasks are being performed at once or concurrently. This requires the availability of three separate processors, one for each subtask. As shown in the diagram, a task is completed at every time step although each task takes five time steps to complete. Thus the total time taken to complete the execution of the three tasks is 7 time steps whereas the total time required to process them sequentially is 15 time steps. In general, the time taken to process n tasks which can be split up into p subtasks is $p+n-1$, assuming that each sub-task takes the same execution time.

This type of concurrency is used in the instruction execution cycle of the CPU where more than one instruction can be processed at a time by splitting the instruction cycle into a number of subtasks and executing different subtasks of consecutive instructions at the same time. Such an organization is able to use separate subunits of the processor to perform the separate subtasks on different instructions concurrently. An example where the processing of each instruction is split into three phases as shown in Figure 13.4.

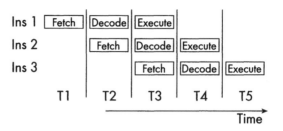

Figure 13.4 Instruction pipelining.

In this example there are three stages to the pipeline, fetch, decode and execute and separate hardware subsystems would be used to implement each stage. Pipelining in the implementation of the processor decreases program execution time but introduces a number of problems, called hazards, which are discussed in more detail in the final chapter of this book. Briefly, since the next instructions in sequence are fetched before the previous one has been completely processed, dependencies between instructions that are close together can cause problems. For example, if the identity of the next instruction is not data dependent, that is, it does not depend on the previous instructions, pipelining will work correctly but when this is not the case, for example, where the current instruction is a conditional branch instruction, then the identity of the next instruction is not available when it is required for the instruction fetch since the conditional branch has not been fully executed at that time. Special consideration must be made for this in the architecture and high performance processors try to predict which way the branch will go and fetch the next instruction into the pipeline based on this prediction. If the prediction is correct then the computation proceeds normally but if not the computation has to be restarted from the correct branch target instruction. This introduces a large number of complications, which are outside the scope of this book; interested readers are referred to the book by Hennessy and Patterson, given in the bibliography, for a detailed discussion of this. An overview of the way in which such problems are overcome in RISC processors is considered in the final chapter of this book.

All modern processors use pipelining in the processor implementation, for example, the Pentium processor contains two five stage pipelines, that is, it is a parallel and pipelined implementation. The number of pipelines and the number of stages in each pipeline determine the maximum amount of concurrency. Increased concurrency results in a faster processor but there is a limit on the amount of concurrency possible due to interaction between instructions as outlined above. The architect has the task of designing a system with as much concurrency as possible subject to the constraints of technology, programs and cost.

13.6 A warning

Concurrency is a very useful tool for the designer but it has a number of drawbacks, especially in debugging. The standard method of debugging sequential systems is to trace the execution, checking the machine state at appropriate points. Future executions will follow the same execution path, given the same inputs. This is not true with a concurrent system since the ordering is relaxed to allow execution at the same time and successive executions may result in different execution orders, especially if the system is interrupt driven since interrupts are unlikely to occur at exactly the same time because they are controlled by the environment, not the system. This makes concurrent systems difficult to debug since errors may disappear due to the differences in the environment rather than changes made to the system. If the error has not been corrected the error may occur again at unpredictable times in the future.

It is the dynamic, time dependent, nature of a concurrent system which causes problems and predictable systems need to restrict this behaviour. For example, a program using polling to perform I/O is equivalent to the same program using interrupts but only allowing the interrupts to occur at that particular point in the program. Restricting the use of concurrency and interrupts makes systems much easier to debug. Thus care should be taken in the use of interrupts and concurrency because, although the system performance may be improved, debugging will be more difficult and system performance will be unpredictable. This can be seen in many operating system most of which still have numerous bugs in them even after many years of use. This can be mainly attributed to the concurrent nature of the operating system.

13.7 Systems with multiple processors

In a previous section the techniques of concurrency were explained. These techniques can be applied to all levels of the architecture hierarchy, both software and hardware, and this section explains the use of concurrency in some of the architectural levels.

Exploiting parallelism and concurrency in hardware above the machine level implies taking multiple processors, multiple memory modules and multiple input–output devices and linking them together in different ways.

13.7.1 Classification of multiple processor systems

There are many different classifications of computer systems with perhaps the most commonly used one based on the classification of Flynn. Flynn classifies architectures into the four types depending on the number of instruction and data streams allowed:

SISD single instruction stream, single data stream

SIMD single instruction stream, multiple data stream

MISD   multiple instruction stream, single data stream

MIMD   multiple instruction stream, multiple data stream

Of these four types, the SISD architectures are the standard sequential architectures with a single instruction stream – a program – and a single data stream – the data operated on by the instructions. The SIMD and MISD architectures are special purpose architectures which are applicable only to special types of applications, for example, a SIMD architecture has a single data stream operating on multiple streams of data. This is an array processor or a vector processor where the instructions operate on an array of data points rather than a single datum and are the type of architectures used for numerical calculations such as weather computations where similar computations are applied to different points in the atmosphere. These applications are sufficiently numerous, important and processor intensive that there is a relatively small market for such machines – called supercomputers – even though they are very expensive. A vector processor is a specialized processor whose machine instructions operate principally on vectors of data items. For example, on such a machine, multiplying a vector of numbers by a constant is a single instruction. The way in which this is implemented using pipelining techniques means that it executes much more quickly than the sequential alternative. An array processor is normally an attached processor which acts as a specialized input–output device to a sequential processor. It performs calculations given to it by the sequential processor in parallel.

The MIMD architecture is the most general type of architecture with multiple processors and consists of many processors and memories interconnected in one of a number of ways. The latest type of MIMD architectures are tending towards independent computer systems that are connected by high speed networks allowing for simple processor interconnection but also high speed communication.

13.7.2 Multiprocessors and multicomputers

There are many different MIMD architectures. A multiprocessor is a system comprising of multiple processors and a multicomputer is a system comprising of multiple computers linked together via communication media. There are many different types of multiprocessor and most can be classified as tightly-coupled or loosely-coupled. Loosely coupled multiprocessors are multicomputers typified by individual computers running their own operating systems, which are connected together via a communication network. These types of systems are becoming increasingly important and are the subject of the next three chapters. Tightly coupled multiprocessors have access to shared memory which is used for communication and the system is controlled by a single operating system. A diagram of a generic multiprocessor system is shown in Figure 13.5.

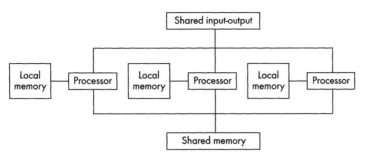

Figure 13.5 Generic multiprocessor architecture

A set of processors is connected to one or more shared memory modules and to a set of shared input–output devices. Each of the processors may have access to a private, local memory and may have direct links to other processors for control purposes. Private input–output devices are allowed on each processor although this differentiates the processors and makes task scheduling more difficult. The simplest form of communication medium between the processors and shared memory is a bus and many computer system allow for multiple processor configurations by having a system bus into which processor boards can be plugged to give the required system configuration. The system is readily extensible and is quite reliable since the bus is a passive device. A bus to support multiple processors must have facilities for arbitration since only one processor can have access to the bus at a time and thus multiple concurrent requests have to be sequenced in some order. The major problem with such systems is one of performance. All communications have to go via the bus and hence there is a need to reduce communication to avoid saturating the bus. Local memory can be used to store information that is private to a particular processor and cache memory (see Chapter 6) can be used to speed up access to shared memory, although this can lead to problems as described later. Another way of speeding up access to the shared memory is to split it into separate memory modules with multiple ports on each module, allowing parallel access to separate memory modules and pipelined access to the same memory module. Even with the use of these techniques, systems with more than a few tens of processors suffer performance degradation because the bus becomes a bottleneck. This means that such configurations are not truly scaleable.

The use of cache in a multiprocessor system is not simple. Cache is used in most modern processors to speed up memory access and, since shared memory access is a bottleneck in multiprocessor systems, the use of cache memory can be very beneficial. However, there is a problem known as the cache coherence problem, which concerns the validity of information in the cache. In a multiple processor system each processor has its own cache which may contain a copy of the same information. If one processor changes the information then the information in the other caches is invalid. Some method of indicating the validity of the information in the caches is required in a multiple processor system. One approach is to use software – a compiler – to analyse the code at compile time and insert instructions to prevent unsafe information from being cached. Preventing all shared information from being cached is too conservative a policy; the compiler must analyse the code to determine safe periods to cache shared information. The alternative approach is to recognize at run-time any potential inconsistency in shared information. This can be done with cache coherence protocols, which are transparent to the programmer and more efficient than compiler-based techniques. There are two approaches to using cache coherence protocols, one of which is centralized and one distributed. The distributed solution is the one that is commonly adopted and is based on each processor watching what other processors are doing via a 'snoopy' protocol. When a processor updates shared information in its cache it broadcasts the fact and other processors 'snoop' on the broadcast messages and take the appropriate action. There are two methods used to provide cache coherence. One method – called write invalidate – just invalidates the relevant cache entries when the processor 'snoops' on a message indicating that another processor has updated the information. In the other method – write update – the processor modifying shared information in its cache broadcasts the modifications it has made, thus allowing other processors to update their copy of the shared information.

The Pentium processor uses the write invalidate method and can be used in multiple processor systems. The most common cache coherence protocol is called MESI, standing for modified, exclusive, shared and invalid. The details of the protocol are outside the scope of this book but basically each line in the cache contains two extra bits, which record the state of the line as one of the four states given by the name of the protocol. Every time a processor accesses information it uses the information in these two bits to decide what to do. For example, if it wishes to write to that line of the cache then if the line is shown as being shared it has to negotiate with the holders of the other copies for them to invalidate their copy before it updates its copy and marks it as modified. If it already has exclusive access it can modify the information without any further action and mark it as modified. If it is marked as modified then it can just modify the block again. Any line that is marked as modified has to be written back to main memory before being deleted from the cache.

13.7.3 Using multiprocessors and multicomputers

In the discussion so far no mention has been made of the grain of the concurrency, that is, the size of the tasks that are being performed concurrently. One possibility is to run a number of different programs concurrently where each program only uses a single processor. Each program will take the same execution time as on a single processor but the overall system throughput will be higher because several programs will be executed concurrently. This type of organization is simple to implement because the only difference from a standard sequential computer system is extra code in the operating system to manage several processors instead of one; the application programs are unchanged. A different organization is to allow a single program to make use of multiple processors in order to improve its execution time. This requires either the application program to be changed explicitly to use multiple processors or for sophisticated system software to be used which can detect and implement the use of multiple processors from sequential code. In practice, the former is the only effective solution, so application programs have to be rewritten with concurrency in mind.

13.8 Summary

Concurrency – multiple actions occurring at the same time – can be exhibited at many different architectural levels in computer systems. Concurrency is used to enhance the performance – the throughput – of computer systems.

Interrupts are a mechanism for implementing concurrency in computer systems by allowing the CPU to be shared between a number of tasks, typically processing and I/O operations. Since interrupts cause the processor to change the task it is performing, they require the processor state to be saved and restored before and after the interrupt is processed. This is known as context switching and is one of the main causes of performance degradation in interrupt based systems.

Pipelining is a technique for executing a sequence of tasks split into sub-tasks on a number of processors so that the overall execution time of the sequence is reduced. It is frequently used in modern CPUs to implement the instruction execution cycle so that more than one instruction can be executed at one time. A major problem occurs when the address of the next instruction cannot be determined until the current instruction completes, since the pipeline implementation requires the address of the next instruction before the current instruction completes. The solutions to this are varied and depend on the processor complexity, but the higher performance processors attempt to predict the outcome of the current instruction and use this to generate the address of the next instruction. This means that processing has to be nullified if the prediction proves to be incorrect.

13.9 Exercises

Exercise 13.1 Order the set of tasks necessary to make a cup of tea to give the maximum concurrency. Take the subtasks to be actions such as: filling a kettle with water, warming the pot, putting tea into the pot, filling the pot, pouring out the tea, adding milk etc.

Exercise 13.2 Devise a concurrent algorithm, that is, a method, for sorting a set of items into a given order, for example, sorting a set of numbers into ascending order.

Exercise 13.3 A task T can be subdivided into three subtasks, t_1, t_2, t_3, which have to be executed in the order given. The subtasks have execution times of 1.5, 3.5 and 3.0 seconds, respectively.

(a) Without pipelining, find the time required to execute five type T tasks.

(b) Using the pipelining described in this chapter, find the time required to execute five tasks of type T.

(c) What modifications would be needed to the decomposition of task T to decrease the overall time required in part (b)?

Exercise 13.4 A number of processes access a queue. The queue is accessed using the procedures read and write outlined below.

Read: Check that there are items to read in the queue
        Remove the item at the front of the queue
        Increment the head of queue pointer to point to new head of queue
Write: Check that there is space in the queue to hold the next data item
        Add the item to the queue
        Increment the queue pointer to include the new item

(a) If multiple processes are allowed to read from the queue concurrently what operations in the read procedure cannot be performed concurrently?

(b) If multiple concurrent read and write processes are allowed, what operations cannot be performed concurrently?

Exercise 13.5 Draw a timing diagram of a pipeline to implement the processing of data through a task which can be split into five separate, equal sized subtasks. From this, compute the speed-up of a large number of cycles through the pipeline. Under certain conditions the second stage of the pipeline can determine if the third and fourth stages are not required for this piece of data. How does this affect the speed-up? If the third and fourth stages could only be omitted for 10% of the data and each stage takes the same time to execute, would it be worthwhile taking advantage of this in the pipeline design? If so, under what conditions? Justify your answer.

Exercise 13.6 Deadlock is a condition that can affect concurrent systems. Suppose a system comprises 15 units of a particular resource. Process A requests 10 units on start-up and process B requests three units. Sometime later process A requests another four units and so does process B. Neither of these requests can be fulfilled so both processes are deadlocked waiting for resources. Can you think of one or more simple ways of avoiding deadlock in this case? Why are the methods you have suggested not generally applicable?

14

Protocols & data transmission

14.1 Introduction

Chapter 7 discussed how typical integrated circuits allow a computer to be interfaced to external devices and how data is transmitted among them. This chapter considers further details of data transmission and the structuring of data transmission in order to introduce ideas on the connection of computers to form computer networks discussed in the next two chapters. An appreciation of the roles of protocols and protocol hierarchies is fundamental to understanding the organization of computer networks and how computers are connected to networks. The remainder of this chapter discusses different kinds of transmission media and how data is transported as physical signals on these media.

14.2 Protocols and protocol hierarchies

The data formats and the rules of message sequencing that characterize message exchanges between two computers are known as protocols. Protocols have been discussed previously, although they were not explicitly given this name. For example, the RS232C serial communications protocol discussed in Chapter 7 is a low-level external protocol. This asynchronous protocol defines the rules for the serial transmission of characters over a point-to-point link between two computers or between a computer and a peripheral device. The transmission of a data stream between a sender and receiver is the basic requirement for a computer network and the RS232C protocol is one of a number of different protocols that can be used for this purpose. The interaction between a CPU and memory, as described in Chapter 6, is also a protocol. This protocol states the voltage levels used to represent logic 0 and logic 1, the sequence of actions that have to be performed over the address, data and control lines to perform read and write operations on memory, including the set-up and hold times required for each signal. This is a low-level internal protocol since it is concerned with the internal parallel transmission of a small, unstructured data item – a word.

Data communication, in general, is the transmission of a stream of data between a sender and receiver across a communication channel. This stream is often broken up into smaller units, called frames, for transmission, in order to make efficient use of the communication systems as illustrated in Figure 14.1. Each frame consists of data accompanied by control information such as the address of the receiver as shown in Figure 14.2. The transmitter accepts a message it is asked to transmit, splits it into suitable sized data units, adds the relevant control information and transmits the frames over the transmission medium to the receiver. The receiver receives the frames, strips off the control information and reassembles the original message.

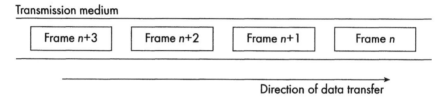

Transmission medium

| Frame n+3 | Frame n+2 | Frame n+1 | Frame n |

Direction of data transfer

Figure 14.1   A sequence of frames implements an efficient data stream.

| control info | data | control info |

Figure 14.2   Frame organization.

Thus, information transfer can be considered as the transmission of a stream of data organized as a set of frames, with the frame format being an important aspect of a protocol. However, a data transmission protocol often involves other complexities. A complex protocol is dealt with in the same manner as any other complex task; by dividing the complex protocol into smaller tasks, which are implemented by a hierarchy of simpler protocols. In data transmission this means splitting the problem of transmitting data between two application processes on different computers into a series of protocol layers with each layer being responsible for specific parts of the overall protocol.

Thus we have a hierarchy at both the sender and receiver, each of which uses a separate protocol to communicate with the same level of the hierarchy at the other end. A message sent by layer N at the transmitter to layer N at the receiver is passed downwards to the lower levels at the transmitter until it reaches level 1. There it is transmitted across the physical channel to level 1 at the receiver and then travels upwards through the levels until it reaches the equivalent level N in the receiver, as shown in Figure 14.3. This is analogous to situations in which humans communicate. Two executives may

5	Logical channel	5
4		4
3		3
2	Physical channel	2
1		1

Figure 14.3 Protocol layers in a sender and receiver.

need to exchange documents, so they send messages and documents to each other as though they were communicating directly, but ask their secretaries to pass on the messages. The secretaries may contact each other by telephone or may use a courier service to send documents. The courier does not interact with the executives but receives the documents from one secretary and delivers it to the other. It is irrelevant to the executives which courier service the secretaries use as long as the message transfer is secure and reliable. This use of layers supports the idea that each layer communicates across a logical channel between the transmitter and receiver at the same level, though this is actually constructed using the lower layer protocols and the actual physical medium connecting the lowest layers.

Every time the message crosses an interface going downwards at the transmitter some protocol (control) information is added to the message and similarly the protocol information is removed when the message travels upwards across an interface in the receiver. For some protocols this requires both a header field (at the start of the data) and a trailer field (at the end of the data) to be added as the control information, whilst other protocols require only header information to be added. The protocol information is used for a number of purposes depending on the nature of the protocol. Some of this information is for ensuring the data is delivered to the correct destination, some to ensure that the data has not been corrupted, and some to allow the receiver to control the rate at which the transmitter sends information to ensure it does not become overloaded. The actual message sent across the physical medium at level 1, therefore, consists of the actual application data wrapped in several layers of protocol information, one for each layer in the transmission hierarchy, as shown in Figure 14.4.

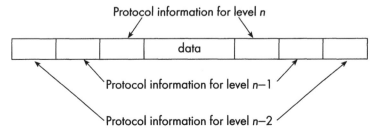

Figure 14.4 Data wrapped in three levels of protocol.

14.2.1 Hierarchies of protocols

The Organization for International Standardization (ISO) developed a seven layer hierarchical architecture model of protocols called the open system interconnection (OSI) to promote compatible operation of hardware and software protocol implementations from different commercial developers. A less complicated four layer hierarchy is used in the pervasive implementations of TCP/IP which give access to the Internet – the World Wide Web (WWW) of internetworked computer networks. We will present a hybrid description using TCP/IP as the model where appropriate and using the OSI model where the TCP/IP model has little to say.

The TCP/IP protocols assume a hierarchy of four layers as illustrated in Figure 14.5. Application programs (such as web browsers or database

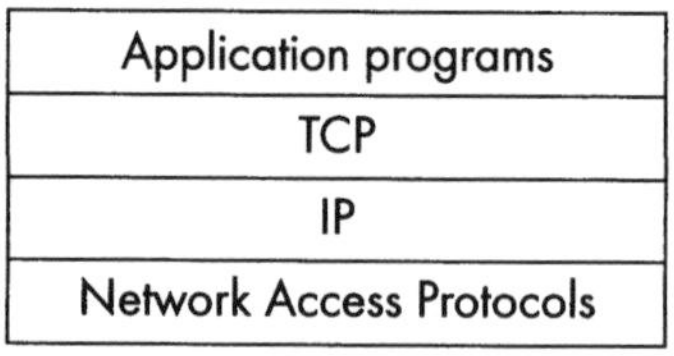

Application programs
TCP
IP
Network Access Protocols

Figure 14.5 The TCP/IP protocol hierarchy.

servers) use the transaction control protocol (TCP) to send and receive messages. The TCP protocol is implemented on top of the Internet protocol (IP) which is implemented on most computer networks. As far as the TCP/IP protocols are concerned, it is irrelevant how these networks themselves actually operate so long as they implement the IP protocol. However for the purposes of the current discussion we wish to gain some insight into the operation of individual networks, hence we will assume the OSI model's further sub-classification of the structuring of individual specific network access protocols as illustrated in the composite diagram in Figure 14.6.

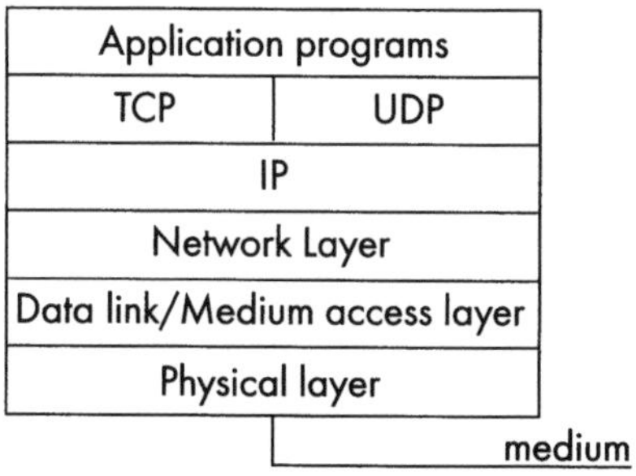

Application programs	
TCP	UDP
IP	
Network Layer	
Data link/Medium access layer	
Physical layer	

medium

Figure 14.6 A six-layer protocol hierarchy.

The lowest layer is known as the physical layer and describes the properties of the physical circuits required to transmit a sequence of signals between sender and receiver over a physical channel. This includes mechanical details such as the type of plug and wiring required and the way that data is represented by signals on the channel. RS232C is a typical example of such a protocol. The IEEE 802.3 Ethernet standard includes specification of operational characteristics at this level as well as higher level characteristics.

Historically, the data link layer has defined protocols for error-free transmission of data between two devices over a single physical link. The devices may be two computers or a host computer and an interface node to a network. In networks with long links involving relatively error-prone media, error-free transmission is achieved by error detection and correction techniques discussed in Chapter 16. However, for highly reliable transmission media, which has become more common-place, particularly over short distances, relatively error-free transmission is the norm and hence it has become more common for low level protocols to assume that transmission media themselves are relatively error-free, hence removing this burden from the data link layer. Chapter 16 discusses the problems of error detection and correction from both a historical viewpoint where these are addressed in the data link layer and the adaptations to such protocols in higher level layers such as TCP.

The network layer's main concern is the delivery of messages across a network between two end point nodes that are not directly connected by a single physical link. Such messages have to be routed through intermediate nodes to reach their destination. Multiple networks may be internetworked in such a way that this in not visible to the outside word. In both cases, routing of messages across a complex network is the major problem to be addressed. Chapter 15 discusses the main distinctions between local and wide area networks and the general problem of routing information.

The Internet protocol is an internetwork protocol designed to operate across an internetwork consisting of a number of very different computer networks. It resolves differences in the operation of lower layer protocols, which could prevent seamless operation.

The transaction control protocol allows for transparent transfer of data between processes running on physically separate computers. It is the main protocol with which application programs intercommunicate over the Internet. However the TCP/IP suite of protocols recognizes the possibility of different needs of different applications and provides a major alternative to TCP known as user datagram protocol (UDP).

Application programs and libraries of common functionality for specific kinds of applications are implemented using the functionality of TCP (and to a lesser extent UDP).

Figure 14.7 illustrates an example configuration of networks and how this hierarchy of protocols is used to solve sub-problems of the overall problem of communicating information between a process on a computer in one network to a process on a computer in another network. Networks A and B

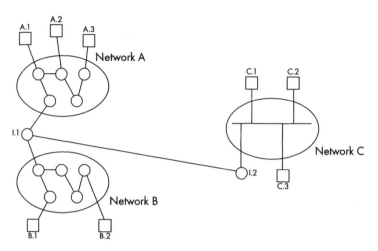

Figure 14.7 An internetwork and the role of a protocol hierarchy.

are connected by the intermediate node I.1. Network C is connected to networks A and B by the route I.1 and I.2. Physical layer and data link layer protocols operate on the individual link between A.1 and the internal node to which it is connected (and similarly between other hosts and internal nodes and pairs of internal nodes). Physical layer and medium access layer protocols govern access by C.1, C.2, C.3 and I.2 on network C. Internal network nodes in network A operate a network layer protocol to route messages between pairs of hosts and internetworking devices (A.1, A.2, A.3, I.1) and similarly for network B, though networks A and B may use different protocols. The internetwork nodes I.1 and I.2 operate the IP protocol in order to route messages between different networks. Applications on host computers (A.1, A.2, ... B.1, ... , C.1, ...) use the TCP protocol in order to achieve error-free message exchange across multiple networks.

Hence, communication within computer networks involves a number of problems that can be factored out into relatively self-contained sub-problems. Computer communication is best conceived (and usually implemented) as a hierarchical collection of hardware and software layers each of which addresses specific problems.

Different protocols are designed for different tasks at different levels of the protocol hierarchy and hence will differ in detail. However, all protocols must define the format of the data and control information for the protocol, which constitute the units of data that are sent and received by that protocol. In addition they need to define rules that govern the sequences of message exchanges that are valid within that protocol. In general, physical layer protocols are usually concerned only with the former aspect. Higher layer protocols generally address both aspects.

The focus of the remainder of this chapter is on the hardware-oriented layers at the bottom of such hierarchies, whose main concern is the characteristics of transmission media that are used to implement physical channels and how transmitters and receivers transmit and receive data as signals over a physical channel.

14.3 Data transmission and the physical layer

At its simplest, transmission of information can be thought of as transmission of a stream of bits between a sender and receiver along a physical link. Physically, the transmission may occur by the propagation of electrical signals along a wire, by the propagation of light waves along an optical fibre or by propagation of electromagnetic waves through the ether. The physical medium of a link thus determines the propagation characteristics and the kinds of signal that are used to represent data. The rate at which a transmitter generates signals, and hence the rate of signal change on the medium, is known as the baud rate. Hardware that implements transmission circuits is known as a transmitter, and hardware that implements reception circuits is known as a receiver. As computers perform internal transfers of data over parallel buses and computer communication is usually across serial links, at the heart of a transmitter is a parallel-in serial-out (PISO) shift register, and conversely the focus of a receiver is a serial-in parallel-out (SIPO) shift register as illustrated in Figure 14.8. During transmission each word is accepted in parallel and then shifted out for transmission one bit at a time; at the receiver a collection of bits are shifted in one bit at a time and once a word is available it is transferred out in parallel.

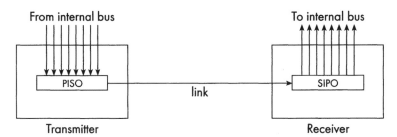

Figure 14.8 Simplified transmitter and receiver hardware.

Transmission between a sender and a receiver may be simplex (unidirectional) or duplex (bi-directional). Duplex channels can be further sub-categorized as those that support transmission in one direction only at any particular point in time (half-duplex), and those that support simultaneous bi-directional transmission (full duplex). Full duplex channels can be constructed from two unidirectional channels, one for each direction. Duplex channels require circuitry for both transmission and reception of signals, collectively know as a transceiver.

The bandwidth of the transmission medium, which is the range of frequencies that can be transmitted over that channel, determines the data transmission capacity of a channel. Generally, the higher the bandwidth the greater the amount of data that can be carried by the channel. The data transmission rate is defined in terms of the number of bits that can be transmitted each second (bits s^{-1}). In situations where a transmitter uses only two different signal levels to denote binary 0 and 1, the bit rate of a channel is the same as the signalling (baud) rate. However, with some data representations there can be more than two distinct signalling levels and in such cases the data rate is higher than the signalling rate. For example, if a channel has four distinct signalling levels then two bits of data can be represented by each signal (any of binary 00, 01, 10, or 11). If the signalling rate is 1200 baud (signals s^{-1}) then the data rate is 2400 bits s^{-1}.

The signals that are sent along a physical channel use either a baseband or a broadband mode of signalling. In baseband mode, the entire bandwidth of the medium is used for a single fast data rate physical channel. In broadband mode the available bandwidth is divided up to support multiple lower data rate channels. Baseband mode allows the medium to be accessed directly so that it can transmit digital signals, for example with electrical cable by manipulating directly voltage levels on the cable. Broadband mode treats the medium as a transmission channel for analogue signals and requires digital data to be encoded in analogue signal representations.

14.4 Multiplexing of signals

It is often the case that the data communication capacity of a channel is significantly greater than the data generation capability of the computers that control the transmitting devices. In such circumstances the bandwidth of the communication medium may be shared among multiple transmitters. There are two main methods of sharing the bandwidth of a physical channel among a number of lower bandwidth logical channels; frequency division multiplexing (FDM) as shown in Figure 14.9 and time division multiplexing (TDM) as shown in Figure 14.10. FDM allocates a proportion of the available bandwidth to each transmitter all of the time and this can be achieved only by using a broadband mode of signalling. The alternative technique, TDM, uses all of the available bandwidth for a single channel that is shared among all stations wishing to transmit by allocating each of them the channel for some proportion of the time.

In FDM different signals are allocated separate frequencies within the bandwidth of the communications medium. The limit to the number of signals that can be sent concurrently depends on the frequency spread of the individual signals, the resolution of the receiver and the bandwidth of the transmission medium. In TDM each communication has the entire bandwidth of the communications medium available to it for a given (short) period of time.

The use of FDM to share the capacity of a single transmission line is possible only with broadband signalling, whereas the use of TDM to share a

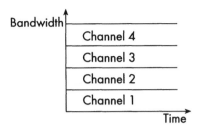

Figure 14.9 Frequency division multiplexing showing channel allocation.

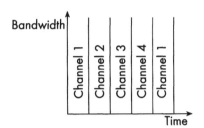

Figure 14.10 Time division multiplexing showing channel allocation.

line is based around baseband signalling. This latter form of signalling can be used to transmit digital data directly. Because of the use of the medium by only a single transmitter/receiver pair at a time, a sophisticated control system is necessary for TDM systems to control the use of the medium. This is not required for FDM systems since each transmitter has a unique frequency range available at all times.

14.5 Types of transmission media

The rate at which data can be transmitted, the regularity with which errors may occur and the transmission cost all depend on the type of media used.

The most common form of medium is copper wire, where transmission takes the form of electrical signals sent along wires. The properties of this type of media are well known as it has been in use for many years. Its main disadvantages are its susceptibility to interference from nearby electromagnetic radiation sources, and its relatively low bandwidth, that is, the small amount of information that can be transmitted in unit time. The most common forms of wiring used are twisted pair and co-axial cable.

Twisted pairs, as the name suggests, consists of a pair of insulated metallic conductors which are twisted together, and data is conveyed in the difference signal of the pair. The reason why a twisted pair is used rather than a flat pair is that the twisted pair has better noise immunity because any external influence is likely to be felt equally by both wires and hence has a reduced effect on the difference signal. Twisted pair cable is used typically for transmission within a building or single site. The reason for this is that the attenuation of the signal is quite high and thus it is necessary to add repeaters to amplify the signal if the transmission line is longer than two or three kilometres.

Co-axial cable is electrical cabling in which a copper core is surrounded by insulating material and an outer conductor and protective covering. It has better immunity from interference and allows higher data rates to be achieved than twisted pair cable. This type of cable is commonly used for distances of up to one or two kilometres. In addition, some countries use co-axial cable as a method of transmitting television pictures to domestic televisions, and though the technology is different, data and voice communication over such installed cabling is possible. For a time co-axial cable was also used for long distance communication boosted by amplifiers or repeaters, but has been superseded in such contexts by optical fibre.

Optical fibres are now the most commonly used medium for high speed transmission with high bandwidth. They are relatively immune from interference since they use light rather than electrical signals to transport the information, they have a high bandwidth and transmission loss is low. Optical fibres are also preferred because they are small and take less space than copper based media. Optical fibres are favoured for long distance communications and for environments where electrical interference is high, for example, in a factory.

Radio waves can also be used to transmit information. Various frequencies of electromagnetic radiation are used for transmission through air and space. This form of communication is important between remote sites since no cables have to be laid. Satellite communication is used for long distances where the information is sent by a ground station to a satellite which then retransmits it to another ground station. Microwave transmission is used for much shorter communication distances since antennae have to be within each other's line of sight.

For long distance transmission, it is usual for a national communication carrier to provide the transmission service and for the customer to have no say in the transmission medium, only the type of service provided. For shorter distances, within a building or site, the users may provide their own transmission facilities. These will usually be electrical cables or optical fibres depending upon the distance involved and the operational environment.

14.6 Framing and synchronization

Whatever transmission medium is used, transmitter and receiver are physically separate and use independent internal clocks to control when they send and receive signals. Signals are delayed by the transmission medium so they arrive later than they are sent, the precise delay depending on the type and length of the medium. These attributes give rise to the problem of synchronization of the transmitter and receiver so that the receiver knows when a data frame starts and finishes, and when to sample the signal for each of bit of data that has been transmitted.

Ideally transmitter and receiver clocks tick at precisely the same rate and therefore the receiver can sample the middle of each transmitted signal. In some schemes, where only a short distance in involved, there may be control lines between the transmitter and receiver in addition to the serial data line (as with one variant of RS232C), and a clock wire may be used achieve this. However, over longer distances typical of computer networks, multiple channels for such control signals are an expensive luxury, and hence with longer distance serial communication only a single communication channel is used.

Independent clocks run at slightly different rates and over a period of time will drift with respect to each other. If the receiver clock is running marginally slower than the transmitter clock (as in Figure 14.11) then eventually the receiver will miss reading a signal or, if the converse is the case, it will eventually read the same signal twice. For this reason, receiver and transmitter clocks have to be synchronized to ensure correct communication.

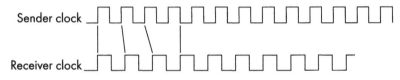

Figure 14.11 Loss of synchronization due to different clock speeds.

Synchronization of the receiver with the transmitter basically involves two sub-problems. The first is concerned with how the receiver recognizes the start and end of a message from the transmitter (frame synchronization). The second is concerned with how the receiver determines the position of the middle of each signal as the most reliable point at which to read the value of the bit(s) of data represented by the signal (bit synchronization).

Frame synchronization is usually achieved by special markers placed at the start and at the end of the data that are detected by the receiver. The start of frame marker is used by the receiver to identify the start of a new data frame which should then be read from the medium. Different approaches to bit synchronization give rise to two different kinds of data transmission. Asynchronous transmission assumes that the data message being transferred is very short and hence that the receiver can remain sufficiently synchronized to the transmitter for the duration of the message. Synchronous transmission assumes much longer messages and hence that additional information has to be embedded within the signals representing the message so that the receiver can periodically resynchronize to continue to sample signals at their mid points.

In the case of the RS232C protocol the 'idle' state, that is, no transmission, is represented by logic 1 (-12 V typically) and logic 0 ($+12$ V typically) is the 'start of transmission' indicator, that is, a start bit of logic 0 is added to the front of the character code transmitted. The data itself typically consists of seven or eight data bits and a parity bit followed by a stop bit (logic **1**). Provided that the receiver knows the rate of transmission and number of bits to be transmitted, which are agreed between the transmitter and receiver before transmission starts, the information can be collected at the receiver.

Asynchronous transmission can be used for sending only a comparatively small number of bits (usually twelve or fewer) in a message. This is because the receiver synchronizes with the transmitter only at the start of the transmission and then relies on its internal clock, whose 'ticks' are determined by the speed agreed prior to the transmission, to determine when the next bit will arrive, relative to the last one. Provided that the number of bits in a single transmission is relatively small, synchronization will not be lost. Asynchronous transmission is normally used for low speed transmission of characters on a serial link as described in Chapter 7. Higher speed transmission normally uses synchronous techniques.

Synchronous transmission, like asynchronous transmission, requires that the transmitter and receiver be synchronized at the start of transmission but, unlike asynchronous transmission, allows the receiver and transmitter to be kept in synchronization for long periods. For long transmissions the problems occur when the representation of the data keeps the signal at the same level for long periods of time with no transitions within the signal. In the case of synchronous transmission, an encoding scheme (such as Manchester encoding) is used which guarantees regular transitions from low to high, or vice versa, even where the transmitted data does not vary. Manchester encoding uses a signal transition from low to high to represent binary **1**, and from high to low to represent binary **0**. Figure 14.12 illustrates the signal encoding of the binary value **11010010**. This allows the receiver to adjust its clock frequency, that is, resynchronize, during the data transfer. The start and stop bits and parity bit of asynchronous communication account for approximately 30% for a 7-bit character. Some schemes that encode binary values as digital signals (like Manchester encoding) use an overhead of 50% for embedding the clocking information for synchronous communication, though there are more efficient encoding schemes that guarantee regular signal transitions. Synchronous transmission is more efficient in requiring proportionally lower overheads for frame start and frame end sequences compared with asynchronous transmission and is preferred for higher transmission rates.

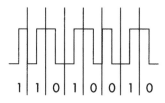

Figure 14.12 Manchester encoding of **11010010**.

14.7 Signal attenuation and noise corruption

A major problem for communication systems is that transmissions are prone to corruption. Signal attenuation and noise are two factors whose effect is to disrupt signals during transmission, as illustrated in Figure 14.12. Attenuation is the tendency for signals to degrade as they propagate further away from the transmitter. Noise is the disruption of a signal due to unfavourable conditions in the surrounding environment, such as the interference that lightning or heavy electrical plant may introduce into electrical signals.

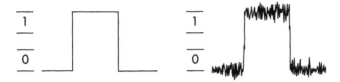

Figure 14.13 An ideal signal and a noisy version.

If attenuation or noise in the transmission system can transform one signal representation into another then the receiver receives corrupted information. Analogue signals can be boosted during transmission using amplifiers, although of course this results in amplification of both the original signal and any noise. Digital signals can be regenerated by repeaters to allow them to be transmitted reliably over greater distances. Repeaters not only boost the signal but can also restore the square wave characteristics of the original signal and thus alleviate many of the problems due to attenuation and noise. For this reason, the modern trend has been for networks to use digital signalling even for data that is originally analogue in nature, such as voice data in telephone calls. Such analogue data can be converted to a digital representation and then transmitted as digital signals to achieve greater reliability.

There are a number of ways to address the residual problems of signal corruption by adding redundant information to the transmitted data so that the receiver can perform checks of the data's integrity. Here simple measures do not suffice and more complicated protocols are required to overcome the problem. A simple form of error detection redundancy is the use of parity bits. This associates an additional check bit with a collection of data bits. In the case of RS232 a parity bit is associated with each 7- or 8-bit character. If a single bit is in error within the character then the parity bit is detected as being incorrect and hence an error is detected.

Though the source of errors occurs at the physical level and error detection can be performed in hardware, error detection and recovery is usually treated as an issue for higher protocol layers. Historically, error detection and correction has been undertaken on each individual link in a combination of error detection hardware at the physical level and error correction in the data link layer. As transmission media have achieved much greater levels of signal integrity (especially with fibre optic links), the modern trend in protocols, such as asynchronous transfer mode (ATM) and integrated services digital network (ISDN and B-ISDN), is to perform data oriented error correction in the higher layers concerned with host machine end-to-end transmission. When data transmission through networks was highly error-prone, performing error detection and correction on each individual link lead to reduced wastage of bandwidth by avoiding further transmission of corrupted data. Now that transmission media achieve greater reliability, the overheads of error detection and correction of data on each individual link are much more significant and are useful in much fewer cases. Error detection and error correction protocols are discussed in Chapter 16.

14.8 Telephone system

Whilst it is possible to connect computers together using dedicated cables to form a network in a single building or site, for example a university network, it is not feasible to do so when the computers to be connected are geographically far apart. For long distance communications it is necessary to use the services pioneered by the public telephone and telegraph (PTT) companies throughout the world. One advantage of this is that these companies realized the need for standardization many years ago and they have promoted many standards so that inter-operation between the telephone and telegraph services of all countries is possible. Thus a basic knowledge of the telephone system, how it works and how it is changing, is necessary to understand general networking techniques.

The telephone system was designed for transmission of analogue speech signals with a bandwidth of 300–3400 Hz. Originally, installed cabling transmitted analogue signals, though there has been an increasing move to the use of digital signalling for voice and digital data internally in such networks. However, the bulk of telephone cabling is in the local telephone subscriber loops, which connect telephones to local exchanges, and these can only gradually be converted to digital signalling.

Digital data can be transmitted over analogue connections by representing binary information within an analogue signal. It is not possible to transmit the digital signals directly as voltage levels because the analogue telephone system will transmit only a small range of frequencies. Binary information is converted to an analogue signal by modulating it on a carrier wave of a particular frequency. The reverse conversion, demodulation, is used at the receiving end to extract the binary information from the received signal. Such modulation techniques make it possible to share the frequency spectrum of a communication medium among several different signals, that is, multiple signals can be multiplexed together on the same transmission medium using frequency division multiplexing (FDM).

14.9 Modulation

There are several modulation techniques that can be used for encoding digital data within analogue signals. The simplest is amplitude modulation (AM) and is illustrated in Figure 14.14.

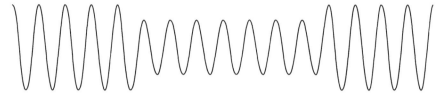

Figure 14.14 Amplitude modulation.

In this modulation scheme, the amplitude (size) of the transmitted carrier wave depends on whether a 0 or a 1 is being transmitted. If a 1 is being transmitted the amplitude is high whereas if a 0 is being transmitted it is low. Hence the waveform in Figure 14.14 encodes the bit pattern 1001 (assuming four cycles are used to represent one bit of information).

Amplitude modulation is susceptible to noise that often manifests itself as variations in signal amplitude. In addition it is more difficult to build highly reliable receivers for amplitude modulation, thus other modulation methods, such as frequency modulation (FM) and phase modulation (PM), are preferred. In frequency modulation the frequency of the carrier wave is changed to reflect the difference between the transmission of 0 and 1 (Figure 14.15), hence a higher frequency signal is used to represent 1 and a lower frequency signal is used to represent 0 (or vice versa). In phase modulation the phase of the signal is changed to distinguish between binary 0 and 1 (Figure 14.16).

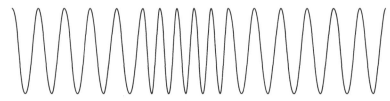

Figure 14.15 Frequency modulation.

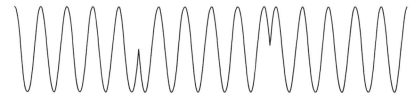

Figure 14.16 Phase modulation with 180° phase shift.

With frequency modulation, the frequency has to be changed by a significant amount to enable the difference to be detected easily by the receiver. Similarly, it is not easy to detect small phase changes and thus large changes of phase are used in phase modulation. Over a 3000 Hz telephone channel these techniques in isolation (using only two level signalling) achieve very conservative data rates, of the order of 1000 bits s^{-1}. In such circumstances the bit rate of the channel is the same as the signalling (baud) rate. However, it is possible to use multiple signal levels and combinations of these techniques, to achieve encodings of multiple bits per signal element. Quadrature amplitude modulation (QAM) uses a combination of phase modulation and amplitude modulation. One version of this is to use eight different phase changes (45° shift of phase) and four different amplitude levels. Theoretically this allows for five bits of information to be encoded in one signal element and thus the data rate to be increased by a factor of five.

14.10 Modems

It is necessary to use modulation to transmit digital data as analogue signals along analogue telephone lines, and to demodulate the signals to reconstruct the data at the receiving end. Thus to connect a computer to a telephone line requires the use of a modulator for sending and a demodulator for receiving. A device to do this is called a modem. Modems work in pairs, one at the sending end performing modulation and the other at the receiving end performing demodulation. The modems send control signals between each other and between the serial interfaces on the computers to which they are attached. It is these control signals that determine the complexity of the serial interface used on most computers. A pair of modems provides a duplex communication channel so that the attached computers can both send and receive information at the same time. The information sent in the opposite directions is modulated on different frequency carrier waves so that the two signals do not interact.

Modems operate at a variety of different line speeds using different modulation techniques at different speeds. For example, the CCITT V.29 standard specifies that a data rate of 9600 bits s^{-1} can be achieved with full duplex operation using the quadrature amplitude modulation technique described earlier. However 16-QAM used in V.29 modems encodes four bits of information per signal element by using one pair of amplitudes for phase shifts of 0°, 90°, 180° and 270°, and a different pair of amplitudes for phase shifts of 45°, 135°, 225° and 315°. Technically, four amplitude levels could be used with each phase shift, allowing five bits of information to be encoded in each signal. However, this redundancy allows greater discrimination at the receiver between adjacent phase shifts which differ not only in phase but in amplitude level. V.29 modems support signalling rates of 2400 baud, but with each signal element encoding four bits of information this achieves a data rate of 9600 bits s^{-1}.

Modems have become increasingly more complex to make them more flexible and to cope with transmission errors. Some modems now contain a microprocessor to provide even greater flexibility by incorporating data compression/expansion and channel multiplexing.

14.11 Example protocol

The lowest level protocol is the physical layer as defined by the ISO OSI model. There are several protocols that can be used at this level but the RS-232C or V24 interface is very common. This protocol, which defines how characters are transmitted between two serial interfaces, has been explained previously in Chapter 7. It was originally devised in the context of a telephone system to define the signals and protocols required for communication between a modem and a computer, as in Figure 14.17. The channels between modems and network switching nodes are telephone lines using analogue signalling. The channels between the computer and modem are short electrical cables that run the CCITT V24 standard and because of the short distances involved use multiple channels to control message exchanges.

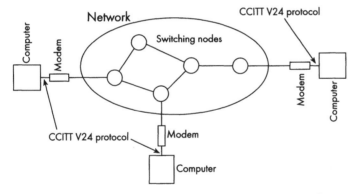

Figure 14.17 CCITT V24 for connection of computers and modems.

The explanation of the interface and protocol given in Chapter 7 was concerned only with direct communication between transmitter and receiver and dealt with three signals – transmit, receive and ground. In that simple description it was assumed a transmitter can transmit information whenever it wishes. However, there are many problems that can arise with such transmissions. For example, there has to be some method by which the receiver can signal to the receiver that transmission is allowed. There is a wide range of such conditions that can arise, some of which are specific to the use of a modem, for example, the loss of the carrier signal implying a break in the transmission across the telecommunications media. When the telecommunications industry, specifically their standards body CCITT, specified the V24 standard, they included a large number of extra control lines and the standard specifies 25 signals, some of which are given in Figure 14.18. Note that

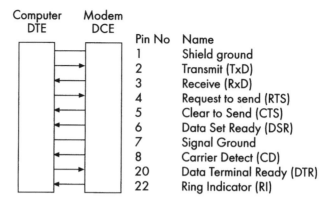

Figure 14.18 Common signals used in the CCITT V24 standard interface.

the computer is called the data terminal equipment (DTE) and the modem is called the data communication equipment (DCE).

Many of these control signals are specific to telecommunications. Thus when computer manufacturers adopted this standard for serial use they were unsure of what to do with all the control signals. Most manufacturers decided to ignore many of them and implemented only the three signals discussed in Chapter 7. No convention for sequencing signals was needed for the use of the three signals; a transmitter could transmit at any time and the receiver had to be capable of receiving data at any time. Some manufacturers decided to implement a larger subset and thus it is not always easy to determine which signals are necessary to control a V24 interface attached to a computer.

For an interface conforming to all the V24 signal definitions, there is a protocol that specifies the ordering of the control and data signals as described below. When a computer and its modem are switched on each acknowledges the other's existence and readiness to establish a connection with another modem. Thereafter a request connection set-up phase and a received connection set-up request phase are used respectively by a call initiator and a call respondent. These are illustrated in the time sequence diagram in Figure 14.19. In time sequence diagrams the vertical sequence of events represents ordering in time, and the caller and the respondent are represented as separate entities horizontally. These diagrams can capture the necessary precision of protocol rules for typical sequences of message exchanges (but are less appropriate for describing a number of possible alternatives).

The message exchanges captured by Figure 14.19 concisely represent the following stages in the communication:

(a) DTE/DCE acknowledge each other's existence.

1. The DTE (computer) sets the data terminal ready (DTR) signal to logic 1 indicating to the DCE (modem) that it is ready to receive data. (On

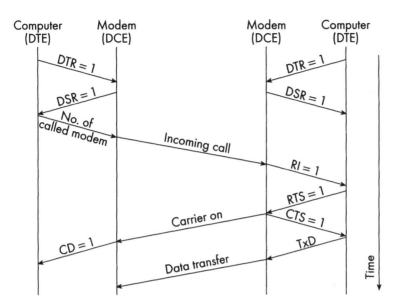

Figure 14.19 Time-sequence diagram for setting up a connection via a V24 interface.

some computers turning on the interface sets this signal and on others the signal is not used.)

2. The DCE (modem) replies by setting data set ready (DSR) to indicate its presence.

(b) Connection set-up phase request.

1. The DTE (computer) informs the DCE (modem) of the telephone number to call.

2. The DCE (modem) calls the specified number.

3. When the called DCE (modem) responds by sending a carrier signal over the telephone lines, the DCE (modem) responds to the DTE (computer) by setting the CD signal to 1. The connection has been set up.

(c) Connection set-up phase received.

1. When the DCE (modem) senses an incoming call, it sets ring indicator (RI) to 1 to inform the DTE (computer).

2. The DTE (computer) replies by setting ready to send (RTS) to logic 1, to which the DCE (modem) responds by accepting the call by sending a carrier signal to the remote calling modem and replies to the DTE (computer) by setting clear to send (CTS) to logic 1. The connection has been set up.

(d) Data transfer.

Once a connection has been established, the DTEs (computers) can send data by transmitting on the TxD data line. The transmitting DCE (modem) converts digital signals used across the RS-232C interface to analogue signals used over the telephone line, and the receiving DCE (modem) converts the analogue signals back to digital signals used on the RxD data line to the receiving DTE (computer). This arrangement can be used in half-duplex mode whereby only one of the modems sets CTS at any one time, or in full duplex mode by both modems setting CTS all the time.

(e) Connection close down.

The connection is closed down by the computer setting RTS and DTR to logic 0 which causes the modem to disconnect the line if there is no carrier signal from the remote modem and set CTS, CD and DSR to logic 0. After a short delay the computer and modem set their DTR and DSR signals to 1 again ready to establish a further connection.

The RS232C/V24 standard has been adopted for serial communication between computers and peripheral devices. Such arrangements are known as null modem configurations and ignore most, if not all, of these control signals but connect each end's TxD line to the other's RxD line for direct data transfers.

It should be noted that there is very little functionality at the physical layer level. The bit stream (represented as a signal stream) is merely transmitted and received, though with the provision for some error detection. FDM and TDM are employed for low-level sharing of a physical link as a collection of multiple logical channels. However, problems relating to use of a logical channel as a shared resource, and sharing of a physical link within a local area network are higher layer issues constructed on top of this primitive functionality. In addition, though error detection is performed in hardware at the physical level, provision for error correction is also treated as a higher level issue addressed in higher protocol layers.

14.12 Summary

Sender and receiver use an agreed protocol or set of rules to be able to communicate with one another. The protocol specifies the format of the data and the control actions to be taken, for example, when errors occur. A set of protocols (rather than a single protocol) is usually employed and the sender and receiver contain layers of software and hardware, which implement different protocol layers. Thus the information is transmitted in frames, which contain data encapsulated in layers of protocol information.

Electronic cable (twisted pair, co-axial cable), optical fibres and radio waves can all be used to transmit signals which encode data. These differ in terms of cost, data transmission capacity and susceptibility to interference.

The current trend is towards installation of optical fibre where high data rate and high reliability are required.

The sender and receiver have to be synchronized in order for them to communicate. Transmission may be performed synchronously in which case the sender and receiver synchronize with each other at the start of frame transmission and then their respective clocks are resynchronized by regular clocking information in the transmitted data encoding. The alternative method, called asynchronous transmission, involves resynchronising sender and receiver for each separate small frame of information transmitted. Typically asynchronous techniques are used for low speed transmission and synchronous techniques for higher speeds.

The telephone system is often used for data transmission but this network was optimized for sending analogue voice signals. Digital data is sent by modulating a standard carrier frequency at the sender, and retrieving the signal from the carrier at the receiver. The device to encode and decode the digital data on to the carrier signal is called a modem and hence computers that communicate over the telephone network each require a pair of compatible modems. There are many different modulation techniques used by modems to encode information, including amplitude modulation where the amplitude of the carrier wave is varied and frequency modulation where the frequency of the carrier wave is varied. Increasingly internal links within such networks have been upgraded to use baseband digital signalling and TDM, however upgrade of consumer local loops progresses slowly and hence connection to a wide area network is often by a modem connection.

14.13 Exercises

Exercise 14.1 Explain what a protocol involves. Discuss why computer communication usually involves a number of protocol layers.

Exercise 14.2 Represent the bit pattern 11010001 as

(a) a digital signal;

(b) an analogue signal using amplitude modulation;

(c) an analogue signal using frequency modulation;

(d) an analogue signal using phase modulation of 180° phase shift;

(e) a Manchester encoded signal.

Exercise 14.3 Why is it necessary to synchronize sender and receiver? How are sender and receiver kept in synchronism using synchronous transmission?

Exercise 14.4 Why is frequency modulation better than amplitude modulation as a modulation technique?

Exercise 14.5 Why is it necessary to use modulation techniques to transmit digital signals across the telephone system?

Exercise 14.6 Consider Figure 14.17. Assume that communication between internal nodes of the network uses digital signalling (but that the links between internal nodes and external computers still use analogue signalling). What functionality has to be built into each internal node that is connected to an external computer so that the computers can still be connected by a modem?

Exercise 14.7 Consider the network in Figure 14.7. Assume that it takes five time units to transmit a frame on each link between computers A.1 and B.2, and that the delay at each node is negligible.

(a) how long will it take for a data frame sent from A.1 to arrive at B.2?

(b) assume that error detection is applied on each link and delays a frame by one time unit at each node, how long will it take for a frame sent from A.1 to arrive at B.2?

Assume that on each link, one out of every n frames is detected as corrupt and can be discarded as soon as this is detected. Discuss the relative merits of incorporating error detection at each node for the cases where (a) $n = 2$, and (b) $n = 200$.

15

Computer networks

15.1 Introduction

In the 1960s and 1970s computers were costly, and hence methods for sharing computer resources were important. One of the first developments that eventually led to the creation of computer networks was the use of timesharing services on computers with typically eight or 16 attached terminals. The processing power of the computer was shared among all users. Each user at a terminal was able to use the full facilities of the machine but only for a fraction of the time. This was a primitive form of network, as each of the terminals was connected via a serial line to the computer, which was usually sited remotely in an air-conditioned room.

However, this only gave users access to the local computer and if they required access to a more powerful one they needed to travel elsewhere. A simple means of giving users access to a remote computer was to install a remote job entry (RJE) station and to connect it to the remote computer via a telephone line. A remote job entry station consisted of a card reader and line printer and thus did not give remote users a time shared service. This led to the eventual development of direct computer-computer links so that users could directly access scarce remote resources such as powerful processors or specialized output devices such as microfilm printers. This was the forerunner of the wide-area network (WAN). As technology improved, terminals were replaced by personal computers, which were still connected to a central computer by a serial link so that work that required significant computing power could be off loaded to the central mainframe. Gradually it was realized that the local network was becoming more important as users wanted to send more and more information not just to the central machine but also to other users in the same building. This generated the interest in local area networks (LANs), which could provide high-speed communication among local computers.

There are several advantages in connecting computers together, all of which involve some form of sharing. One form involves hardware resources where some particular resource can be shared by a group of users. For example, in many companies a considerable amount of computing power exists in the personal computers that many employees have on their desks. Where these PCs are networked, mechanisms exist whereby it is possible for one user to use the CPU of a remote idle machine to perform extra processing. Often, items of equipment that are required on an irregular basis, such as printers, are provided as shared resources. A more common form of sharing is the sharing of data. For example, a database of customer names and addresses may be made available to all the salesforce in a company who can update the database with new names and addresses. A very important form of sharing is the use of electronic mail whereby users of the network can communicate with other users sending messages that would previously have been communicated by post or telephone. The advantages of electronic mail are that the recipient does not have to be present at the receiving end (the message will be stored until it is read) and it is much faster than the post (often delivered in a matter of minutes).

To connect a computer to a network requires a method of interfacing the computer to the transmission medium. The simplest method is to use a modem, as described in the previous chapter, to connect the computer to the telephone system. This method is suitable for low speed long distance communications but is unsatisfactory for local high-speed communications. For such communications dedicated lines are required with more sophisticated interfaces, which are implemented in separate interface boards within modern personal computers. A special communications processor is often dedicated to supporting communication and computers that wish to communicate with each other do so via the communications processor, as in Figure 15.1. In the case of local area networks, instead of using a separate communication processor for local communication, interface processor boards in the host computers implement a local area network medium access control (MAC) protocol to give access to a shared communication medium. In this context the communications processors giving access to wide area networks are usually known as bridges, routers or gateways depending upon the functionality they embody. The speed of a local area network is typically 10 to 100 Mbits s^{-1} as opposed to 64 kbits s^{-1} for a typical connection to a wide area network.

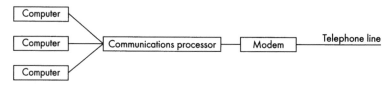

Figure 15.1 Connection via a communications processor.

A useful property that can be used to classify communication systems is whether it uses point-to-point or broadcast communications. In point-to-point communications, as used in the telephone system, messages are routed through the network by setting switches in the intermediate nodes so that the information travels along a particular communication pathway. Broadcast communication is sent to all receivers at once and it is the task of the intended receiver to recognize and copy those messages that are intended for it and ignore those that are intended for others. Point-to-point communication is used in wide area networks and broadcast communication is used in many isolated local area networks. This distinction is usually closely related to the topology of the network.

15.2 Topology

The topology of a network is the physical configuration of the interconnected nodes. There are many possible topologies and some of the more common ones are discussed below.

15.2.1 Mesh and reduced mesh networks

A (totally connected) mesh topology, Figure 15.2, connects every node to every other node by a bi-directional point-to-point connection. In this case,

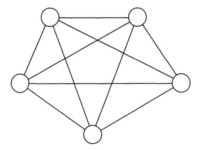

Figure 15.2   A mesh (totally connected) network.

routing of messages from one node to another requires selecting only the appropriate outward channel, but this configuration is very expensive of interconnecting media. In addition, expansion to more nodes requires an extra communication line from each existing node to the new one. For these reasons totally connected networks are rare. However it should be noted that the purpose of higher layer protocols in computer networks organized on other topologies is to give an illusion that the underlying topology is a mesh (that is, to behave from an application program/user viewpoint as though there is a direct connection to any other computer).

A form of reduced mesh with fewer connections is normally used for wide area networks. Such networks have a topology that is an arbitrary graph of nodes, as shown in Figure 15.3. The connectivity of a particular graph of

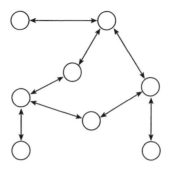

Figure 15.3 Arbitrary graph of nodes.

nodes depends on a number of factors, such as the cost of lines, the distance between the nodes, and the amount of redundancy that has to be built into the network to ensure all nodes remain connected even if a node or link between nodes becomes inoperable. They do not have a regular structure, since additions to the network, inevitable as the system grows, are largely unplanned and unknown when the system is initially designed. Such networks require a complicated routing algorithm since the number of connections that have to be traversed to get from one node to another depends on the connectivity of the network and the relative positions of the nodes that wish to communicate. Often however the routing is handled internally in the connecting nodes rather than as a concern of host machines connected to the network. In this way, the underlying network presents an illusion to the host machines connected to the network that there is a direct connection to any machine with which it wishes to communicate.

15.2.2 Star networks

A simpler topology still is the star network in which a central node acts as a switch connecting all the other nodes together, as in Figure 15.4.

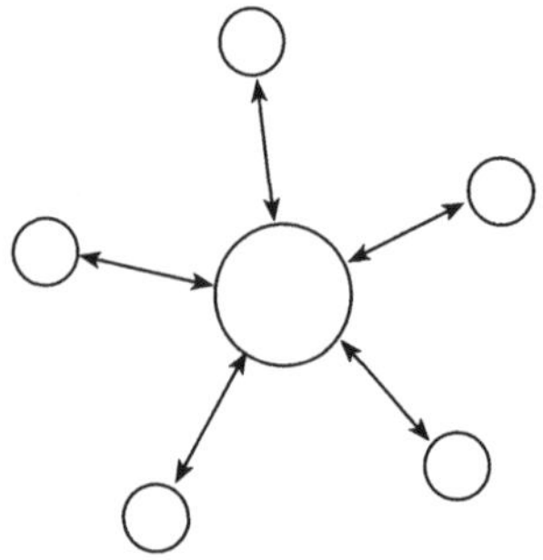

Figure 15.4 A star network.

Conceptually this is very simple and involves only the addition of one extra line to connect an additional node, but it suffers from the weakness that failure of the central switch causes the whole network to fail and that overloading of the switching device can significantly degrade performance. As electronic switches are reasonably reliable, this topology is quite frequently used in practice.

15.2.3 Ring networks

A ring, Figure 15.5, consists of a set of nodes, each of which is attached to its own host and its two nearest nodes. The set of nodes form a closed loop (ring), which make routing simple since propagation of a message around the circumference of the ring takes the message to all nodes. Failure of a single node causes the whole system to fail, so braids, connections that bypass one or more nodes, are sometimes inserted to provide a second pathway in the case of failure of the primary one.

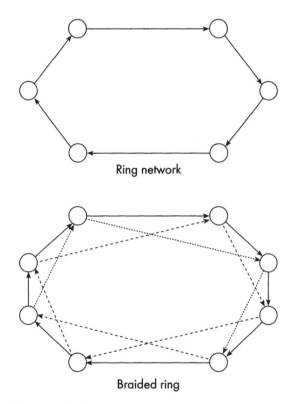

Ring network

Braided ring

Figure 15.5 Ring topologies.

15.2.4 Bus-based networks

Another common topology is based on the use of a bus or group of buses, illustrated in Figure 15.6. The best known example of this type of topology is the Ethernet developed at Xerox PARC in the 1970s. In this network, the bus is a coaxial cable with the nodes tapped on to the cable at intervals along its length. Messages propagate away from the transmitter in both directions

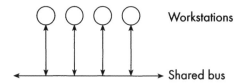

Figure 15.6 A bus network.

along the cable so that all nodes see them. As with the internal CPU bus, only one transmitter should be active at any one time and in the Ethernet system there is no central controller; each transmitter/receiver (called a transceiver) detects if another node is transmitting and, if so, does not transmit itself. More details of the Ethernet system are described later in this chapter.

In general, wide area networks have an irregular topology of an arbitrary graph of connected nodes in which routing of messages from source to destination is a major issue. Conversely, local area networks have more regular topologies that initially were based around star, bus or ring topologies and in which broadcast communication is the main technique. Increasingly, however the tendency is towards having multiple local area networks within a single site and to organize these as an arbitrary graph of interconnected LANs. Such so-called 'internetworking' means that routing between individual LANs becomes an issue, as broadcast communication is restricted to each individual LAN.

In addition, though bus and ring topologies have been common place for the past decade or longer, there is an increasing shift towards cabling topologies that are star-like. Changes and advances in technology often have significant effects and here we note just a few that have significant impact on the design of LANs. Bus-based topologies have been popular due to the success of Ethernet on coaxial cable for 10 Mbits s^{-1} networks. However faster data rate versions of Ethernet, based upon electrical cabling and fibre optic cabling, are usually based around a star topology due to the restrictions that operation of the Ethernet medium access control protocol (MAC) requires at fast data rates. In addition, faster and more reliable switching technologies have reduced the fragility of star based topologies so that these are becoming more common. Finally, ring based networks are often cabled in a fashion similar to star based networks in order to isolate faults on individual links and at individual nodes on the ring. Hence the potential reduced cabling costs of ring topologies in comparison with star topologies are often not realized in practice due to reliability factors.

15.3 Local area networks (LANs)

A local area network is a network over a small geographical area, for example, a building or site, and is usually owned and run by a single organization. Typical topologies are rings, stars and buses. LANs are characterized by comparatively high information transfer rates and relatively low error rates.

LANs are suitable for supporting distributed computing services where a computation is distributed over several nodes of the network. Most companies and organizations now have internal LANs to which they connect personal computers.

For each kind of a LAN, a physical layer standard defines the way that data is represented as signals on the link and usually involves some constraint on the maximum length of a data frame which can be transmitted. In addition, it defines signal sequences which indicate the start and end of frames and the state of the medium when it is idle. In general, LANs use baseband digital signalling, thereby using the entire medium bandwidth to support a high data rate single physical link between computers. (Notable exceptions to this are broadband based networks which use existing cable TV technology to support multiple analogue channels on the physical link.)

Consequently, most isolated LANs use a broadcast protocol for data transmission. Senders and receivers are connected by physical links (channels) that form the transmission routes between senders and receivers. In a broadcast system, the physical link (channel) is shared among multiple senders and thus a medium access control (MAC) protocol has to be designed to allow a maximum of one sender or transmitter to be active at any one time. The MAC layer protocol is constructed on top of the physical layer protocol. Whereas the physical layer provides raw functionality for generating data on the link, the MAC layer protocol is designed to give fair and efficient access to each computer connected to the network link. There are two main classes of techniques for sharing the channel, contention based and allocation (or permission) based methods.

In contention based systems, senders are allowed to try to transmit whenever they have data to send and a mechanism is used to detect corruption of messages when multiple senders transmit simultaneously. Allocation systems are based upon a notion of negotiated permission to transmit. Permission to transmit, usually in the form of a control token, is passed from workstation to workstation. Workstations are allowed to transmit only when they have the control token. Both of these strategies have their advantages and disadvantages. The contention strategy works best when traffic is light, since there will be few occasions when information is corrupted by multiple transmissions at the same time, but aborted transmissions become much more common under heavy loading. The allocation strategy works better when there is heavy traffic on the transmission medium since senders can get a fair share of the bandwidth, but under light loading the overhead of stations periodically relinquishing the control token to other stations with no data to transmit becomes significant.

15.3.1 Contention based systems

The first system to use a contention method of access control was the ALOHA system implemented at the University of Hawaii in the 1970s. This system was based on transmission of radio signals because the university is based over a number of islands. The transmitter repeatedly re-transmits the frame and waits for some random period until it detects that the complete frame has been sent without corruption, that is, without any other transmitter trying to transmit at the same time. This is a very crude system but it can be shown theoretically that up to 18% of the available bandwidth can be successfully used, that is, up to 18 frames in 100 transmitted are successfully received. In fact this system can be improved substantially by a very simple change – the channel is slotted into time slots and the transmitters are allowed to transmit only at the beginning of each slot rather than at any arbitrary time.

15.3.2 CSMA

A further refinement of this scheme requires a transmitter to sense if another station is trying to transmit before attempting to transmit. If the medium is busy then it must defer to the other station already transmitting. This is known as a carrier sense multiple access (CSMA) protocol, and is often characterized as a 'listen before talk' protocol. Variants of this arrangement are classified in terms of how enthusiastically each station insists on trying to transmit if it finds the channel is free, and how enthusiastic each is in trying to be the next station to transmit if it finds the channel busy. There are three different types of CSMA system – non-persistent, p-persistent and 1-persistent (though the third is a limiting case of the second).

In the non-persistent system the transmitter checks before it transmits that the channel is free and if so transmits immediately. However, if the channel is busy the transmitter backs off and transmits later after a random amount of time. The problem with this is that the channel may become free after one station has transmitted but no other transmitter then starts to transmit because all waiting stations are still waiting for the random amount of time to elapse. Surprisingly, this kind of system can achieve high levels of throughput over the channel with heavy loading because it avoids multiple waiting stations each enthusiastically transmitting after another station has finished. However this is at the expense of unwarranted (and possibly long) delays for individual transmitters before they transmit.

The p-persistent version of this system checks whether the channel is free before transmitting. If it is free it makes a decision on whether to use the channel, with probability p, or not, with probability $1-p$. If it does use the channel, it will do so immediately, otherwise it will wait a predetermined period of time before making the decision again. This predetermined period of time treats data transmissions on the channel as occurring in discrete time slots. If the channel is being used, then it waits until it is free, and then makes its probabilistic decision on whether to transmit or not. The choice of exactly what probabilistic function to use is difficult to make. The two extremes are that the transmitter will wait indefinitely for the channel to be free, and at the other extreme that the transmitter will never wait but always try and transmit when the channel is free. This latter case is known as 1-persistent CSMA because when the channel is free, a transmitter sends data with a probability of 1 and hence dispenses with the need for time to be slotted. It is often treated as a separate case (rather than the extreme of p-persistent CSMA) due to this attribute and because of its high profile as the technique utilized in the IEEE 802.3 (Ethernet) protocol discussed below. The 1-persistent scheme achieves faster response for individual transmitters at the expense of poorer performance at heavy loading. The more polite the scheme in terms of delaying transmission in case another transmitter wishes to do so, the better the throughput under heavy loading, but this is achieved at the expense of poorer response times for each individual transmitter.

The most widely used family of protocols is called CSMA/CD – carrier sense multiple access with collision detection. Such protocols include a further refinement to increase performance. The CSMA schemes require a transmitter to 'listen before it talks', but once transmission has begun, corrupted data is not detected until the frame of data has been received. The inclusion of collision detection is a requirement that each transmitter monitors the signal on the medium while it transmits and aborts as soon as it detects that the signal on the medium is being corrupted due to multiple transmissions. This 'listen while talking' action significantly reduces the loss of bandwidth due to continued transmission of long frames after corruption.

CSMA/CD is the basis of the IEEE standard, IEEE 802.3. In these protocols the transmitter abandons a transmission as soon as it detects a collision has occurred. Again, there is a choice of persistent and non-persistent protocols. Ethernet, the most famous of the family, is a 1-persistent version of CSMA-CD. This means that it will always try to start frame transmission immediately that the channel is free. Currently, the most common variant of the standard operates at a speed of 10 Mbits s^{-1} using a bus topology, Figure 15.7.

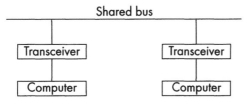

Figure 15.7 Ethernet local area network.

Whenever a collision is detected, transmission immediately stops and the transmitter waits a random amount of time before attempting retransmission. This random period is determined dynamically by an exponential back-off algorithm. Initially a random value in the range 0 to 1 is chosen and the transmitters wait either 0 or 1 times the period to transmit the smallest Ethernet frame (512 bits). If a further collision occurs then the range of values is increased to 0 to 3 and each transmitter generates a value in this range and then retries after that number of 512-bit times. The process continues with the range 0 to 2^{c-1} increasing as the number of collisions, c, increases. For this process to work, it is necessary that data frames have a minimum size (512 bits) which ensures that when a collision occurs the corrupted signal propagates back to each of the transmitters whilst they are still transmitting the frame. The minimum size is determined by the maximum distance (2.5km) between transmitting and receiving computers.

The IEEE 802.3 defines operating characteristics for a number of variations of this CSMA/CD protocol over different media, including 200m thin-coaxial cable segments (thin Ethernet, 10Base2), 500 m thick-coaxial cable (thick Ethernet, 10Base5), 100m twisted pair cable segments (10BaseT), and 2km optical fibre segments (10BaseF). All of these operate at 10 Mbits s^{-1} and use baseband (digital) signalling. As the short segment lengths can be restrictive, repeaters are used to join cable segments and boost the signal. However, such cable sequences are restricted to have a maximum length of 2.5km so that they satisfy the CSMA/CD requirement that the transmitter is still transmitting a data frame when a collision propagates back to it.

More recently this standard has been updated to include faster data rate operation at 100 Mbits s^{-1}, either multiplexed onto four sets of telephone-quality twisted pair cables (100BaseT4), or on a single high-quality twisted pair cable (100BaseTX), or over fibre optic cables (100BaseF). The 10Base2 and 10Base5 variations use the shared bus topology illustrated in Figure 15.7. However the other variants all use a star topology based around either a central shared or switching hub with dedicated point to point links connecting each workstation's transceiver to the hub as illustrated in Figure 15.8. In the case of a shared hub, only one transceiver can be

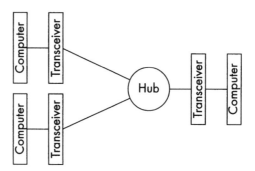

Figure 15.8 Ethernet hub based local area network.

transmitting at any one time and the normal collision detection applies at the hub, which propagates collisions back to the transmitting devices. In the case of switched hubs, which are necessary for faster data rate fibre optic versions and desirable for faster data rate electrical cable versions, data frames are buffered for the point to point links at the hub and collision detection and recovery is localized within the hub. Consequently, switched hubs allow multiple transmitters to be transmitting at once over their point-to-point links, and the switch schedules and routes packets through the switch transparent to the transmitters and receivers involved.

15.3.3 Allocation systems

These systems work on the principle that collisions, and recovery from collisions, waste bandwidth and that avoidance of collisions can be at least as efficient in the use of bandwidth. The most widely used system of this type is the token ring protocol.

Token ring

This protocol has been standardized as IEEE 802.5 and is used on LANs that are physically organized as rings. Though ring topologies theoretically require less cabling than a star topology, in practice they are often cabled in a comparable fashion to a star topology centred on a device that connects incoming to out-going links so as to form the ring, as illustrated in Figure 15.9. This has the advantage that if one station fails, or a link to or from one station fails, then the wire centre can reassign port connections to isolate the offending portion of the ring and re-establish a smaller ring excluding it.

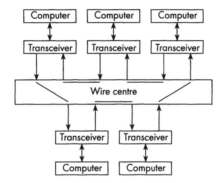

Figure 15.9   Token ring architecture.

The basic operation of the token ring protocol uses a token, a small unique control frame, which continuously circulates around the ring when it is idle. Any transmitter that wishes to transmit can claim the token by removing it from the ring and then transmit its data frame. Since the physical organization of the system is a ring, the data transmitted is seen by every receiver attached to the ring and eventually returns to the sender who then removes the data frame and replaces it by the token frame.

The main problems with a token based system are the ring management functions that are required to ensure that the token is not lost or corrupted either due to errors in the system, (for example, a transmission error) or a malfunctioning transmitter or receiver. To handle these problems, token rings have a network monitor known as the active ring monitor whose purpose is to monitor the operation of the ring and generate a new token if it is lost or remove duplicate tokens should they arise. In addition this monitor station watches for data frames that propagate around the ring for a second time. Such a situation arises if a transmitting station crashes during transmission and thus is not able to remove its transmitted data frame. It then becomes the task of the ring monitor to drain the ring of this frame and generate a new token. Each station connected to a token ring network can potentially fill this role, but only one station performs the function at any one time. However, as the active ring monitor is equally prone to failure as any other station, the token ring protocol and its implementation within workstations are complicated by the need for a distributed algorithm that allows the stations to negotiate a new monitor station when one or more stations notice that the previous monitor station is no longer fulfilling this role.

Contention based protocols are simpler in the sense that they do not require any centralized monitoring function and consequently do not need comparable management protocols. However, in the token ring protocol, each transmitter gets a fair chance to transmit as the token is passed around the ring in order, whereas in CSMA systems the transmitter that wins in the contest to transmit next is elected on a random basis.

The IEEE 802.5 standard originally defined operational characteristics for token ring networks operating at 1 and 4 Mbits s^{-1} using twisted pair cable. Subsequently IBM developed a 16 Mbits s^{-1} version, and more recently the fibre distributed data interface (FDDI) is a fibre optic variant operating at 100 Mbits s^{-1}. The slower token ring protocols (1 and 4 Mbits s^{-1}) require the transmitter to regenerate a token once it has drained the data frame it sent and for short, slow rings this is reasonable. However in the case of faster rings operating over longer distances, this delay leads to significant wastage of available bandwidth. In the case of large FDDI rings it is possible that the ring circumference is sufficient to hold multiple data frames one after another but which would be precluded if token release only occurred once a data frame had been returned to the original sender. The 16 and 100 M bits s^{-1} variants therefore require a transmitter to release the token immediately after transmitting the last bit of a data frame, which permits the next station wishing to transmit to send a data frame before the first has drained its data frame.

A further more recent version of FDDI (FDDI-II) supports transmission of both synchronous and asynchronous data frames. In general, older LAN protocols have supported only asynchronous data frames, where unpredictable delays between successive frames may arise. Synchronous data frame transmission is required by real-time applications that must be guaranteed specific data transfer rates. This involves a form of reservation of a proportion of the available bandwidth or prioritization of data transfers. Asynchronous data frames are used for data where the timing is not so important. When the transmitter receives the token, it transmits synchronous data frames before asynchronous data frames.

15.3.4 LAN frame formats and addressing

Each kind of local area network specifies the frame format for that particular kind of LAN. Figure 15.10 shows the frame formats for the IEEE 802.3 (CSMA/CD) and IEEE 802.5 (token ring) standards. The size of fields within the frames

	7	1	2/6	2/6	2		4
(a)	Preamble	Start of frame	Destination	Source	Length	Data	FCS

	1	1	1	2/6	2/6		4	1	1
(b)	Start of frame	Access control	Frame control	Destination	Source	Data	FCS	End of frame	Frame status

Figure 15.10 (a) IEEE 802.3 (CSMA/CD) frame format;
(b) IEEE 802.5 (token ring) frame format.

are indicated in numbers of bytes (often called 'octets' in communication documents). Both use Manchester encoded signals to represent binary data. In 802.3 the start of the frame is signalled by the eight byte preamble and start of frame fields and the length field determines where the end of the frame will occur. In the 802.5 standard the start of frame and end of frame sequences are illegal Manchester encodings of binary data which cannot occur within the data field. The access control, frame control and frame status fields include information for the detailed operation of the token ring protocol (such as distinguishing between token and data frame, indication if a data frame is circulating for a second time) whose detail we omit. Both protocols use a 32-bit frame check sum (FCS) for error detection of any corruption within a frame (though the calculation of the FCS may be different).

In both protocols, a network is configured to use either 16-bit or 48-bit station addresses. Each station has its own unique address, which it uses as the source address for frames it generates and which it compares with the destination field of frames broadcast on the network in order to determine which to copy from the network. Such addresses have only local significance, they must be unique within the LAN but there is no guarantee (and it is highly unlikely) that the same MAC layer address bit patterns are not used for other stations in other networks in the world. In addition, both kinds of LAN have physical restrictions on the overall size of a LAN which also restrict the numbers of stations that can be connected to a single LAN.

15.3.5 Interconnecting LANs

The growth of local area networks has been fast and many organizations now have all their computers connected to a LAN. Local control of LANs brings a number of benefits, but it also has led to uncoordinated installation of LANs by different departments within the same organization. Consequently, many organizations have many different LANs to which computers are connected. In addition, there is a physical limit to the number of machines that can be connected to a specific LAN, both because of addressing problems and, more importantly, because of limited available bandwidth. Thus there are several reasons why an organization might wish to connect multiple LANs together.

The simplest way to interconnect two LANs together is to use a bridge or router as shown in Figure 15.11. This is a device that is connected to two

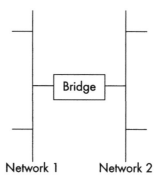

Figure 15.11 Use of a bridge to connect two LANs.

separate LANs and detects frames transmitted on one LAN whose destinations are on the other LAN. In such cases, it removes these frames from the originating LAN and subsequently transmits them on the other LAN. The complexity of such interconnecting devices depends upon the extent to which the protocols of the two LANs differ. If the differences are negligible then the device is relatively straight-forward. However, if the differences are more profound then the device will have to reformat data, recalculate error detection information and even segment large frames from one LAN into a number of smaller frames for the other LAN. Minimally such devices have to be able to receive and transmit data frames on each LAN.

Two LANs that use the same protocol (such as two Ethernet networks) can be connected via a bridge. The bridge monitors the source and destination address fields of each data frame, looks these up in a table and ignores frames whose source and destination are on the same LAN. For situations where the source and destination machines are not on the same LAN, it removes the data frame from the originating LAN and transmits it onto the destination LAN. However, as the frame formats are the same on each LAN, it does not need to perform any frame conversion. Interconnecting two Ethernet LANs is an alternative to connecting then by a repeater as two segments of the same LAN. The use of a bridge, and appropriate assignment of stations to each LAN such that communication across LANs is relatively rare, results in more efficient use of bandwidth and can be used to enhance security (by isolating use of more sensitive data within one of the LANs).

Bridges, however, must buffer the frames in transit, since there is no guarantee that a frame can be immediately transferred from one network to the other. The bridge needs to obtain access to the receiving network as a transmitter using the appropriate media access control protocol of the destination LAN. In addition, when the protocols are very different (such as connecting an Ethernet network to a token ring network), the bridge has to buffer sufficient frames to be able to accommodate local congestion that may arise from trying to forward frames from a faster network onto a slower network. Finally it should be noted that, whereas an isolated LAN broadcasts data frames to all stations on that LAN, interconnection of multiple LANs requires that bridges forward on frames appropriately, and hence they often perform a routing function using techniques comparable to those described for wide area networks below and are often called routers or brouters (bridge routers).

An alternative and more structured method of connecting a number of separate LANs is to use a high-speed backbone to which bridging devices are connected. Currently this is the typical use for high data rate (100 Mbits s^{-1}) technologies. The backbone may be either a fast Ethernet hub, a FDDI token ring network or a distributed queue dual bus (DQDB, IEEE 802.6 standard) network. The speed to the backbone usually needs to be greater than the speed of individual isolated LANs, as potentially it must service a larger number of workstations (via bridges), and in addition it is usual for backbones to be connected to further interconnecting devices (known as gateways) which give access to wide area networks.

DQDB is a dual bus system in which the buses transfer information in different directions as shown in Figure 15.12. Thus stations can transmit information to stations to their left or right by using the appropriate bus. The bus is treated as a slotted medium with the head of each bus generating 53 byte slots that can hold a single DQDB data frame plus protocol control information.

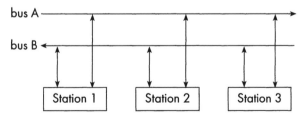

Figure 15.12 Distributed queue dual bus system.

DQDB uses a permission based medium access control layer protocol, which is relatively complex since an attempt is made to be fair to all transmitters. A transmitter cannot just acquire an empty slot as it goes by, as this would be unfair to downstream transmitters who are waiting to transmit. To give transmitters equal chances of acquiring a slot, requests are registered by upstream neighbours by using the opposite direction bus. Slots transmitted on a bus have two bits signifying whether the frame contains data and whether a frame upstream from this station has requested an empty frame. Each station can have only a single outstanding request for an empty slot and each station keeps track of the number of requests for empty slots made for each direction.

Let us assume that a station X wishes to transmit to another station Y to its right (that is downstream on bus A). It registers the request with stations upstream from it on bus A by setting the request bit of the first slot with its request bit unset on bus B. Each station downstream of X on bus B (to its left) counts the number of such requests from upstream stations. Hence, each station allows an appropriate number of empty slots to pass by on bus A before trying to transmit its own data frame. The cumulative effect of these counters is to implement a distributed queue, in which the order of the frames transmitted by all stations is fairly handled on a first come first served basis.

The channel is used fairly and efficiently in a DQDB system. If only a small number of stations are trying to transmit, then a station will count only a few outstanding requests and thus can access the network quickly. In one that is heavily loaded, any station only has to wait for a frame with the busy bit unset, which it can then use to reserve a frame on the opposite direction bus at a later time.

15.4 Wide area networks

The main problems that LAN medium access control protocols address is fair access to a shared transmission medium and efficient use of available bandwidth. As each workstation sees all frames transmitted on an isolated LAN, routing a message from a source to a destination becomes a problem only once multiple LANs are connected together. However, routing is a major concern in wide area networks (WANs) since they do not use broadcast protocols. In addition, as WANs can introduce more significant data transmission delays, greater concern is given to the quality of service that a WAN offers to user applications running on host machine connected to it.

WANs internally consist of an arbitrary graph of internal network nodes, as shown in Figure 15.13. The complexity of the nodes depends upon the operation of the WAN. Each WAN is under the control of a single authority, which administers and controls it. Individual WANs often encompass entire countries. However just as LANs may be internetworked into larger configurations, so WANs are usually interconnected both to other WANs and to LANs. The world-wide network of such interconnected networks is known as the Internet and uses the TCP/IP protocols to achieve communication independent of the underlying networks.

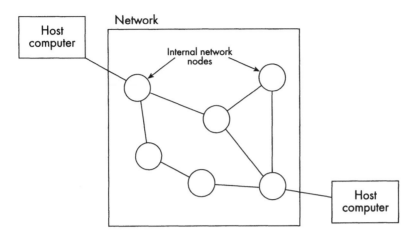

Figure 15.13 Host computers connected to a WAN.

Initially we will consider the organization of an isolated WAN, and some of the options that are available in terms of its internal organization, the kinds of service it provides and the ways in which it routes messages from one host station to a destination host station.

15.4.1 Circuit and packet switching

In the early days of wide area networks, communication was based upon use of existing analogue telephone lines for data transfer. Such telephone networks allocated a collection of channels and switches to establish a path from the station initiating a message to a required destination. Communication starts by setting up a dedicated path between sender and receiver. Each intervening node reserves a channel to the next node so that eventually a complete path is established between sender and receiver. This path is maintained for the duration of the message transfer and can be used only by the two parties involved in the communication. Once the path has been established, messages sent along the pathway do not need the global address of the receiver, only the correct output channel at the source as the channels along the path have been reserved. When the message transfer is finished, a disconnect message is issued along the path and this has the effect of releasing all the intermediate channels and switches. Such circuit switching is used for voice information with telephone calls, though the underlying technology has changed. Circuit switched data communication uses identical techniques to reserve resources that establish a dedicated path through the network.

Circuit switching has the advantage that once the path has been established, data transfer is delayed only by the propagation delay along the channel, and is therefore almost immediate. The disadvantage of circuit switching, however, is that it is not a perfect fit to the usual requirements of data transfers. Often messages to be transmitted are generated in bursts for some period followed by an idle period before further messages are sent. Circuit switching, however, reserves resources (channel bandwidth and switches) for the duration of a call. Users are generally charged for connect time rather than the volume of data transmitted. From the communication carrier's perspective, though it receives revenue for periods when communication is idle on an established call, this wastes bandwidth that could be offered to other customers.

To compensate for these shortcomings, subsequent WANs were designed to use store and forward devices as switching nodes. Data transfers are then achieved by each switching device receiving (a part of) a message and then forwarding this on to the appropriate successor switching device when a channel to it becomes available. Two main variants of this are possible, namely message switching where entire messages (no matter how long) are stored at each switching node, and packet switching where long messages are segmented into fixed length packets which can be stored in main memory at each switching node. Message switching results in much longer delays within the network, and hence packet switching has become the preferred technique within WANs. However, both techniques have the advantages that the destination does not necessarily have to be available as the message can be delivered at a later time, and that users are charged for volume of data transmitted rather than connect time.

15.4.2 Datagrams versus virtual circuits

Packet switching itself can be sub-categorized based upon two different implementation techniques that are used within the switching nodes, datagram oriented and virtual-circuit oriented.

In a datagram oriented network, each packet is dealt with separately so individual packets can be routed along different paths to the destination, as shown in Figure 15.14. Consequently, packets may arrive at the destination in a different order to that in which they were sent.

The virtual circuit implementation uses virtual circuit identifiers to identify the particular path used for messages associated with a sustained connection between two host computers, as in Figure 15.15. In essence, this is a packet switched simulation of circuit switching. A connection set-up phase determines an appropriate path to the destination and establishes entries in virtual circuit tables at each node along the path to appropriately route packets that contain that virtual circuit number to the correct destination. Packets for a multi-packet message are then transmitted with this virtual circuit number rather than with source and destination addresses and follow the same path. Old packet switched networks used error correcting techniques (such as those to be discussed in Chapter 16) in order to guarantee error-free in-order delivery on each individual link between pairs of nodes in the network. If in-order error-free delivery is guaranteed over each individual channel between pairs of nodes on the path, and

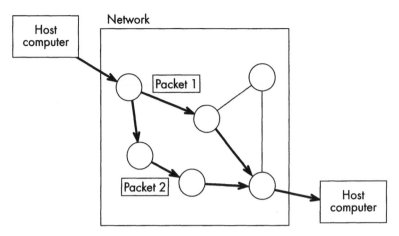

Figure 15.14 Datagram routing in a WAN.

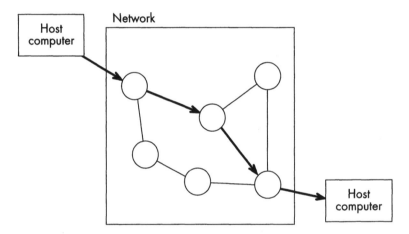

Figure 15.15 Virtual circuit routing in a WAN.

packets for the same message follow the same path, then this achieves in-order error-free delivery from the source to destination host computer.

The internal implementation is not visible to the host machines that are connected to the network. Rather, host computers are concerned with the quality of service that a network provides. The quality of service of connections supported by a network involves a number of factors, one of which is discussed below.

15.4.3 Connectionless and connection-oriented services

A connectionless service does not guarantee error-free nor in-order delivery. Packets are delivered on a best-effort basis, in isolation. This correlates well with the natural service a datagram implemented network can achieve. However, there are also circumstances where a connectionless service needs to be implemented over a virtual circuit network with the potential overhead of a connection set-up and close-down for each packet.

A connection-oriented service is comparable to the functionality supported by a circuit-switched system. Packets are delivered in-order and error-free, and it is the responsibility of the internal network to achieve this. This corresponds naturally with a virtual circuit implemented network, although such a service can also be implemented over a datagram implemented network (or any connectionless service) by buffering in-coming frames at the receiver and passing packets to higher layer protocols only once they are in order.

The assumption behind early WANs and the OSI reference model has been that WANs should offer high integrity connection-oriented services to user applications. Historically, WANs were more liable to errors than LANs, due to the longer distances, greater number of switching nodes, less predictable operating environments and relatively higher error rates of copper cabling. Consequently, the nodes in the network were designed to recover from errors and use robust error and flow control protocols (discussed in Chapter 16). This manifests itself in the OSI expectation of heavy-weight low-level protocols to provide error-free in-order delivery on each internal link at low levels of the protocol hierarchy.

In contrast, the most common hierarchy of protocols used on the World Wide Web (WWW) use an internet protocol (IP) which provides a connectionless service over all underlying kinds of networks, and then supports higher layer protocols that build upon this service. The most common of these are TCP (transmission control protocol) and UDP (user datagram protocol) which support connection-oriented and connectionless services respectively. In OSI terms, this assumes only that communication carriers' network layer can provide connectionless services and that host implementations enhance this service where necessary through use of TCP, a higher layer connection-oriented service.

In addition, the more recent use of fibre optic links has contributed to this change in emphasis. More modern protocols (such as ISDN and ISDN-II) rely to a greater extent on the reliability of the underlying medium and the provision for error-correction in host computers to provide more light-weight fast high-capacity data channels.

15.4.4 Routing in WANs

Broadcast protocols that are typical of LAN media access control protocols are inherently inefficient because they use bandwidth to send frames to stations that do not need to receive the information. For large networks this inefficiency cannot be tolerated and a new mechanism has to be used, so that frames are sent only to the required receivers. This is the purpose of the routing function of WANS.

As mentioned above, messages between stations on a wide area network are sent by means of point-to-point communication channels. These channels pass through intermediate nodes, as shown in Figure 15.13, and the intermediate nodes are responsible for routing the information to the eventual destination. Hence, one of the main functions of the intervening nodes is routing.

Network nodes in a WAN are dedicated processors with memory that deal with the lower three layers of the OSI model. The physical layer and data link layer are concerned with data transmission over a single channel to the next adjacent node. The network layer is concerned with routing packets through the network (and, in the case of virtual circuit implementations, with managing virtual circuits). The network layer is thus concerned with conventions for addressing connected host machines and with techniques for routing packets.

Host computers connected to a network are identified by a host address and these addresses are used to route packets through the network. All routing strategies are based upon tables that map host destination addresses to information that allows an appropriate path to be determined. However, strategies differ on where these tables exist and the entries for each host.

Routing strategies can be categorized by their ability to accommodate changes in topology and traffic volume as either static (non-adaptive) or adaptive. Alternatively, they can be categorized in terms of where the responsibility lies for determining the route a packet follows; either source routing or network routing.

(a) Source routing versus network routing

In source routing it is the responsibility of the host computers to maintain tables that map each destination to an appropriate path (a sequence of switching nodes) for packets to follow through the network to the destination, as illustrated in Figure 15.16. This path is then embedded within the header for the packet and each node extracts from the packet the routing information to determine which node should receive the packet next. This scheme can use either static or dynamic techniques for maintaining the host tables determining the routes, although source routing is most generally used only to over-ride network routing if a network's routing tables are severely corrupted. In other circumstances, the disadvantage of source routing is that the internal topology of the network has to be visible outside the network. In addition, the overhead of each packet containing the full path wastes available bandwidth. Network routing locates the responsibility for determining an appropriate path for a packet inside the network, requiring only that packets identify the destination station. Nodes internal to the network determine an appropriate path.

Whereas source routing considers the routing problem as the determination of a global path (sequence of switching nodes) to be taken through the network, network routing views this problem as a collection of local decisions at each node. For each packet received, the node determines the appropriate output link (and hence successor node) for the packet. Hence

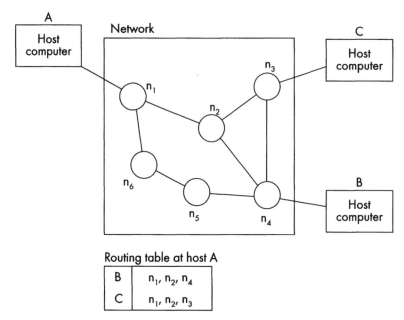

Figure 15.16 Routing tables in source routing.

each node requires only a routing table, which associates each destination with a list of the best output link(s) to be used to route packets to that destination, as illustrated in Figure 15.17. A packet from node A with a destination field containing host C's address is sent initially to n_1, whose routing table determines it should forward this to n_2. Node n_2's routing table determines that packets destined for C should be forwarded to n_3. (Usually, the links are identified by link names, rather than the node at the other end of the link.) The combination of such decisions at each node determines an appropriate path.

(b) Static versus adaptive network routing

Maintenance of these routing tables can be handled on a static or dynamic basis. Static routing requires only that appropriate routing tables be computed and then loaded when network and host computers are started. Various graph algorithms for determining the connectivity of a graph of arbitrary nodes and shortest and minimal cost paths within a graph can be used to determine the routing tables. Once computed and loaded into the switching nodes, the routing tables remain static and the same path(s) to a particular destination will continue to be used. Such arrangements however, do not take account of failures of nodes or channels within the network.

Adaptive routing algorithms employ techniques that allow these tables to be updated if the topology of the network changes (due to either internal node or channel failure) and, in some cases, as responses to the volume of packets at nodes and over links.

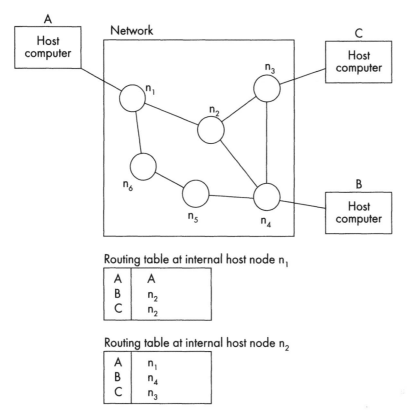

Routing table at internal host node n_1

A	A
B	n_2
C	n_2

Routing table at internal host node n_2

A	n_1
B	n_4
C	n_3

Figure 15.17 Routing tables in network routing.

15.4.5 Adaptive routing strategies

There are three main adaptive routing strategies, isolated routing, centralized routing and distributed routing.

In the case of isolated routing, each node makes a routing decision based on local information within the node. For example, the 'hot potato' algorithm routes an incoming packet to the output link with the shortest output queue of packets waiting to be sent on that link. This takes no account of direction and hence a packet may be routed in an inappropriate direction.

Centralized routing uses a special routing node that periodically collects information about the state of the network, calculates the best routes to use and distributes routing tables to each node. The problem with this technique is the same as any centralized system; the possibility of failure of the special node and the local build up of traffic around this centralized node. Centralized routing can be regarded as a refinement of static routing with periodic recalculation of routing tables that are then transmitted to each node.

Distributed routing is more complex, as each node is responsible for maintaining and updating its routing table when it receives information from adjacent nodes regarding node connectivity and traffic density known to its neighbour. A node in the network continually assesses the cost of sending packets along each of its output lines. One popular version of this kind of algorithm derives the cost to send to a destination from the information about the cost of each of its neighbours to send information to that destination plus the cost to pass information to that neighbour. Often the cost is calculated as one unit per link between nodes, and hence the minimum cost route is the one with the fewest nodes on it. This allows nodes to become aware of lost channels or failed nodes, but is not responsive to parts of the network becoming over-loaded. Other variants take into account the distance of each link and the volume of data currently queued to that link to allow the cost to reflect the loading in parts of the network. In practice, distributed algorithms require adjacent nodes periodically to exchange their routing tables. A node (X) receiving a routing table from an adjacent node (Y) updates its routing tables so that for each destination its new entry is either the output link it currently uses or the link to Y if this is a better (lower) cost. Though each switching node is more complicated, the resulting network adapts more quickly to changes in topology and network traffic.

15.4.6 Congestion

Though adaptive routing can reduce the problem of congestion, it is not a full solution to the problem. Congestion is the localized build up of too much traffic within some part of the network. It is due either to nodes that are too slow for the volume of traffic, or to local channel bandwidth saturation. However, as both these problems are countered by local buffering of frames, the overall problem is one of insufficient buffering for temporarily storing packets in transit. If packets are received at a faster rate than they can be transmitted, eventually memory in the node will be exhausted and the node will fail.

In connection-oriented systems there is a simple solution to congestion. When a virtual circuit is established, buffer space within nodes is pre-allocated to the connection and the information flow between sender and receiver is controlled by the number of allocated buffers. Some flow control techniques (discussed in Chapter 16) allow dynamic alteration of the number of packets that can be in transit over a particular virtual circuit, and hence a more sophisticated dynamic determination of the number of packets that may need to be handled by a node.

With datagram implemented networks, there has to be a way in which a node can prevent its memory becoming full. This can be achieved by the node discarding packets when its memory is full. Perhaps surprisingly, this technique works well; however, it does mean that the network is not reliable, that is, information transmitted through the network may be 'lost'. In such cases a higher layer protocol must detect the loss of packets and request retransmission, as in the protocols discussed in Chapter 16.

15.4.7 Addressing in WANs and internetworks

Each host computer connected to a WAN needs to have a unique address on the network so that packets can be routed to it appropriately. Within a single WAN, as with an isolated LAN, this can be achieved by the controlling authority allocating the unique address.

However when LANs and WANs are internetworked to former larger internets, some further organization is needed to ensure that stations have unique addresses on the internetwork. Thus, it is usual to treat network addresses as hierarchically structured with a format <network field> <host field>, where the network field identifies a particular network and then the host field identifies the host machine on that network.

15.4.8 Connecting WANs together

Within a single LAN or WAN a particular MAC layer protocol or network layer protocol is used to deliver messages to the appropriate destination. However across multiple networks, different protocols are typically used and thus it is necessary for higher layer services to support a common set of protocols across different kinds of networks. Nodes that are connected to networks that use very different protocols are called gateways (or routers), and these nodes have to be able to transmit and receive using the protocols used on both networks and translate between them.

There are a number of problems that occur when connecting dissimilar networks together and which can be classified as:

1. Addressing problems. Ideally the joined network should have a uniform addressing structure. Unfortunately different networks usually have different addressing conventions, for example, different address formats and different positions in the packet. This means that the gateway has to be able to convert between different conventions.

2. Service compatibility. Joining a network that does not support reliable connection-oriented communication to one that does might require the gateways to adopt a protocol to enable the unreliable network to support reliable communication between gateways. Alternatively the network layer protocol may assume the lowest available service as the norm for all connected networks, assuming only a connectionless service, as with IP.

3. Packet size. Different networks may use different packet sizes and this can cause problems if packets from one network have to be split into smaller packets for transport across another network. This is known as fragmentation. Splitting a packet into smaller packets is not difficult but managing the receipt of packets that may be out of order is more demanding on storage management. Packets may have to traverse several networks between sender and receiver and hence they may have to travel through several gateways. There are several options for dealing with fragmented packets in such situations. Fragmented packets can be

forwarded immediately and re-assembled at the final destination or they may be reassembled into the original packets at each gateway before onwards transmission. One of the main problems here concerns how packets with errors are dealt with, since if a packet has been fragmented several times across several networks all the smaller packets will have to be discarded and the transmitter asked to re-send the original larger, offending packet.

15.5 Example – the Internet

The most successful collection of protocols are the TCP/IP protocols used on the world wide Internet. Technically, the Internet protocol (IP) is a network layer protocol in the OSI reference model terms. However, as it was specifically designed with the intent of running over different kinds of wide and local area networks, it is conceptually simpler to consider this as a separate 'internetworking' layer that can run on top of a number of different wide and local area network protocols. Figure 15.18 illustrates such an internetwork. When

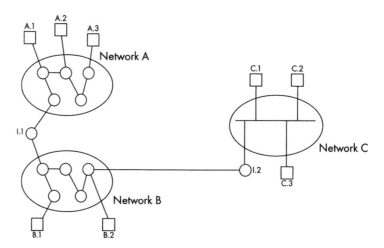

Figure 15.18 An internetwork.

A.2 wishes to send data to C.2, network A determines that the destination is not on this network and the internal routing tables of network A route the message to I.1. I.1 uses its internetwork routing table to determine that I.2 is the best internetwork node to which to send the message, but network B's routing algorithm determines the best way to deliver this to I.2 is through its internal nodes. I.2's routing table indicates the link to network C as the best link on which to forward the packet. The internal LAN protocol of network C (here a bus based Ethernet protocol is assumed) determines the Ethernet address for the corresponding IP host address on this network and sends the IP packet inside an Ethernet frame to C.2.

The hierarchy of protocols allows the separation of different aspects of the protocol to be solved by different hardware devices and software layers. In practice, actual implementations might not separate these aspects as cleanly as the discussion here implies. Nonetheless, these simplifications illustrate the underlying principles reasonably accurately.

15.5.1 IP addressing

Each station has a 32-bit address, which is structured as a pair of values consisting of a network identification field and a host identification field. There are three different classes of address, A, B and C, which allocate the 32 bits differently between the network and host fields as shown in Figure 15.19.

A	0 nnnnnnn hhhhhhhhhhhhhhhhhhhhhhhh

B	10 nnnnnnnnnnnnnn hhhhhhhhhhhhhhhh

C	11 nnnnnnnnnnnnnnnnnnnnn hhhhhhhh

	Max number of networks	Max number of hosts per network
A	128	16 777 216
B	16 384	65 536
C	2 097 152	256

Figure 15.19 Internet addressing structure.

The 32 bits for Internet addresses are usually written using a dot notation for four groups of values. Each value is eight bits of the address but is written as a decimal value between 0 and 255, for example,

$$140.101.160.80$$

The first two bits of the first number determine the class of the address, for example, if the first bit is **0** (that is, the decimal value is less than 128) then it is a class A address, if the first two bits are **10** (that is, the decimal value is between 128 and 191 inclusive) it is a class B address, and if the first three bits are **110** (that is, the decimal value is between 192 and 223 inclusive) it is a class C address. Values in the range 224 to 255 inclusive are used for multicast broadcast communication to multiple destinations or are reserved for future use. To connect a new network to the Internet, an organization needs to contact the Internet Network Identification Centre that assigns a unique network address. The host portion of the address can be assigned by the organization as required.

15.5.2 The IP packet

The Internet protocol (IP) supports a connectionless service for IP packet transmission. Reliable transmission is provided by the higher level TCP protocol implemented in host computers connected to the Internet. UDP is a protocol that implements a connectionless service directly on top of IP.

IP packets are packets that are transported inside the data fields of individual WAN and LAN packets and frames. IP packets, therefore, have a header field (which contains protocol information) and a variable size data field (the transported message). The IP header contains IP addresses of the source and destination of the message and additional protocol information. The destination address is used to route the packet through the internet, although the division of IP addresses into two component fields means that gateways (routers) that connect different WANs need use only the network portion of the address initially to route the packet. When the packet reaches the destination network, then the host portion of the address is used to route the packet to the appropriate host. If the original source and destination exist on the same network then only the host portion of the address is needed and the internal broadcast protocol or internal routing mechanism is used to deliver the message to the destination. The full IP packet is detailed in Table 15.1.

Table 15.1 The IP packet

Word no.	Field description
1	4 bit – protocol version number
	4 bit – header length in 32 bit words
	8 bit type-of-service – identifies routing requirements
	16 bit byte count of bytes of data in packet
2	16 bit identification number
	3 bit flag – required for packet fragmentation
	13 bit offset to identify next fragment if packet fragmented
3	8 bit time-to-live – max no of nodes a message may traverse
	8 bit protocol number – identifies transport level protocol used
	16 bit header frame check sum
4	32 bit source address
5	32 bit destination address
6	Optional fields
7	Data – 1 to (64k – header size) bytes

The protocol version number is included to allow different versions of the protocol to be in use at different parts of the Internet at any one time, so that up-grading can take place on an incremental basis. The header length field allows the standard five 32-bit word header to be increased by additional optional fields.

Of the eight bit type-of-service field only four bits are used. Each is a Boolean value specifying whether the following parameters are active or not:

minimize delay   get this datagram to its destination as soon as possible. This is typically used is sending control packets.

maximize throughput   set if a large amount of data is to be sent. Specifies that a large number of datagrams can be in transit at any one time, that is, network congestion should be avoided.

maximize reliability   routing is performed to minimize the number of retransmissions required. This is typically set for transmissions within a single network.

minimize monetary cost   mainly used for sending news bulletins.

The time-to-live field is set typically to 32 or 64, to ensure that datagrams do not circulate in the network forever. Each hop within the network decrements this by 1 and packets whose time-to-live value drops to 0 are discarded.

The protocol handles fragmentation by the identification field and the fragment offset field. A packet that has to be fragmented results in multiple packets with the same value in the identification field but a fragmentation offset which allows the destination to determine the position of the fragment in the original packet. An immediate forwarding policy is used so that the destination station is responsible for reassembling any fragmented datagrams. Usually the data field is restricted to a field of less than 10,000 bytes to reduce the prospect of fragmentation.

The eight bit transport layer protocol field distinguishes whether TCP, UDP or another protocol is being used on the data in the IP packets data payload. This allows the receiver to deliver the packet to the appropriate process to handle that protocol.

The header checksum is a 16-bit checksum that verifies the header information only, but in so doing checks for corruption of the destination address particularly to avoid delivery to the wrong address. As the time-to-live field changes on each hop the checksum has to be recalculated on each hop.

15.6 Summary

There are two main types of networks: local area networks (LANs), which cover a small geographical area such as a building or site and wide area networks (WANs) which cover a wide geographical area such as a country or continent. The networks differ in almost all their characteristics at lower protocol levels. One of the major differences is that LANs often use broadcast transmission techniques where every receiver is able to 'see' each message sent and uses the address in the message to decide whether it is the intended recipient. WANs normally use point-to-point routing where a message is routed to the addressed recipient only.

There are many different topologies possible for networks. WANs typically have no regular structure as they have grown in an unstructured manner. LANs are usually more structured either as buses, rings or stars.

LANs often use contention-based MAC protocols such as CSMA-CD which is used in the common Ethernet LAN. In this system, transmitters transmit when they sense that no other transmitter is transmitting and abandon the transmission if they detect collisions between competing transmitters. This works well for lightly loaded systems but less well under heavy loading. A token ring LAN is a permission based LAN protocol where each station has to wait for a token before it is allowed to transmit. This method is more efficient than the contention method for heavily loaded systems.

Networks can be connected together to form larger networks. The simplest form of interconnection is to use a router or bridge, but this can be used only when the networks to be connected together use similar protocols. Connecting dissimilar networks is more difficult since the interconnecting node has to perform protocol conversion.

Originally, wide area data transmission used facilities provided by telephone networks, which used circuit switching. Contemporary WANs are usually packet switched networks in which routing is a major problem.

Two main kinds of service are provided in packet switching, connection-oriented service and connectionless service. Connection-oriented services provide reliable in-order delivery of packets and are suited to long messages, which need to be sent as multiple packets. A connectionless service delivers an isolated packet as best it can.

Internal to a network, packets can be routed in isolation (datagram implementation) or can be based upon a virtual circuit implementation where a path is determined and then used for all subsequent packets on that virtual circuit. A virtual circuit implementation gives an external impression of circuit switching though bandwidth on specific channels is not reserved in a comparable way to circuit switching. Connection-oriented services are typical requirements for many applications, hence datagram implemented networks support such services by protocols which buffer packets at the receiver so that they can be passed on in the correct sequence. IP is similar to this latter approach in assuming underlying networks are unreliable datagram networks and therefore offering a connectionless service to higher layer protocols. TCP uses the facilities of IP to implement a connection-oriented service on top of IP which it can offer to applications.

15.7 Exercises

Exercise 15.1 How do the addressing requirements differ among a broadcast network, a single WAN and an internet?

Exercise 15.2 What is meant by a contention method for access control to a network? Why does this method become less efficient when the network loading is high?

Exercise 15.3 How is token loss detected in a token-ring network? Suggest policies by which the token could be regenerated. What happens if a token is inadvertently generated in error by one of the nodes?

Exercise 15.4 Describe the kinds of problems that arise when trying to connect two dissimilar networks together. Identify the different kinds of devices for doing this and for what kinds of internetwork connection they are appropriate.

Exercise 15.5 What is meant by the terms virtual circuit and datagram network implementations. Briefly discuss the relative merits of each.

Exercise 15.6 Describe what is meant by the terms 'connection-oriented service' and 'connectionless service', and identify which kind of service is supported by each of IP, TCP and UDP.

Exercise 15.7 Describe the differences between static routing, centralized adaptive routing and distributed routing. Briefly discuss the relative merits of each.

Exercise 15.8 Consider Table 15.18 and assume that networks A, B, C have been assigned the IP network addresses 160.101.hhh.hhh, 183.80.hhh.hhh and 204.65.103.hhh respectively, and assume the stations on networks A, B and C have host numbers as indicated in the diagram.

(a) What class of network are networks A,B and C?

(b) What is the IP address of C.2?

(c) Do internal network nodes of networks A and B need IP addresses?

(d) Briefly illustrate an IP packet for a message to be sent from A.1 to C.2

(e) Discuss the similarities and differences between the internal routing tables of nodes in network B and the routing tables of the internetwork nodes I.1 and I.2 (assuming they both use network routing).

16

Error correction

16.1 Introduction

Chapter 14 introduced the idea that hardware implementations of error detection are a function of the physical layer and that user applications eventually require connection-oriented services which guarantee in-order error-free delivery of packets. In this chapter we discuss in more detail the principles behind some common protocols that specifically address the issue of error correction.

Error correction is not an issue that is specific to one particular protocol layer. In some WANs, especially ones that use less reliable media over long distances for internal links, error detection and correction is performed over each individual link to avoid subsequent internal transmissions of an erroneous packet. In these contexts error correction is treated as a layer 2 (data link layer) issue. WANs that use high reliability media (such as fibre optic cables) tend to avoid the overheads and delays inherent with such a heavy-weight data link layer. Such WANs prefer to treat these issues on an end-to-end basis in higher protocol layers. LANs, which transmit data over significantly shorter distances than WANs and thus achieve higher reliability on electrical cabling, also tend to treat error-correction as a higher level notion above the MAC protocol. In the TCP/IP protocol, error correction and the provision of connection-oriented services are the province of the TCP protocol constructed on top of IP. It aims to provide error-free in-order delivery of packets on an end-to-end basis between one host station and another.

It should be noted that error detection and correction techniques are not perfect. They can reduce the number of errors but some small residual number of errors will go undetected. Often the required level of reliability is a facet of the application programs that are run across networks. Some applications can tolerate errors and noise in the transmitted data (as with much voice and video data). Some applications are inconvenienced by an occasional character which is wrong but do not have potentially catastrophic consequences (as with many text file data transfers). Some applications require total accuracy (as in process control or numerical data that is the basis for highly significant decisions). Applications that require high data integrity usually distrust the reliability of the underlying network even if there is significant levels of error detection and correction within the network and require high-level protocols to be responsible for data integrity themselves.

Two problems that have to be addressed in communication systems are the occurrence of errors and the differing speeds of processing at senders and receivers. Error control and flow control mechanisms are used to overcome these problems. Error control involves error detection and error-recovery. Flow control is concerned with regulating the speed of transmitters so that they do not overload a possibly slower receiver. Previously we assumed that the transmitter can send data at the maximum media transmission rate. However, when frames are received, the information is first stored in an internal buffer and later transferred to main memory. If the rate at which the information can be transferred to main memory and processed is lower than the rate at which information is transferred across the medium, then information will be lost. Thus a mechanism is needed to ensure that the sender does not transmit information at a faster rate than the receiver can deal with it. This is known as flow control and again it is of note that this applies at a number of different levels, such as between adjacent nodes with a WAN and between host computers connected across a network or internetwork.

16.2 Error control

It is rare for communications systems to be completely error free. Packets of data may be corrupted and protocols have to be able to recover from errors. In addition, errors may occur in the packet header control information and control packets of the protocol. Error control is differentiated by use of either forward or backward error correction techniques. Both require an error detection mechanism but differ in how the error is then corrected. Initially backward error correction is considered as it is the more commonly used technique.

16.2.1 Error detection

The standard techniques for error detection require the transmitter to apply some function to the transmitted data and to send the resulting value with the data. The receiver applies the same function to the received data and compares the result with that sent by the transmitter. If the two values are not the same then an error must have occurred in the transmission. Parity bit calculations and frame check sequences (FCS), sometimes called cyclic redundancy checks (CRC), are two such functions. Frame check sequences are usually calculated over larger items of data than parity bits.

(a) Parity check

The simplest error detection calculation is computation of a parity bit. The sum of the individual bits of the data is calculated to determine a parity bit which is then appended to the data. For odd parity the total number of bits, including the parity bit, has to be an odd number. Thus, the parity bit will be set to zero if the number of 1 bits in the data is odd or one if the number of 1 bits in the data is even. For even parity the reverse is true. For example, in Figure 16.1(a) a data unit of eight bits is to be transmitted. With even parity a further bit set to 1 is appended to the data, as in Figure 16.1(b). With odd parity a 0 bit is appended to the data, as in Figure 16.1(c).

(a)

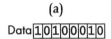

(b)   (c)

Figure 16.1   (a) a data byte;
(b) even parity;
(c) odd parity.

Parity bits can detect an odd number of bit errors in a bit string, for example, a single bit whose value was 1 but which has been corrupted to be a 0, or vice versa. However it cannot detect an even number of corrupted bits. For example, if the first two bits in the string were inverted, the appropriate parity bit for the original and the corrupted strings are the same. Thus parity checks are useful if only infrequent isolated errors occur, but are poor if errors are frequent or are bunched together. In such cases a more comprehensive check is required and a polynomial code, also known as a cyclic redundancy check, is more frequently used.

(b) Frame check sequence (cyclic redundancy check)

A generator polynomial is used to generate a value called the frame check sequence (FCS) or cyclic redundancy check (CRC) which the transmitter calculates and transmits with the data. The transmitter treats the data string to be transmitted as a bit string for a very long binary number and divides the data by the polynomial generator. A 17-bit polynomial produces a 16-bit remainder, and the remainder (the FCS) is transmitted at the end of the data. A FCS is typically a 16-bit or 32-bit value generated by a 17-bit or 33-bit polynomial generator respectively. The receiver performs the same computation on the received data as the transmitter performed on the transmitted data and compares it with the FCS sent with the data. If the two values do not match the data received is in error, is discarded and the frame has to be retransmitted.

Arithmetic division using arbitrary long bit patterns is an expensive operation to implement in hardware and is slow in software. Implementations optimize the above characterization by using modulo-2 division which can be implemented efficiently by XOR gates. (Rather than perform subtraction in the standard division algorithm, exclusive OR operations are used, thus two 0s or two 1s produce 0, otherwise 1.) The FCS is calculated as follows. The data to be transmitted is treated as a bit string that is divided using modulo-2 division by some predetermined division sequence g. The remainder of this division is the frame check sequence for the frame and is appended to the data. g is called the generator polynomial and is normally specified as a polynomial in x. The receiver divides the received frame including the transmitted remainder by g and generates a result of 0 if no error has occurred.

Example

Suppose the data to be sent is 10101110 and the generator polynomial is $x^4 + x^2 + 1$. The data is shifted four bits to the left since the generator polynomial is five bits long (10101) and 0s are introduced in the positions which the FCS will eventually occupy. Thus the transmitter divides 101011100000 by 10101 (using modulo-2 arithmetic)

```
            10000111
     10101 )101011100000
            10101
            0000011000
                  10101
                  011010
                  10101
                  011110
                  10101
                  01011
```

This gives an FCS of 1011 and the message sent is 101011101011.

The receiver performs the modulo-2 division of the received data (including the FCS) by the same generator polynomial. If the remainder is zero the frame has been received correctly otherwise it is in error.

```
            10000111
     10101 )101011101011
            10101
            0000011010
                  10101
                  011111
                  10101
                  010101
                  10101
                  00000
```

In general, the larger the polynomial generator, the greater its ability to support error detection.

16.2.2 Error correction

The techniques described above allow many of the errors that can occur in transmitted data to be detected. How can these errors be corrected? There are two ways of doing this:

- re-send information in error, or

- add additional redundancy to the information so that the correct data can be recovered.

In most cases, re-sending the information is the more efficient because the majority of information is transmitted without error and adding redundancy to all information substantially increases the amount of information that has to be sent. This technique is known as backward error correction (BEC) as it requires the receiver to inform the transmitter of the need to re-send data. In a few cases, for example, satellite transmission, where the transmission times are very long, re-sending the data causes a long delay and such cases use methods based on forward error correction (FEC) where redundant data is sent. This technique uses a coding technique, such as Hamming encoding (see Section 16.5.1), that is able to detect and correct multiple errors by adding extra bits to the data.

16.3 Backward error correction

Backward error correction (BEC) requires the receiver to inform the transmitter that a frame has been corrupted and request retransmission of the frame. In order for the sender and receiver to co-operate, they must both be able to send and receive messages to and from each other, that is, full duplex communication is required between them with a transmission channel in each direction. Hence both are capable of transmitting and receiving frames and are known as transceivers (transmitter/receivers), however we will continue to refer to one of these as the transmitter because it is transmitting data to the other which is receiving the data.

When the receiver receives a frame, it checks it for errors, tells the transmitter whether the frame has been received correctly or not, and hence whether the frame needs re-transmitting. A number of different kinds of errors can arise, and there are a number of different variations on schemes whereby the receiver and transmitter negotiate re-transmission.

When a frame is corrupted an error may have occurred in any of the start of frame sequence, the data itself or the end of frame sequence. If the error is in the data itself then it is detected by the error detection technique applied at the receiver, typically by detecting an incorrect frame checksum described earlier. If the error is in the end of frame sequence then the receiver will continue to accept erroneous signals as part of the data, but as frames usually have a maximum size, receipt of a frame that is too long implies that the end of frame sequence was corrupted. Each of these cases can be detected by the receiver. An error in the start of frame sequence however results in the receiver never recognising the transmitted frame. To handle all three cases, two techniques are required. The in-data and end of frame errors are handled by the receiver's discarding erroneous frames and sending messages back to the transmitter indicating which frames have been correctly received and which have not. These messages back to the transmitter are known as acknowledgements. The start of frame errors are handled by the transmitter's inferring from the absence of an acknowledgement that the frame was corrupted and therefore must be re-sent. When the transmitter sends a frame, it expects an acknowledgement within some pre-set maximum time, and if such an acknowledgement fails to arrive it re-sends the frame.

There are two main variations of the conventions that transmitters and receivers can use regarding acknowledgements. These conventions are known as acknowledgement schemes and the main variations are a full acknowledgement scheme and a positive only acknowledgement scheme.

A full acknowledgement scheme allows the receiver to send back control messages for both a correctly received frame by an acknowledgement (ACK) and an erroneously received frame by a negative acknowledgement (NAK). When the transmitter receives a NAK it re-transmits the corrupted frame. In addition, it may re-transmit a frame if it times out not having received an ACK because of a start of frame error. A positive only acknowledgement scheme supports the receiver sending ACKs only for correctly received frames. Thus, from the original transmitter's point of view, all frame corruptions appear to be start of frame corruptions, but the desired effect (re-transmission of the corrupt frame) is the same whatever the source of the error. The absence of an ACK results in the transmitter re-sending the frame. In general the transmitter is aware of a corrupted frame earlier with a full acknowledgement scheme compared to a positive only scheme, but the positive only scheme is simpler in implementation terms because the one technique (time-out on non-receipt of an ACK) handles all three sources of error. Frame corruption is depicted on time sequence diagrams as the non-arrival of the frame at the receiver as in Figure 16.2.

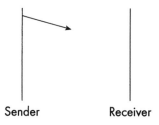

Sender   Receiver

Figure 16.2   Transmitted frame lost.

These techniques alone, however, are unable to ensure correct data transmission. Not only must the rules of messages exchange guarantee re-transmission of lost frames, they must also prevent receipt of duplicated frames (or at least provide a way to detect duplicate frames so they can be discarded). The ACK and NAK control messages are themselves bit patterns that are transmitted over the channel and may be corrupted as illustrated in Figure 16.3. If such control information is corrupted then eventually the

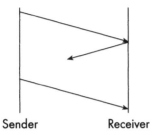

Sender   Receiver

Figure 16.3   Frame acknowledgement lost.

transmitter will re-transmit the unacknowledged frame, and in the case of a lost ACK the receiver will receiver this data frame for a second time. Hence it is necessary for the receiver to be able to determine whether a data frame it receives is a new frame or whether it is a duplicate data frame which resulted from a lost acknowledgement. Data frames hence contain frame sequence numbers that allow the receiver to determine if an in-coming frame is a new frame or one that it has already received and that should be discarded. If sequence numbers on successive data frames had always to be increasing, an unlimited size field within the data frame would be necessary. However, the information which the receiver needs to be able to detect duplicates can be defined in terms of a set of numbers for frames that it currently is willing to accept, and a set of frame numbers it will discard. These two sets can be relatively small and hence a restricted range of values, and hence field size within the data frame, will suffice to allow the receiver to detect duplicates.

In summary, transmission of (negative) acknowledgements, time-out on unacknowledged frames, and sequence numbers within frames are the fundamental techniques of different backward error correction protocols. The following sections discuss different ways these techniques are used in different protocols.

Stop and wait protocol and sliding window protocols

A stop and wait protocol is a simple backward error correcting protocol, which requires that the transmitter send a data frame and then wait for an acknowledgement from the receiver before sending the next data frame.

Let us assume the conventions of a positive only acknowledgement scheme with 1-bit sequence numbers that can differentiate between two frame numbers 0 and 1. Both transmitter and receiver maintain a 1-bit counter, the send window at the transmitter and the receive window at the receiver, both initially set to 0. The send and receive windows are both incremented using modulo-2 arithmetic (hence for successive frame transmissions the send window has successive values of 0, 1, 0, 1, ...).The send window is the frame number of the next frame to be sent. The receive window is the frame number of the frame that will be received next. When a frame is sent the value of the send window is copied into the data frame. When a frame is received the frame number is extracted from the frame and compared with the receive window, if they are the same then the frame is accepted and the receive window incremented using modulo-2 arithmetic, otherwise it is discarded. When an acknowledgement is sent the value of the receive window is copied into the acknowledgement frame, hence ACK(0) is a message back to the transmitter meaning the receiver has received frame 1 and next expects frame 0. When an acknowledgement is received the send window is set to be the value in the acknowledgement frame, and the transmitter is in a position to send the next data frame. The transmitter can have only one unacknowledged frame in transit at anyone time, but must retain this frame within a buffer in case it is not acknowledged and has to be re-transmitted. The receiver knows that it will not have to deal with more than one particular frame at a time and therefore the amount of buffer space required can be restricted to a single frame.

Fig 16.4 illustrates the basic operation of this protocol as a time sequence diagram. The solid arrows indicate the propagation of the first bit of the data frame and the dotted arrows represent propagation of the last bit of the data frame. As the frame check sequence is typically at the end of the data frame, an acknowledgement cannot be sent until the entire frame has been received and checked. The dotted line will be omitted in subsequent time sequence diagrams. When the receiver has received an uncorrupted frame, it checks its sequence number against the receive window and accepts the frame if they are the same and increments its receive window. When the transmitter receives an acknowledgement, it moves its send window on to the value in the acknowledgement.

Figure 16.5 illustrates the operation of this protocol with data frame and acknowledgement corruptions. On the first transfer, the data frame is corrupted and then retransmitted. The second data frame's acknowledgement is corrupted and data frame 1 is re-sent and acknowledged but discarded by the receiver. Note that the single bit sequence number allows the receiver to distinguish between a duplicate copy of the previous frame and the currently expected frame.

This protocol is very inefficient, as can be seen from a simple analysis. If the frame propagation time is long compared to the time taken to generate and process the data, then most of the time is spent waiting for the frame and acknowledgement to arrive, that is, the sender and receiver are idle for much of the time. In such circumstances, more efficient protocols based on sliding

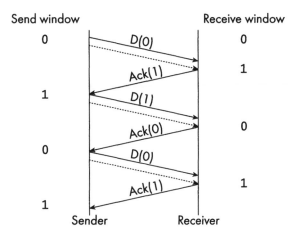

Figure 16.4 Stop and wait protocol.

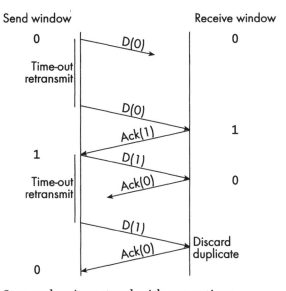

Figure 16.5 Stop and wait protocol with corruptions.

window protocols are used. These allow a transmitter to have multiple unacknowledged frames in transit at any one time rather than the single frame in transit which stop and wait permits. The transmitter has to buffer the frames that it has sent and for which it has not yet had an acknowledgement since it may have to retransmit them if they are lost in transit or received with errors. The send and receive windows can specify a range of sequence numbers, which can be transmitted and are currently expected, respectively. In addition, the interpretation of acknowledgements has to be generalized so that, rather than each frame requiring its own acknowledgement, one acknowledgement can acknowledge all frames up to (but excluding) the sequence number in the ACK frame.

The idea is that the sender sends frames, with sequence numbers permitted by the range of its send window, without waiting for acknowledgements. When the receiver detects an error in a frame there are two possible ways of subsequently proceeding. The receiver can request that the transmitter retransmit all the frames from the erroneous frame onwards. This is known as 'go-back-N', and is illustrated in Figure 16.6. This has the advantage that the receiver can merely discard out of sequence frames knowing that such frames will be automatically re-transmitted and hence does not need to buffer frames.

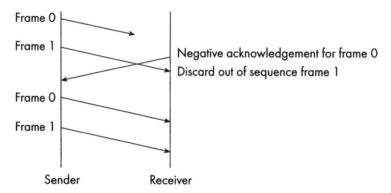

Figure 16.6 An example of a sliding window protocol using go-back-N.

The alternate scheme is known as 'selective repeat', and is illustrated in Figure 16.7. This requires the receiver to request retransmission of the erroneous frame but continues to accept uncorrupted out-of-sequence frames by buffering these until the re-transmission of the lost frame arrives when it can be inserted in its correct position in the buffered sequence of frames. This is more efficient in terms of transmission bandwidth as only lost frames are re-transmitted, but it requires more resources at the receiver to buffer out-of-order frames.

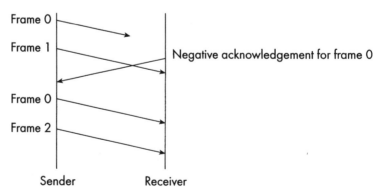

Figure 16.7 An example of a sliding window protocol using selective repeat.

Consider an example with a 3-bit sequence number for values 0-7. A Go-Back-N scheme splits this set of values into seven unacknowledged frames that the transmitter can have in transit (send window) and one that the receiver expects (receive window). The transmitter can initially send up to seven frames before it must wait for an acknowledgement. The receiver initially expects a frame with the sequence number set to the initial value, say 0. Only the frame with this sequence number will be passed to the receiving process. Once this frame has been received, the receiver increments its receive window (modulo 8 so that after frame 7 a new frame 0 is expected). Thus, if there are no errors, the transmitter and receiver communicate by sending and receiving frames in ascending sequence number order (modulo 8). With the selective repeat scheme, the send and receive windows are half the range of the sequence numbers.

The constraints on how these schemes use these sub-sequences of sequence numbers described above are determined by the worst case scenarios, illustrated in Figure 16.8. In both cases, the sender has as many unacknowledged frames in transit as possible and the acknowledgement for these has been corrupted. In such cases the receiver's receive window values (frames it next expects) must be disjoint from the frames that the transmitter may retransmit, so that the receiver may differentiate duplicates from genuine new frames.

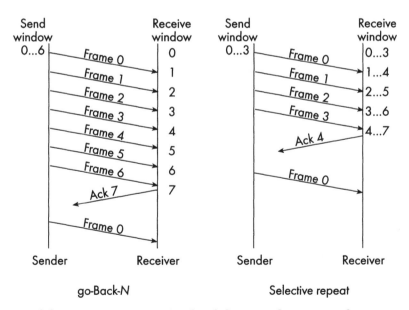

Figure 16.8 Worst case scenarios for sliding window protocols.

This discussion illustrates operation of these protocols in only one direction. Over duplex links the same protocol is applied to reverse direction traffic also. This complicates the description but adds little additional conceptual complexity. However in these circumstances acknowledgement messages do not have to be sent as separate frames but can be included in a field of frames flowing in the opposite direction. This technique is called 'piggybacking' acknowledgements and leads to greater efficiency in two respects. Piggybacked acknowledgements are much smaller and therefore take less bandwidth. Secondly, as a field for each piggybacked acknowledgement is reserved in each frame, the receiver might as well acknowledge whatever frames it can whenever it has reverse direction traffic to transmit. This can lead to more timely sending of acknowledgements than having to wait for a time out. As receipt of acknowledgements allows the transmitter to progress its send window, this can lead to subsequent frames being sent earlier and a net impact that the channel is used more efficiently. Perhaps strangely, heavier reverse direction traffic allows these protocols to operate more effectively.

16.4 Time-out control

Time-outs are implemented by a transmitter starting a clock when information is sent. If the time expires before a response is received, the communication is deemed to have timed-out. The time-out action is normally to abandon the transmission or to try again.

It is very difficult to decide what the time-out period should be, since it will depend on a number of factors, some of which change dynamically. Over a single point-to-point communication link the propagation delay of the link can be calculated and the two way propagation delay will determine a minimum value for a time-out period. If the time-out period is too long then time is wasted when an error occurs, but if it is too short unnecessary re-transmissions may be incurred. In practice, time-out periods are usually set generously.

The time a receiver takes to respond will depend on its workload and this may vary dynamically. In addition, over multi-channel routes of paths through wide-area networks, delays at intermediate nodes are less predictable, so that operation of such protocols on an end-to-end host computer to host computer basis over a WAN requires much longer and conservative time-out periods. In such circumstances, full acknowledgement schemes with the provision for negative acknowledgements allow receivers to provide more timely information to senders of data.

16.5 Forward error correction

Forward error correction (FEC) is based upon a principle that redundant information is sent with the frame so that the receiver can not only detect an error, but can also locate the position of the error and therefore correct it. In comparison with backward error correction, the amount of redundant information is more extensive and consumes a higher proportion of the available bandwidth. However, the use of special codes, known as Hamming codes, involve redundancy of sufficiently low levels as to be acceptable in some contexts. The choice between forward and backward error correction depends on the likelihood of error and the speed of transmission. Local area networks generally have a very low error rate and hence use backward error-correcting retransmission techniques.

16.5.1 Forward error correction and Hamming codes

Hamming codes work on a principle that the encoding of 'successive' or 'adjacent' data values can differ from each other in ways that can be measured as a distance between such adjacent values. For example, character codes such as ASCII or EBCDIC are codes in which adjacent values differ by only a single bit. In general, the relationship between error detection and error correction can be expressed in terms of the distances between values in such codes as

$$Hdist = NerrorsToDetect + NerrorsToCorrect + 1$$

where *Hdist* is the Hamming distance, *NerrorsToDetect* is the number of bits that can be detected and *NerrorsToCorrect* is the number of bits that can be corrected. This formula is also constrained such that $NerrorsToCorrect \leq NerrorsToDetect$, N-bit errors can be corrected only if N-bit errors are detected. On this basis, the ASCII and EBCDIC codes are unable to support either error detection or correction on their own. The addition of a parity bit to an ASCII 7-bit code results in a set of valid values, which differ in two bits. For example, using even parity the values **0001110** and **0001111** have different parity bits giving 8-bit bit patterns that differ in two bits from each other, **00011101** and **00011110** respectively. Using the above formula, ASCII supplemented by a single parity bit is able to detect 1-bit errors but not correct them. Other codes can be designed, for example one which can detect all 2-bit errors and correct those which involve only 1-bit errors.

The principle of Hamming codes requires that for detection of N-bit errors a distance of at least N+1 is needed between any two codewords. Correction of N-bit errors requires a distance of at least 2N+1 since this guarantees that N changes to a codeword will still leave it closer to the correct codeword than any other codeword.

Hamming invented a method for generating the check bits, which is convenient for processing purposes. The bits of the codeword are numbered starting with 1 at the left hand end and with those positions that are a power of 2 used as check bits and the rest for data bits. Each check bit is the parity of some combination of the data bits. Each data bit contributes to the parity bits with positions that sum to the position of the data bit in the code word. For example the data bit at bit position 6 in the code word contributes to the parity of the parity bits at positions 2 and 4 in the codeword. The receiver checks the parity bits to see if they are the correct value. If they are not, it adds the positions of all parity bits that are incorrect in a counter. If the counter is zero when all the bits have been checked then the data is correct, otherwise the bit whose position is in the counter is the bit in error. Note that if a single parity bit has been corrupted, this technique also identifies the error to the parity bit.

Example

Consider the 4-bit data item 0001. Three parity bits are calculated and interleaved with the data bits on the following basis. Bits 1, 2 and 4 are (even) parity bits (P1,P2,P3). Bits 3, 5, 6 and 7 are the data bits (D1,D2,D3,D4). Hence (assuming bits are numbered from the right) parity bits are calculated and inserted into the codeword **000X1XX** for this data item.

Bit 1 (P1) is even parity for the data bits at positions 3, 5 and 7.
Bit 2 (P2) is even parity for the data bits at positions 3, 6 and 7.
Bit 4 (P3) is even parity for the data bits at positions 5, 6 and 7.

Figure 16.9 illustrates the format and how even parity is calculated for bit 4 (P3). Once even parity bits for bits 1 and 2 (P1 and P2) are determined, the codeword is **0000111**. Note that the data bits contribute to different combinations of parity bits. Data bit 1 (codeword bit 3) contributes to codeword bits 1 and 2. Data bit 2 (codeword bit 5) contributes to codeword bits 1 and 4. Data bit 3 (codeword bit 6) contributes to codeword bits 2 and 4. Data bit 4 (codeword bit 7) contributes to codeword bits 1, 2 and 4.

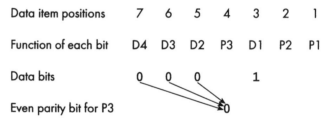

Data item positions	7	6	5	4	3	2	1
Function of each bit	D4	D3	D2	P3	D1	P2	P1
Data bits	0	0	0		1		
Even parity bit for P3				0			

Figure 16.9 Hamming code parity determination for P3.

Assume that the bit pattern received is **0000011**. The receiver checks the parity bits. Bits 1 and 2 are incorrect and 4 is correct for the data bits within the codeword. By adding the positions of the parity bits in error, the receiver can determine the data bit in error. The receiver calculates 1+2 locating the erroneous data bit as bit 3, that is, the correct pattern is **0000111**. This algorithm works for errors in the check bits also. Assume the receiver receives the bit pattern **0000110**. The check determines that only the first bit is in error, that is, the error is in bit 1 and the correct pattern is **0000111**.

Consider a simple parity check on a 4-bit value which adds a single binary digit to make the number of bits even for even parity or odd for odd parity. To provide the same amount of error checking – single bit errors – and error correction using a Hamming code requires three extra bits and thus the Hamming code requires extra bandwidth to provide the forward error correction. In fact the Hamming code requires, for d data bits, a minimum of c check bits where

$$2^c - c = d + 1$$

Hence for $d = 4$ the minimum value of c is 3 and for $d = 100$ the minimum value of c is 7.

This Hamming code can correct only single errors but can be adapted, by using additional parity bits, to correct multiple bit errors (burst errors), that is, a series of errors adjacent to one another. In practice, codes that detect multiple bit errors in long data words use up to 50% of the bandwidth for parity bits, which compares unfavourably with backward error correction except with highly unreliable channels (where retransmissions would dominate) or long distance extra-terrestrial channels (where re-transmission is too slow). However high-bandwidth fibre-optic media has brought increased interest in the use of networks for time-critical applications where delays inherent in re-transmission cannot be tolerated. These are likely to increase the provision for forward error correction to support such applications.

It should also be noted that where a duplex link is available, forward and backward error techniques are not mutually exclusive. Codes can be designed to correct single bit errors but detect multiple bit errors, hence FEC can be used for the former but BEC (and therefore re-transmission) can be used for the latter, thereby reducing the frequency with which re-transmission is necessary.

16.6 Flow control

The model of a communication system is a producer process generating data that is stored in a buffer to be transferred to a distant receiver. The transmitting process takes the data from the buffer and sends it along the transmission medium to the receiver, which stores the input in a buffer after verifying it is correct. A consumer process at the receiver consumes the data sometime later. Because the transmitter and consumer processes run asynchronously there is a possibility that the transmitter will send data at a faster rate than it is consumed and hence the buffer storage in the receiver may be exhausted.

Flow control techniques tackle the general problem that the rate at which a transmitter can generate and send data may be faster than the rate at which the receiver can receive and pass on the data. The stop and wait and sliding window protocols discussed earlier can address this problem over a single channel connecting two computers or switching nodes. The send window determines the largest number of unacknowledged frames that can be in transit at any one time, and hence refusal to acknowledge by the receiver will slow the transmitter down and prevent it transmitting new frames. For such channels, the number of frames that can be accommodated in the length of twice the distance of the link determine an effective upper-bound on the number of unacknowledged frames in transit to permit. Typically a 3-bit sequence number allowing up to seven frames in transit is sufficient.

Over multi-channel routes of paths through WANs or internetworked LANs the propagation delay of frames from the source to destination is much less predictable and often much longer. Typically 8-bit sequence numbers are used with sliding window protocols in these contexts to allow up to 127 frames in transit at any one time. However, short paths with low propagation delays are also possible between two arbitrary host computers attached to a WAN, and in such cases allowing the transmitter to send a hundred or more frames before any have been acknowledged can swamp the receiver. Hence in WAN contexts, sliding window protocols alone are insufficient for flow control. Usually additional protocols are used to allow the receiver to control the number and rate of frames that the transmitter can send before further information from the receiver is available. One such technique is a system of 'credits' whereby the receiver periodically informs the transmitter of the number of unacknowledged frames in transit it can handle and dynamically increases and decreases this depending upon the buffer space and processing power for incoming frames available at the receiver.

16.7 Error and flow control in HDLC

As mentioned previously, the data link layer protocols have historically been concerned with providing an error-free channel between the host computer and its associated network node in order to ensure only correct data is transmitted across the network. In addition, many older networks employ error correcting protocols on each link between pairs of nodes. Many protocols at this level are based on the HDLC (high-level data link control) protocol developed in the 1970s and use backward error correction. HDLC is a sliding window, synchronous, bit-oriented protocol designed for wide area networks. It provides three different modes of operation depending on whether a node may be a master, a slave or both. A master node may initiate communication whereas a slave may only respond to requests from the master. The standard mode used with computer networks is called ABM (asynchronous balanced mode) when both ends of the link are equal in status and either may initiate transmission.

The frame structure of HDLC is given in Figure 16.10.

The start and end of a frame is indicated by the bit pattern 01111110. The use of such bit patterns to indicate control information means that these bit patterns must not occur within the frame itself in order to achieve what is termed 'data transparency'. A technique known as 'bit stuffing' is used to ensure that this pattern is not transmitted as part of the frame. The data sent is monitored and if five consecutive 1s have been transmitted then a 0 is inserted before the next bit. Similarly the data received is monitored and if a 0 is received after five 1s it is removed.

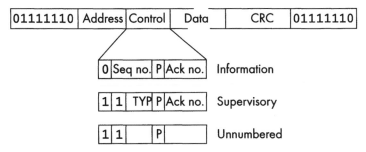

Figure 16.10 Frame structure for HDLC

The control field specifies the modes of operation and deals with acknowledgements and errors as described below. The cyclic redundancy check (CRC) field is 16 bits long and uses the generator polynomial $x^{16} + x^{12} + x^5 + 1$ which enables it to detect all single bursts of errors less than or equal to 16-bits in length and greater than 99.99% of longer error bursts. The poll/final bit is not used in ABM.

The SEQ NO and ACK NO fields are the number of the current frame being sent and the number of the last frame being acknowledged respectively as used in the sliding window protocol.

There are three types of control field as shown in Figure 16.10. The information control field is used for information (data) frames. The supervisory control field allows for four different kinds of control information to be transmitted to the receiver as shown below:

(a) acknowledgement of correct receipt of frames;

(b) indication that the receiver is not ready;

(c) rejection of frame due to an error condition – 'ack no' field specifies the sequence number of frame to restart transmission;

(d) selective repeat – 'ack no' field specifies the sequence number of the frame to be resent.

Unnumbered frames, which allow for up to 32 commands and responses, are used to establish and disconnect the link.

When there is no information to be sent continuous 1 bits may be sent. Between seven and 15 continuous 1 bits are used to signal abort and greater than 15 1 bits are used to signal idle.

There are many different subsets of HDLC including a series called LAP and one called LLC. The LAP (link access protocols) subset are based on the ABM mode of operation of HDLC and LAPB is used in the standard X25 set of protocols for wide area networks. LLC (low level link control) is an IEEE standard and is used in local area networks.

16.8 Transaction control protocol (TCP)

The Internet transaction control protocol (TCP) incorporates many of the aspects of the HDLC protocol but adapts these to operate on a host computer to host computer basis across multiple network links transported in IP packets. A simplified form of the TCP packet is illustrated in Figure 16.11 (with field sizes in bits). TCP provides a connection oriented service, where

Source process port (16)
Destination process port (16)
Sequence number (32)
Acknowledgement number (32)
Control field (32)
Checksum (32)
Other (48)
User data

Figure 16.11 The TCP packet.

initially a logical connection through the network is established and is closed down at the end of the communication. The source and destination addresses of the TCP packet are local process port identifiers for application programs. As IP provides only a connectionless service, both host machines' TCP layers maintain a mapping of TCP connection addresses to IP addresses. Once connection set up has established the association between the process ports and station IP addresses, TCP messages to be sent to a remote port are embedded inside IP packets with the appropriate IP addresses inserted, as indicated in Figure 16.12. Connection set-up also allows each party to inform the other of the initial values for sequence numbers that it will use with sliding window protocols.

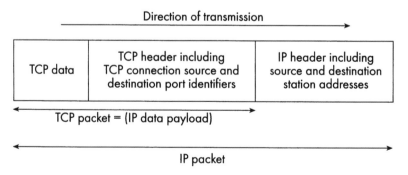

Figure 16.12 TCP packets embedded in IP packets.

The sequence number and acknowledgement numbers of the TCP packet are comparable to the sequence number fields we have discussed previously.

However, TCP chooses to number the octets (bytes) of data rather than individual packets, hence if there are 500 octets of data in each packet the sequence numbers increase in increments of 500 (rather than 1 as we saw earlier). Thus the sequence number fields are much larger in TCP packets, however these are used with a go-back-N sliding window protocol as discussed previously though the send window size is negotiated at connection set-up stage.

The checksum field is a 16-bit 'longitudinal parity check'. Bit 0 of the parity word is an odd parity check of all bit 0s of the header and data, and similarly for all other bits of the parity word. Note that, in contrast to the IP packet where the checksum is calculated only over the IP header, the TCP checksum covers the data as well. The IP checksum is intended to ensure only that corruptions do not prevent the packet reaching the correct destination; the TCP checksum is for validating that the data is received correctly.

16.9 Summary

Errors detection and correction are unavoidable subproblems that communication protocols must accommodate. Backward error correction using stop and wait and sliding window protocols are common techniques that are used over single channels between adjacent computers or nodes. In addition, these kinds of protocol can also be used across entire networks though requiring longer timeouts prior to automatic re-transmission and for pipeline protocols requiring larger ranges of frame sequence numbers. Forward error correction is an alternative technique, which uses codes that can detect and correct errors thereby avoiding re-transmissions. Currently the use of this technique is restricted, though it might well become more commonplace if limited bandwidth is less of a problem as high data rate media become more commonly installed.

Flow control allows receivers to control the rate at which senders transmit information to them. To some extent this is achieved by stop and wait and sliding window protocols. However, over WANs, additional techniques are often needed to support flow control adequately.

16.10 Exercises

Exercise 16.1 Describe the differences between backward error correction and forward error correction and discuss the situations for which each is most appropriate and why.

Exercise 16.2 Assuming a polynomial generator of `10101` and a data sequence `100100100`, determine the frame checksum for this data sequence. Describe how the receiver determines if the received bit sequence has been corrupted or not.

Exercise 16.3 Consider the simple stop and wait protocol. Normally, only one frame is in transit at once so the frame does not need a sequence number. What is the flaw in this argument?

Exercise 16.4 Assume that a sliding window protocol is used. What is the minimum set of frame number values required for the link to recover from intermittent transmission errors, (that is, loss of occasional frames), but also to allow the transmitter always to transmit if acknowledgements are received in sufficient time?

Exercise 16.5 Assume a Hamming code with eight data bits and four parity bits is to be used to construct a code word **1010x101x0xx** where bit numbers are numbered from 1 at the right left hand end of the codeword. For each data bit position, state the parity bit positions that check it. Assuming odd parity is used, determine the values for each of the parity bits and hence the value of the transmitted codeword. Assume that the received data has codeword bit 10 in error as a **1**. Describe how the receiver will detect and correct this error.

Exercise 16.6 Explain in detail how error control works in the HDLC protocol.

Exercise 16.7 Transmission across a slow data link causes a propagation delay of 200 milliseconds. The maximum rate at which frames, which consist of 452 bits of data and 48 bits of protocol, can be transferred across this link is 10 million bits/sec. What is the maximum rate at which data can be transferred across this link, assuming that a stop-and-wait protocol is used?

Assuming that acknowledgements are piggybacked on to reverse direction data frames, determine the delay between sending the first bit of a data frame and receiving the last bit of the data frame containing the acknowledgement. Hence propose a minimum send window for a sliding window protocol that would avoid the transmitter having to wait for an acknowledgement and allow it to send frames immediately after each other (assuming acknowledgements are returned in sufficient time).

17

Architectural trends

17.1 Introduction

In previous chapters of this book the components of a simple computer system, both hardware and software, have been described with examples from typical microcomputer systems. The hardware and software presented is one possible design of computer but there are many others, since the design space is large. A driving factor in architectural change is the continuing improvement in technology, which makes new forms of architecture attractive. One consequence of the improvements in networks over the past few years has been the emergence of true distributed computing systems where many processors are used to solve a problem.

Before considering architectural trends it is worth summarising the features of technology and software which underlie these trends. Technology is driven by Moore's Law, named after the founder of Intel. This law states that the amount of circuitry that can be placed on a given chip area doubles approximately every 18 months. Thus a circuit designed 18 months ago can be implemented in half that chip area today or, alternatively, a circuit twice the size can be implemented on the same chip area. The yield, that is, the percentage of the circuits produced that actually work correctly, increases as the size of the circuit decreases thus making smaller circuits cheaper. Smaller circuits also operate more quickly since signals do not have so far to travel. Thus reducing the size of a circuit is very attractive. Larger circuits allow more integration of components thus reducing the total number of separate chips required for system implementation, which, in turn, reduces the total system cost and increases the system reliability. Moore's law has held since the early 1970s and is expected to apply for several more years, although there are limits to the miniaturization that can be achieved, since physical laws start to break down at very small sizes. Processing and storage technology have changed very quickly in the past due to the effect of Moore's Law and are expected to do so into the future. In contrast, communications bandwidth changes very much more slowly; according to some authorities about one order of magnitude per century. The speed of information transmission is directly related to how far the information has to travel and hence the smaller the circuit the faster it will be. Also, intra-chip communications are significantly faster than inter-chip communications and hence the higher the integration of a circuit the faster it will be. Thus the technology trends are to make the electronic components of the system smaller so making faster and more powerful systems for the same or reduced costs. This trend can be seen in the increasing functionality and speed of personal computers whose cost has fallen substantially in real terms over the past ten years. From a total system viewpoint, software costs dominate hardware costs and hence the architecture should be designed to reduce the cost of software as far as possible. There are a number of ways of achieving this. Firstly, software development costs are high and duplication costs low so the more of a particular product that can be sold, the larger the number of copies over which the development cost can be amortised. Making software portable allows it to be used on multiple hardware platforms and making software reusable allows it to be used in multiple products. Portability can be enhanced by developing the product in a 'standard' high level language. The use of object oriented design techniques and languages can also increase the reusability of the design and code. Favoured high level object oriented languages in use include C++ and Java, with the latter having the advantage of being highly portable and integrated with the Internet. With the improvements in the technology of compilers the programmer can now assume that a high level program will be efficiently implemented on the available hardware. Thus the computer architect has to ensure that the underlying machine architecture is one for which compilers can produce cost effective code, that is, code that makes the 'best' use of the machine resources. A corollary of this is that the architect does not have to make the machine code architectural level simple for a human being to understand or program, since access to all the machine resources will be via a high level language and efficient compiler.

In this first section, two comparatively recent trends in computer architecture are examined.

17.2 Reduced instruction set computers (RISC)

The specific microprocessors described in this book – the Motorola 68oxo series and the Intel 8ox86 series – both belong to the class of computers called CISC machines. CISC – complex instruction set computers – are a class of computers which are characterized by:

- a large number of addressing modes;

- a large number of instructions;

- different instructions take differing amounts of time to execute;

- different instructions having different formats and occupying different amounts of memory space.

A typical CISC machine will have about 10 to 20 addressing modes, more than 100 different instructions and a wide range of sizes and instruction times for different instructions.

The increasing complexity of CISC computers can be followed from the development of the first computers in the 1940s and 1950s. As technology improved so the designer was able to add more complexity to the architecture of the computer and, as high level languages developed, the general opinion was that the best way to improve the execution performance was to provide more and more high level features in the underlying architecture. An example of this is the inclusion of the switch statement in the DEC VAX instruction set, which mimics the CASE statement found in a typical high level language. The DEC VAX architecture, an architecture very common in the 1980s, was perhaps the culmination of this design approach and this computer contained a large number of instructions, several hundred if all the different variations with different sized data types are counted. It also had up to 16 different addressing modes available.

In the 1980s some designers began to question this trend to increasingly complex architectures and set out to investigate if a different approach would be more cost effective. The architecture that resulted from this research is called a reduced instruction set computer (RISC) and has the following characteristics:

- all instructions execute in a single machine cycle;

- all instructions have the same length;

- only a few different types of instruction format are supported;

- access to main memory is via load and store instructions only – all other instructions operate on operands in registers;

- the instruction set is designed specifically to support high level languages.

The first two characteristics in the list mean that the architecture can be simple, since all instructions are treated identically. Also, the implementation can be hardwired rather than microcoded since it is relatively simple. The fourth characteristic means that instruction execution will be fast since most instructions will not access main memory but will operate on operands in on-chip registers. A corollary of the final characteristic means that it is not necessary for a programmer to be able to write machine code programs easily and efficiently, since the normal mode of programming for these architectures is via a high level language. Thus this type of architecture is entirely dependent on high level language compilers for the generation of efficient code.

The approach taken by RISC designers was to examine the way in which high level languages used the instruction set of a computer and to measure the use of the instruction set in a typical set of high level language programs. Patterson and Sequin, two of the early pioneers, studied a range of programs written in Pascal and C and discovered that the percentages of the different types of instruction, weighted for the number of machine code instructions required to implement each statement, was approximately 45% for procedure call and return, 30% for loops, 15% for assignment and 10% for conditional statements with other statements occurring a minimal amount. They also discovered that scalar variables were the most frequent data type. From this they concluded that the most important features of an architecture to execute high level languages efficiently are an efficient procedure/call mechanism and fast access to variables.

To provide fast access, variables should be accessible in registers on the processor rather than in memory on a separate chip. This implies that the processor should include a large number of registers. Making procedure call and return efficient implies making the transfer of parameters efficient. Invoking a procedure involves copying any parameter from the caller's environment to the called environment, saving the contents of any register that may be used in the called procedure and jumping to the procedure code. Similarly, returning from the procedure involves restoring the environment of the caller, copying the parameters back to the caller and returning to the correct place in the caller's code. Patterson and Sequin suggested the idea of using register windows where the set of registers accessible to a procedure are split up into a number of sets called high, local, low and global. Register windows of caller and callee overlap so that parameters are passed between two procedures with no copying overheads.

The operation of register windows can be explained using Figures 17.1 and 17.2, which relate to the RISC-1 processor designed by Patterson and Sequin.

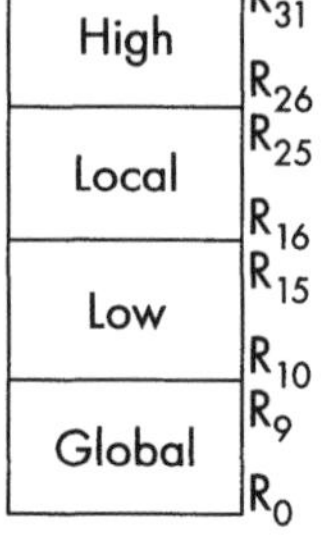

High	R_{31}
	R_{26}
Local	R_{25}
	R_{16}
Low	R_{15}
	R_{10}
Global	R_9
	R_0

Figure 17.1 Register set for a procedure.

The processor contains a large number of registers but only a small subset are accessible at any one time, in this case 32. The lower 10 registers, R_0 to R_9, are called the global area and this part of the register address space is always mapped to the same physical registers, giving a globally accessible register

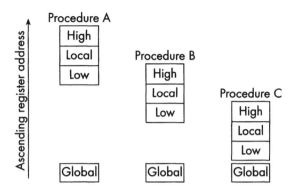

Figure 17.2 Overlapping windows of procedures when A calls B calls C.

set. The area containing registers R_{10}–R_{15} is called the low area and contains temporary variables and parameters passed to/from 'lower procedures', that is, procedures called by the present procedure. The local area, R_{16}–R_{25}, contains variables local to the current procedure and the high area, R_{26}–R_{31}, contains parameters passed to/from this procedure and a calling procedure. When a procedure call is executed, the register set used for the high, local and low areas 'slides' over the total set of registers so that the old low area becomes the new high area and new registers are allocated for the new low and local areas, as shown in Figure 17.2. If the hardware register file is completely allocated then the file is extended into main memory with a consequent loss of performance. The size of the register file is tailored to the expected depth of nesting of procedure calls by measurement of a typical workload. It appears that good performance can be obtained by a register set of about 100 registers since procedure nesting rarely exceeds seven.

This technique of register renaming is now commonly used in new architectures and Sun Microsystems have incorporated register windows into their RISC-based SPARC (scalar processor architecture). Most other manufacturers have adopted a different approach of providing a reasonably large number of registers, typically 32, and have used increasingly sophisticated compiler technology to map program data to processor registers in the most efficient and effective way.

One technique that is almost universally employed in making RISC-based processors fast is the use of instruction cycle pipelining as explained in Chapter 13. Using pipelining, it is possible to process more than one instruction at a time by overlapping the execution of one instruction with succeeding instructions. A major problem with the use of pipelining is that instructions, in general, are not independent. For example, consider the assembly code sequence

```
bne   label   ; jump to the instruction labelled label if the result of
              ; the previous instruction resulted in a non-zero result
add   #1,r4   ; add 1 to the contents of register 4
```

The instruction to be executed following the conditional branch (bne) will be either the next instruction (add) or the instruction labelled label, depending on the result of the previous instruction. Thus the next instruction cannot be determined until the result of the bne test is known, that is, the execution of the bne instruction and the following one cannot be overlapped. Conventional (CISC) high speed processors that use pipelining techniques in their implementation use elaborate mechanisms to overcome this problem, but these techniques are, in general, too complex for RISC processors which rely on simpler solutions to overcome the problem. A simple solution to the problem above is to delay the execution of the instruction following the branch so that its address will be available when the instruction has to be fetched. This can be done by inserting one or more no-operation opcodes into the instruction stream after every branch. In the example above this would result in the code:

```
bne    label
noop
...
...
noop
add    #1,r4
```

which would cause the noop instructions to be executed, which have no effect, between the bne and the add instruction. The number of no-operation instructions that needs to be added depends on the degree of overlap between consecutive instructions, that is, how many stages there are in the pipeline, and the stage of the pipeline in which the required quantity is computed. If there are n stages in the pipeline and the required quantity is computed in the final stage then n-1 noop instructions will be required, for example, for a 2 stage pipeline only a single noop will be required. The problem with this solution is that instruction execution is slowed down by the additional no-operations. In many cases it is possible to rearrange the code so that there is no need for an extra no-operations. An example illustrating this for a two-stage pipeline is shown in Figure 17.3 but the techniques for such code reorganization are too specialized to describe here. Interested readers are referred to [Hennessy and Patterson]. The algorithms for code reorganization are built into the high level language compilers for RISC machines but they are difficult for programmers to apply by hand, hence programming of RISCs at the assembly code level is rarely attempted since high level language compilers can usually produce more efficient code.

Using the techniques outlined above it is possible to implement a very simple processor that executes instructions very efficiently and quickly even though each instruction does not do as much work as a CISC instruction. Studies have shown that simple RISC architectures can perform at least as well as conventional architectures and this is the reason that most

Example code for non-pipelined processor		Code with NOP for pipelined RISC with two stages		Rearranged code with only one NOP	
	CMP	D0,D3	CMP	D0,D3	CMP	D0,D3
	BNE	L1	BNE	L1	BNE	L1
	ADD	D1,D0	NOOP		NOOP	
	JMP	L2	ADD	D1,D0	JMP	L2
L1:	ADD	D2,D0	JMP	L2	ADD	D1,D0
			NOOP		L1: ADD	D2,D0
			L1: ADD	D2,D1		

Figure 17.3 An example of delayed jumps.

manufacturers have adopted the RISC approach in the design of their current processors, for example, the PowerPC and SPARC processors.

17.2.1 The PowerPC architecture

Several years ago Motorola entered into an alliance with IBM and Apple Computer to develop the POWER architecture, which emerged from development work on RISC architectures by IBM. As a result of the collaboration, extra features were added to the architecture, resulting in a RISC superscalar architecture. This architecture has now been realized in many different forms from the processors that power Apple computers to the processors that control the engine management systems on Ford cars. The PowerPC 601, the first member of the family, was a 32-bit processor but later members of the family are 64-bit processors

The programmers view
The PowerPC has 32 64-bit general registers called R_0 to R_{31}, which can hold integer values and which can be operated on by integer arithmetic and logical operations. R_0 is special in that it is assumed to contain the value zero when used as the source operand with many instructions. Zero occurs frequently in many programs and this justifies having special provision for its requiring fewer bits to encode than the equivalent immediate value. There is a 32-bit exception register associated with the integer general registers, which is used, among other things, to record whether overflow occurred during an operation. The PowerPC also has 32 64-bit floating point registers which are used with floating point operations. There is an associated control and status register which is used to control the operation of the floating point unit and to record its status.

The PowerPC differs from the 680x0 in how it saves the result of an instruction for use with conditional branches. Instead of there being a single status register which has individual bits for carry, overflow etc. the PowerPC has a single 32-bit condition register which is split into eight sets of four bits, each set of four bits serving to record the status after an instruction. Integer instructions affect only one set of four bits and floating point operations affect another set while comparison instructions can affect any set of four bits since the identity of the set to be used is included in comparison instruction. Similarly, conditional branches include the identity of the set of bits to be tested and can thus depend on instructions other than the last instruction executed. The reason for allowing conditional branches to depend on instructions other than the immediately preceding instruction is to allow instructions to be executed out of order. The four bits that are used to store the status after an instruction are:

bit 0: set if the result is less than zero for an arithmetic operation or for source operand1 being less than source operand2 for a comparison operation;

bit 1: set if the result is greater than zero for an arithmetic operation or for source operand1 being greater than source operand2 for a comparison operation;

bit 2: set if the result is equal to zero for an arithmetic operation or for source operand1 being equal to source operand2 for a comparison operation;

bit 3: set if the result of the operation resulted in zero.

There is also a 64-bit link register used for call and return instructions. Typically when a call is performed the return address is to the instruction following the call and there is an instruction to perform a call loading this return address into the link register. The return instruction copies the contents of this link register to the program counter which returns execution to the instruction immediately after the call. An associated 64-bit count register is used as an efficient way to provide a loop count. Every time the count register is accessed the count is decremented by one. Thus if the count register is loaded with the loop count prior to the beginning of a loop and tested for zero at the end of the loop, the loop will exit after the requisite number of iterations.

There are two registers for holding the system state for interrupt processing. When an interrupt occurs, the program counter value is copied to one register and the machine status to the other. On a return from interrupt instruction being executed the program counter and machine state are restored.

Instruction set and addressing modes

The instruction set of the PowerPC is much simpler than the 680x0 described earlier, since it has a RISC architecture, but it does cater for floating point instructions as well as integer operations. All integer arithmetic and logical operations operate only with immediate or register operands and hence these are the only addressing modes supported for these type of operations. Load and store instructions are used to copy information to/from main memory and registers and these can use indirect and indirect indexed addressing modes. Branch instructions can use absolute, relative and indirect addressing modes. Floating point instructions operate only on register values and support only this addressing mode.

The instruction set is compact. For example, there are only four types of integer arithmetic operations (add, subtract, multiply and divide) and five types of logical operation (compare, and, rotate, shift and bit count). The only type that does not occur in the 680x0 is the bit count operation, which counts the number of 0 bits in a register. There are a number of different types of load and store operation to load and store varying numbers of bits, for example, word, double word and strings of bytes.

Because of the small number of addressing modes allowed and the small number of instruction types there are relatively few instruction formats:– three for branch instructions, three for load/store instructions, nine for integer instructions and one for floating point instructions. The format for an integer operation using register addressing mode is given in Figure 17.4.

Opcode 1	Dst	Src 1	Src 2	0	Opcode 2	R
6 bits	5 bits	5 bits	5 bits		9 bits	

Figure 17.4 Format of a PPC arithmetic instruction using register mode addressing.

Each register field, src1, src2 and dst occupy five bits since there are 32 integer registers. There are 15 bits available for the opcode specification but these are spread over two fields. The reason for this is that the immediate form of integer operations allows only a 6-bit opcode and uses the other nine bits as part of the immediate field. By splitting the opcode field, it is possible to reduce the complexity of the decoding algorithm required. The R field is used to determine whether the instruction sets the condition bits. The reason for including such a facility is that a conditional branch cannot be directly dependent on an instruction that does not set the condition bits and the hardware can reorder non-dependent instructions if desired.

Processor implementation

The PowerPC implementations are superscalar, that is, more than one instruction can be issued per clock cycle. In order to be able to do this, the processor must have multiple functional units and the PowerPC 601, the first implementation of the architecture, contained an integer unit, a floating point unit and a branch unit. This means that the processor can execute a maximum of one instruction of each of these three types simultaneously. Later processors have more functional units and hence potentially can have higher parallelism.

A block diagram of the 601 processor is shown in Figure 17.5. The processor contains a fetch unit, which pre-fetches up to eight instructions to a cache which holds both instructions and data. A dispatch unit retrieves instructions from the cache and loads them into an instruction queue which can hold eight instructions. The three functional units are fed from the bottom four items in the queue, the bottom four items being used just to

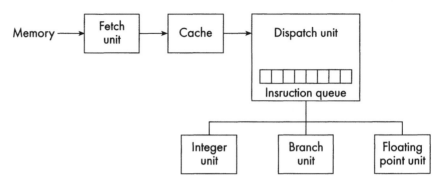

Figure 17.5 Block diagram of the PowerPC 601 processor.

buffer the instructions from the cache. Branch instructions and floating point instructions may be issued out of order but only if they are in the top four items in the queue. This helps to keep the functional units busy and improves processor throughput.

Instruction implementation is pipelined and different instructions have different numbers of stages. In the PowerPC 601, a branch instruction requires two stages, an integer instruction four stages, load/store instructions take five stages and floating point instructions take six stages. The instruction queue is examined every cycle and up to three instructions are dispatched.

Because instructions can be executed out of order, a mechanism has to be provided to ensure that when dependencies between instructions exist they are executed in the correct order. The PowerPC 601 stalls the pipeline, that is, introduces no-operation instructions, if necessary, to provide the correct execution order.

The handling of branch instructions is very important to the efficiency of the processor and the PowerPC has attempted to optimize the architecture to handle branch instructions. The techniques used to optimize the handling of branch instructions are outside the scope of this text. However, it should be noted that handling of transfer of control instructions in superscalar systems is the subject of much current research since it is thought to be the key to high performance processors.

The PowerPC architecture has numerous similarities with the 680x0 family described earlier in this book. The major differences are an increase in the number of registers, a decrease in the number of instructions and addressing modes and an increase in the complexity of the implementation.

17.2.2 The future of RISC processors

It is in the area of processor design where the architect has perhaps the most choice. The decision as to which is the 'best' architecture is not a simple choice as it depends on a large number of factors, including the application area and the perceived future trends in hardware and software technology.

There has been a great deal of debate about whether the RISC or CISC approach is the best for current architectures. The basic difference between the two approaches concerns the architectural level at which system functionality is assigned to implementation levels. RISC designers put the functionality at a higher level in the architecture than CISC designers, assuming that the language translators will perform an efficient mapping to low level code. CISC designers build more functionality into the lower level architecture.

The trend is for any architecture to get more complex with time. The reasons for this are many and varied but include the following.

- New models of a computer system are required to be upwardly compatible, that is, they must include as a subset features of previous models so that they can execute software from the older model. This can be seen in the Intel Pentium processor, which includes features which can be traced back to the Intel 8-bit processors of the 1970s.

- Reduction in the 'semantic gap' between the user's programming language and the native language of the target machine. This is desirable as it reduces the software complexity which is the major factor in computing system costs. Reduction in the semantic gap requires low level architectural support for high level languages via compilers.

- The desire of the manufacturer to increase the speed of execution by migrating features from software to hardware.

- The technology improvements which allow the designer to increase the complexity of the circuit on a chip at very little extra cost.

These arguments suggest that any design, including RISCs, will get more complex as time passes. In fact RISCs and CISCs are just two points in the design space which have proved to be cost-effective in the past; there is no guarantee that they will be the most efficient in the future as technology improvements significantly change costings.

Perhaps the largest area of debate between CISC and RISC concerns the effect of the large register file on the performance of the RISC architectures. Would the use of a large register file increase the performance of a CISC machine? Undoubtedly it would, but the designers of RISC argue that the space required by the register file reduces the space for the processor logic on the chip and thus only a RISC machine is small enough to fit. However, technology improvements mean that the amount of circuit that can be placed on a chip is predicted to continue increasing at its present rate for the next decade so the complexity of the processor that can be implemented is also increasing. It will therefore be possible – in fact, it already is possible – to implement a CISC processor with a large register file.

Although the debate between RISC and CISC designers has been useful in focusing attention on processor design, the design space parameters are still changing so fast that there is no one 'best' design over time. Perusal of manufacturers' information on current processors at the time of writing shows that even though many manufacturers advertise their processors as RISC machines, many of them contain features of CISC processors, for example, microcoded RISC processors are appearing and processors with increasing instruction sets and increasing numbers of addressing modes. In the future it is likely that architects will take the best features from all designs, CISC or RISC, to produce the most effective architecture to execute current applications.

17.3 Webcentric computing

One of the major developments in computing in the 1990s was the growth of the Internet and the World Wide Web (WWW). The Internet is a network of networks and has grown steadily since the ARPAnet was developed in the US by the Department of Defence in the early 1970s. Gradually more and more networks in different countries from all over the world were connected together and the result is the world-wide network, the Internet, of today. The topology of the Internet is irregular because of the way in which it has developed but it allows computers all over the world to communicate with one another. The World Wide Web (WWW), designed in 1989 by Tim Berners-Lee, provides a method of organising and searching through information stored in many different computers across the Internet using hypertext and hypermedia. Hypertext is text which may contain links (pointers) to other hypertext documents which may be on the same computer or any other connected computer, that is, on the Internet. This allows a network of documents to be generated, usually in some form of hierarchy. Hypermedia is the term given to hypertext which has been extended to include other forms of media such as graphics and sound.

The basis of WWW is the use of HTML – hypertext markup language – which allows the creator of information to annotate the text with pointers to other documents, images, graphics and sounds. The hypertext or hypermedia is stored on a server computer linked to the Internet. Each hypertext or hypermedia document has a unique address called a URL – uniform resource locator – and it is the URLs which are used to link the resources together. Users of the WWW need client software called a web browser on their networked computer. The browser displays the contents of the current URL on the screen and highlights links to other hypermedia. Users can follow the links and display the information pointed by a simple action, for example, by clicking the mouse when the cursor is over a link. The two most common web browsers are Netscape Navigator and Microsoft Explorer.

A newer development is the object oriented Java programming language, a language that has been designed for programming WWW applications. A distinctive feature of the language is that many implementations are interpretive – although there are an increasing number of Java compilers – and the run time system is small and can be easily ported to a wide variety of platforms. The interpreter is included in browsers and thus Java code can be distributed and run across the WWW. This provides a simple way of distributing programs across the Internet and gives greater functionality to the WWW as dynamic information as well as static information can be displayed via a browser, for example, a moving image such as a simulation can be included in a hypermedia document.

These – and other – developments mean that much of the future of computing is seen as being intimately tied up with networking and distributed computing across the Internet.

This introduction to the Internet and WWW is deliberately brief as this book is concerned primarily with computer architecture rather than the development of the Internet. The interest from a computer architecture point of view is how this webcentric view of computing will influence the future of computer architectures. A number of experts see the future as consisting of simple computers running browser software being attached to the Internet which will contain a large collection of information including programs such as word processors and spreadsheets. A user will start up the simple browser machine which will communicate with the network to obtain copies of whatever information – data and programs – the user requires. In this view of the future the user's network machine needs very little in the way of resources itself as it can obtain everything it requires from the network. The argument is that this will substantially reduce the cost of computing, and this in turn will lead to new applications and significantly higher sales. This simple computer is known as a network computer and several companies have plans for such machines. These computers are expected to cost between one half and one third of the cost of a typical PC since they do not require a hard disc and use a television screen as the output device, thus removing the need for a VDU. With the advent of Java and similar languages the network computer may be able to run just with browser software as programs written in these languages can be embedded in hypermedia. Thus these computers could be Java machines, that is, they could be simple Java interpreters. In terms of computer architecture, a Java machine is very similar to the current model of a computer so there would be very little change except that the architecture could be tailored to a single language and therefore be more efficient. Thus, at present, it appears that the architecture for future machines will be a simple, RISC-like processor with a large amount of RAM to cache information from the Internet. The computer will have a minimum amount of disc space as this will be provided elsewhere on the Internet. The interface to the Internet will be crucial for performance and thus the emphasis on architecture will be on the communications structure of the machine rather than processor design.

The major problem with this model of computing is that present network response is comparatively slow. This comes about for a number of reasons.

Firstly, many computers are connected to the Internet by slow communication links, for example, telephone lines with modems. This can be overcome by the use of higher speed links which are available now but they are too expensive for most applications. Secondly, the present growth of the network is exceeding the pace at which the network components are being upgraded and hence the performance is degrading. Proponents argue that these problems will be overcome in the short term by the growth of cable networks and by the introduction of large, geographically local centres which will cache copies of frequently used information so that remote access will be required infrequently. Whilst these developments will undoubtedly take place it is unclear how effective they will be and how quickly they will be implemented.

One trend that has become apparent over the past few years and which will undoubtedly continue into the future is the increase in computing power required to service the human computer interface. This will be required whether or not the computer is attached to the Internet or whether it is stand alone, since the user will expect to have a complex interface with full multimedia including sound, video and 3D graphics. This requires substantial computing power and some manufacturers are currently defining extended instruction sets and special purpose interfaces to cope with multimedia, for example, the MMX instruction set and data type extensions to the Intel Pentium architecture. These type of extensions will be included in future architectures and specialized I/O processors will be developed to deal with the human computer interface. These developments may transform system architectures over time but they are unlikely to change processor architectures substantially.

Thus while webcentric computing appears to be the future of computing, it does not appear that this will have a great effect on computer architecture except to decrease the need for local storage and increase the need for fast, reliable remote services. The growth of webcentric computing and its influence on the present use of personal computers will depend critically on the development and introduction of fast, cheap telecommunication systems.

17.4 The future of architectures

17.4.1 Processor architectures

The cost of implementing a new processor architecture is very high and it is not commercially worthwhile unless there are substantial gains to be made. Additionally, if current applications are to be run on the new architecture, then there are many constraints on the architect, for example, some of the features of the original Intel microprocessors can be found in the latest Pentium designs. These features have been included in later designs for backwards compatibility. Thus new designs tend to be evolutions of old designs rather than completely new designs. The Intel Pentium processors conform to this model whereas RISC processors do not. The implementation of the architecture will continue to evolve provided it does not impact on the compiler's model of the architecture. For example, Pentium processors use considerably more concurrency in their implementation than the earlier models, for example, the 80486, although they both have the same basic processor architecture. Thus it is unlikely that processor architectures will change rapidly or markedly with the current implementation technology.

17.4.2 System architecture

Whereas processor architecture is unlikely to change radically in the near future, changes in system architecture are more likely, since these changes are largely hidden from the programmer and compiler. The object of building a system is to balance the performance of each component so that no one component is the system bottleneck all the time. In modern systems the number of integrated circuits is kept to a minimum because this reduces the number of system failures and also results in a system that is comparatively fast since intra-chip communications are generally very much faster than inter-chip communications. The system architecture is thus the configuration of the circuits comprising the system. Most systems are bus-based, as this results in a system that is easy to customize and expand, although the overheads of the protocol for setting up the communication can be high for short communications. It is unclear what the future holds for system architecture as it will be possible to build complete systems on a single chip, although this makes expansion difficult. It is likely that systems, other than very simple, cheap ones, will consist of interconnected subsystems, probably bus-based, to make them expandible.

17.4.3 Other implementation techniques

This book has concentrated on the conventional implementation of a computational model based on the processing and communication of electrical signals. However, there are many different ways of implementing a computer model. Remember that the original attempts to implement a computer were based on mechanical devices where information was represented by the position of cogs and information was transmitted by connecting cogs together. Although the electrical implementation has served us well for the past 50 years it is not at all clear that this will be the best model in the future, especially since the limits on miniaturization may not be far off. One new method of implementing a computational model which is starting to be explored is based on the use of DNA. The 0s and 1s of the binary system can be coded into a string of the four basic components of DNA. Thus a DNA molecule can represent data and the data can be processed by chemical methods that allow different pieces of data to interact. As an example, the basic 'machine code' of a DNA computer would involve 'instructions' such as:

- amplification, that it making copies of a DNA string;

- extraction, that is, extracting DNA strands that contain a given pattern;

- cutting, that is, using a chemical to break the DNA strand at a given point;

- detection, that is, confirming the presence or absence of a given DNA string in a sample.

Using chemical analysis of the result it is possible to determine the outcome of the computation. The reasons for so much interest in this implementation technique are that:

- it is very fast because computations are performed in parallel;

- the amount of energy required to perform the computation is very much less than using electronic technology;

- the information can be stored at much higher densities than electronic media.

There are a number of problems to overcome before a DNA-based computer becomes economically feasible. Firstly, at present it is not possible to mimic all the components of a universal computational model but it is expected that this will become possible in the next few years. Secondly, the implementation is based on biochemical techniques and these need to be automated and miniaturized.

These techniques are still only at the research stage but it is likely that the dominant method of implementing a computer later in the 21st century will not use the current electronic-based technology.

17.5 Summary

Two major recent developments in computer architecture have been the introduction and growth in the number of reduced instruction set computers (RISC) and the growing use of the Internet and World Wide Web (WWW) to provide distributed computing.

Reduced instruction set computers are computers with a relatively small number of instructions and addressing modes. They were developed because designers saw that conventional architectures were getting large and complex and much of the complexity was not used by most compilers and applications. RISC architectures are deliberately kept small and simple to enable small, fast implementations to be produced. Complex compiler technology is used to generate efficient code for these processors, which are designed to be programmed in a high level language. Most recent architectures are RISC based, although many are hybrid RISC/CISC designs.

The largest growth in computing at present is in the use of the WWW. Architecturally the WWW can act as a distributed computing system with the nodes of the network acting as processors and data sources. There is considerable debate about what effect the use of the WWW will have on the future of computing. As far as computer architecture is concerned, the debate concerns whether future computers need all the resources of present computers or whether a cut down version with less storage and facilities will suffice. It appears unlikely that the WWW will have a substantial effect on computer architectures in the near future; architectures are likely to be influenced far more by technological developments in integrated circuit technology.

In the more distant future it is likely that new methods of implementing a computational model will be developed and the DNA-based computer is one of these which is currently under investigation.

17.6 Exercises

Exercise 17.1 What are the essential characteristics of RISC machines?

Exercise 17.2 Most RISC machines use pipelining as part of the processor implementation. What problems does this cause for the programmer? How are these problems overcome by compilers?

Exercise 17.3 Why do you think that most RISC machines do not use the sliding window technique for register allocation but, instead, allow the compiler to allocate registers to particular tasks?

Exercise 17.4 Search the WWW to find information on different ways of implementing a computer architecture.

Appendix

This appendix gives more details of the instruction sets of the Motorola 68000 and the Intel 80x86 ranges of computers. The instruction sets of both these machines are quite complex, for example, not all addressing modes can be used by all instructions and even what appear to be similar instructions sometimes take different addressing modes. Since the intention of this book is not primarily to teach assembly code we have taken the liberty of generalising the instruction sets to make them simpler to comprehend but there is enough detail for the exercises at the end of Chapter 12 to be attempted. Those readers who wish to know the details of the instruction set for a given computer should consult the manufacturer's literature or one of the books quoted in the bibliography.

Motorola 68000 family instruction set

Two operand instructions

MOVE	src,dst	copy contents of src to dst
ADD	src,Dn	add contents of src to data register D_n
ADD	Dn, dst	add contents of data register D_n to dst
ADDI	#n, dst	add literal value n to contents of dst
SUB	src,Dn	subtract contents of src from D_n
SUB	Dn, dst	subtract contents of data register D_n from dst
SUBI	#n, dst	subtract literal value n from contents of dst
MULU	src, Dn	unsigned multiply of D_n by src
MULS	src, Dn	signed multiply of D_n by src
DIVU	src, Dn	unsigned divide of D_n by src

DIVS	src, Dn	signed divide of D_n by src

ROL	src, Dn	rotate D_n left src number of bits
ROR	src, Dn	rotate D_n right src number of bits

LSL	src, Dn	logical shift D_n src bits left
LSR	src, Dn	logical shift D_n src bits right

ASL	src, Dn	arithmetic shift left D_n src bits
ASR	src, Dn	arithmetic shift right D_n src bits

CMP	src, Dn	set condition codes on result of $D_n - $ src
CMPI	#n, dst	set condition codes on result of dst $- n$

One operand instructions

CLR	dst	set dst to 0
NOT	dst	replace dst by its 1's complement
NEG	dst	replace dst by its 2's complement
TST	dst	set condition codes on contents of dst

Transfer of control instructions

JMP	dst	jump to dst
JSR	dst	jump to subroutine at dst
RTS		return from subroutine

BRA	addr	branch to addr
BSR	addr	call routine at addr

BCC	addr	branch to addr if carry $= 0$
BCS	addr	branch to addr if carry $= 1$
BEQ	addr	branch to addr if zero bit $= 0$
BNE	addr	branch to addr if zero bit $= 1$
BPL	addr	branch to addr if negative $= 0$
BMI	addr	branch to addr if negative $= 1$
BVC	addr	branch to addr if overflow $= 0$
BVS	addr	branch to addr if overflow $= 1$

BGE	addr	branch to addr if result of last instruction ≥ 0
BLT	addr	branch to addr if result of last instruction < 0
BGT	addr	branch to addr if result of last instruction > 0
BLE	addr	branch to addr if result of last instruction ≤ 0

Other instructions

LEA	src, An	load effective address of source operand to address register A_n
SWAP	Dn	swaps upper and lower 16 bits of D_n; operates only on longwords
BCLR	src, dst	clears bit src of dst
BSET	src, dst	sets bit src of dst
BCHG	src, dst	changes bit src of dst (0 to 1 or 1 to 0)
BTST	src, dst	tests bit src of dst and sets condition codes

Notes

1. Src = source operand, dst = destination operand, addr = address (label in assembly code).

2. All one- and two-operand instructions can operate on longword, word or byte data. The data type for an instruction is denoted by .L, .W or .B following the opcode.

3. Addressing modes supported for src and dst are

   Register direct (data or address register) – D_n or A_n
   Indirect (address register only) – (A_n)
   Autoincrement (address register only) – $(A_n)+$
   Autodecrement (address register only) – $-(A_n)$
   Based or indexed – $n(A_n)$
   Based indexed – $n(A_n, D_n)$
   Immediate – $\#n$
   Absolute – address
   Relative

4. Assemblers for 680x0 will usually convert to the most efficient or required form, for example, MOVE   #2000,A2 would be changed to MOVEA #2000,A2 which is the required form of move to an address register. Also if a jump or branch is to a near location, the addressing mode will be changed from absolute to relative.

Intel 80x86 family instruction set

Two operand instructions

MOV	dst,src	copy data from src to dst
MOV	dst,data	move given data to dst
ADD	dst,src	add contents of src to dst
ADD	dst,data	add data to dst
ADC	dst,src	add contents of src to dst with carry
ADC	dst,data	add data to dst with carry
SUB	dst,src	subtract contents of src from dst
SUB	dst,data	subtract data from dst
SBB	dst,src	subtract contents of src from dst with borrow
SBB	dst,data	subtract data from dst with borrow
CMP	dst,src	subtract contents of src from dst and set flags
CMP	dst,data	subtract data from dst and set flags
AND	dst,src	logical AND of contents of src with dst
AND	dst,data	logical AND of data with dst
OR	dst,src	logical OR of contents of src with dst
OR	dst,data	logical OR of data with dst
XOR	dst,src	logical exclusive OR of contents of src with dst
XOR	dst,data	logical exclusive OR of data with dst
TEST	dst,src	set flags as a result of ANDing dst with src
TEST	dst,data	set flags as a result of ANDing data with dst
SHR	dst,cnt	logically shift right dst by cnt bits
SHL	dst,cnt	logically shift left dst by cnt bits
SAR	dst,cnt	arithmetic shift right dst by cnt bits
SAL	dst,cnt	arithmetic shift left dst by cnt bits
ROL	dst,cnt	rotate dst left cnt bits
ROR	dst,cnt	rotate dst right cnt bits
RCL	dst,cnt	rotate dst left cnt bits including carry
RCR	dst,cnt	rotate dst right cnt bits including carry
XCHG	dst,reg	exchange register contents with dst

One operand instructions

INC	dst	increments contents of dst by 1
DEC	dst	decrement contents of dst by 1
NEG	dst	replace contents of dst by its 2's complement
NOT	dst	replace dst by its 1's complement
MUL	src	unsigned multiply of AL or AX by contents of src
IMUL	src	signed multiply of AL or AX by contents of src
DIV	src	unsigned divide of DX, AX by contents of src
IDIV	src	signed divide of DX, AX by contents of src

Transfer of control instructions

JMP	addr	jump to address addr
JMP	src	jump to address in src
CALL	addr	call subroutine at address addr
CALL	src	call subroutine at address in src
RET		return from subroutine
RET	n	return from subroutine, add n to stack pointer
JC	addr8	jump if carry flag = 1; go to PC + addr8
JNC	addr8	jump if carry flag = 0; go to PC + addr8
JS	addr8	jump if sign flag = 1; go to PC + addr8
JNS	addr8	jump if sign flag = 0; go to PC + addr8
JZ	addr8	jump if zero flag = 1; go to PC + addr8
JNZ	addr8	jump if zero flag = 0; go to PC + addr8
JP	addr8	jump if parity flag = 1; go to PC + addr8
JNP	addr8	jump if parity flag = 0; go to PC + addr8
JO	addr8	jump if overflow flag = 1; go to PC + addr8
JNO	addr8	jump if overflow flag = 0; go to PC + addr8
JL	addr8	jump if last result was less than 0
JGE	addr8	jump if last result was greater than or equal to 0
JLE	addr8	jump if last result was less than or equal to 0
JG	addr8	jump if last result was greater than 0
LOOP	addr8	decrement CX and jump to addr8 if not CX = 0
LOOPZ	addr8	decrement CX and jump to addr8 if not CX = 0 and ZF = 1
LOOPNZ	addr8	decrement CX and jump to addr8 if not CX = 0 and ZF = 0

Other instructions

PUSH	src	push src on to stack
POP	dst	pop the top of stack to dst
LEA	reg,src	load reg with effective address of src
CBW		convert byte in AL to word in AX
CWD		convert word in AX to double word in DX, AX
CLC		clear carry flag
CMC		replace carry by its 1's complement
STC		set carry
HLT		halt processor
NOP		no-operation

Notes

1. The 80x86 family supports a number of string processing instructions not included here.

Further reading

This book covers a wide range of material at an introductory level. Readers may wish for more information on some of the topics and this bibliography contains a list of references that supplement material introduced this book. It is not exhaustive but contains references that the authors recommend even though some of the references are several years old.

A very good web site as a starting point for information on topics covered in this book is webopedia, URL http://webopedia.internet.com.

Electronics

Horowitz, P. and Hill, W. (2e 1989) *The Art of Electronics*, Cambridge University Press. This book is an extensive, readable and practical electronics text aimed at first year undergraduates covering both analogue and digital electronics.

Very large scale integration (VLSI)

Taur, Y. and Ning, T. (1998) *Fundamentals of Modern vlsi Devices*, Cambridge University Press. A recent book on the fundamentals of VLSI design.

Pucknell, D. A. and Estraghian, K. (1994) *Basic VLSI Design – 3rd Edition*, Prentice-Hall. A very good introductory text on VLSI design.

Digital logic design

Roth, C. C. (1998) *Fundamentals of Logic Design*, PWS. This comprehensive textbook covers the whole spectrum of digital logic design from first principles through to combinational and sequential logic systems. The book contains a chapter on sequential design with programmable logic devices. Each chapter concludes with a full set of problems.

Katz, R. H. (1994) *Contemporary Logic Design*, Benjamin-Cummings. This is also a very comprehensive digital logic design text covering essentially the same material as the Roth text, but with more emphasis on implementations with programmable logic and gate arrays. The book also contains chapters on computer organization and control unit design. It is part of a complete teaching package which includes an instructors guide, transparencies available over the Internet, as well as access to software design tools.

Interfacing

Stone, H. (2e 1992) *Microcomputer Interfacing*, Addison Wesley. An excellent book on interfacing. Although quite old, most of the material is still very relevant.

Motorola 68000

There is the usual manufacturer's literature on this processor, its software and support chips. For beginners a better approach is to consult a textbook such as the ones mentioned below.

Wakerley, J. F. (1989) *Microcomputer Architecture and Programming: The 68000 Family*, John Wiley and Sons. This is one of the most comprehensive textbooks on the 680x0 processors. It is particularly good on programming aspects and contains many code examples.

Clements, A. (3e 1997) *Microprocessor Systems Design: 68000 Hardware, Software and Interfacing*, PWS. A predominantly hardware-based text on the 68000. It covers all the hardware characteristics including the bus and support chips.

Bramer, B. (1986) *M68000 Assembly Language Programming*, Arnold. One of the many textbooks on low-level programming for the 68000 series. This is one of the better ones at a moderate cost.

Intel 80x86

Ayala, K. J. (1995) *The 8086 Microprocessor: Programming and Interfacing the PC*, West Publishing Company. This book covers the architecture and programming of the 8086 series microprocessors. It also covers the interfacing of external devices to the standard ports of a PC and the interfacing of devices to the system bus.

Jones, D. S. (1988) *Assembly Programming and the 8086 Microprocessor*, Oxford Scientific Publications. This is a concise book, which concentrates on assembly code for the 8086 range of processors. It is an excellent introduction to assembly code for this range of processors.

Messmer, Hans-Peter (1997) *The Indispensable PC Hardware Book*, Addison-Wesley. This is probably the most comprehensive book on the hardware of the complete range of PC systems from the 386 onwards. An excellent reference book.

Networks

Stallings, W. (5e 1996) *Data and Computer Communication*, Macmillan. This is a comprehensive textbook on both data communications and networking and contains material on the techniques for data transmission as well as computer networking techniques.

Tanenbaum, A. S. (1996) *Computer Networks*, Prentice Hall Inc. This is one of the larger and more comprehensive textbooks on computer networks. It includes material on recent developments such as the World Wide Web.

Beauchamp. K, (3e 1995) *Computer Communications*, ITCP. This is one of the best moderately priced textbooks on both data and computer communications but it does not have the coverage of either of the two previous texts.

Advanced computer architectures

Hennessy, J. L. and Patterson, D. A. (1995) *Computer Architecture A Quantitative Approach*, Morgan Kaufmann Publishers. This text covers the detailed quantitative arguments a designer has to evaluate when designing a new computer architecture. The major architectures in use today are considered.

Hwang, K. (1993) *Advanced Computer Architecture*, McGraw-Hill Publishers. A detailed text on computer architecture with particular emphasis on parallelism, scalability and programmability.

Computer arithmetic

Scott, N. R. (1985) *Computer Number Systems and Arithmetic*, Prentice Hall Publishers. This is one of the most comprehensive books on computer arithmetic and still a useful reference work.

Gosling, J. B. (1980) *Design of Arithmetic Units for Digital Computers*, Springer–Verlag. This book considers the hardware design of ALUs and contains a wealth of material of different algorithms for implementing common computer arithmetic.

DNA Computer

Adelman, L. (1994) *Molecular computation of solution to combinatorial problems*, Science 266, pp 1021–1024.

URL http://dna2z.com/ contains a good introduction to DNA computing.

Glossary

Absolute address: actual memory address used to access data or instructions in memory

Access time: delay between time supplying address to memory and receiving data

Accumulator: special register in the CPU, often the destination of arithmetic and logical operations and, sometimes, one of the source operands

ACK: a positive acknowledgement to a transmitted frame

Adaptive routing: a technique whereby the route taken by a communication depends on the overall traffic flow through the network

Addressing mode: method of specifying the address of an operand from the address bits in the instruction

Algorithm: sequence of steps required to solve a problem

ALU: arithmetic and logic unit

ASCII: American standard code for information interchange

Arithmetic and logic unit:
a hardware unit that performs operations, such as addition, on its operands according to the function supplied

Array processor: an attached processor that performs parallel computations

Assembler: the program that converts input in assembly language to machine code

Assembly code: representation of machine instructions where bit patterns are replaced by symbols

Asynchronous: not synchronized – in communication systems the sender can send to the receiver at any time

Asynchronous transmission:

transmission where the sender and receiver resynchronize at the start of the transmission of each piece of data

ATM: asynchronous transfer mode – a high speed networking system

Backward error correction:

a method of correcting errors in transmitted data by retransmission

Bandwidth: the range of frequencies that a communication medium can support

Base: the radix of the number system, for example, 2 for binary

Baseband: only a single signal can be transmitted which occupies the whole frequency spectrum of the medium

Baud rate: a measure of information transfer rate, often equivalent to bits per second

BCD: binary coded decimal

Binary: representation of numbers in base 2, that is, using the digits 0 and 1 only

Binary coded decimal:

a method of number representation where each decimal digit is encoded into 4 bits

Bit: binary digit, taking one of the values 0 or 1

Bridge: a node which connects two networks using similar protocols

Broadband: several signals can be transmitted at the same time using different frequencies

Broadcast: the sending of a message to all possible receivers

Bubble jet printer: a printer using ink bubbles sprayed on the paper to produce the image, synonymous with ink jet printer

Bus: a group of wires carrying information between subsystems

Cache: small, fast memory between the processor and main memory

Cache coherence: the problem of keeping shared information in more than one cache valid

Central processing unit:
the arithmetic and logic unit together with registers and control logic for decoding and executing instructions

Channel: any medium that carries information

Chip: an integrated circuit; a circuit etched on a substrate such as silicon

Circuit switching: a switching technique in which a route is set up, used for data transmission and closed down

Clock: source of regular pulses to control system operation

Combinational : a circuit whose outputs depend only on the current circuit inputs

Combinatorial: another term for combinational

Compiler: a program that translates a high-level language program into the equivalent low level code, usually machine code

Complement: 1's complement is inverting all bits;
2's complement is 1's complement +1

Condition flags: flags normally used to indicate carry, sign, overflow and zero as the result of the last instruction executed

Congestion: situation where messages on networks are delayed because the traffic density is very high

Contention system:
used in local area networks; method of accessing the communication medium whereby control is distributed

CPU: central processing unit

CRC: cyclic redundancy check; value added to message to aid detection of errors

CSMA: carrier sense multiple access

CSMA–CD: carrier sense multiple access–collision detect

Cycle stealing: taking control of the bus away from the CPU for a number of bus cycles

Datagram: a message routed through a network using the address in the message for routing from node to node

Data selector: a programmable switch

Deadlock: a state in which no action is occurring because two or more processes are stopped waiting for one of the other stopped processes to respond

DCE: data communication equipment

Direct memory access:

method of transferring large quantities of information between memory and input–output devices without CPU intervention

Distributed computing:

computations spread over several processors

DMA: direct memory access

DNA computer: a model of computation based on encoding information into strands of DNA – chemical techniques are used to process the DNA and hence perform the computation

DQDB: distributed queue dual bus

DTE: data terminal equipment

duplex: in both directions at once

ethernet: the IEEE 802.3 networking standard

FCS: frame check sequence; same as CRC

FDDI: fibre distributed data interface – a network protocol

FDM: frequency division multiplexing

FEC: forward error correction

Fetch: that part of the instruction cycle concerned with transferring the next instruction to be executed from memory to the instruction register in the CPU

Flash memory: low powered memory which can be built into devices or provided as small accessory cards

Flip-flop: a single-bit memory device

Forward error correction:

a method of correcting errors in transmitted data by the addition of extra information in the transmitted signal

Frame: a unit of information transmitted along a communication channel

Full adder: a circuit that accepts two single-bit operands and a carry producing their sum and a carry out

Gateway: a node that connects together two dissimilar networks

Half adder: a circuit that accepts two single-bit operands and produces their sum and carry

Hamming code: a code that allows the correct information to be recovered in the presence of an error – used in forward error correction

Handshake: one or more signals controlling (synchronising) the transfer of data between a sender and receiver

Hardware: that part of the computer implemented in mechanical and electronic components

HDLC: high level data link control; a level 2 OSI protocol uses to communicate between host computer and network node

Hexadecimal: number system using base 16 with the digits 0 to 9 and the letters A to F as the character set

High level language:
a language where each statement corresponds to several machine code instructions; a language which is more expressive than machine code

Host: a computer attached to a network

HTML: hypertext markup language; a language for marking text to include pointers to other text in other documents

Indirect address: an address that refers to a location containing the address of the required value

Input–output: the interface and devices by which the computer communicates with the outside world

Instruction: a collection of bits containing an operation code and, possibly, one or more operands

Instruction register:
register in the CPU used for holding the current instruction whilst it is being decoded

Instruction set: the repertoire of instructions available on a particular computer

Internet: the world-wide network formed by linking national networks

Interpreter: a program that directly executes statements in a language without prior translation

Interrupt:	a signal from a device to the CPU signalling that it requires attention
I/O:	input–output
IP:	Internet protocol
Java:	language for programming applications that are portable across the internet
LAN:	local area network
Laser printer:	a printer based on photocopying technology
Link editor:	program that fills in the cross references between separately compiled subprograms and performs relocation
Literal:	any symbolic value representing a constant
Loader:	program that loads a binary program into memory
Local area network:	network that extends over a small area such as a building or single site
LSI:	large scale integration – integrated circuits large enough to hold a microprocessor on a single chip
MAC:	medium access control
Machine code:	a representation of the bit pattern of an instruction, often in hexadecimal
MAN:	metropolitan area network
Memory mapped I/O:	an addressing scheme where the registers concerned with input–output have addresses in the memory address space
MESI:	a cache coherence protocol
Microprocessor:	a CPU implemented in LSI or VLSI
Mnemonic:	a symbol representing a bit string
Modem:	a modulator/demodulator used to encode digital signals to send along a telephone line
Modulation:	the altering of one signal to carry another
Monitor:	a device in a token ring LAN that checks for errors in the system, for example, loss of a token

Moore's Law:	a 'law' which states that the amount of circuitry which can be manufactured on to a fixed size piece of silicon doubles roughly every 18 months
MOS:	metal oxide semiconductor
Multicomputer:	a computer system comprising several machines linked together via communication lines
Multiplexer:	a switch that allows several inputs to share the same output but not at the same time
Multiprocessor:	a computer with multiple processors operating on shared memory
Mutual exclusion:	one task excluding all others from the same action
NAK:	a negative acknowledgement to a transmitted frame
Node:	a switch in a network
Operand:	a value that is operated on by the opcode of an instruction
Operation code:	opcode
Opcode:	that part of the instruction that defines the operation to be performed
OSI model:	a standard model for protocol levels in networks
Packet switching:	a technique for sending messages across networks as fixed-size units
Page:	a contiguous block of memory space
Paging:	a mechanism for swapping information between main memory and backing store
Parity:	a bit added to a bit pattern to make the number of bits odd for odd parity or even for even parity
Peripherals:	input–output devices
Pipelining:	a technique for processing multiple tasks concurrently
PLA:	programmable logic array - a regular array of AND and OR gates which may be connected together (programmed) to produce the required logic function
Polling:	interrogation of a device to find its status
Port:	an external entry or exit point from an interface
Process:	a program or subprogram in execution; also called a task

Program counter: a register in the CPU holding the address of the next instruction to be executed

PROM: programmable read-only memory – a reusable programmable memory which can be programmed by special equipment and erased by ultra-violet light

Protocol: a set of communication rules that sender and receiver have to obey in order to communicate

PTT: public telephone and telegraph

RAM: random access memory, often used for read/write memory; access to any location takes the same time irrespective of address

Refresh: a process whereby a dynamic memory that loses information after a short time has its memory contents rewritten

Register: a fast memory location in the CPU or an interface circuit

Register window: a set of registers used in a RISC computer design

Relative address: an address relative to the current contents of the program counter

Relocation: the process of moving code or data from one part of memory to another

RISC: reduced instruction set computer

ROM: read-only memory

Rotate: see shift

Routing: the process of directing a message through a network

RS232C: a standard for communication

Sequential: in sequence, that is, one after another

Sequence numbers: numbers added to a frame to identify it

Serial: one after another, often with reference to communication

Shift: to move sideways in a register

Sliding window: a method of controlling the flow of information across a communication link

Software: sets of instructions which tailor the computer for a particular application

Stack:	memory or a data structure that is accessed in the order last-in-first-out
Stack pointer:	register that contains the address of the current top of stack
Static RAM:	memory that needs no refreshing
Status:	condition
Synchronization:	the co-ordination of actions between two or more entities
Synchronous transmission:	transmission where the sender and receiver are always in synchronization
TCP/IP:	transmission control protocol/internet protocol; common network protocols
TDM:	time division multiplexing
Token:	a special bit pattern which gives the holder permission to transmit a message
Token ring:	a type of local area network organized as a ring with tokens circulating
Time-out:	an event which occurs when a clock which is counting down reaches zero
Transceiver:	a combined transmitter and receiver
Trap:	interrupt
Tristate:	three state, usually logic 0, logic 1 and high impedance
V24:	a standard for communication, virtually identical to RS232
VDU:	visual display unit
Vector processor:	a specialized processor whose primary data type is the vector
Virtual circuit:	a shared point-to-point path set up through a network
VLSI:	very large scale integration
WAN:	wide area network
Wide area network:	a network over a large geographical area such as a country or continent
Word:	a group of bits, usually the size of the data bus

WWW: World Wide Web – network of interlinked information
                        sources made available via the Internet

Answers to selected exercises

[Solutions to all the exercises are available to academic staff via the McGraw-Hill web site.]

Chapter 2

2.1 (a)
$$\overline{A.B} + A.B + \overline{A}.B$$

Combining terms 1 and 3 gives

$$\overline{A}(\overline{B} + B) + A.B = \overline{A} + A.B$$

Using the simplification theorem

$$A + \overline{A}.B = A + B$$

then gives

$$\overline{A} + B$$

i.e.

$$\overline{A}.\overline{B} + A.B + \overline{A}.B = \overline{A} + B$$

The result may be checked by the truth table method.

2.1 (b)
$$\overline{A}.B.C + A.\overline{B}.C + A.B.\overline{C} + A.B.C$$

The term $A.B.C$ can be combined with each of the other terms. If two extra $A.B.C$ terms are ORed with the original expression, i.e.

$$\overline{A}.B.C + A.\overline{B}.C + A.B.\overline{C} + A.B.C + A.B.C + A.B.C$$

then combining terms 1–3, 2–4 and 3–6 gives

$$B.C.(\overline{A} + A) + A.C.(\overline{B} + B) + A.B.(\overline{C} + C) = B.C + A.C + A.B$$

2.9   Working backwards from the output the expression for Z is

$$Z = \overline{C.(A.(\overline{A+B}))}$$

$$= \overline{C.A.(\overline{A+B})}$$

Using de Morgan's theorem gives

$$Z = \overline{C.A} + A + B$$

$$= \overline{C} + \overline{A} + A + B$$

$$= \overline{C} + B$$

i.e. the expression does not depend on A.

Chapter 3

3.3   The input range of 0 to 7 decimal requires three binary inputs, labelled X, Y and Z. The square of the input is obviously a number in the range 0 to 49, which requires six binary lines, labelled A, B, C, D, E, F. The truth table for the system is:

Input		*Output*	
Decimal	**XYZ**	*Decimal*	**ABCDEF**
0	000	0	000000
1	001	1	000001
2	010	4	000100
3	011	9	001001
4	100	16	010000
5	101	25	011001
6	110	36	100100
7	111	49	110001

The outputs required are then

$$A = \sum 6,7$$

$$B = \sum 4,5,7$$

$$C = \sum 3,5$$

$$D = \sum 2,6$$

$$E = 0$$

$$F = \sum 1,2,3,5,7 = Z$$

The expressions can be simplified algebraically as follows:

$$A = X.Y.\bar{Z} + X.Y.Z = X.Y$$
$$B = X.\bar{Y}.\bar{Z} + X.\bar{Y}.Z + X.Y.Z = X.\bar{Y} + X.Y.Z$$
$$= X.\bar{Y} + X.Y$$
$$C = \bar{X}.Y.Z + X.\bar{Y}.Z = Z.(\bar{X}.Y + X.\bar{Y})$$
$$D = \bar{X}.Y.\bar{Z} + X.Y.\bar{Z} = Y.\bar{Z}(\bar{X} + X) = Y.\bar{Z}$$

The circuit implementation is then:

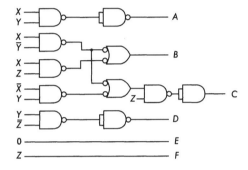

3.8 The truth table for the 3-input majority function is:

Inputs			Output
a	*b*	*c*	*M*
0	0	0	0
0	0	1	0
0	1	0	0
0	1	1	1
1	0	0	0
1	0	1	1
1	1	0	1
1	1	1	1

The K-map is:

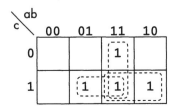

So $M = a.c + b.c + a.b$. The implementation with NAND gates is:

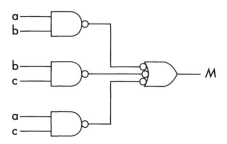

Majority function circuits with four or more inputs are best implemented with an iterative circuit.

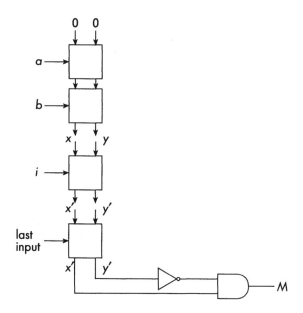

An iterative circuit contains a number of identical cells.

In this example a cell has three inputs; input i (for the ith cell), which is an external input (a, b, c etc) and two inputs x and y, which contain information from the previous cell. The cell has two outputs x' and y' which pass on information to the next cell according to the following code:

x'	y'	
0	0	No previous inputs are set
0	1	One previous input is set
1	1	Two or more previous inputs are set

The truth table for the *i*th cell is then:

Inputs				Outputs	
x	y	i		x'	y'
0	0	0		0	0
0	1	0		0	1
1	0	0		1	0
0	0	1		0	1
0	1	1		1	0
1	0	1		1	0

Giving the equations

$$x' = x.\bar{y}.\bar{i} + \bar{x}.y.i + x.\bar{y}.i$$
$$y' = \bar{x}.y.\bar{i} + \bar{x}.\bar{y}.i$$

For the first cell $x = y = 0$.

For the last cell the logic required to generate M is $M = x'.y'$

3.10 The truth table is

Input		Output		
Decimal	bcd	Decimal	bcd digits	
	xywz		**abcd**	**efgh**
0	0000	0	0000	0000
1	0001	5	0000	0101
2	0010	10	0001	0000
3	0011	15	0001	0101
4	0100	20	0010	0000
5	0101	25	0010	0101
6	0110	30	0011	0000
7	0111	35	0011	0101
8	1000	40	0100	0000
9	1001	45	0100	0101

The outputs required are:

$$a = 0$$
$$b = \sum 8,9$$
$$c = \sum 4,5,6,7$$
$$d = \sum 2,3,6,7$$

$$e = 0$$

$$f = \sum 1,3,5,7,9 = z$$

$$g = 0$$

$$h = \sum 1,3,5,7,9 = z$$

The PLA may be programmed directly from these equations.

If it is necessary to minimize the number of product terms, then the expressions for b, c, d and f can be minimized algebraically, or by using the K-map technique.

Chapter 4

4.1 The first step is to define the state diagram:

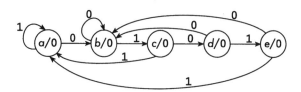

The state table is:

Present state	Input	Next state
a	0	b
a	1	a
b	0	b
b	1	c
c	0	d
c	1	a
d	0	b
d	1	e
e	0	b
e	1	a

The output z is a 1 if the system is in state e.
Assign the states as follows:

$$a = 000$$

$$b = 001$$

$$c = 010$$

$$d = 011$$

$$e = 100$$

The state diagram is then rewritten

Present state ABC	Input x	Next state A'B'C'
000	0	0 0 1
000	1	0 0 0
001	0	0 0 1
001	1	0 1 0
010	0	0 1 1
010	1	0 0 0
011	0	0 0 1
011	1	1 0 0
100	0	0 0 1
100	1	0 0 0

where **A**, **B** and **C** are state variables.
Then from the state table:

$$A' = \bar{A}.B.C.x$$
$$B' = \bar{A}.\bar{B}.C.x + \bar{A}.B.\bar{C}.\bar{x}$$
$$C' = \bar{x}.(\bar{A}.\bar{B}.\bar{C} + \bar{A}.\bar{B}.C + \bar{A}.B.\bar{C} + \bar{A}.B.C + A.\bar{B}.\bar{C})$$

The expression for C' can be reduced using a three-variable Karnaugh map to:

$$C = \bar{x}$$

The output is

$$Z = A.\bar{B}.\bar{C}$$

The implementation is then:

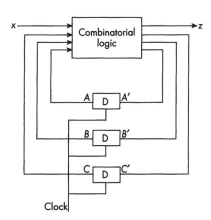

Three D-type flip-flops are required to store the state variables A, B and C. The combinatorial logic can be either random logic or a PLA.

4.4   The state table for the modulo-3 counter is

Present state	Next state
0	1
1	2
2	0

If the states are represented by

$$0 = 00$$

$$1 = 01$$

$$2 = 10$$

i.e. the normal binary sequence then the state table becomes

Present state $a\ b$	Next state $a'\ b'$
0 0	0 1
0 1	1 0
1 0	0 0

4.4 (a)   Two D-type flip-flops are required to store the state variables a and b, which are also the counter outputs. The logic required for the D-inputs is read directly from the state table and is

$$D_a = \bar{a}.b$$

$$D_b = \bar{a}.\bar{b}$$

so the implementation is

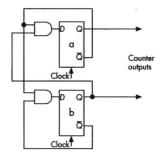

4.4 (b) The logic required for the JK flip-flop implementation is determined using the state change table of Table 4.6, ON PAGE 73. The state table becomes:

Present state				Next state			
a	b	a'	b'	J_a	K_a	J_b	K_b
0	0	0	1	0	×	1	×
0	1	1	0	1	×	×	1
1	0	0	0	×	1	0	×
1	1	0	0	×	1	×	1

Note that an extra row has been added, namely row 4. If the present state ever becomes $ab = 11$ then the next state is always 00. In practice state 11 should never be entered but if it is the counter moves to state 00 on the next clock pulse. The addition of this extra row also simplifies the logic for the flip flops, namely:

$$J_a = b \qquad K_a = 1$$
$$J_b = \bar{a} \qquad K_b = 1$$

Chapter 5

5.1 Only one device can transmit on a bus at any one time because a bus is a shared transmission medium and thus if two devices transmit at the same time their transmissions will interfere.

In a system with multiple transmitters on a single bus, an arbitration system is used to ensure that only one device transmits at a time. When a device wants to transmit it requests use of the bus from the arbitration system, which will either grant or refuse the request depending on whether another device is using the bus. If two devices request use of the bus simultaneously then the arbitrator will grant use of the bus to the highest priority device.

5.5 Processor registers are not necessarily the same size because they hold different types of information. Address registers will usually be the same length as the size of the address bus. Data registers will usually be the same size as the data bus of the machine. For example, a 16-bit machine will have data registers 16 bits long and a 32-bit machine will have data registers 32 bits long.

Chapter 6

6.1 (a) 16 address lines are required to access 64K words of memory since $2^{16} = 65536 = 64K$.

6.1 (b) 20 address lines will address $2^{20} = 1048576$ (or 1024K) words of memory.

6.3 Consider a processor executing 100 instructions. With a hit rate of 0.9, 90 instructions will be found in the cache and 10 in main memory. The total number of memory read cycles is then

$$(90 \times 3) + (10 \times 5) = 320 \text{ cycles}$$

If there is no cache memory then the total number of read cycles is

$$100 \times 5 = 500.$$

The speed up factor is thus

$$(500 - 320) \times 100/500 = 36\%$$

Chapter 7

7.2 The total number of bits transmitted per character is 10, consisting of 8 data bits, 1 start bit and 1 stop bit.

The effective data rate is 9600/10 = 960 characters/second.

7.7 When an interrupt occurs the processor has to perform the following tasks:

(i) recognize and acknowledge the interrupt;

(ii) save the program counter and status register;

(iii) execute the interrupt handler;

(iv) restore the status register and program counter.

The total time for all this is 4 + 10 + 70 + 10 = 94 microseconds. Interrupts must not occur more frequently that every 94 microseconds so the highest interrupt frequency is $1/(94 \times 10^{-6}) = 10638$ Hz, that is, about 10kHz.

Chapter 8

8.4 (a) The architecture shown in Figure 8.1, ON PAGE 170 actually has no direct means of clearing the accumulator. Indirectly it could be done by the instruction and #0, that is, ANDing the accumulator with the contents of the next location in memory, zero in this case. In practice the accumulator would probably have an extra control line which will zero the contents of the accumulator when activated. This line would be controlled by an extra bit in the microinstruction word.

8.4 (b) After the processor has fetched and decoded the LDA instruction it has to perform a second fetch to transfer the operand value 10 from memory to the MBR. The microinstruction sequences for the execute cycle are then:

(i) MBR → bus2, bus2 → bus3, bus3 → ACC

(ii) PC → bus1, '1' → bus2, ADD, bus3 → PC

(iii) As in (b) above the operand has to be fetched from memory to the MBR. The microinstruction sequences for the execute cycle are then:

(i) ACC → bus1, MBR → bus2, ADD, bus3 → ACC

(ii) PC → bus1, '1' → bus2, ADD, bus3 → PC

Note that it is assumed that data is output from registers such as the ACC or PC on the rising edge of the clock onto bus1 (or bus2 in the case of MAR). Data is latched back into a register on the falling edge of the clock.

Chapter 9

9.1 The original system has a 16K word RAM at addresses 0–16383 and a 16K ROM at addresses 16384–32767. The memory map is shown below.

A_{15}	A_{14}	A_{13}	A_{12}	A_{11}	A_{10}	A_9	A_8	A_7	A_6	A_5	A_4	A_3	A_2	A_1	A_0	
0	0	×	×	×	×	×	×	×	×	×	×	×	×	×	×	RAM
0	1	×	×	×	×	×	×	×	×	×	×	×	×	×	×	ROM

For partial decoding the two sets of address patterns can be distinguished by the value of A_{14} and hence the chip select signal on the RAM can be driven from A_{14} and that of the ROM from NOT(A_{14}) or, if the chip select signal is active low, from the inverse of these signals.

For full decoding both A_{15} and A_{14} need to be considered. These two signals can be fed into a 2-to-4 decoder and output 0 connected to the chip select on the RAM chip and output 1 to the chip select on the ROM chip.

The difference is that using full decoding the RAM chip will only respond to addresses between 0 and 16383 and the ROM to addresses between 16384 and 32767 whereas with partial decoding the RAM chip will respond to addresses between 0 and 16383 and between 32768 and 49151 and the ROM chip will respond to addresses between 16384 and 32767 and between 49152 and 65535.

Chapter 10

10.1 (a) $(27)_{10} = (11011)_2 = (1B)_{16}$

10.1 (b) $(96)_{10} = (1100000)_2 = (60)_{16}$

10.1 (c) $(1032)_{10} = (10000001000)_2 = (408)_{16}$

10.1 (d) $(1111)_{10} = (10001010111)_2 = (457)_{16}$

10.3 (a)

$$
\begin{array}{ll}
\quad 000101 & \qquad 5 + 7 \\
\quad 000111 \;\; + & \\
\hline
\quad 001100 &
\end{array}
$$

10.3 (b)

$$
\begin{array}{ll}
\quad 001100 & \qquad 12 + (-3) \\
\quad 111101 \;\; + & \\
\hline
\quad 001001 &
\end{array}
$$

10.3 (c)

$$
\begin{array}{ll}
\quad 010100 & \qquad 20 + 16 \\
\quad 010000 \;\; + & \\
\hline
\quad 100100 &
\end{array}
$$

overflow since two positive numbers give a negative result. This can be overcome by performing computation in different order

$$
\begin{array}{ll}
010000 & 16 + (-5) \\
\underline{111011} \ + & \\
001011 & \\
\underline{010100} \ + & 16 + (-5) + 20 \\
011111 & = 31
\end{array}
$$

10.3 (d)

$$
\begin{array}{ll}
000111 & 7 + (-30) \\
\underline{100010} \ + & \\
101001 & 7 + (-30) - 12 \\
\underline{110100} \ + & \\
011101 &
\end{array}
$$

underflow since two negative values add to a positive. The computation cannot be reorganized here since the result cannot be represented in 6-bit 2's complement form

10.3 (e)

$$
\begin{array}{ll}
001100 & 12 \times 5 \\
\underline{000101} & \\
110000 & \\
\underline{001100} & \\
111100 &
\end{array}
$$

which is overflow since multiplying two positive values has given a negative result. Needs more bits to store result, typically twice the number of bits for the operands.

10.7 (a) 0 00000000 00000000000000000000000

10.7 (b) 1.0 in binary is $1.0 = 0.1 \times 2^1$
0 10000000 00000000000000000000000

10.7 (c) −10 in binary is $-1010 = -0.1010 \times 2^4$
1 10000011 01000000000000000000000

10.7 (d) $123.4375 = (1111011.0111)_2 = 0.11110110111 \times 2^7$
0 10000100 11101101110000000000000

Chapter 11

11.3   Subtract is implemented by adding the 2's complement so the same answer should result in both cases.

11.5   There are several solutions involving looking at the bottom bit of the data, which is zero for an even value

(i)
```
        MOV  AX, 0    ; set result to zero
        CLC           ; clear carry bit
        ROR  BX, 1    ; rotate bottom bit of BX into carry bit
        JCS  L1       ; if carry = 0 result = 0
        INC  AX       ; else result = 1
    L1:
```

(ii) One solution is
```
        move.w  #0,D0    ; clear result, assume even
        and.w   #1,D1    ; see if bottom bit of D1 is zero
        beq     L1       ; branch if bottom bit clear
        move.w  #1,D1
    L1:
```

Chapter 12

12.2   Symbol table would contain

Symbol	Value
Start	0
L1	8

12.4   Assumptions for 68000 solution:

All data items are 16-bit words
LARGEST = d0
INDEX = d1
LIMIT is defined as a constant elsewhere
NUMBER is a vector with a0 pointing to the first element

```
        clr.w  d0              ; LARGEST = 0
        clr.w  d1              ; INDEX = 0
    L1: cmp.w  #LIMIT, d1      ; WHILE (INDEX<LIMIT)
        bmi    L2
        cmp.w  0(a0, d1), d0   ; IF (NUMBER[INDEX]>LARGEST)
        bpi    L3
```

```
        move.w  0(a0, d1), d0  ; LARGEST = NUMBER[INDEX]
   L3:  add.w   #1, d1         ; INDEX = INDEX + 1
        bra     L1
   L2:
```

Chapter 13

13.1   One possible solution using concurrency – concurrent tasks are shown in groups side by side

Fill the kettle	Fetch teapot and cups
Boil water	
	Warm teapot
Reboil water	Add tea to teapot
Pour water into teapot	
Leave to brew	Add milk to cups
Pour into teacups	
Add sugar	

13.3 (a)   40 secs

13.3 (b) $7 \times 3.5 = 24.5$ secs

13.3 (c)   Each stage time is the maximum of each subtask. To reduce the overall time means reducing the maximum stage time. For example, if the 3.5 sec subtask is divided into two subtasks of 2 secs and 1.5 secs then there would be 4 subtasks and these could be pipelined in $8 \times 3 = 24$ secs. Further if the 3 sec subtask could be split in half, the complete task could be performed in $9 \times 2 = 18$ secs. The ideal is to have equal sized subtasks.

Chapter 14

14.3   The sender and receiver run on independent clocks which will run at slightly different rates. If left unsynchronized they will eventually be sufficiently out of step with each other that the receiver will either lose bits or read the same bit twice. Frame synchronization introduces transitions into the signal before the start of a frame to allow the receiver to resynchronize its clock to that of the transmitter. Bit synchronization is used with synchronous transmission to guarantee regular subsequent transitions with each bit in the transmitted data.

14.6   If a WAN uses digital signalling internally but still has local subscriber loops which support only analogue transmission then the internal nodes must demodulate the analogue signals injected into the network, transmit these internally as digital signal and then modulate them as they exit at the other side. In effect a modem is needed between each station and the node to which it is connected.

Chapter 15

15.3   The central control monitor monitors the medium for the presence of the token. If the token does not appear within a fixed period of time it generates a new token. One such policy would be to determine the maximum period it should take for the token to circulate, assuming there is the maximum number of stations on the ring and each has data to transmit. Alternatively, this theoretical maximum may be reduced by considering average circulation times over some period, and setting the period to be the average period plus some leeway.

Generation of a spurious token leads to the possibility that multiple stations may transmit. As a station transmits it also drains the ring of in-coming bits so that it also removes its own frame from the ring. In this exceptional circumstance, each transmitting station can monitor the ring for in-coming bits and if these define an incoming frame other than its own returning then it can detect this anomaly and take corrective action. Corrective action could be either that the station with the higher address wins and the station with the lower address aborts its transmission, or that it reports this to the central monitor.

15.6   Connection-oriented services support the notion of a virtual connection and guarantee error-free in-order delivery of packets on it.

Connectionless services merely support the notion of un-ordered packet delivery.

IP and UDP provide connectionless services. Packets are delivered independently of each other.

TCP provides a connection-oriented service. As it is implemented on top of IP, which provides only a connectionless service, buffering at the receiver is necessary to guarantee in-order delivery of packets.

Chapter 16

16.1   Backward error correction requires error detection and correction by re-transmission. It is appropriate on duplex links where the medium is relatively reliable (so that re-transmissions are relatively few in number).

Forward error correction requires sufficient redundancy in the transmitted data to not only detect errors but also correct them without re-transmission. It is appropriate on simplex links or highly unreliable duplex links. As real-time multimedia applications become more common on data networks, this is also appropriate on reliable duplex links where there is sufficient bandwidth to accommodate the redundancy.

16.5   Codeword bit 3 is checked by bits 1 and 2
Codeword bit 5 is checked by bits 1 and 4
Codeword bit 6 is checked by bits 2 and 4
Codeword bit 7 is checked by bits 1, 2 and 4
Codeword bit 9 is checked by bits 1 and 8
Codeword bit 10 is checked by bits 2 and 8
Codeword bit 11 is checked by bits 1, 2 and 8
Codeword bit 12 is checked by bits 4 and 8

Codeword bit 1 is the odd parity for bits 3, 5, 7, 9, 11 (0, 1, 1, 0, 0) therefore is 1
Codeword bit 2 is the odd parity for bits 3, 6, 7, 10, 11 (0, 0, 1, 1, 0) therefore is 1
Codeword bit 4 is the odd parity for bits 5, 6, 7, 12 (1, 0, 1, 1) therefore is 0
Codeword bit 8 is the odd parity for bits 9, 10, 11, 12 (0, 1, 0, 1) therefore is 1

Thus the full codeword is 101011010011.

If bit ten is received as a 1, then codeword bits 2 and 8 are incorrect as odd parity for the sets of bits each checks, therefore the receiver detects the error at bit position 2 + 8 = 10, and therefore inverts the bit back to a 0.

Chapter 17

17.3   The sliding window technique works well but it is fixed, that is, the number of registers in each region is fixed by the designer who has to go on statistical data to decide what size they should be. It would be better if there was some other technique which allows for registers to be renamed but also allows for variable numbers of registers to be used for each region. Recent compiler technology allows the compiler to deal with some of the renaming problems and some are dealt with by more flexibility in the architecture.

Index

1-bit memory cell   90
2–4 line decoder   52
3-state buffer   89
4–1 line multiplexer   53
680x0   186–189, 366
   addressing modes   234–239
   assembly code   215–252
   assembly code examples   244–252
   processor   108
   programmer's model   219–220
7-segment decoder   43, 54
80x86   86
   abstract machine   6
   addressing modes   234–239
   assembly code   215–252
   assembly code examples   244–252
   memory organization   131
   processor   105
   programmer's model   219

A

abstraction   2
acknowledgement (ACK)   350
   scheme-full   350
   scheme-positive only   350
adaptive routing   335–336
addition
   binary coded decimal   206
   floating point   211
   two's complement   203
addressing modes   234–240, 366–367
   absolute   234–235
   autoincrement   236
   autodecrement   237
   direct   234–235
   immediate   238–239
   indexed   237–238
   indirect   235
   relative   238
   uses of   240–244
allocation protocols   323–324

Altera
   EP330 EPLD   81
   EP330 EPLD macrocell   82
   FLEX 10K EPLD   82
ALU   98
amplifier   303
amplitude modulation   305
analogue
   data   304
   signals   304
AND gate   14
ARPAnet   376
ASCII code   197
assembler   222
   directives   222–223, 257
   one pass   259
   two pass   259–261
assembly code   221–223, 255–257
assembly language, see assembly code
asynchronous counter   87
asynchronous data frames   324
asynchronous sequential circuit   64
asynchronous transfer mode (ATM)   304
ATM, see asynchronous transfer mode

B

back plane   96
backbone   327
backward error correction   349–356
   acknowledgement (ACK)   350
   go-back-N 354
   receive window   352–353, 355
   selective repeat   354
   send window   352–353, 355
   sequence numbers   351–356
   sliding window   352–356
   stop and wait   351–352
   time-out   350, 356
bandwidth   297
baseband signalling   298, 322
baud rate   297
BCD, see binary coded decimal

big endian   114, 220
binary arithmetic   195
binary coded decimal   200–201
bipolar transistor   28
Boolean algebra   17
bridge   326
broadband signalling   298
broadcast communication   315
bubble technique   21,43
buffer   13
bus   96
   parallel   135
   protocol   320–323
   topology   317–318
byte   94

C

c   368
c++   366
cache memory   124
CAD system   83
carrier sense multiple access   320–323
carrier sense multiple access/collision
     detection   321–323
   frame format   325
carry   202
CCITT V24   307–310
CD-ROM   163–165
circuit
   miniaturization   365, 379
   yield   365
circuit board   95
circuit switching   329–330
CISC, see complex instruction set computer
clock   65
CMOS   33
coaxial cable   299, 322
combination door lock   66, 75
combinatorial circuit   39
communication
   broadcast   315
   point-to-point   315
communications processor   314
compatability   8
compilation   268–269
compiler   370
complex instruction set
     computer   366–367, 380
concurrency   6, 277–287
condition tests   227–228
congestion   336
connection
   close down   310
   set up   309
connection oriented service   345
connectionless service   331–332
connection-oriented service   331–332
contention protocols   319–323
control information in frames   92
control unit   173–177

copper wire   299
counter design   84
CPU   97
CSMA, see carrier sense multiple access
CSMA/CD, see carrier sense multiple access/
     collision detection
cycle time   116
cyclic redundancy check   346, 347, 361

D

data direction register   138–139
data link layer   295
data streams   292
datagram   330–331
datatypes
   characters   196
   integers   196–200
De Morgan's theorem   18, 22
Dec Vax architecture   367
decoder   52
decoding   181–185
demultiplexer   52
design language   83
digital
   data   304
   signals   304, 322
direct memory access   149–150
disks
   floppy   159–161
   hard   161–163
distributed queue dual bus   327–328
distribution   6
division   206
   floating point   211–212
DMA, see direct memory access
DNA   379–380, 381
DQDB, see distributed queue dual bus
duplex   297
dynamic memory (DRAM)   116

E

electrically programmable logic device
     (EPLD)   58, 80
emulation   178
encoding   239–240
EOR gate   16
erasable programmable memory
     (EPROM)   117
error correction   295, 303–304, 345–362
   backward   349–356
   forward   356–359
error detection   295, 303–304, 345,
     346–349
   cyclic redundancy check   46, 347
   frame check sequence   346, 347
   generator polynomial   347–349
   modulo-2 division   48
   parity bit   346, 347

Ethernet   295, 338
    frame format   325
execute cycle   94, 104
exponent   208

F

fall time   28
fan-out   29, 31, 34
FDDI   324
FET, see field effect transistor
fetch cycle   94, 103
fibre distributed data interface, see FDDI
field effect transistor (FET)   24
    NAND gate   27
    NOR gate   27
    switch   24
finite state machine (FSM)   77
fixed point numbers   207
flash memory   117
flip–flop
    D   71
    JK   71
floating point numbers   208–212
flow control   346, 359–360
forward error correction   356–359
    Hamming codes   357–359
fragmentation   340–341
frame check sequence   346, 347
frame check sum   340–341
frame format
    end of frame   302
    start of frame   302
frame sequence numbers   351–356, 360, 362–363
frequency divider   87
frequency modulation   305
full adder   99
functional decomposition   3
fuse   57

G

generator polynomial   347–349, 361

H

half-adder   17, 99
half-duplex   297
HDLC, see high-level data link control
hierarchy   2
    of protocols   291–297
high level languages   5, 265–268
high-level data link control   360–361
Hitatchi 2764 EPROM   121
Hitatchi 6264 SRAM   119
HTML, see hypertext markup language

hypertext   376
    markup language   376

I

I/O mapping   136
IEEE 754   209–210
IEEE 802.3, see Ethernet
IEEE 802.5, see token ring
in-order delivery   345
input–output interface   136–144
instruction cycle   147
instruction set   215–217
instructions
    arithmetic and logical   224–225
    bit manipulation   225–226
    branch   228–229
    data movement   223–224
    input–output   230–231
    program control   226–230
Intel   65
    80x86 see 80x86
    21014 DRAM   120
    8088   185–186
    Pentium   375, 378
Internet   338–341, 366, 376–378, 380–381
Internet protocol   94, 328
    addressing   339
    network class   339
    packet   340–341
internetwork   295, 325–328
    backbone   327
    bridge   326
    local area network   325–328
    protocol   295
    wide area networks   337–339
interpretation   4, 268–269
interrupts   145–149, 279
    multiple   148–149
    software   279
IP, see Internet protocol

J

Java   366, 376–377

K

Karnaugh maps   46
keyboard   150–152

L

LAN, see local area network
language translation   269–271

latch
  D   70
  SR   68
linking   262–264
liquid crystal display   156
list   241
little endian   114, 220
loading   264–265
local area network   313, 318, 318–328
  errors   345
logic levels   30
logical channel   292

M

machine code   5
macrocell   58, 80
magnetic input   153–154
magnetic tapes   165
Manchester encoding   302, 325
mantissa   208
medium access control (MAC)   314
  allocation protocols   323–324
  contention protocols   319–323
  CSMA   320–323
  CSMA/CD   321–323
memory
  address   113
  address register (MAR)   97
  buffer register (MBR)   97
  byte   118
  hierarchy   122
  interleaving   123
  mapping   129, 136
  matrix   119
  modules   122
  structure   220
mesh topology   315
microcoded architecture   367
microprogramming   169–179
  horizontal   177–178
  vertical   177–178
Microsoft Explorer   376
microwave   300
miniaturization   365, 379
minimization   45
modem   306–310, 314, 378
modulation
  amplitude   305
  frequency   305
  phase   305
  quadrature amplitude (QAM)   306
Moore's law   7, 365
Motorola 680x0, see 680x0
mouse   152–153
MSI circuits   50
multimedia   378
multiple processor systems   278, 283–287
multiplexer   53
multiplication   204–206
  floating point   211–212

N

NAND gate   15
NAND/NOR logic   20
negative acknowledgement (NAK)   350
negative clock transition   65
negative logic   23
Netscape Navigator   376
network
  local area   313, 318, 318–328
  wide area   313, 318, 328–342
  layer   295
  routing   333–334
noise   303
  immunity   29, 30
NOR gate   15
NOT gate   13
number systems   191–195
numbers
  binary   192
  octal   93–194
  hexadecimal   93–194

O

one's complement   198
opcode   215–217
open systems interconnection (OSI)   294
  seven layer model   94
operands   215, 231–234
optical fibre   300, 304, 322, 359
OR gate   15
Organization for International
    Standardization (ISO)   294
overflow
  integer   201
  floating point   209

P

packet switching   330–331
parallel in serial out (PISO)   297
parallel port   137–140
parallelism   280–281
parity
  bit   303, 346, 347
  even   347
  generator   41
  odd   347
Pascal   368
Pentium   375, 378
peripheral devices   150–165
phase modulation   305
physical channel   292
physical layer   294, 297–311, 345
pipelining   281–282, 369–370
point-to-point communication   315
polling   144–145

positive clock transition   64
power dissipation   28
PowerPC   371–374
  addressing modes   372–373
  instruction set   372–373
  superscalar   373
printers   156–159
  ink-jet   157
  laser   158–159
procedure call   368
program   93
programmable logic array (PLA)   56
propagation delay   28
protocol   291
  addresses   292
  allocation based   323–324
  bus based   320–323
  contention based   319–323
  control information   292
  distributed queue dual bus   327–328
  Ethernet   320–323
  frame format   292
  header information   292–293
  hierarchy   291–297
  IEEE 802.3   320–323
  layers   292–297
  medium access control (MAC)   314
  token ring   323–324

Q

quadrature amplitude modulation   306
quality of service
  connectionless   331–332
  connection-oriented   331–332
queue   243
Quine–McClusky   50

R

random access memory (RAM)   115, 118
read only memory (ROM)   59, 77, 116, 117
read operation (68000)   109
read operation (8086)   106
real numbers   207–212
receiver   297
reduced instructions set computer
      (RISC)   366–376, 380
register   368
  bank   88
  file   375
  floating point   371
  link   372
  window   368
relocation   261–262
repeater   303
residue function   55
ring topology   317
ripple counter   87
RISC, see reduced instruction set computer

RISC-1   368–369
rise time   28
routing   295, 332–336
  adaptive   335–336
  network routing   333–334
  source routing   333–334
  static   334
  tables   334–336
RS232C   291, 295, 307

S

scalar processor architecture (SPARC)   369
scanner   153
segment register   106
sequential logic circuit   63
serial in parallel out (SIPO)   297
serial port   140–144
service, see quality of service
shift register   102
signal
  attenuation   303
  corruption   303
  frequency division multiplexing
        (FDM)   299
  multiplexing   298
  propagation   297
  time division multiplexing (TDM)   299
signalling   297
  baseband   298
  baud   297
  broadband   298
simplex   297
sink current   32
sliding window protocols   352–356
source current   32
source routing   333–334
SPARC, see scalar processor architecture
specification   40
stack   242–243
star topology   316
state   63
  diagram   64
  table   65
  variables   65, 68
static memory (SRAM)   116
stop and wait protocol   351–352
stream of data   292
subroutine call and return   229–230
subtraction
  binary coded decimal   206
  floating point   211
  two's complement   203
subtractor   100
sum-of-products   19
superscalar   373
switching
  circuit switching   329–330
  datagram   330–331
  packet switching   330–331
  virtual circuit   330–331

synchronisation
  asynchronous 301
  bit 301
  frame 301
synchronous 302
  data frames 324
  counter 84

T

table 240
TCP, see transaction control protocol
telephone system 304
  local loop 304
time sequence diagram 352–353
token 323
token ring
  active monitor 323
  frame format 325
  management 323
  protocol 323–324
topology
  bus 317–318
  graph 315–316
  mesh 315
  reduced mesh 315
  ring 317
  shared hub 322
  star 316
  switching hub 322
trackball 153
traffic light controller 63, 73
transaction control protocol 294, 328
  errors 345
  packet format 362–363
transistor-transistor logic (TTL) 30
translation 4
transmitter 297

tri-state buffer 89
TTL, see transistor-transistor logic
twisted pair cable 299
two's complement 199–200

U

universal synchronous/asynchronous
    receiver transmitter 135, 142–143
universal resource locator (URL) 376
universal serial bus 143–144
up-down counter 85
URL, see universal resource locator
USART, see universal synchronous/
    asynchronous receiver transmitter
USB, see universal serial bus
user datagram protocol (UDP) 295

V

V24 141–142
VDU, see visual display unit
virtual circuit 330–331
virtual memory 128
visual display unit 154–156

W

WAN, see wide area network
wide area network 313, 318, 328–342
  errors 345
world wide web 376–378, 380–381
  browser 376–378
WWW, see world wide web